Postcolonial Perspectives
on Women Writers
from
Africa, the Caribbean, and the US

POSTCOLONIAL PERSPECTIVES ON WOMEN WRITERS FROM AFRICA, THE CARIBBEAN, AND THE US

Edited by

MARTIN JAPTOK

Africa World Press, Inc.

P.O. Box 1892
Trenton, NJ 08607

P.O. Box 48
Asmara, ERITREA

Africa World Press, Inc.

P.O. Box 1892   P.O. Box 48
Trenton, NJ 08607   Asmara, ERITREA

Copyright © 2003 Martin Japtok
First Printing 2003

Book design: Getahun Seyoum Alemayehu
Cover design: Ashraful Haque

Library of Congress Cataloging-in-Publication Data

Postcolonial perspectives on women writers from Africa, the Caribbean,
and the U.S. / edited by Martin Japtok.
p. cm.
Includes bibliographical references and index.
ISBN 1-59221-067-8 (hardcover)--ISBN 1-59221-068-6 (pbk.)
1. Literature--Women authors--History and criticism. 2. Literature,
Modern--20th century--History and criticism. 3. African
literature--History and criticism. 4. African literature
(English)--History and criticism. 5. Caribbean literature--History and
criticism. 6. American literature--African American authors--History
and criticism. I. Japtok, Martin.

PN471 .P67 2003
809'.89287'0904—dc21
                                                        2002152573

ACKNOWLEDGEMENT:

I wish to thank NOVEL for allowing me to reprint Karen Jacob's essay. It originally appeared in NOVEL: A Forum On Fiction 30.3 (1997). Copyright NOVEL Corp. ©1997. Reprinted with permission.

CONTENTS

INTRODUCTION

In a 1989 essay entitled "Speaking in Tongues: Dialogics, Dialectics, and the Black Woman Writer's Literary Tradition," Mae Gwendolyn Henderson proposes a theory for reading black women's texts. Such texts are characterized by a "rewriting or rereading of the dominant story," Henderson says, "resulting in a 'delegitimation' of the prior story" (35). The metaphor she suggests for this transformative power is a "'womblike matrix' in which soundlessness can be transformed into utterance, unity into diversity, formlessness into form, chaos into art, silence into tongues, and glossolalia into heteroglossia" (36). Her theory results from a reading of U.S. African American women's texts, but the essays in this collection show that similar transformative powers may be ascribed to texts by women writers across the African Diaspora and from Africa itself. Though Henderson does not employ the term, these texts may be said to engage in the postcolonial project of revisioning the past and re-envisioning the present.

When comparing texts over geographical, temporal, and cultural boundaries, one always encounters the danger of making undue generalizations; this is a problem particularly pertinent for postcolonial criticism when comparing cultural phenomena on the grounds of their common context in, for example, British imperialism, most other variables being different. Tejumola

Olaniyan addresses this concern in his introduction to the 1993 special issue of *Callaloo*, "On Post-Colonial Discourse." He maintains that while one should "insist that the term 'post-colonial' account for its spatio-temporal manipulations at the expense of historical specificity, we must learn to be auto-critical about our own (investments in the) sacralization of such 'specificity.' Historical specificity is an identity that should be a staging, not a sacrosanct ground" (746). If the demand for such specificity were to prevent comparisons across time, space, language, or culture, it could just as easily become a version of "divide and conquer," as Olaniyan suggests; it might obstruct necessary alliance building in the political realm, and the study of overarching cultural dynamics in the scholarly one. Strictly speaking, does not even such a movement as Pan-Africanism ignore historic and local specificity in the name of nonetheless existing common experiences and interests?

The term "postcolonialism" continues to undergo rigorous analysis and critique: what does the "post" signify? Does postcolonialism overrely on metropolitan theories? Is it a new, possibly invidious, form of perpetuating Western hegemony through relating all "peripheries" to a "center" like the spokes of a wheel, thus constricting their ability to interact with one another as long as attention is focused on the West? Despite continuing and justified doubts about the term, no replacement for it has been found, and something like postcolonial criticism keeps being practiced; and for all one knows, this lack of theoretical cohesiveness (even the spelling—hyphen or not—is not standardized yet) might be a strength, even an expression of resistance to some grand unifying meta-narrative, the very "seamless methodological universalism" R. Radhakrishnan implies postcolonialism might set itself up to be in a context of continued Western dominance (751). Francoise Lionnet's formulation might be useful here: after acknowledging that the "post" in postcolonial might lead to the misunderstanding that postcolonialism denies the existence of neocolonialism, she proposes a usage that "refers to more than the static periodization that the "post-" implies. In fact, I find it useful to think of "postcoloniality" in terms of "postcontact": that is, as a condition that exists within, and thus contests and resists, the colonial moment itself with its ideology of domination" (4). In this view—and it is a view this collection subscribes to—, postcolonialism serves as an umbrella term including all the effects and ramifications of the encounters between colonized and colonizers. Such dynamics are not restricted to Western colonialism, of course, and though in practice they have been predominantly studied in that historical context, the field needs by no means be limited to it.

However specifically postcolonialism or postcolonial criticism might be defined—a definitive answer to that question remains and will, I hope, remain elusive—most of its practitioners would be likely to see themselves as opposed to the continuance of colonialist/imperialist dominance, both theoretically and, perhaps, practically, however that praxis might manifest itself. What postcolonial criticism means in terms of this collection of essays is that it represents a variety of critical approaches that have in common that they interrogate colonialism and its aftermath in an attempt 1) either to analyze what has happened, to reach for new levels of truth beyond the stories offered by colonialism itself, to support the truth-seeking mission of the author's work they analyze; or 2) to examine and critique strategies for overcoming colonialist domination in whatever form, as those strategies are offered by the texts in question. In this way, this collection intends to prove as correct Tejumola Olaniyan's suspicion that "'Post-colonial' thus appears to be an open warrant to rifle through the history of Empire— before, during, and after—*from the perspective of the victims*" (744). One unifying element in postcolonial criticism, therefore, is its opposition to colonialism and its effects.

This does not imply, though, that postcolonialism turns into an automatic celebration of whatever it might be that follows colonialism. However good the "post" in postcolonialism might be in that it implies at least an end to direct occupation, the conflicted state of societies and peoples after colonialism of whatever form appears to require multiple perspectives. Several phenomena and scenarios open themselves to analysis, and what follows is merely an excerpt from what could easily be a longer catalogue: aftershocks of colonialism (political, economic, etc.); psychological leftovers requiring "decolonization of the mind," to use Ngugi wa Thiong'o's famous phrase; continuing forms of (neo)colonialism; the viability of traditions and/or a critique of traditions; new and possibly indigenous forms of oppression arising in the aftermath of colonialism; the role of nationalism. Since this collection focuses on women writers, critical perspectives on postcolonial conditions are inevitable, given that liberation of territory from occupying forces did not necessarily bring about positive results for women other than the disappearance of one layer of oppression.

Even though Africa and its Diaspora are now often taken for granted as forming a continuity, examining the core of commonalities on which this essay collection is founded will illuminate some of the sometimes unspoken assumptions on which postcolonial comparisons are based; rather than assuming that comparing women writers from Africa and the African Diaspora is a self-justifying undertaking, the following will explore, if only briefly, what the grounds for such a comparison are.

There are two obvious bases of comparison: the first consists in gender. All the writers examined here are women, and their texts largely focus on women as well. But is this in and of itself a valid basis? It is dangerous to "universalize" women's role, since such "universalizations" have often taken place in the context of Western dominance, and women's lives in one place, or writings about women's live in that place, may be misunderstood if unconsciously measured against women's lives in another place. Patriarchy appears in differing permutations in differing cultures, for one. All of this points to the difficult role feminism has played in an assessment of women's literatures and women's lives outside the West. The recent controversy surrounding Alice Walker's involvement in the campaign against excision—or genital mutilation—illustrates the conflict. Can a "Western" feminism intervene in a debate internal to a traditional culture? Or is feminism a Western construct? At times, that debate has ignored the presence of indigenous feminisms, which may actually predate the emergence of Western ones. Sisterhood may be global, to adapt the title of Robin Morgan's 1984 essay collection, but it does not take place in a de-politicized space, and thus the problem of Western hegemony impacts cross-cultural assessments of women's texts. Nonetheless, in a parallel to Tejumola Olaniyan's advice concerning historical specificity, one might say that ignoring similarities in women's lives and literatures for fear of treading on politicized ground could cause more damage than good. Such explorations, given proper caution concerning the critic's own cultural baggage, are indispensable for coalition building, and they often mutually illuminate problems only partially understood before. While Alice Walker's literary and political foray might have blundered at times, it has also heightened cross-cultural awareness of the degree to which women's sexuality is politicized, to what degree it might even be perceived as a threat by the powers that be, and to what degree women participate in their own oppression.

The second ground for comparison consists in "race," a generally problematic concept, given its roots in the history of colonialism and racism, further complicated here by "ethnicity," by the fact that people of African descent live in a variety of cultures. However, as Carole Boyce Davies has said, "Pan-African scholars seem unified on the issue that the export of Africans to the 'New World' unified Africans across their ethnic differences as it cut them off from their past." Colonialism and slavery created bonds between Africans who would have otherwise not thought of each other as "Africans," as having a common identity. At the same time, the Diaspora was also cut off from a common fount of culture and forced to create cultures of its own. "The Pan-African community thus created the conditions for another 'imagined community,' on the one hand a unified homeland, on the other a diaspora" (Davies, *Black Women* 20). The shared histories of contact and conflicts with Europeans and their descendants therefore established a new basis for a kind of "nation," both in Africa and in the Diaspora. The danger in the Pan-African approach, of course, lies in the tendency of nationalism to invent and/or idealize a common past and culture that, in fact, was not common. Cultural differences existed and exist in Africa as well as in the Diaspora, and there is the danger, too, of putting an overemphasis on "racial" difference in the study of diasporic cultures, in only seeing "racial" commonalities but overlooking existing exchanges and influences between peoples of African, European, and Native

American descent. Such "an overemphasis on dissimilarities," as Francoise Lionnet warns, "is likely to lead from racial and biographical determinism into an essentialist impasse" because it subscribes to an "erroneous view of culture wherein difference is rigidly valorized for its own sake" (14).

Nonetheless, parallels exist, cultural (deriving from common origin in Africa) and otherwise. Gay Wilentz, in discussing West African cultural retentions in the U.S., mentions "the Yoruba churches in Harlem, Igbo, Akan, and Mende names in the southern coastal areas, and food preferences and folklore throughout the Southeast." Beyond the cultural bridges, there are socio-economic and ideological considerations. In her essay "African Feminism: A Worldwide Perspective," Filomina Chioma Steady describes the status of black women in Africa, the Caribbean, the U.S. and Europe, summarizing that women of African descent tend to occupy the lower social rungs on a world-wide scale, particularly in the Diaspora, as a result of the combination of racism and sexism. As she says, in "Africa, independence did not bring about significant changes in the social, sexual, and racial inequalities perpetuated by colonialism mainly because many of the economic structures of colonialism remained intact and, in some cases, became even more exploitative" (10). Her essay shows that similar statements— with local adjustments—can be made about the situation of women of African descent in the Diaspora as well so that she concludes that "[f]or the majority of black women poverty is a way of life" (17). At this juncture, it is useful to remember Carole Boyce Davies reminder that "[i]f we see Black women's writing only as gender- and race-based ... then we miss a major understanding of the very specific critique of imperialism that many [black women writers] are offering" (*Black Women* 25). "Race" and gender are uniting elements in writings of women of African descent, but colonialism and its aftermath provide a context in which "race" and gender are situated. Thus the appropriateness of adopting a "postcolonial" approach to the writers discussed in this collection.

And it is "colonialism" in its various forms which provides a third connection between African American, Caribbean, and African literatures. While the shape of Western colonialism has differed significantly from locale to locale, for example in the degree to which it has penetrated a culture or dislocated its inhabitants, a "racial" and racist component has been common to all, and so has an insistence that Western culture is the yardstick by which all others are to be measured, and that the experiences of Europeans and their descendants can stand in as the experiences of all of humanity. The concept of "internal colonialism" might be appropriate here, because it helps clarify the historical and ideological background for a cross-cultural comparison of this kind. In his classic 1972 study *Racial Oppression in America*, Robert Blauner—in an attempt to justify his use of the term "internal colonialism" with reference to people of color in the U.S.—identifies certain "common core elements... which make up a complex I shall call *colonization*." He preambles a listing of those core elements by providing a crucial context for them:

> The common features ultimately relate to the fact that classical colonialism of the imperialist era and American racism both developed out of the same historical situation and reflected a common world economic and power stratification. The slave trade preceded the imperialist partition... of Africa; in fact, it may have been a necessary prerequisite for colonial conquest, since it helped deplete and pacify Africa, undermining resistance to direct occupation.... Because classical colonialism and America's internal colonialism developed out of similar technological, cultural, and power relations, a common *process* of social oppression characterized the racial patterns in the two contexts—despite the variations in political and social structure. (83/84)

The four core components he proceeds to list are the typically forcible entry that characterizes the beginning of colonialism, colonialism's "impact on culture," which manifests itself by a disturbance or destruction of "indigenous values, orientations, and ways of life," a "special relationship to... the legal order" for people of color, and, as final component, racism (84). In the 1970s, proponents of the concept of "internal colonialism" and of the usage of "Third World" with reference to African

Americans and other peoples of color within the U.S. had to defend this usage against charges of generalization and ahistoricism. Postcolonialism does as well, and it seems that merely the terms of the debate have changed; but as long as the basis for cross-cultural analyses remains solidly established, such analyses should continue to be produced, because there is a political and cultural necessity for them.

But, as usually, it is the writers themselves who perceived and emphasized the bridges between Africa and the various parts of the Diaspora and who adopted a "postcolonial" approach (with a focus on women) before there was such a term. Paule Marshall, a pivotal figure in this as in many other respects, has said about Merle, a character from her 1969 novel *The Chosen Place, the Timeless People*, that she "envision[s] her striding restlessly up and down the hemisphere from Argentina to Canada, and back and forth across the Atlantic between here and Africa" (109); Marshall's 1961 collection of short stories *Soul Clap Hands and Sing* considers the African Diaspora in a hemispheric sweep, from "Barbados" to "Brooklyn," from "British Guiana" to "Brazil." A growing number of writers, such as Jamaica Kincaid and Edwige Danticat, to name just two, or Toni Morrison in *Tar Baby*, stress the interconnectedness of the North American and the Caribbean diasporas; the "flight back to Africa" plays an important role in Morrison's *Song of Solomon* and Marshall's *Praisesong for the Widow*; and Simi Bedford, in *Yoruba Girl Dancing*, tells of recent Nigerian arrivals in England and their connections to the home country. Thus, in considering black women writers in a hemispheric and transatlantic light, critics have followed the lead of the novelists themselves.

Carole Boyce Davies' work must be mentioned as being of particular importance in a cross-cultural assessment of literature by women of African descent. Her 1994 work *Black Women, Writing and Identity* forges a theoretical framework within which such writings can be examined by taking "migration" both literally and metaphorically, by looking at the real disruptions of women's lives, often as the result of colonialist intrusions of one kind or another, and by seeing the psychological and ideological "migrations" against this background. Gay Wilentz' *Binding Cultures* (1992) examines the central role of women in transmitting cultures in works by African and African American novelists and is an important early book-length study making such a connection. In many ways, the work of these authors has been enabled by earlier attempts to apply feminism beyond color lines and globally, such as the pathbreaking 1979 anthology *Sturdy Black Bridges*, edited by Roseann Bell, Bettye Parker, and Beverly Guy-Sheftall; Gloria Anzaldua and Cherrie Moraga's classic anthology *This Bridge Called My Back: Radical Writings of Women of Color* (1981); Filomina Chioma Steady's collection *The Black Woman Cross-Culturally* (1981); and Rosalyn Terborg Penn's and Andrea Benton Rushing's *Women in Africa and the African Diaspora* (1987) which appeared in an expanded second edition in 1996. I wish to bow to these and other unnamed pioneers who have established a field that continues to be one of the most exciting fields in the academy, not least because its insights challenge almost everything the academy has taught in the past by focusing on what the academy has neglected in the past—it is here that postcolonialism and cross-cultural feminism are united.

Postcolonial criticism, as a result of its interdisciplinarity, has adopted a methodological pluralism. Though the essays in this collection focus on literature, that pluralism is reflected in the variety of approaches they employ. Bart Moore Gilbert maintains that

> Postcolonial criticism can still be seen as a more or less distinct set of reading practices, if it is understood as preoccupied principally with analysis of cultural forms which mediate, challenge or reflect upon the relations of domination and subordination—economic, cultural, political—between (and often within) nations, races or cultures, which characteristically have their roots in the history of modern European colonialism and imperialism and which, equally characteristically, continue to be apparent in the present era of neo-colonialism. (12)

The unity of the essays collected here goes beyond their analysis of and/or context in European colonialism and their Pan-African interests and sympathies: they are united by their focus on oppositional strategies, on attempts to create alternative value systems. Many of the strategies postcolonial texts pursue have to do with a kind of healing: re-writing history, re-imagining culture, re-visioning the role of women and men, re-constructing identity. The essays collected here examine such coping strategies through various theoretical approaches. Their common intent, not their methodological unity, and their focus on related themes make it possible to group these analyses under the heading "postcolonial."

Joy Viveros' essay "In a Shattered Glass: Harriet Jacobs's Archeology of Slaveholder Subjectivity" opens this collection because it reaches back in time furthest, to just before the U.S. Civil War. Her project, guided by the spirit of Jacobs' narrative, also undertakes a particularly daring task: to rewrite slaveholder subjectivity from the point of view of the person most qualified to do so—the slave. No one was more qualified because it was the slave's subjectivity which slavery sought to deny. Subjectivity has been an important concern in postcolonial criticism, not least thanks to the Subaltern Studies project, but this essay is an original application of the concept to a slave narrative. In showing Jacobs' awareness of the tenuous nature of the slavery system's constant denial of the slave's humanity, a denial that was in constant need of reaffirmation and yet constantly self-contradictory, Viveros focuses on a dimension of the text which reveals its postcolonial nature: through keen analytical resistance and exposure of the tactics used to deny her humanity, Jacobs' subjectivity ultimately proves more powerful than Flint's, and it is hers which literally has had the last word. Viveros subtly explores the psychological nuances of that "last word" as it reveals insights into the captor's tortured and self-defying strategies of self-validation. In the end, it is the captor's subjectivity that is in question.

Can anthropology be turned into a "neutral" tool of exploration or is its "exoticizing" and "othering" tendency so deeply inscribed that it turns against its African American practitioner? This is the question underlying Karen Jacobs' essay "From 'Spy-Glass' to 'Horizon': Tracking the Anthropological Gaze in Zora Neale Hurston." In Jacobs' words, the "spy-glass [Hurston's metaphor for the anthropological method] evokes not just the penetrating male gaze of science but the imperial white gaze of colonialism, both of which inform the ambiguous history of anthropology and its consolidation as a discipline in the 1920s and 30s." Hurston as anthropologist is thus, potentially, also the object of anthropology. Despite the relatively progressive politics informing Boasian anthropology, and despite its attempt at "cultural relativity," it assumed an "objective," implicitly "white" observer as "guest" of the observed culture. Hurston, however, was also a member of the observed culture. Furthermore, the hierarchy of "civilized" and "primitive" assumed by anthropology put Hurston in a difficult position in a cultural climate in which African Americans were striving for equal participation in U.S. society. As Jacobs observes, Hurston attempts to resolve such problematics, for example in her essay "Characteristics of Negro Expression," by making an "overt concession to perceived white standards of aesthetic value, contradicted by a covert endorsement of black practices as the crude but infinitely more vital form of cultural expression." Jacobs then turns to an extended reading of *Their Eyes Were Watching God* to show that artistic discourse, rooted in a kind of Emersonian transcendentalism, though it seems to offer an escape from primitivist Eurocentrism, is still compromised through philosophical assumptions "underpinned by a white male body." Jacobs illustrates the ambiguities and tradeoffs postcolonial subjects may face when attempting to adopt Western strategies for their own liberation.

Representation is at the heart of Venetria Patton's essay "'Yes, Anyone With Half an Eye Could See that It Wasn't She': Helga Crane's Artistic Decolonization." Helga Crane, the heroine of Nella Larsen's *Quicksand*, attempts to resist the mold her beholders are trying to cast her in in Denmark and in the U.S.: that of a sexualized exotic being, ultimately one-dimensional and derived from Western fantasies of African Americans. As Patton shows, the novel depicts Helga's battle to control image production about her, to shape her own image. However, she becomes trapped in a kind of "perceptual colonization," a process maybe most clearly symbolized by the painting a Danish painter produces of her. He interprets her as a completely sensual being, foreclosing her own attempts to come to terms with her sexuality—an embattled field in image production, as Patton illustrates by discussing the "Jezebel" stereotype derived from the ante-bellum South. Helga thus finds herself caught in a Catch-22 situation: if she rejects the sexual stereotypes, she might find herself caught in Victorian prudery, a Western straightjacket for healthy self-expression. But healthy self-expression might be interpreted as licentiousness by whites, as the Danish portrait shows. And what form is self-expression to take? Patton's essay navigates through this maze and illuminates a postcolonial theme—the search for self definition, accompanied by attempt to counter stereotypes—in this Harlem Renaissance novel.

Tanya Monier discovers a postcolonial dimension in Greek mythology. Her essay "Recontextualizing Women's History: Ursa Corregidora as a 'Blues Arachne'" employs Arachne as a template for a counterhistorian, one who refuses to let the history of the conqueror stand and insists on creating her own version, no matter what the prize. Such innovative bridge-building between African American literature, Greek mythology, and postcoloniality opens up possibilities of connections across time and space, linkages between stories of oppression and resistance from women's point of views; Gayl Jones' novel itself, of course, makes such connections between two parts of the African Diaspora—Brazil and the U.S—, and in spanning this hemispheric arc, she shows how past wrongs cannot be denied but must be confronted. The haunting quality of that past and the sexual transgressions it contains may still have destructive power in the present if it possesses the inheritors of that past. As Monier shows, the blues may offer a way out of this conundrum, and thus Ursa Corregidora becomes a kind of blues historian, a modern-day Arachne spinning her tales in the face of continuing oppression.

Like Tanya Monier, Tracey Thornton, in "Breaking Canonical Chains: Gloria Naylor's *Linden Hills*," is concerned with "writing back" to the metropolis, with the re-writing of a classical European text—Dante's *Inferno*—, a strategy that has been utilized by a number of postcolonial writers (one might think here of Walcott, Achebe, Baraka, Lamming, or of Marlene Nourbese Philip, as explored in Shara McCallum's essay). Gloria Naylor's answer to Europe in *Linden Hills*, as Tracey Thornton explains, focuses not only on power structures with regard to "race" but on gender as well, and replaces an individualistic struggle for happiness, spiritual and material, with "a notion of identity based upon the communal sharing of cultural traditions that allow the African American community to become a resource, a network, for its own people." In Thornton's view, the *Inferno* is part and parcel of a cultural tradition that has been used to assimilate, often forcibly, the cultures and traditions of colonized peoples and societies. The re-writing of the *Inferno*, and, by extension, of European American culture, to fit the cultural needs of African Americans is thus an "African Americanization" of it. *Linden Hills* sets out to illustrate the destructive results of wholesale adaptation of unwholesome cultural attitudes, but it also shows that mere reaction to Eurocentric standards, whether affirmative or negative, is not enough. The novel thus centers on the reclamation of spiritual practices. Religion is at the center of Dante's *Inferno* as well, but Naylor encourages "the rejuvenation of a personal and communal religion," thus moving spirituality into the spotlight of postcolonial concerns.

Like *Corregidora*, Jamaica Kincaid's *Lucy* is concerned with legacies of the past, both personal and historical, and their continued impact on the present. Both novels also illustrate that personal and historical past are inextricably interwoven. In "'Can't Leave Home Without It': The Paradox of Memory in Jamaica Kincaid's *Lucy*," Paulette Brown-Hinds explores the conflicted nature of home by analyzing it as a construct of memory as well as a place. Caught between two places— Antigua and New York—and "at home" in neither one, the novel's protagonist finds that it is difficult to forge an identity while simultaneously trying to forget the past—symbolized by her mother—and refusing to be cast into the role of the exotic colonial by her employers. The very colonial past Lucy attempts to repress resurfaces in her relationship with Mariah, one of her employers, as Paulette Brown-Hinds subtly illustrates through a reading of what might be called the "daffodil sequence" in the novel. In re-reading Wordsworth's poem "I Wander Lonely Like the Clouds" through Lucy's eyes, the reader is made to understand not only the nature of colonialist education but also the cultural contingency of literary works and how even an apparently innocuous text may become a tool of ideological domination. While the novel does not offer an unambiguous escape route from such domination, and while Lucy cannot escape either her personal or larger colonial past, she does break free of the neo-colonial relationship to her employers, and the narrative makes clear that only a reckoning with the past, whether personal or historical, may provide Lucy with a vision of her future which she lacks at present.

Shara McCallum revisits a classic question of postcolonial criticism in her essay "Remaking the Wor(l)d: A Poetics of Resistance and Transformation in Marlene Nourbese Philip's *She Tries Her Tongue: her silence softly breaks*": can the choice of language, in this case Creole, in and of itself serve political ends beyond its use for aesthetic purposes? To answer this question, McCallum "investigate[s] to what extent Creole has the ability to go beyond resistance and become transformative, that is, to what extent it is capable of redefining the world/self and our understanding of the same." As Gloria Naylor in *Linden Hills*, Philip utilizes a canonical Western text—the Proserpine-Ceres myth—and bends it to her own needs, Caribbeanizes it. She does so, as McCallum explores, both through content-based alterations and through linguistic changes, through selectively employing Creole. McCallum reads Philip's poems closely and makes transparent the politics that inform them as conveyed through their innovative language use. The poems, both in content and style, see Caribbean identity as "fluid" and use the reciprocal mother-daughter relationship as their main metaphor for mutual influence—mother searching daughter, daughter searching mother. Philip's poems move beyond resistance to transformation. Philip "changes the reader's conception of the world...but...she also changes the reader's conception of how the world is created through the word."

The land and the body—both are subjects of investigation in Joy M. Lynch's "'Beyond Recognition': Heritage and Identity in Paule Marshall's *The Chosen Place, the Timeless People*." The landscape becomes a kind of body in the novel as it appears alive, and the bodies of characters become a kind of landscape in that they are marked, both landscape and bodies revealing the signs of the past, of centuries of exploitation still vividly present. But, as Lynch says, the landscape resists: despite continued efforts at "modernization," which is really a euphemism for more efficient exploitation, Bournehills, the poorest region of Marshall's fictional island, remains virtually unchanged. The novel's main character, Merle, is at the center of Lynch's argument. As in Paulette Brown-Hinds' essay, memory is revealed as inescapable; but here, memory manifests itself physically. Through Merle, Lynch illustrates "how our bodies carry personal and historical memory forward, and how our bodies may be the conduits through which our subjectivity becomes integral to the landscape which bears memory as well."

Carmen Nge—in "Rising in the Ashes: Reading *Krik?Krak!* as a Response to 'Can the Subaltern Speak?'"—puts to the test Gayatri Spivak's theory developed in "Can the Subaltern Speak?", one of postcolonial theory's most famous documents, by reading it through selected stories of Edwidge Danticat's short story collection *Krik? Krak!*. Nge asks whether the subaltern is indeed as disempowered as Spivak implies, a claim that simultaneously makes the postcolonial critic the agent through whom the subaltern can speak. But even the "speechless" act of suicide, discussed in Spivak's essay, is not of necessity as silent and ineffectual as Spivak claims. Focusing on "A Wall of Fire Rising" and "Children of the Sea," Nge explains her discomfort with the categorical powerlessness of the act of suicide and the primacy of the word as written by the critic. In reading these stories, Nge shows how the suicides occuring in both of them are not acts without impact but affect communities who know how to interpret these deaths as they were meant: as acts of political resistance. While not arguing for the "agency" of all suicides, Nge insists that subaltern deeds can have impact and be remembered without having found "speech," without the posthumous intervention of the critic.

In "(Re-)writing the Marginalized Body: Grace Nichols's *The Fat Black Woman's Poems*," Melissa Johnson employs an eclectic mixture of European literary theory—mainly Bakhtin and Cixous—to analyze a Caribbean text. She does so self-consiously, however, aware of the "threat of theoretical colonization" and informed by postcolonial critics such as Ketu

Katrak and Wilson Harris, who have examined the potential dangers of such a procedure. Since Johnson focuses on the "Carnivalesque" quality of Nichols' poems, and Carnival represents an important facet of Caribbean culture, Bakhtin lies close at hand, and her analysis is further tempered by taking into account the cultural specificities of Caribbean Carnival. As in Carnival, which suspends and/or reverses the prevailing order, so in Nichols' poems: "When we enter this world through the poetry of Grace Nichols, we must check all Western patriarchal and philosophical baggage at the door." Her poems are concerned with European notions of beauty, patriarchy both African and European, racist anthropology, and, of course, language and its cultural and political implications. In close readings of individual poems, Johnson comes to the conclusion that "'The Fat Black Woman's Poems' are a hopeful and powerful vision of a new syncretic heritage and future which combines all the disparate strands of postcolonial culture."

Merri Lisa Johnson approaches Mariama Ba's *So Long a Letter* in the manner of philosophical hermeneutics, by being aware of her own "horizon" of cultural expectations so as to be able to interact with that of the literary work, as she shows in "Ramatoulaye's Letter: Cross-Cultural Reading Strategies & the Criticism of Mariama Ba's *So Long a Letter*." This is consistent with her project, which is to read critical responses to Ba's novel, responses in which she detects "projections of American women's desires, fears, and culturally-specific histories of oppression." In her metacritical analysis, Johnson decries the lack of cultural sensitivity and specificity in many readings of *So Long a Letter*, commenting that few critical discussions "read Ba's fiction in terms of Black feminism." She juxtaposes such readings with a variety of approaches she judges to be more constructive and which do not view any adherence to tradition as inherently reactionary and antifeminist. A section of Johnson's essay discusses the feminist and empowering potential of the written word—a discussion which might be fruitfully read against Carmen Nge's essay, which doubts the primacy of the word and emphasizes the efficacy of action.

In "Self-Colonization and Racial Identity in Ama Ata Aidoo's *Our Sister Killjoy or Reflections from a Black-Eyed*

Squint," James M. Ivory examines the continued impact of the
era of colonialism (and subsequent history) on the psyche of the
formerly colonized. He does so through an analysis of Aidoo's
novel and its exploration of "exile," of Africans residing in
Europe. At the same time that Aidoo's polemic calls on Africans
to return and put their expertise into the service of building their
home-countries, it works through the reasons why some—or
many—might not. James M. Ivory's reading of the novel focuses
on "self-colonization" as one of the answers, on the possibility of
internalizing colonial values—and the destructive results of such
an internalization.

The utopia at the center of the postcolonial project—the wish
to overcome and go beyond (neo)colonialism—is what interests
Su Fang Ng in her essay "Women's Utopic Impulses in Buchi
Emecheta's *Destination Biafra*." Though Emecheta's novel is
anything but optimistic, Ng argues that it is nonetheless informed
by a utopian vision and that Emecheta "insists on the integral
role of utopia and utopic vision in the decolonization project."
The novel's main character is central to the novel's development
and, ultimately, transformation of utopic vision, as Ng maintains.
Through a series of disillusionments that serve as a harsh
education in political realities, the protagonist's utopic vision is
altered but not lost. At the end, utopia is "[n]o longer a move to
recuperate native wholeness or an idealized world... [but]
becomes a faith in the possibility for genuine political action,
and that action must be at the grass-roots level where people are
forced to defend their very lives."

Jennifer Poulos Nesbitt's "'Loose or decent, I don't know':
Space, Self, and Nation in Tsitsi Dangarembga's *Nervous
Conditions*" discusses the interplay of the forces of tradition and
of Western-style modernization as they impact women's "place"
in society. Jennifer Poulos Nesbitt focuses on the role of
geography in relation to gender. Recognizing (post)colonial
nation-building as an often male-centered enterprise, *Nervous
Conditions* asks what a challenge to the patriarchal order means
for the development of Rhodesia/Zimbabwe. Poulos Nesbitt
examines a little-explored undercurrent of that challenge: the
question of landownership. Colonialism has already altered the
relationship of the Shona to the land and established "spatial

inequalities." Her essay explores to what extent space is gendered, closely reading—as the centerpiece of her analysis— the protagonist's, and, by extension, other women's connection to the river Nyamarira. Nesbitt shows that even what might be taken as the very image of freedom and unrestraint—a river— does not escape the historical forces of colonialism, its response, nationalism, and a sexism shaped by both.

Chinyere G. Okafor's essay "Location and Separateness in African and African-American Drama: A Study of Hilda Kuper's *A Witch in My Heart* and Lorraine Hansberry's *A Raisin in the Sun*" concludes this collection by spanning a bridge between the U.S. and Swaziland. Putting gender in the foreground, Okafor examines cultural similarities in a play centering on an African family in Swaziland and an African American family in Chicago. Referring to a number of other African and African American plays as well, Okafor finds that the "subordination of women and women's struggle against it cuts across spatial setting and social structure." The factor of "race" and forms of colonization serve as background for gender-based oppression in these plays and give it a distinctive dimension. Going against recent injunctions against cross-cultural readings and skepticism about cross-cultural feminism, Okafor insists that it is the common bond of gender (and gender-based oppression) that causes the parallels between these plays, despite geographical distance, and despite the fact that one playwright is white and from Zimbabwe and the other African American. In effect, the essay argues for a kind of global sisterhood and, in that respect as well, makes for a befitting ending.

The essays have been organized according to geographical origin of the authors of the literary works examined, mainly for the convenience of readers predominantly interested in the literature of one of the regions. Despite the fact that Africa leads its Diaspora in the title of this collection—a choice made for political and symbolic reasons, countering the neglect Africa experiences in Western media and scholarship—African American literature starts the collection because the African Diaspora in the Americas found itself in a postcolonial situation, formally speaking, before Africa itself; Caribbean literature begins the journey back to the continent itself, which occupies the last section, ended by an essay comparing an African and African American plays. Different lines of organization are possible following connections between essays in separate sections. Thus, Tanya Monier's, Tracey Thornton's and Shara McCallum's essays are all concerned with revisions of canonical European texts. Both Melissa Johnson's and Merri Lisa Johnson's essay self-consiously focus on (European) theory and its appropriateness or applicability for postcolonial texts, as does Karen Jacobs, who examines what happens when European theory underwrites the anthropological work of an African American author. Carmen Nge's essay takes an almost opposite stance on the role and importance of the written word as resistance as Merri Lisa Johnson's essay. Both Joy Lynch's and Jennifer Nesbitt's analyses concern themselves with landscape and geography, and in both essays, landscape almost becomes a kind of character. Joy Viveros and James Ivory are concerned with the psychological dimensions of oppression (though they use very different approaches), as are Tanya Monier and Paulette Brown-Hinds, whose essays discuss the impossibility of escaping the past. Melissa Johnson, James Ivory, Chinyere Okafor, and Su Fang Ng derive direct political lessons from the readings of their chosen texts, while Venetria Patton, Jennifer Nesbitt, and Karen Jacobs analyses are of a more philosophical-theoretical character (which does not make them devoid of political implications, of course). Many of the essays are fruitfully read side-by-side, and together they illustrate both the diversity and ultimate coherence of the postcolonial project.

Carol Boyce Davies mentions the "automatic equation of black women's writing with U.S. African-American women's writing," in great part due to the hegemonic role the U.S. plays in the global economy (*Moving* 1). While this picture has begun to change, as both African and African American Studies are moving towards a more integrative, transatlantic approach, this collection hopes to contribute to a growing awareness of the diversity of writings by women of African descent as well as draw attention to the powerful analyses provided by them.

* * * *

I'd like to thank the contributors for their hard work and all of those who have, over the years, encouraged me in my enthusiasm for African, Caribbean, and African American literature and culture. They are too many people to name here, but I will name a few: Adetona Akindes, Susanne Becker, Paulette Brown-Hinds, Beverly Chandler, Maureen Eke, Anna Marie Evans, T. Ford-Ahmed, Winfried Herget, Dale Herndon, Matthew , Hobson, Beverly Horton, Christine Henderson Kennedy and the entire Kennedy family, Kathleena Kennedy, Michael Kramer, Joy Lynch, Clarence Major, Shara McCallum, Abainesh Mitiku, Linda Morris, James Natsis, Tayoba Ngenge, Myrna Nurse, Venetria Patton, Joy Viveros, Ernest Sekabunga, Carol Taylor Johnson, Litchfield O'Brian Thompson, Patricia Turner, and all my students in African American or African Literature classes I have taught in California and West Virginia. At least my part of the work on this volume is dedicated to Nagadya Mutawe—Segadya wo akwagala ennyo!

Works Cited

Blauner, Robert. *Racial Oppression in America*. New York: Harper & Row, 1972.

Boyce, Carol Davies. *Black Women, Writing and Identity. Migrations of the Subject*. London and NewYork:Routledge, 1994.

——, ed. *Moving Beyond Boundaries. Vol. 2: Black Women's Diaspora*. New York: New York UP, 1995.

Henderson, Gwendolyn Mae. "Speaking in Tongues: Dialogics, Dialectics, and the Black Woman's Writer's Literary Tradition." *Changing Our Own Words. Essays on Criticism, Theory, and Writings by Black Women*. Ed. Cheryl A. Wall. New Brunswick: Rutgers UP, 1989. 16-37.

Lionnet, Francoise. *Postcolonial Representations. Women, Literature, Identity*. Ithaca: Cornell UP, 1995.

Marshall, Paule. *Reena and Other Stories*. New York: Feminist Press, 1983.

Moore-Gilbert, Bart. *Postcolonial Theory: Contexts, Practices, Politics*. London: Verso, 1997.

Olaniyan, Tejumola. "On 'Post-Colonial Discourse': An Introduction." *Callaloo* 16.4 (1993): 743-749.

Radhakrishnan, R. "Postcoloniality and the Boundaries of Identity." *Callaloo* 16.4 (1993): 750-771.

Steady, Filomina Chioma. "African Feminism: A Worldwide Perspective." *Women in Africa and the African Diaspora. A Reader*. 2nd ed. Eds. Rosalyn Terborg-Penn and Andrea Benton Rushing. Washington, DC: Howard UP, 1996, 3-21.

Wilentz, Gay. *Binding Cultures. Black Women Writers in Africa and the Diaspora*. Bloomington: Indiana UP, 1992.

1: AFRICAN AMERICAN WRITERS

IN A SHATTERED GLASS: HARRIET JACOBS'S ARCHAEOLOGY OF SLAVEHOLDER SUBJECTIVITY

Joy Viveros

As Christopher Wise and Cora Agatucci remind us, "African-American literature differs from most post-colonial literatures in that it is written by members of a minority community who reside within a nation of vast wealth and military power."[1] Wise and Agatucci's observation is particularly apt with respect to the narratives of antebellum household slaves because these narratives materialize from the covetously shielded interior spaces of the antebellum South. This genre emerges as an innovative form of "postcolonial testimonial"[2] because the history of their authors' access to the intimate lives of captors allows them to become agents of illumination from within the realm of the colonizers.[3] In her 1861 autobiographical narrative, *Incidents in the Life of a Slave Girl*,[4] Harriet Jacobs brings into relief that although domestic slaves lived at the outermost margins of power, they also lived within the colonial family and as such were uniquely positioned to speculate on the characterological effects of holding captives on the slaveholders themselves.

In reconstructing the psychological dynamics of the slaveholding household as Jacobs invites us to do, it is important to apprehend that cultural categories failed to entirely explain away the experience of those defined as property. The social death[5] of the enslaved was a construct that demanded perpetual nurture because it centered on emotive, psychological beings endowed with memory and the capacity to create their own moral categories. Although slaveholding ideology denied that the interior resources of the enslaved had any bearing on their sociojuridical erasure, the reaction of the enslaved to their legal and cultural effacement, and to the exercise of virtually unregulated power among slaveholders, was in unrelenting friction with the fictions slaveholders lived by.

Abdul JanMohamed has argued for the existential implications of social death: that it functioned in part to negate the subjectivity of the enslaved.[6] I would add that this negation was necessarily justified on the basis of its own morality. Antebellum juridical categories had to be equated with justice not simply for the slaveocracy to sustain its ideological integrity, but for the individual slaveholder to sustain a sense of the legitimacy of his or her subject position. Apologias for Southern slavery could be viewed as directed not only to abolitionists, the North, and the international community, but also to the slaveholding community itself. George Fitzhugh's 1857 *Cannibals All!*, for example, justifies effacing the identity and will of the enslaved by arguing that, at an interpersonal level, the "perfect... subordination" of the will of the powerless to that of the powerful leads to the "greater... happiness" of them both.[7] Attempts such as this to fortify slaveholders' subjectivity obliquely point to the pressures of identity conceived in relation to the inherently self-contradictory logic of the subject position "human chattel." The practice of social death demanded of captives an emptying out of interiority in the interests of a self-presentation that did not appear to deny its own legal and social erasure. This ideal was, however, unachievable. No manner of self-presentation could be entirely devoid of affect and, therefore, self-reference. Slave affect, of itself, eroded the subject position of the slaveholder. Every definition that increased the ontological distance between enslaved and enslaver shored up the moral position of the latter. But emotion, whether suppressed or not, registered the alikeness of captive and captor. And this alikeness threatened the integrity of a moral order predicated on difference.

Critical to the intrapsychic efficacy of the ideology of difference was the degree to which slaveholders could limit their exposure to slave affect. This attempt was relatively effective in relation to enslaved populations outside the slaveholder's immediate environs. The slave at a physical distance on the plantation could be apparently contained within social constructs and ultimately pushed outside the first horizon of the slaveholder's consciousness. Even the perceptual blurring of the humanity of field slaves facilitated by their separate living quarters and sheer numbers was insufficient, however, to overcome the draining effect of their presence on the focus necessary for the slaveocrat to extract from them their maximum use value. Field slaves were therefore forced to further their own erasure by their participation in work songs which served to drown out the affect latent in their silence. Frederick Douglass observes in his second narrative that,

> Slaves are generally expected to sing as well as to work.
> A silent slave is not liked by masters or overseers.
> *"Make a noise," "make a noise"* and *"bear a hand,"* are
> the words usually addressed to the slaves when there is
> silence amongst them. This may account for the almost
> constant singing heard in the southern states.[8]

My discussion here is not intended to overlook the lyrical and spiritual qualities infused into these songs by the enslaved, but to underscore Douglass's observation that singing in the field often occurred not as an organic response to the emotive states of the enslaved, but to suit the needs of slaveocrats. The traumas enslavement presented—the sale of offspring, shortened life span, sleep deprivation, hunger, radical exposure to the elements, sexual exploitation, coercive violence and murder, and their ever present threat—necessarily created a palpable environment of psychic noise around the enslaved: a noise amplified by their numbers. Requiring field slaves to sing yielded two-fold gains for the slaveocrat: the rhythmic qualities of song increased the productivity of a work force always in the grip of grief and depression, and the momentum of song carried enslaved workers out of the vortex of introspection to other emotive states. This coerced performance masked grief, rage, and depression in the enslaved and thus decreased the psychic pressure of these emotive states on the slaveocrat.

Jacobs demonstrates that the attempt to limit exposure to slave affect was considerably less efficacious within the slaveholding household. Here, the emotional shocks resulting from the murder, abuse, torture, and sale of the enslaved were driven into bifurcated fields of repression: the slaveholding family denying anything out of the ordinary had occurred, and demanding in turn an identical repression of each member of the enslaved family. Although repression was also demanded of plantation slaves, Jacobs's narrative demonstrates that captives within the slaveholding household were subject to relentless performative demands. Jacobs introduces the rigors of minimizing the effect on one's captors of one's own subjectivity in a scene pivoting on her brother as a helpless witness of her humiliation by Dr. Flint. She notes, in this regard, the consequence of her brother's failure to "keep back" his responsive tears:

> This manifestation of feeling irritated the doctor. William could do nothing to please him. One morning ... [a] circumstance afforded his master an opportunity to vent his spleen. He was put in jail. (61)

What William is ultimately punished for is his failure to pretend insensibility to his sister's degradation. This failure asserts a realm of human connection Flint attempts to force back into the shadows of his and William's consciousness by giving them both something worse to remember.

This incident can be understood more completely in light of Jacobs's earlier delineation of the competitive tension between the affects of captor and captive. Jacobs tells us that on the day following her father's death, she is forced to divert herself from the "dead body of [her] father" and ordered, instead, to "gath[er] flowers and weav[e] them into festoons" for Mrs. Flint's "evening party" (10). Mrs. Flint's insistence on "festivit[y]" appears somewhere in the range between stupendous self-absorption and belligerent cruelty. But Jacobs' narrative as a whole demonstrates that these behaviors are also compensatory: that "manifestation of feeling" on the part of the enslaved is itself threatening to slaveholders. Slaveholders are at pains not only to dominate their captives, but to demand that captives deny, disown, and silence their own emotive states. Paradoxically, Mrs. Flint's festooned gala must go forward, and Jacobs must participate in Mrs. Flint's effacement of her interior concerns, *because* Mrs. Flint cannot see herself as cruel or selfish. Clearly, Mrs. Flint has committed herself to an ideological construct in which the interiority of the enslaved is absolutely irrelevant. She acts as she does because it is only deep within this construct that she is safe from Jacobs's grief and its dilating implications.

Violence within the slaveholding home is of particular import here because it does not simply signal efforts—consistent with slaveholding ideology—to regulate the behaviors of the enslaved; it also points to fissures in that ideology. Rather than illustrating the protected sphere of paternalistic care touted in apologist lore, slave narratives often portray the slaveholding home as a locus of chronic, episodic escalations of violence. Clearly, one function of slaveholder violence within the slave-holding household was to emphasize *to the enslaved* the immutability of the demarcation within it between enslaved and enslaving families. But slaveholders were also drawn to violence against captives in their own homes because the intimate terms of common living quarters and shared resources worked against *their own* certainty of this immutability. Minor incursions into this demarcation thus gave rise to bizarre forms of retribution. Jacobs recalls of Mrs. Flint that,

> If dinner was not served at the exact time on that particular Sunday, she would station herself in the kitchen, and wait till it was dished, and then spit in all the kettles and pans that had been used for cooking. She did this to prevent the cook and her children from eking out their meager fare with the remains of the gravy and

other scrapings. The slaves could get nothing to eat
except what she chose to give them. (12)

As this and other passages in *Incidents* indicate, the radically
disparate distribution of material resources and foodstuffs did not
occur tactfully somewhere outside the slaveholding household.
The measurement and allotment of provisions was performed at
regular intervals (thrice daily in the case of Mrs. Flint) by either
the slaveholding husband or wife. The slaveocrat's desire to
sustain a sense of well-being in the face of the nutritional
deprivation of household slaves necessitated great psychological
maneuvers. The palliative often utilized was to compound
institutional violence with retributive violence. In this case, for
example, whether Mrs. Flint is viewed as "correcting,"
"punishing," or "retaliating against" her captives, it is clear that
her attempt to make her leftovers revolting or inedible to the
hungry is an attempt to underscore that she perceives herself as
the wronged party amongst them. Retributive violence can be
seen as a kind self-assuring behavior, justified by the
slaveholder's interior litany of inequities suffered at the hands of
the enslaved—not the least of which is the unnamed uncertainty
simmering beneath the slaveholder's bravado.

Another significant aim of reactive violence within the
slaveholding household was to exclude attachments outside it.
The intrapsychic turmoil precipitated by slaveholder's inability
to delimit both sides of emotional attachments formed between
household slaves and others is nowhere clearer than in the rage
provoked by the attachment of female slaves to free African
American men. Consider, for example, Dr. Flint's incensed
response to Jacobs's request to marry a "free born" suitor (37).
After offering Jacobs the option of coupling, instead, with one of
his slaves, he asks whether she "love[s] this nigger?" (39). In
response to Jacobs's plain, "Yes, sir," Flint explodes with an
incredulous, "How dare you tell me so!," tremulous with a wish
to un-know what Jacobs has made explicit between them (39).
Slaveholders exercised the power to determine the sexual
pairings of all slaves; this should not eclipse that their investment
in this power possessed a different charge when the slaves shared
with them their homes, and in a real sense, their private selves.
Since such attachments imposed no sociojuridical limits on

slaveholder sexual prerogative, their rage clearly issued from a threat of another order. The enslaved woman's emotional attachment to someone other than those who possessed the power to govern her body signified her hunger for voluntary relations. This hunger exposed every interaction between enslaver and enslaved as necessitating a performance from the latter, and thus undermined any fantasy that the performance could be taken at face value. Slaveholders' exercise of the power to sunder such attachments was an effort to blot out awareness of what their power had already rendered inscrutable. Slave narratives are thus replete with descriptions of an almost obsessive desire on the part of slaveholders of both genders to interject themselves into the interiority of the slave experience. Dr. Flint, for example, does not want for venues for his sexual pursuit of Jacobs. She nevertheless recalls,

> If I went out for a breath of fresh air, after a day of unwearied toil, his footsteps dogged me. If I knelt by my mother's grave, his dark shadow fell on me even there. (28)

Flint's interposition of his sexual demands and threats into the brief moments when Jacobs is manifestly turned toward her own experience demonstrates that at some level he experiences her interest in anything or anyone outside himself as a threat. The insistence on obtaining the absolute emotional attention of the enslaved masked one of the rigors of the slaveholding relationship: having severed ties captives might have had, slaveholders often felt compelled to sunder further ties since these attachments were of themselves an indictment of the slaveocrat's subjectivity.

Whenever slaves failed to conceal their judgments, rage, sorrow, grief, longings, and attachments to others, or even allowed their attention to wander from the demands of servility, they spoke their humanity through the mask of servitude. This evidence could not be incorporated by the prevailing ideology and its consequences could only be addressed in the psychological structure of the slaveholder by a move toward recognition of that humanity or by intensifying cruelty toward the slave. Mrs. Flint says as much when forced to confront the unrestrained grief of an enslaved child. Following Jacobs's escape from the Flint plantation, several members of her family are incarcerated, including her two-year old daughter Ellen. Shortly thereafter Mrs. Flint retrieves Ellen from jail in the hope of training her for household service. On the day of her relocation to the Flint household, Ellen, too immature to dissemble, "scream[s] and sob[s]" unrelentingly (102). In reaction to this Mrs. Flint has Ellen incarcerated, noting that had Ellen remained, she "should either [have] kill[ed] her or spoil[ed] her" (102). The choice Mrs. Flint presents between "spoil[ing]" and "kill[ing]" is a compelling one. An unwilling spectator to her effect on her captive, Mrs. Flint predicts she will be driven to neutralize Ellen's distress in some way: either by rendering her no longer distressed ("spoiling" her) or by rendering *her* no longer (erasure of her reactive sentience by murder). Opting instead to remove her captive from her sight and hearing, Mrs. Flint seems to posit recognition of her enslaved's humanity as equally distasteful to her as killing her enslaved.

While cruelty by slaveholders certainly issued from their absolute power in relation to their human chattel, it was also symptomatic of a desperate attempt to shore up a viable image of the self. Slave actions and affect that pressured fissures in slaveocratic ideology placed the slaveholder in an impossible position. These implicitly stripped the slaveholder's exercise of power of its ideological undergirding and exposed the largest part of his or her psychology in terms of naked self-interest. The only refuge from the nonviability of the binary capabilities assigned by the slaveocracy to slaveholder and slave was in the transfer of this binarism to rudimentary theological constructs. Theological constructs were particularly ripe for this purpose since they could dissolve logical and moral dilemmas into matters of faith. Thus the slave had to be punished not for calling into question constructs which justified and sanctioned the morality of the slaveholder's exercise of self-interest, but for his or her essential badness. The slaveocrat's move was not necessarily to the formal justification of the persecution of dark skinned peoples as descendants of Ham, but rather an intuitive movement to the sanctuary of primal logic.

For the slaveholder, the household thus became the site of a moral war, with the slave embodying the native evil in the human condition, and the enslaver its inherent virtue. All activity between enslaver and enslaved was thereby reendowed with the lofty aims of religious drama. Although Jacobs does not depict the Flints as particularly pious, she does hint at the relation between slaveholders' religiosity and their assault on household slaves in a passage about Mrs. Flint which moves abruptly from one subject to the other:

> "She ... could sit in her easy chair and see a woman whipped, till the blood trickled from every stroke of the lash. She was a member of the church...." (12).

What I wish to point out here is not so much any contradiction between Mrs. Flint's actions and her theological beliefs, but rather the interaction Jacobs is pointing to between violent assaults on slaves and the explanatory power of religious constructs. Although there may be contradictions between slaveholder behavior and particular biblical injunctions, my point here is that slaveholders brought the imaginative weight of theology to bear on their own understanding of their attacks on their captives.

The inherently contradictory logic of the term human chattel nevertheless always acted to destabilize the slaveholder's interpretive scheme. Because the slaveocracy was structured at some points to provide for total dependency on slave labor, and because the slave was simultaneously viewed as nominally visible, slave presence, particularly in the home, was ubiquitous. Jacobs points to the atypical character of conversations out of the hearing of household slaves by her numerous references to conversations overheard by the enslaved, as well as by her description of a "closeted" conversation between Mrs. Flint and her daughter-in-law, alarming to her in part because it took place behind closed doors (93). Although slaveholders tended to know relatively little about the psychological and spiritual lives of their captives, there was for them an ever present awareness of and reliance on slave knowledge of their personal and family histories and psychological characteristics. For the enslaved, acquiring expertise in this area was a matter of survival, and dedication to this project a consciously motivated daily agenda. For the enslaver, however, this knowledge existed at the threshold of consciousness, blended into the environment of comfort and burden provided by the presence of the enslaved. Aunt Nancy's impending death, for example, is experienced by the Flints as a dreaded loss of a valued slave. Their apprehension surrounding this prospect is clearly incompatible with any knowledge that she has consistently encouraged Jacobs to escape enslavement, or that even on her death bed she is helping to conceal Jacobs.

The opposing functions and uses by slaveholder and enslaved of the latter's knowledge of the former's personality and modus operandi is exposed in some detail in Jacobs's description of Dr. Flint's extended struggle to make her his sexual partner. My discussion here focuses on Flint's un-willingness to rape or sell Jacobs who grew up in his household from age eleven or twelve. While Flint's coercive tactics are a hair's breadth from physical rape, the significance of his desire to obtain Jacobs's quasi-consensual assent to a sexual liaison with him is particularly relevant to this discussion. Jacobs speculates that Flint refrains from literal sexual assault because he is concerned to maintain his respectability within his family and as a physician in their small town. This speculation does not fully explain the doctor's reluctance to physically rape her since so many factors mitigate against him suffering any consequence whatsoever as a result of this act. This is particularly true after Flint's false confession to Mrs. Flint that he and Jacobs have already been having an affair and Mrs. Flint's subsequent gossip within the town about Jacobs's participation in her marital difficulties. Flint's confession blocks any recourse Jacobs might have had against him should he physically rape her by compounding her sociojuridical erasure with the erasure of her credibility.

The fact is, neither Jacobs nor Flint completely fathoms his reluctance to exercise his virtually unlimited power to exploit her sexually. Nevertheless, Jacobs's apprehension of this reluctance permits her to maneuver it within her means. Dr. Flint's only public description of Jacobs contained in *Incidents* is his advertisement for her arrest that describes her as:

> ... an intelligent, bright, mulatto girl ... , 21 years of age.
> Five feet four inches high. Dark eyes, and black hair
> inclined to curl ... [that] can be made straight. Has a
> decayed spot on a front tooth. She can read and write,
> and in all probability will try to get to the Free States.
> (97)

Their mutual history indicates, however, that even if he does not
consciously value her as more than this bare description
indicates, she certainly symbolizes more than this to him. To
begin to understand the nature of what she signifies, we must
return to the slaveholding household and name what slaveholders
could not: that it existed as both separate, oppositional kinship
relations and as a partially acknowledged blended family of the
slaveholders and their captives. Jacobs underscores this relation
in her depiction of a conversation between her grandmother Aunt
Martha and Dr. Flint wherein Aunt Martha reminds him that in
spite of the conflict between their families, she could wish no ill
to his wife who is her own "foster-child," and the "foster-sister"
of her daughter Nancy (145).

The experiences shared within the single and irreparably
bifurcated slaveholding family accrued over generations. The
presence of the enslaved through celebrations, births, suckling
infancy, illness, infirmity, feuds, intrigues, and deaths increased
their symbolic value for the slaveholder. The household captive
became a repository of familial and personal history. The value
of such a repository, somewhere between object and person,
tended to increase as time and his or her knowledge of family
affairs accrued. This accounts in part for the occasional outrage
over the sale of captives such as Jacobs's grandmother, held in
the family over a period of generations:

> When the day of sale came, she took her place among
> the chattels, and at the first call she sprang upon the
> auction-block. Many voices called out, Shame! Shame!
> Who is going to sell *you*, aunt Marthy? Don't stand
> there! That is no place for *you*." (11)

What this protest registers is slaveholders' experience that as
decades accrued their humanity in some way invested itself in
their household captives. If this sort of investment were not

perceived, there would be no reason whatsoever for community outrage over treating chattel who had served a particular slaveholding family for years any differently from one who had not. The "*you*, aunt Marthy," echoed here refers to a subject who has become absorbed into the slaveholding community to such a degree that her sale constitutes a kind of amputation of communal memory. This is not to argue that this sort of amputation did not regularly occur, but to note the slaveholding community's introjection of this enslaved woman, an incorporation precipitated by her prolonged exposure to the intimate lives of slaveholders.

The intimacy facilitated by the slaveholding relationship centered on the absolute power of the enslaver over the enslaved. This perfect power left no need for secrets between enslaved and enslaver as to the latter's personality. The slaveholder's liberty to bare to the enslaved all desires, licit and illicit, taboo and sanctioned, fostered a climate of intensified intimacy between them. The value of this intimacy was that it was a site where taboo aspects of the slaveholder's personality could be experienced and known by another. The fact that this other could be regarded and treated as a literal object afforded the slaveholder the opportunity to act upon his or her own thriving ambivalence about this taboo self inscribed in the mirror of another's sentience.

In addition to signifying taboo personal history, the captive became the site for reenacting the trauma of family life riddled with abuse of the sociojuridically helpless. Parents who routinely sexually exploited, tortured, and persecuted those they enslaved left their children with the legacy and memory of who they had been. Reenacting parental patterns of abuse against the enslaved was one way the adult child could continue to idealize and honor the significance of their parents' lives. When young Emily Flint, new to adulthood, takes up the task of attempting to lure Jacobs back to slavery, she makes the point that in doing so she is acting "independently of [her] father"(186). It is an interesting assertion given that her desire to return Jacobs to the interior of the Flint family is consistent with her father's quest from the time of Jacobs's escape. That Emily Flint was in conflict with her father on the issue of Jacobs's ownership should not obscure that the subterfuge she engages in to recapture Jacobs[9] also mimics her father's obsession with Jacobs, or that it is of a piece with the spirit of his earlier prediction about Jacobs's relation to their family: "She shall be my slave as long as I live, and when I am dead she shall be the slave of my children" (109).

The slaveholding family's tendency to utilize the enslaved to release pent-up affect and discharge taboo sexuality often resulted in emotional abandonment of the household's non-slaves. The emotional needs of the Flints' youngest daughter, then four years old,[10] for example, could not have been adequately honored during her mother and father's tug-of-war over the doctor's desire to take her into his bedroom at night in order to justify the alleged necessity of having Jacobs with him throughout the night. For this reason, the slave intimate was vulnerable to being perceived as the site of the interruption of intrafamilial bonds and emotional support within the slaveholding family. Mrs. Flint registers that she views Jacobs as exactly this when she refuses to believe Dr. Flint's suggestion that their daughter is emotionally attached to Jacobs. Lillian Smith's memoir of life in the post-Reconstruction South is helpful in understanding Mrs. Flint's insistence that rather than caring for Jacobs, young Emily merely fears her. In her memoir, Smith describes the Southern mother's resentment toward the female servant who has garnered her children's love: "Of all the humiliating experiences which Southern white women have endured, the least easy to accept ... was that of a mother who had no choice but to take the husk of a love which her [child] in [its] earliest years had given to another woman."[11] Even before Jacobs becomes an object of her husband's sexual attention, Mrs. Flint braces herself against any suggestion that their captive has garnered part of what Mrs. Flint considers her own.

Hostility over the enslaved's cathectic function in the family was easily transposed to his or her perceived active role in undermining the sanctity of family life. This accounts in part for the vicious treatment slaveholding wives meted out to enslaved women who gave birth to children fathered by the slaveholding husband. The interpsychic familial turmoil precipitated by slave-holding husbands' exploitation of female slaves was often managed by scapegoating the enslaved woman. The enslaved mother and her offspring became the reification of the breakdown of emotional and sexual intimacy in the slaveholding marriage. More often than not, the parties to that marriage nominally repaired damage to it sustained as a result of the slaveholding husband's infidelity by dis-owning the evidence of this damage. Jacobs documents several instances of this pattern of denial of extramarital sexual conduct by way of the sale of enslaved mother and child. Of particular interest is the following passage recounted by Jacobs's grandmother about an enslaved woman who had just given birth to her slaveholder's child:

> Her mistress had that day seen her baby for the first time, and in he lineaments of its fair face she saw a likeness to her husband. She turned the bondwoman and her child out of doors, and forbade her ever to return ... The next day she and her baby were sold to a Georgia trader. (122)

Removal of the mother and child by their sale acted to remove the emblems of the failure of intimacy in the slaveholding marriage. Sale of mother and child constituted both an act of aggression against the enslaved family and an act of appeasement within the slaveholding marriage. By implicitly agreeing the presence of a particular enslaved woman precipitated a rupture in the slaveholding marriage, husband and wife joined in the fantasy that her removal could in some way repair the rupture. This kind of logic, tinged as it is with magical ideation, accounts for Mrs. Flint's vow, following Jacobs's removal to "a small house ... in a secluded place, four miles away from the town" (53) that she would "kill" Jacobs should she "[come] back" to the Flint household (76). The fact that Jacobs, as chattel, has been relegated to the role of a decisive actor in this domestic drama is no less fantastic than the fact that Mrs. Flint and her husband have somehow concurred that her desires are being met, in part at least, by removing from her view evidence of his desire to be unfaithful to her—particularly because this relocation multiplies his opportunities for sexual contact with Jacobs. In instances such as these, aversion transformed into amnesiac strategies. The slaveholding marriage reestablished a tenuous equilibrium based on the efficacy of this amnesia, which was inevitably undermined by another enslaved woman or the birth of another of the slaveholder's mulatto children.

A not uncommon consequence of this manner of fortifying the slaveholding marriage is that the parties to it sought the level of each other's cruelty. In these cases, the marriage survived at the cost of the mutual brutalization of the parties to it. Jacobs's narrative records the evolution of Mrs. Flint's transformation from injured wife to Dr. Flint's co-conspirator against Jacobs. Although Jacobs makes explicit that Mrs. Flint was never "a very refined woman" (34), it is clear that the wife who "wept" and "groaned" to hear of her husband's lascivious invitations to the fifteen-year old Jacobs (33) is delicate by comparison to the wife who, years later, has joined her husband in his quest to recapture Jacobs and "see her broke in yet" (102).

The radical plasticity of the slaveholding relationship permitted the slaveholder avenues of self-expression unthinkable in their relations with equals. A chattel could become for some intents fully human, and this status and all considerations attendant upon it instantaneously collapsed at the will of the enslaver. This plasticity could not help but undermine the truth claims the slaveocracy asserted for its social constructs. The few extant records of private conversations between slaveholders and slaves reveal how the demonstrated artificiality of slaveocratic constructs impacted the slaveholding relationship. One of the most striking features of these conversations is their way of addressing the captive's articulation of his or her own experience as a violation of the rules of the game. Consider this conversation between Jacobs and Dr. Flint:

> ... I [Jacobs] exclaimed, "You have struck me for answering you honestly. How I despise you."
>
> There was silence for some minutes. ... Finally, he [Dr. Flint] asked, "Do you know what you have said?"
>
> "Yes, sir; but your treatment drove me to it."
>
> "Do you know that I have a right to do as I like with you,—that I can kill you, if I please?"

"You have tried to kill me, and I wish you had; but you
have no right to do as you like with me."

"Silence!" he exclaimed, in a thundering voice. "By
heavens girl, you forget yourself too far! ..." (39-40)

This interchange is arresting in that the players have stepped
outside their assigned roles. Jacobs and Flint are at once in the
pitch of a power struggle, and dispassionate observers of their
private positions within the slaveocracy. Although records of
private exchanges are relatively rare, scholars such as Fox-
Genovese have documented numerous incidents indicating that
movement outside roles assigned by the slaveocracy was not.
(See, for example, her description of an enslaved woman who
cut off her hand and threw it at her enslaver, and another
involving a young slaveholding male who struck a household
captive who had suckled him in his infancy, in response to which
he was beaten by her and told why).[12]

The movement to unsanctioned terrain openly acknowledged
what was always just beneath articulation in relations between
slaveholders and their captives: a charade in which brutal force
acted to keep half the actors in character. This charade was
between them no matter whether captives broke character or
were so deeply shaped by the terms of their bondage that they
believed their own performances. What slaveocrats beheld of
themselves in the enslaved profoundly undermined the terms of
self-articulation given them by the slaveocracy.

Slaveocrats' perception of themselves as participating in a
hideous charade lent urgency to contradictory desires: to be
completely rid of the enslaved, and to possess them totally and
forever.[13] In some cases, the latter aspiration involved ensuring
perpetual ownership of the enslaved and compounding that
ownership with a turning of all affective attention toward the
slaveholder. The fulfillment of either scenario revitalized the
charade: in the former instance by silencing the sentience of the
enslaved, in the latter by ensuring the continued containment of
the secrets they embodied. In a relationship such as the one
sustained between Jacobs and Dr. Flint, an added benefit of
perpetual possession was that it permitted the slaveholder
unlimited access to a person whose radical disinvestment in her
assigned role in the slaveocracy allowed him to experience

himself in a territory outside of his. Thus, Flint swears, "You are mine; and you shall be mine for life" (81). This declaration furthers his conscious vengeful aims; it also registers her subjective value to him, a value which, paradoxically, he can never experience in any real sense since his ownership of Jacobs collapses this possibility.

In the rare instances of manumission, a given slaveholder's perception of the humanity of a given chattel was forced upon the entire slaveholding community. Manumitted slaves were for many slaveocrats the embodiment of the danger of personal history unearthed, of the pretensions attendant upon the tyrannical exercise of power revealed. Thus when in the height of an argument with Jacobs's grandmother Martha, Dr. Flint asks, "Do you know whom you are talking to?," his incredulity registers a desire to retreat to the safety of his normative role and the spell it usually casts. Her plain answer, "Yes, I know very well who I am talking to," underscores that since it is her status and not his that has undergone a change, it is he who has forgotten to whom he is talking (82). Jacobs recounts numerous instances of slaveholders' fear of the gaze of former chattel and chattel momentarily outside the slaveocrat's personal purview. When Mrs. Wade dies, for example, she "entreat[s] her husband not to permit any one of her slaves to look on her after her death" (48). Palpable in this request is Mrs. Wade's impending loss of the power to deflect the gaze of her captives. For his part, Dr. Flint is all but haunted by his "aversion to meeting slaves after he has sold them" (82). It is in this context that Dr. Flint's vow that Jacobs shall "always be" his slave is best understood (60).

Slaveocrats' fears were not irrational. Dr. Flint had reason to fear the witness in Jacobs. Ernesto Laclau posits that the oppressed "cannot assert [their] identity without asserting that of the oppressor as well."[14] Jacobs, I believe, goes beyond a reflexive representation of those who held her in captivity or even a rendering of her "lived moment of resistance."[15] She has brought to the public stage a theory of slaveholder subjectivity. In her portrait of the "cultural unconscious"[16] of the slaveholding cohort, Jacobs renders subjectivities profoundly determined by the captivity in which they kept others, and perpetually frustrated in their private fantasies of omnipotence. Inside slaveholding intimacy Dr. Flint could unabashedly display this fantasy—confidently promising that his captive could obtain the freedom she "desire[d]" (and by implication, everything worth desiring), "only through [him]" (83). In her examination of the layered registers of struggle between captor and captive, Jacobs has left a record not only of slaveholders' belief in their own power to nullify the threat of the subjectivity of their enslaved, but also of their wish that it could be so.

Notes

1. Christopher Wise and Cora Agatucci, "Historical Review of African-American Literature," *English Postcoloniality: Literatures from Around the World*, ed. Radhika Mohanram and Gita Rajan (Westport: Greenwood Press, 1996), 135.

2. Wise and Agatucci 137.

3. I am expanding here on Edward Said's assertion that Commonwealth literature "contribute[s] massively as the ... agent of illumination within the realm of the *colonized*." (My emphasis.) Edward W. Said, "Figures, Configurations, Transfigurations," *From Commonwealth to Post-Colonial*, ed. Anna Rutherford (Sydney: Dangaroo P, 1992) 3.

4. Harriet Jacobs, *Incidents in the Life of a Slave Girl: Written by Herself*, ed. Jean Fagan Yellin (Cambridge: Harvard UP, 1987).

5. My use of this term derives from Orlando Patterson's observation that a feature of all slaveholding societies is the imposition of "social death" on the enslaved—that is, a condition of social nonexistence except as an extension of the will of the slaveholder. Orlando Patterson, *Slavery and Social Death* (Cambridge: Harvard UP, 1982) 5, 38.

6. Abdul R. JanMohamed, "Negating the Negation as a Form of Affirmation in Minority Discourse: The Construction of Richard Wright as Subject," *The Nature and Context of Minority Discourse* (New York: Oxford UP, 1991).

7. George Fitzhugh, *Cannibals All! Or, Slaves Without Masters*, 1857 (Cambridge: Belknap Press of Harvard UP, 1960).

8. Frederick Douglass, *My Bondage and My Freedom* (1855; New York: Dover Pub., 1969) 97.

9. Yellin, Jean Fagan. Introduction. *Incidents in the Life of a Slave Girl* by Harriet Jacobs (1861; Cambridge: Harvard UP, 1987) xvii.

10. Elizabeth Hannah Norcom is not identified by name in *Incidents*. See note 3 to Chapter VI.

11. Lillian Smith, *Killers of the Dream* (New York: Anchor, 1963) 138.

12. Elizabeth Fox-Genovese, *Within the Plantation Household: Black and White Women of the Old South* (Chapel Hill: U of North Carolina P, 1988) 329, 314.

13. My analysis of these polar desires is not identical with, but in many respects agrees with Joel Kovel's discussion of "dominative and aversive" racism, particularly in his chapter "The Fantasies of Race" in *White Racism*. Kovel's analysis centers on the elaborative fantasies of race as projected onto the historical figure of the enslaved African American man or woman, and the historical shift from "phallic and oedipal" dominative racism to the more contemporary "anal sadism" of aversive racism which he asserts is the "cardinal manifestation of modern American racism." Joel Kovel, *White Racism: A Psychohistory* (New York: Random, 1970) 83-85.

14. Ernesto Laclau, "Universalism, Particularism and the Question of Identity," *The Identity in Question*, ed. John Rajchman (London: Routledge, 1995) 102.

15. Homi Bhabha, "Freedom's Basis in the Indeterminate," *The Identity in Question*, ed. John Rajchman (London: Routledge, 1995) 60.

16. Michel Foucault, "Rituals of Exclusion," qtd. in Judith Butler, "Subjection, Resistance, Resignification: Between Freud and Foucault," *The Identity in Question*, ed. John Rajchman (London: Routledge, 1995) 229.

FROM "SPY-GLASS" TO "HORIZON": TRACKING THE ANTHROPOLOGICAL GAZE IN ZORA NEALE HURSTON

Karen Jacobs

The "spy-glass of Anthropology," Zora Neale Hurston's telling metaphor for her anthropological training under Franz Boas during her Barnard years, is perhaps the most quoted and least interrogated image in a body of work remarkable for its rich figuration. Used in Hurston's introduction to her first published ethnography, *Mules and Men* (1935), the image is most obviously meant to signal the enabling distancing of perspective and self-regard which that scientific apparatus afforded her in her efforts to record the African American folklore of her southern childhood.

> From the earliest rocking of my cradle, I had known about the capers Brer Rabbit is apt to cut and what the Squinch Owl says from the house top. But it was fitting me like a tight chemise. I couldn't see it for wearing it. It was only when I was off in college, away from my

> native surroundings, that I could see myself like somebody else and stand off and look at my garment. Then I had to have the spy-glass of Anthropology to look through at that. (1)

The "tight chemise" is a revealing trope in which to drape those familiar cultural stories. Hurston chooses an unambiguously female garment that both reveals the form and conceals the surface of the black body beneath through a form of mediation. It's the chemise's decisive mediating function which Barbara Johnson emphasizes when she remarks that "[i]nside the chemise is the other side of the chemise: the side on which the observer can read the nature of his or her own desire to see" (182). But the chemise is not, I think, so easily separable from the body that's wearing it, which at least competes with it and may become the chief, if unspeakable, object of visual interest in the scene. Hurston is clearly playing on the to-be-looked-at-ness of the female body in all of its erotically charged materiality here; what the phrase, "I couldn't see it for wearing it" sets us up for is striptease—to see the chemise clearly, the logic of the phrase suggests, she'll have to take it off. Heading off this scandalous possibility is another visual feint, in which an objectifying rhetoric of *self*-reflection ("see[ing] myself like somebody else") is pressed into the service of seeing *the garment*, neatly displacing Hurston's body and making cultural stories the real object of the gaze. By the time she's peering with proper detachment through the spy-glass, that objective instrument of science, Hurston has managed to dodge the problem of embodiment altogether—her own, and that of the stories'— which she confronts us with at the start. Given the problematic nature of that embodiment, in which the black female body must stand as both maker and interpreter of cultural meanings against , more prevalent significations—the primitive, sexual excess— Hurston's strategy shouldn't surprise.[1] But the body remains as afterimage, reminding us of the personified nature of cultural materials and of the gendered, voyeuristic and objectifying underpinnings of the spy-glass as investigative instrument. The spy-glass evokes not just the penetrating male gaze of science but the imperial white gaze of colonialism, both of which inform the ambiguous history of anthropology and its consolidation as a discipline in the 1920s and 1930s.[2] One might ask, to what varieties of striptease, in the form of identity positions, would the black female viewer be subject when aspiring to organize her world through that lens?

This essay tracks the patterns of such divestitures and reappropriations of identity positions, and the problems of embodiment each foregrounds, to demonstrate the path through which Hurston carves out a visionary territory to which she may lay claim to in her work. The story I wish to tell highlights two crucial and conflicting aspects of Hurston's most publicly claimed identities—those of social scientist and novelist—which she occupied by turns over the course of her career; and it dwells on the challenges that each of these identities posed for Hurston in the context of discourses about African-American cultural development and attainment in circulation in the 1920s and 1930s—discourses inseparable from conceptions of the primitive which pre-date and define the terms in which such cultural notions were broadly conceived.[3] Hurston's 1937 novel, *Their Eyes Were Watching God*, positioned as it is chronologically between her two ethnographies, *Mules and Men* (1935) and *Tell My Horse* (1938), and written during Hurston's fieldwork in Jamaica, powerfully encodes the intersection of these identities and discourses; it thus provides a multi-layered "testimony" about African-American cultural forms, both in itself as a species of the African-American novel, and through the conflicting discursive trajectories it contains and works precariously to resolve. I frame my reading of *Their Eyes* between what I argue are the two most prominent of those discourses for Hurston, one of which takes its bearings from the name of science and the other from art.

I begin, as the initial image of the spy-glass may suggest, with Boasian anthropology, whose participant-observer method, theory of cultural relativism, and critique of the comparative method of anthropology cumulatively reframe primitivist discourse in ways which are at once enabling and disabling for Hurston. Boasian theory, that is, provides a fully realized conceptual basis from which to revalue African-American expressive forms, but it accomplishes this through a problematically objectifying distance from its selected objects of study;

moreover, it retains a concept of the primitive still tainted by its derivation from evolutionary biology, however much it was reformed by Boas, thereby reinscribing the very forms of cultural hierarchy it elsewhere works to discredit. Using this framework, I read *Their Eyes* as Hurston's attempt to revise anthropological method in ways that initially privilege active participation in and celebration of African-American folk culture; however, Janie Crawford's transformation from folk heroine to visionary at the conclusion of the novel, I argue, demonstrates how Hurston's revision moves beyond a critique of anthropological methods, and towards an idealist model of individual transcendence. I conclude, then, by tracing the roots of that model to a second, historically anterior, and perhaps unanticipated discursive source, Emersonian Romanticism, through which I delineate the specifically transcendentalist terms in which Janie's trans-formation from folk heroine to visionary artist is effected. Like Boasian anthropology, Emersonian theory figuratively gives and takes away its cultural capital with the same paternalistic hand, as it situates its notion of the primitive within a paradigm of cultural development and aesthetic currency. Emerson's cele-bration of the poetic, picturesque language of "children and savages," provides an alternative and aesthetically particular discourse through which Hurston can reclaim African-American linguistic practices; however, her attempt to refashion the dimensions of Universal Being and transcendence associated with cultural and artistic maturity into a viable visionary consciousness for her folk heroine, Janie, obscures the specific history of black embodiment which prefigures and, for Emerson, disqualifies her from those achievements. We may see the appeal of Emerson's disembodied seer through which Hurston elevates Janie at the end of the novel, therefore, as an imaginary, if not outright false, resolution to the real social contradictions Hurston inhabited, a "solution" which paradoxically suggests the intrac-table nature of black embodiment as an ontological problem for her. Yet, without contradiction, we may equally understand Hurston to be adapting Emersonian paradigms to suit her own needs: through her appropriation of them, Hurston arguably exposes Emerson's blindness to the situated nature of embodi-ment, and complicates his account of "primitive" artistry, at the same time that she reclaims that portion of the American literary inheritance that he theorizes and personifies for her own. In Hurston's adoptions and modifications of these central Western discourses and their engagements with "the primitive," in other words, we can grasp the tradeoffs and challenges which she faced, as a kind of postcolonial subject, in her effort to retool them into liberatory narratives.

I. Through a Spy-glass Darkly: The Participant-Observer of Boasian Anthropology

Unlike Boas' other famous female students, such as Margaret Mead and Ruth Benedict, whose foreign, exotic fieldwork experiences conformed with disciplinary prestige and expectation, Hurston is unique for pursuing fieldwork not merely in the southern United States but in her own home town—the first incorporated black township, Eatonville, Florida.[4] Even in her second ethnography, *Tell My Horse* (1938), in which she investigates Voodoo practices on the foreign soil of Jamaica and Haiti, Hurston apparently views those populations as sharing some of the same West African cultural influences as African Americans, a perspective which may explain both her interest in those countries, and her willingness to break with anthropological convention by considering two distinct nations together. The spy-glass passage, then, is important for what it reveals about Hurston's equivocal position as both subject and potential object of the anthropological gaze as she pursued her research into African American folklore and African-influenced religious and cultural practices. Hurston's facile placement and displacement of her material body in the opening sentences of *Mules and Men* operates both as a condensed illustration of anthropology's participant-observer method and as a send-up of its detached and neutral pretensions by exposing the ways in which the bodies on either side of the lens are "material" to the insights it's credited with producing.[5] I want to consider the principal features of that method here, particularly its complex relations to notions of the primitive, the better to grasp the equivocal rewards anthropology offered Hurston in the early part of her career.

The participant-observer method, the conventions of which, according to James Clifford, had won international acceptance by the mid-1930s, combines general theory with empirical research, cultural analysis with ethnographic description, in a practice through which the personal experience of the ethnographer is framed and filtered through scientific method.[6] Particularly for Boas, the participant-observer method was meant to produce a wealth of empirical ethnographic data from which theory could only tentatively be derived, and never at the data's expense. There were, of course, numerous unacknowledged limitations to the method. The fieldworker, mythically and presumptively white and male,[7] must set aside his own cultural biases and assumptions in order to see from a monolithically conceived "native point of view"; the fruits of this perspectival reorientation could then be translated culturally, linguistically and generically, into the newly standard ethnographic document, the monograph—purified by science beyond the subjectivist distortions of the diary, the travelogue and other degraded narrativizing procedures. A recurrent feature of the monograph, often born of the necessity for efficiency in the face of limited fieldwork time, was the selection of a single individual or institution to represent larger cultural truths; this synecdochical logic clearly exerts a homogenizing force against cultural variety, conflict and difference. Even bracketing such translations, as a chorus of post-Geertzian anthropologists have made clear, the dirty little secret of the participant-observer method is its masking or denial of the complexity of the intersubjective encounter between fieldworker and native, and its inevitable power relations, by seriously proposing what Hurston only burlesques: that cultural assumptions and biases can be taken on and off at will, like clothing. Boas himself, arguably anthropology's most enlightened and methodologically scrupulous early 20th-century practitioner, makes the taint of this objectivist mirror readily visible in an early, rapturous account of cosmography in which the cosmographer "holds to the phenomenon which is the object of his study... and lovingly tries to penetrate into its secrets until every feature is plain and clear. This occupation with the object of his affection affords him a delight not inferior to that which the physicist enjoys" ("Study"

645; qtd. in Krupat 139). The translation of data into text evidently could be stimulating, not to say perilous.

The Boasian professional fieldworker was further distinguishable from his predecessors—the amateur, the tourist, the missionary, the untrained observer—by his attitude of cultural relativism. With his theory of cultural relativism, Boas maintained the equality of different cultural formations while detaching them categorically from race, thus countering an overtly racist evolutionary discourse that positioned blacks as atavistic precursors to white civilization. Cultural relativism was thus a blow to the thinking that arranged racial development hierarchically and unchangeably, and to the very idea of "primitive" culture altogether, whether expressed in the respectable, scholarly form of Freud's *Totem and Taboo* (1913) with its evolutionist vision of the ways the rituals and prohibitions of "primitive peoples" are reconfigured as "complexes" in modern, civilized man; or in the openly racist and jingoistic form of Lothrop Stoddard's *The Rising Tide of Color* (1921) with its conception of successive waves of the "savage" colored races swamping white civilized strongholds.[8] In a cultural moment in which Darwinian and Lamarckian evolutionary theories were vying for adherents (Kuper 129),[9] Boas was conducting anthropometric studies—he had Hurston measuring heads on Harlem streets in 1926 (Hemenway 88)— which he used to prove that the categories of race and culture were not co-extensive, and therefore, that racial "characteristics" have no essential or genetic basis.[10]

Beyond its anomalously progressive racial politics (it would take until WWII for cultural relativism to gain wide acceptance as a theory), what is so striking about Boasian anthropology is its retention of an almost positivist insistence on the untainted, unmediated scientific gaze as a tool for producing reliable knowledge. Relative to its contemporaries in the hard sciences, for example, which had to contend with the relativization of observational postures previously conceived of as neutral in such theories as Heisenberg's Uncertainty Principle, Boasian anthropology kept faith with a doctrine of observable truths made possible by proper fieldwork methodology. Hurston herself celebrates Boas' "genius for pure objectivity" and his passionate allegiance to facts over theory in her autobiography (*Dust Tracks* 127). However, if we are tempted to view Boas himself as a kind of throwback in the evolution of twentieth-century science, Arnold Krupat complicates this portrait. While Boasian anthropology seems to resist what has been characterized as the epistemological crisis of 1885-1915 and its shift toward relativity, it doesn't ignore so much as selectively implement relativist discourse:

> Boas and his students seemed to find the new relativity not the foreclosure but the promise of objectivity, scienticity, and realism. Relativism, for Boas, was understood primarily to mean cultural relativism, and a stance of cultural relativism (which was not taken as implying a general epistemological relativism) as enabling a satiric method by which to expose the abundant undocumented generalizations indulged in by practitioners of "the comparative method of anthropology." (134, 137)

Exposure to cultural difference then, for Boas, would have a relativizing impact that would yield a defamiliarized, objective view of culture without impugning the scientific purity of the anthropological gaze itself. However, Boas' insistence that individual cultures be studied on the basis of their distinctiveness and particularity did not insulate him from producing distorting cross-cultural analogies himself, anymore than his adherence to the participant-observer method prevented him from compromising "pure" observation with subjective perspectives. The primary vehicle for such distortions, I am arguing, is Boas' retention of the cultural category of the primitive, the institutional origins of which were inevitably linked to an evolutionary model of cultural and racial development, and which were arguably methodologically imbricated in the objectifying gaze of anthropology's participant-observer practice and its structurally implicit hierarchies as well.

While Boas could argue that the difference between primitive and civilized was more apparent than real in his 1911 work, *The Mind of Primitive Man*, he nevertheless supplies a wealth of criteria which uphold the distinction. Primitives, he argues, do not properly differentiate between the human and animal, adhering instead to idiosyncratic, irrational classification systems that arise from unconscious processes; they reify attributes as objects and engage in anthropomorphism; and they are the captives of traditional ideas unamenable to advancing civilization through conscious betterment. One hesitates to find a folk literature in any culture that would not match all but the last of these criteria; and, of course, what constitutes advancing civilization is a highly subjective judgment. Moreover, the rationality of mythic systems has been defended by later anthropologists such as Claude Lévi-Strauss, who has argued that the logic of mythical thought "is as rigorous as that of modern science, and the difference lies, not in the quality of the intellectual process, but in the nature of the things to which it is applied" (1963, 230). Boas understood such distinctions to be scientifically derived, and offered them by way of disputing the popular, and implicitly racist, characterization of the primitive as unable to inhibit impulses, and as having neither the powers of attention, originality of thought, nor the ability to reason that civilized man enjoys. He concludes that the transition from primitive to civilized is marked by the "lessening of the number of emotional associations, and an improvement of the traditional material that enters into our habitual mental operations" (*Mind* 250)—a definition which endorses the twin virtues of scientific rationality and progress that are the hallmarks of Enlightenment thought, and subject, therefore, to a by now familiar critique of the mechanisms of power and repression which underwrite it.

By dwelling on Boas' engagement with the category of the primitive here, I by no means intend to identify him as an especially pernicious voice in the history of primitivist discourse. Indeed, even an avowedly progressive thinker like Marianna Torgovnick makes a case for the ongoing utility of the concept, and the futility of substituting more "value-free" terms (Torgovnick 20-21). Adam Kuper notes the remarkable persistence of the concept *despite* such contributions as Boas,' and its rapid dissemination beyond the preserves of social anthropology to infuse "the political and historical consciousness of several generations" (Kuper 14). Torgovnick explains the immense attraction of the concept to be its chameleon-like, dialectical ability to represent the Other for the cultural imaginary in positive *and* negative terms, as Edenic social palliative or "barbarian at the gate" as the cultural moment warrants. Michael North makes a similar observation about the attractions that racial masquerading and the appropriation of black dialect held for white modernist writers, demonstrating the latitude it afforded them "to play at self-fashioning" through rebellion against linguistic and cultural standardization, at the same time underscoring the conceptual slide between primitivism and blackness in the discourse (North 11).

The grip of evolutionary thinking on the concept of the primitive and its overdetermined spectrum of racialization is evident in a diversity of cultural documents, from white Bloomsbury critic Roger Fry's celebration of the superior freedom of expression and formal aesthetic success of the "savage" in a 1920 essay on Negro sculpture;[11] to the assurance Alain Locke found it necessary to offer his readers with in his 1925 anthology of the Harlem Renaissance, *The New Negro*, namely, not to expect represented in its pages "the mind of a savage" but rather, individuals who have achieved "cultural adolescence and the approach to maturity"; to William Stanley Braithwaite's ridicule of the formula of "atavistic race-heredity" as the recurrent plot of fictional depictions of Negroes by whites, in the same volume (Locke xxvi, 35). (As late as 1950, in one of her last essays, Hurston would herself renew this complaint against "the folklore of reversion to type" ["White Publishers" 953]). In this cultural climate, little wonder that the only way Boas-trained anthropologists could find to implement cultural relativism's presumption of cultural equality and difference with regard to African Americans, according to John Szwed, was to view them as lacking any culture at all, as the victims of cultural stripping accomplished through a legacy of slavery which left them with only a deplorable cultural deficit.[12] A glance at the Contents page of Niles Newbell Pucket's *Folk Beliefs of the Southern Negro* (1926), the work of Hurston's leading contemporary in the field, reveals the sedimentation of concepts of the primitive in a formal ethnographic context, in which a version of the Boasian notion of traditional ideas sits side by side with popular notions of uninhibited impulses; among the topics

Puckett addresses are "Laziness, Humor, and Sexuality," "Mutilated English," "Fewer Restrictions upon Self-gratification," and "Fossilized Customs" (xi).

Trained by Boas in anthropological theory and methods, partaking in the literary milieu of the Harlem Renaissance and debates about its modernist qualifications, exposed to popular discourses of the primitive, and immersed in African American folk culture by personal history and profession, Hurston was situated in a conflictual vortex of hierarchical discourses involving race, artistry and cultural attainment. Boas' participant-observer method, his theories of cultural relativism and of the independence of racial and cultural variables, and his critique of the comparative method of anthropology, all clearly helped Hurston gain sufficient purchase on African American folk materials to revalue them as complex cultural forms worthy of study and record. At the same time, Boas' theories posed peculiar problems for this African American woman. First, the participant imagined by the participant-observer method was clearly a guest, not a member, of the community he documented, and possessed a world of tacitly superior cultural differences—including a talent for objectivity—to temporarily suspend; not so, Hurston. Second, the expected translation of oral materials into written texts, whether into the monograph of anthropological science or into the novel of Western literature, could only be a vexed one, the division of oral from written expression being inseparable from its historical use as a litmus test to police the boundaries of primitive and civilized.[13] Arguably, to commit folklore to paper in any form was to participate in a hierarchy of cultural representation; Hurston's dilemma, staged for the length of her career, was to choose between the hierarchy of science and "objective" knowledge mandated by the conventions of the monograph, and the hierarchy of individuated high culture epitomized by the novel, over and against "lower'" collective expressive forms. To collect, record and otherwise make use of the folklore of her childhood, then, involved Hurston's anxious positioning as both an interloper in the world of anthropology, and as an insider willing to sell-out African American arts—a dilemma exacerbated by the fact that her wealthy, white patron,

Mrs. Charlotte Mason, retained legal ownership of her scholar-ship during the collecting trips that led to *Mules and Men*.[14]

Given these pressures, Hurston's preference for rehearsing folk songs, for example, until she learned them by heart, or undergoing Voodoo initiations that involved her in extended fasts and body marking to learn its mysteries, can appear to be ways of "proving on the flesh" knowledge which had the potential to be reproving once made text.[15] Hurston's sporadic sponsorship of folk-oriented theatrical and musical events likewise suggests the attractions that embodiment held for her over that of "pure" textualization. Deborah Gordon explains the much observed absence of interpretation and analysis in Hurston's ethnographies as the result of Hurston's method-ological division between *two* mentors—Mrs. Mason, who herself in her work with Native Americans used a more documentary style of fieldwork collecting which excluded larger cultural references, and Boas (160-1). But it seems possible that Hurston was simply resistant to what amounted to a self-reflexive interpretive enterprise mandated by Boasian methods, and actively preferred to let her subjects speak for themselves. Compared with her white modernist peers—Faulkner, for instance, or West, Nabokov and Woolf—who presume a subjectively governed visual world and self-consciously explore its consequences, Hurston was initially drawn to a more stable, confidant model of visuality in Boas, which lent her preoccupations the prestige and validation of science; but her radicalizations of that model, at least in the early part of her career, produce effects that come to resemble those of her white literary contemporaries. It is noteworthy that in her long career, Hurston wrote only one entirely *interpretive* ethnographic piece—"Characteristics of Negro Expression"—and in it, Hurston makes use of primitivist discourse herself.

"Characteristics of Negro Expression" (1934) is a curious document for many reasons, not least because it combines something like aesthetic theory with an essentialist compendium of racial "features," some of which, like Hurston's speculation on the relationship between Negro lip form and dialect, literally link the black body with types of expressivity. What makes "Characteristics of Negro Expression" a difficult and perhaps undecidable text are the ways in which it attempts simultaneously to deploy and rehabilitate the category of the primitive and its corollary, the imitative, as artistic resources. The essay opens by developing an analogy between the evolution of language as a medium of exchange and monetary systems: "Language," Hurston tells us, "is like money." Hurston offers three equations of presumed ascending complexity between the two terms: she links "primitive" descriptive language with the bartering of goods in comparably "primitive communities"; highly developed languages, replete with "words for detached ideas," correspond to the "legal tender" of a money system based on abstract equivalence; and "cheque words, like 'ideation' and 'pleonastic,'" which take abstraction to the next stage, Hurston associates with a specifically literary language, exemplified by the Milton of *Paradise Lost*. She concludes that "the white man thinks in a written language and the Negro thinks in hieroglyphics" (175). Now, this analogy lends itself most obviously to a progressive narrative in which Negro hieroglyphics, however affectively colorful and rich, are manifestly backward, indeed "primitive," compared with the elevated language of literature—represented, ironically enough, by personification.[16]

But this hierarchical ordering is less innocent and straightforward, I would suggest, than it first appears, shaped as it inevitably is by larger discourses about monetary and aesthetic currency in circulation during the 1920s and 1930s. When "Characteristics of Negro Expression" was published in 1934, five years into the Great Depression, the appeal of abstract monetary systems over barter was arguably no longer self-evident; as Melchior Palyi points out in a book about the collapsing gold standard, "more than one half of the 30,000 banks operating in 1921 had closed by the end of 1933, more than 8,000 between December 1930 and June 1933, *wiping out $14 billion of deposits* in those two and a half years" (217). Indeed, it is on the grounds of its abstracted detachment from concrete standards of value that Ezra Pound would condemn the apparently autonomous power of money in the practice of usury, first in "Hugh Selwyn Mauberley" (1919-20), and later, in the Usury Cantos and in his 1935 polemic, *Jefferson and/or*

Mussolini. The new aesthetic "currency" of simplified language use that Pound developed with H.D. in the early teens as the Imagiste movement could be construed as merely a poetic correlative to Pound's insistence on the integrity of concrete objects and the dangers of abstraction in the monetary sphere; Imagism advocated "direct treatment of the thing" and to "go in fear of abstractions," while privileging the Image that had been defined, famously, as the presentation of "an intellectual and emotional complex in an instant of time" (Flint 198-200; Pound 200-6). Pound's later preoccupation with the Chinese ideogram in the *Cantos,* understood (following Fenollosa) as a "thought-picture," and H.D.'s poetic hieroglyphs and palimpsests, all more closely resemble Hurston's hieroglyphic in spirit than Milton.[17] Moreover, the hieroglyphic itself is a richly suggestive figure, evoking complexity, poetic condensation, and cultural and historical depth through its allusion to Egyptian civilization.

Although no one, to my knowledge, has identified Hurston as a devotee of Imagism, such a discourse on the image, complete with its rhetorical repudiation of the literary habits of the past, was certainly available to her and to the Harlem Renaissance milieu of which she was a part. Yet I would hesitate to maintain that Hurston's endorsement of the hieroglyphic as the quintessence of Negro expression is all an elaborate ruse meant to deconstruct hierarchical categories at the moment they are invoked by capitalizing on its high culture caché and the suspicion now attached to abstract monetary systems—that sort of reclamation strategy seems more convoluted than it is worth. With all of the attention Hurston has received restoring her place as an advocate of African American cultural traditions, it is important not to idealize her contributions at the expense of understanding the historical constraints under which she wrote.[18] I would suggest, however, that such counter-currents operate in the passage to complicate and potentially revalue the status of the "primitive" and its aesthetic currency, against "the stark, trimmed phrases of the Occident" ("CNE" 178) which make up the alleged standard. That they remain counter-currents is made clear by Hurston's very reliance on the sort of cultural evolutionary theory Boas worked to discredit, a theory that sought to distinguish "primitive" from "highly developed" languages in the first place.

The same kinds of contradictory valuations are at work in Hurston's discussion of originality and imitation. At first redefining imitation as fundamental to artistic process, Hurston stresses Negroes' facility for adapting white cultural forms for their own use, thereby stressing their innate artistic resourcefulness; she then points out that Negro interpretations of whites' musical instruments have been *re*-interpreted by whites themselves, transitively shifting the imitative burden to whites, while draining it of its primitivist connotations: "Thus," she determines, "has arisen a new art in the civilized world, and thus has our so-called civilization come." But ultimately, Hurston restricts the black imitation of white culture to a self-despising middle class, who "apes," as she puts it, "all the mediocrities of the white brother," in a phrase that both strips imitation of its artistic endowment and reinscribes its primitive associations, but for the new reason of its repudiation of a now-authentic black culture ("CNE" 181-2).[19] What emerges in Hurston's treatment of the concepts of the "primitive" and "imitation" in "Characteristics of Negro Expression" is an overt concession to perceived white standards of aesthetic value, contradicted by a covert endorsement of black practices as the crude but infinitely more vital form of cultural expression. Like "the truly cultured Negro" and the "Negro 'farthest down'" whom she celebrates in the essay, Hurston means to "like her own things best"; she only lacks an agreed upon, sanctioned aesthetic standard through which to validate her preferences. What remains in suspension to the end of the essay is whether Hurston is arguing that Negro people and Negro arts really *are* primitive but nonetheless powerful and compelling, or that beneath the face of the so-called primitive lies an unlooked-for, alternative standard of civilization and aesthetic accomplishment.

Hurston's reliance on racial, cultural and aesthetic hierarchies, here and elsewhere, is as striking as its overall instability in her thought. Reading across her ethnographies and autobiography, numerous contradictory statements implicating those hierarchies emerge which arguably testify as much to Hurston's internal conflicts and divisions as to her elusive,

editorially shaped and constrained position as a speaking
subject.[20] For the purposes of this argument, I am primarily
interested in the ways Hurston locates herself as a participant and
observer in these works, because of what these locations reveal
about her relationship to hierarchical positioning. As many
readers of her ethnographies have noted, Hurston breaks with the
conventions of the monograph in ways that anticipate postmodern methods and assumptions, by foregrounding her
membership and participation in the communities she is
studying, and parading the often intrusive means by which she
managed to collect materials.[21] Beyond this crucial issue of her
placement, Hurston's statements about her methods and
materials reveal an inconsistent relationship to them. In *Mules
and Men*, for example, one of Hurston's opening moves consists
in reassuring the reader that her return to her home town of
Eatonville is not motivated by her desire "for the home folks [to]
make admiration over me because I had been up North to college
and come back with a diploma and a Chevrolet" (2); Hurston
revisits this scene in her autobiography, *Dust Tracks on a Road*,
with quite a different eye, conceding that "I did not have the
right approach. The glamor (sic) of Barnard College was still
upon me" (127), interfering, as she explains, with her ability to
represent herself as one of the folk and easily collect materials.
Whereas in *Mules and Men*, Hurston makes solemn
pronouncements about the efficacy of hoodoo rites, and
expresses her sorrow at the necessity of refusing a "two-headed
doctor's" offer to remain as his partner, both of which would
indicate her belief in hoodoo practices (211, 205), Hurston
adopts the decidedly detached, secular perspective of a scientific
observer in *Dust Tracks*, explaining that "[f]eeling a weakness in
the face of great forces, men seek an alliance with omnipotence
to bolster up their feeling of weakness, even though the
omnipotence they rely on is a creature of their own minds"
(201). In *Tell My Horse*, Hurston excoriates Haitians as liars and
thieves in one breath, and ends her chapters in apparent cultural
solidarity with the exclamation, "Ah Bo Bo!," in the next (101).

In every case, Hurston uneasily vacillates between speaking
as and for the given group, as insider and outsider, participant
and observer, divisions which are inevitably laced with implicit

standards of cultural value. Significantly, the most memorable images from the two ethnographies are those that enact a predatory or ventriloquizing relationship to cultural materials. Hurston closes *Mules and Men* with the story of Sis Cat, who is tricked out of dinner by a lecture on table manners delivered by her main course, a rat, and learns to eat first and wash later; Hurston concludes: "I'm sitting here like Sis Cat, washing my face and usin' my manners" (246), having dined, we must imagine, on a banquet of folk tales and songs, the proverbial rat in the analogy. Hurston's allusion to her "manners" here, I should add, invites us to reconsider her consumption of those materials as mediated by conventions which mask, perhaps, the essential violence of the encounter. Hurston's second ethnography, *Tell My Horse*, gets its name from the Haitian god GuedÈ's habit of "mounting" human visitants or "horses" through whom or to whom he speaks, frequently in a spirit of social criticism; GuedÈ instructs his listeners to "tell my horse" a message which, in Hurston's view, should be understood as a selective opportunity for the masses to criticize their social betters in an otherwise rigid class structure. Hurston represents this practice of borrowing an authoritative voice to express otherwise inarticulable truths about social hierarchy as an enabling rather than violent relation, and clearly, it held for her sufficient resonance and power to motivate her selection of it as the book's title (219-21); arguably, the two halves of the relation together epitomize Hurston's own position relative to black culture, as the borrower and representative of an anthropological authority used alternatively to maintain and dispute high and low cultural divisions.

II. The Road to Horizon: The Turn from Boas in *Their Eyes Were Watching God*

It is in the light of Hurston's hierarchical preoccupations and their origins in the anthropological gaze of the participant-observer method that I want to reread *Their Eyes Were Watching God*. While much has been written about the centrality of voice in the novel, little attention has been paid to its visual registers, a striking neglect in a text featuring "eyes" and "watching" in its title, and which ends with the word "see," signaling a new, visionary consciousness for its protagonist. That *Their Eyes* is concerned with hierarchy has been more frequently noted, an observation based on its apparently celebratory depiction of the rural life of the African American folk. My own reading is most indebted to those of Hazel Carby, Henry Louis Gates, Jr., and Sharon Davie, each of whom foregrounds Hurston's struggle with hierarchical structures, although coming to quite different conclusions about their larger significances. For Carby, the substance of the novel is rooted in hierarchy, so that "critics are incorrect to think that Hurston reconciled 'high' and 'low' forms of cultural production"; instead, "Hurston could not entirely escape the intellectual practice that she so despised, a practice that reinterpreted and redefined a folk consciousness in its own elitist terms" (75-6). Through readings particularly of its folk materials, Davie describes Hurston's "explosion of societal, narrative and linguistic hierarchies in *Their Eyes*," arguing that the novel "not only inverts the terms of accepted hierarchies (black over white, female over male) but—more significantly— allows readers to question, if only for a moment, the hierarchical mode itself" (447). To be sure, many materials work to complicate and destabilize hierarchy in the novel, but Davie's case for its inversion, I would argue, is more utopian than the case warrants. For instance, while Davie characterizes Gates' powerful reading of Hurston's formal innovations in *Their Eyes* as "upsetting a linguistic hierarchy" (448), Gates himself describes Hurston's "speakerly text"—one in which free indirect discourse mediates between dialect and standard speech in the novel—as merely "resolv[ing] the implicit tension" between them (*Signifying* 192). This is an important difference, and one which points to the contradictory character of *Their Eyes*.

What I hope to suggest, through a reading of the visual metaphors of cultural hierarchy in *Their Eyes* and Janie's positioning within them, are the ways in which the novel engages with anti-hierarchical fantasy despite its larger constitution through hierarchical structures—what may be regarded as a classic post-colonial dilemma. Through such structures, vertical, hierarchical forms intersect with horizontal, democratizing figures in uneasy co-existence, thereby spatializing Janie's equivocal posture at the center and margins of the folk community, as well as her evolution from object of the gaze to visionary figure. Such intersecting structures point also to Hurston's unstable position as cultural participant and observer, and as the producer and collector of oral stories who ultimately reifies them in print. Through its resolution of these myriad instabilities and conflicts, the novel can be read as a repudiation of the rationalized "language of visuality" of the anthropological gaze and a retreat from the problems of objectification and embodiment its empirical methods pose, in favor of a Romantic idealism that re-establishes Hurston's artistic project on new, seemingly universalist foundations. The American representative of that Romantic idealism is Ralph Waldo Emerson, whose notions of subjective transparency and poetic language help us to comprehend Janie's transformations at the end of *Their Eyes*.

I want to begin with Janie's retrospective narrative that occupies the body of the novel, because it introduces a set of hierarchical "problems" that the materials within the frame device are designed to resolve. The largest formal, organizational, and figurative structures the novel employs are hierarchical; and Janie is persistently presented in hierarchical terms as well. Again, formally, as Gates describes it in his argument about free indirect discourse, the novel negotiates a discursive path between dialect and standard English. Organizationally, it is unavoidable that the division of Janie's life into relational stages be interpreted hierarchically, since Janie provides such a commentary herself when she repudiates Nanny's high chair and community custom to live her own way (108). Whether we chart the novel's progress through Janie's acquisition of a voice; through her discovery of a genuine romantic love represented by the pear tree; as the ascension of racial authenticity over a false, white bourgeois ethos; or as the emergence of democratic over autocratic forms of social organization, the novel inescapably charts a descent from, or an ascent to, an identifiable ranking of values, at least until the complicating reversals of the hurricane and its aftermath.[22] Excluding its frame, the novel can also be read as a triumph of participation over observation, by tracking Janie's descent from Nanny's "high chair," associated with white women's privilege, detached observation and abstract contemplation, to the democratized space of the muck, where land and water, male and female, dark and light skins meet and co-mingle, and where Janie shares in work and storytelling against the expectations, raised by the combination of her money, light skin and femininity, of her "class[ing] off" (135). From Janie's initial positioning in the novel at her grandmother's front gate, "gaz[ing] up and down the road" and "[w]aiting for the world to be made" (11), to her ultimate self-identification as a "delegate to de big 'ssociation of life" (6), Janie's development and increasing freedom is marked by the broadening range of her participation in activities initially cordoned off by racial, gender and class hierarchies.

The novel's two central images, the horizon and the pear tree, likewise seem designed to foreground issues of hierarchy. The horizon, as the place where "ships carrying wishes" sail in the novel's opening (1), remains a transcendental image of freedom and possibility in the text—"the biggest thing God ever made" (85)— which defines the outer limits of vision literally, and figuratively suggests it through the homonym, "her-eyes-on." The horizon's axis suggests a leveling democratic force, a spatialized equilibrium, for the novel. But the horizon is frequently cut across by the vertical figure of the road or highway which promises to lead to it and its possibilities, but points to the obstacles of hierarchy instead. Hurston employs the road this way in her adaptation of the Exodus story to narrate Nanny's flight from slavery to freedom, when she describes her intent to "throw up a highway through de wilderness" for her daughter, but "got lost" (15), en route, one imagines, to the horizon as promised land. Horizons and roads, it seems, may work at cross purposes in the text.[23] The pear tree, a visionary figure of self-discovery and eroticism in the novel, also spatializes the intersection of horizontal and vertical forces through its network of branches and roots. Hurston employs it as a tree of life, with "dawn and doom... in the branches" (8), and as a genealogical tree, when Nanny describes "colored folks as branches without roots" (15). In both images, vertical and horizontal axes are in conflict, with life threatened by doom, and the branches of the present cut off from their past. Hurston also uses the tree to isolate Nanny from the branches' horizontal promise, describing her head as "the standing roots of some old tree...torn away by storm" (12), a Medusan image both vertical and inverted, the very image of destructive hierarchy to which she'll be linked elsewhere in the novel, particularly through the vertical iconography of the "high chair." As figures constituted through visual condensation, the horizon and the pear tree can be understood as a species of hieroglyphic which encapsulates the larger cross-currents in the text, and recalls the "primitive" hieroglyphics Hurston linked with black expressivity in "Characteristics of Negro Expression." Ultimately, I will argue, they forge a link between the strictly visual and a visionary epistemology in the novel.

The intersection and obstruction of horizontal with vertical structures also tells a larger story of Janie's positioning within her marriages and communities in *Their Eyes*. The novel is endlessly engaged with reshuffling Janie's social status and its nominal causes, suggesting the significance of that instability as a key to her social relations. Because it is framed through a heterosexual romance plot, the hierarchical structure most overtly foregrounded is that of gender, with the couple functioning as a primary space of power; but the structure is inseparable from the inflections of race and class as they are defined by the community. By making the free wheeling, gambling, box-picking folk hero, Tea Cake, the culmination of Janie's romantic career, Hurston would seem to be positioning Janie to evolve into a corresponding folk heroine. But her inability to sustain that posture reveals Hurston's own ambivalent relationship to the folk, as its sometime member and chronicler, and exposes her treatment of the folk as far more critical than the idealized love relationship at first indicates. Hurston's two apparent aims in *Their Eyes*—to make a heroine of Janie and to celebrate the folk—run parallel only briefly because the two projects fundamentally conflict. Following the hurricane's exposure of the folk ideal as predicated on egalitarian fantasy, Hurston's efforts to produce Janie as a folk heroine collapse in a sequence of irreconcilable divisions: poor versus middle class, black versus mulatto, male versus female, collective versus individual, and finally, embodied folk versus disembodied visionary.

Although Janie is the bastard child of a mother who has been raped by a white man and turned to drink, and ends her story in a pair of dirty overalls, Janie is a folk heroine who will not stay folk. True, her early life with her grandmother living in "de white folk's back-yard" leads school children to regard her as "low," but the whites' hand-me-downs she wears make her seem too "high" as well (9). After her first marriage, her husband Logan Killicks says much the same thing, noting that she was "born in a carriage 'thout no top to it" but still thinks she's "white folks" (29). In some sense, this is quite literally true, as Janie's childhood misrecognition of herself in a group photograph would indicate: the "truth" that the objective, technological medium produces—that she's "colored" (9)—is not one she recognizes; indeed, it seems to instigate an alienated sense of identity or even its loss, as one of the white children's remarks makes clear: "'Dat's you, Alphabet, don't you know yo' ownself?'"[24] Among other things, the moment underscores the enormity of what the objective camera eye (or any other objective "apparatus") can't see, just as the name "Alphabet," standing in for the many names Janie is sometimes called, conveys the scope of what language cannot say, in its abstracted attempts to name the self. And the moment draws attention to Janie's belief that she occupies a recognizably "white" position as universal subject which the discovery of being "colored" destabilizes. The continuity of Killicks' observation that Janie thinks she's "white folks" is worth noticing in the novel—when Janie returns to the community in the frame narrative which marks the end of her story, a neighbor sums her up: "She sits high, but she looks low" (3).

The novel equivocates about how she got up there. As a black woman, at least as her grandmother tells it, Janie occupies the very bottom of the social order, as "mule uh de world" (14), and is therefore obliged to try to raise her status through the traditional means of marriage and property. Nanny attests to how Janie's marriage to Logan Killicks secures her respectability ("everybody got tuh tip dey hat tuh you and call you Mis' Killicks" [22]), one which is substantially enhanced by his much touted organ and sixty acres. Hurston works to distance Janie from Nanny's materialism by depicting Janie's indifference to Killicks' land, but other details suggest her immersion in her grandmother's standard of values. Unlike at the end of the novel when, on the muck, Janie seems to interpret her husband's invitation to share the spheres of work and domesticity as an opportunity for gender and class parity, she greets Killick's intention to buy her a mule of her own to plow with as a violation of her newly won status; when Killicks asks her to help in the fields, she counters, "Youse in yo' place and Ah'm in mine" (30). Her decision to leave Killicks for the prosperous Joe Starks seems attributable, in part, to Joe's vision of a future in which she rocks on the front porch and eats "p'taters dat other folks plant just special for you" (28), restored to the high chair of which Killicks deprived her. At the moment of her departure from her marriage and property, even en route to more of the same, the status Janie could be said to derive from her husband would seem to be moot; however, it is clear that she continues to be perceived in elevated terms, confronting us with an underlying standard of value which the text, perhaps unconsciously, endorses.

That the first men Janie and Joe encounter in Eatonville instantly recognize Janie's high status suggests that her appearance is decisive, since Joe has not yet had the opportunity to prove himself as an economic and political force, and the men are not awed enough by marital sanctity to prevent their trying to steal another man's wife. Still, they recognize the futility of the job, as Lee Coker explains to Hicks about Janie: "There's some women dat jus' ain't for you tuh broach. You can't git *her* wid no fish sandwich" (37). Separate from her share in her husbands' property, Janie's value is made legible in the text through her "heavy," "plentiful," long hair, a marker not merely of female eroticism but of her mixed racial heritage as well (26, 28). It's this asset that Joe attempts to bank through Janie's enforced restriction from community life, save in an ornamental capacity as the "bell cow" (39); the hair, Janie's chief currency, must be tied up in the store to keep other men from "spending" it and diminishing its value. Joe's possession of Janie and her physical assets means control of their circulation, and predictably issues in Janie's exclusion from the public sphere—from speech-making and porch "lying sessions," to the dragging out of Matt Bonner's mule and games of checkers. In the marriage to Joe, in short, Janie does not acquire so much as herself become property, the value of which is legible only through an imposed hierarchy of racial characteristics. Janie is thus highly valued and totally devalued, as the prized object in her conventional marriage. Her association with Joe strengthens the linkage between materialism and whiteness which contributes to Janie's "value" in this section of the novel. Joe's habits and preferences are identified as white, from the imperious "I god" which punctuates his speech to the plantation-style "big house" surrounded by "servants quarters" that Joe builds, and his style of compulsion which reminds townspeople of slavery days (44-5).

The position of observer to which Janie is restricted then, in this section of the novel at least, could not be less associated with a masterful gaze save in an entirely self-reflexive way as contemplation, since Janie is herself her only possible object. Only white women, Janie argues, have a natural occupation in the high chair, presumably because their elevated cultural position enables them to be subjects of the sovereign view it affords them (107). Hurston stresses Janie's formal compliance but internal resistance to her objectification and subordination by multiplying images of her self-division. Janie develops "an inside and outside now and suddenly she knew how not to mix them" (68); a "shadow of herself" has come to "prostrat[e] itself before Jody, while all the time she herself sat under a shady tree" (73). Such images of Janie's "inside" are clearly meant to suggest Janie's development of an alternative, self-generated standard of value, but they also curiously interiorize the subject/object relations now disrupted with her husband. As Janie acquires a form of autonomy through these mechanisms, she initiates a reversal of subject/object relations, significantly, through the subjective prerogative of the gaze, by objectifying and feminizing Joe's aging body through the apparently fatal pronouncement: "When you pull down yo' britches, you look lak de change uh life" (75).[25] When Joe seems uncomprehending of the insult, Hurston signals the conflation of visual and verbal registers with Walter's phrase, "'You heard her, you ain't blind'"

(75);[26] Janie follows up her objectifying image of Joe with a speech explicitly condemning his autocratic rule (82). However, these various signs of Janie's emerging subjectivity—her expanding interiority, and her brandishing of the gaze and voice, may lead us to forget that Janie has also internalized herself as object. After Joe's death, in a scene clearly intended to affirm Janie's new status as a subject, she appropriately turns to the mirror in a moment of self-reflection: "The young girl was gone, but a handsome woman had taken her place. She tore off the kerchief from her head and let down her plentiful hair. The weight, the length, the glory was there. She took careful stock of herself, then combed her hair and tied it back up again" (83). As Janie takes "stock" or inventory of her material assets here in order to claim ownership of them, "tying them up" herself, her primary standard of value in her own eyes as well as others seems unchanged—the "glory" of her hair remains a signifier of her elevated place in a racial hierarchy, for the moment eclipsing the economic status derived from her husband that she now enjoys in a class hierarchy.

Interestingly, it is in the Joe Starks section of the novel, presided over by precisely the sort of self-despising middle class black whom Hurston condemns in "Characteristics of Negro Expression,"[27] that folk materials make their presence most keenly felt. The section features mule stories, the self-contained buzzard fable, seemingly gratuitous depictions of courting rituals among dispensable characters and a caution/nurture debate, and culminates in Joe's dark hints about Janie's involvement with voodoo rites. While the materials are more or less subsumed within the fabric of the larger fiction, their presence and content raise larger questions about their functions in the text. To the extent that the mule is explicitly identified with the labor of black women and is implicitly identified with black folk tales through the numerous stories it inspires, it can be understood as a rough symbol of the larger folk community; Davie stresses the influence of the eighteenth-century derived discourse of black animality on the mule's meaning as well (449). Joe's perch atop the distended belly of the dead mule which he has formerly freed "like Lincoln," and over which he is delivering a mock funeral oration, literally dramatizes his position above the lowly folk, through an iconic and parodic enactment of the chain of being. Joe leads with a eulogy of the town's "most distinguished citizen," and Sam Watson preaches a sermon articulating for the first time the novel's fantasy of hierarchical inversion through a vision of mule-heaven, in which "mule-angels would have people to ride on" (57). But if we are tempted to take that vision seriously, we should remember that Hurston frames the scene by assessing its value for consolidating Joe's status, making him "more solid than building the schoolhouse had done" (57). When the world is really turned upside-down in the novel, I will argue, it only reveals hierarchy. Just as Janie does, the folk materials in the Joe Starks section serve both as yardsticks against which to measure Joe's greater power and prestige and, through their native interest and complexity, as indicators of possible alternative standards, standards which *Their Eyes* works to elevate through the world of the muck. It is in the Tea Cake section, particularly on the muck, that Janie's identification with the folk becomes most intimate, although the association is unstable and temporary; ultimately, Janie's positioning relative to the folk will be virtually indistinguishable from Joe's.

The hierarchical positioning of the Tea Cake section is complicated initially by its connection with the visionary, specifically, with Janie's vision under the pear tree and the spiritual transcendence with which it is associated. As Gates notes, Tea Cake's full name, Vergible Woods, or veritable woods, identifies him as the incarnation of the pear tree's promise (*Signifying* 191). Their affiliation thus elevates them: Tea Cake is named "a glance from god" (102); Janie has the "keys to de kingdom" (104). But the spiritual elevation in this section is counterbalanced by the physical movement southward, and mediated by a material and social leveling between Janie, Tea Cake, and the agricultural workers whom they join on the muck, all of which spatially and conceptually averages into a kind of social mean. In this section, the now well-off Janie blames her former "classing off" on Joe (107), and the novel dives headlong into a fantasy of a post-hierarchical world, in which the social strata Janie classed off from in Eatonville—the story-telling, gambling, dwellers in the present—here emerge as the ubiquitous standard. Differences of age, gender, class and race are here dismissed as purely conventional: youth is redefined as a state of mind; Janie is invited to partake and becomes adept at male-defined activities like checkers, fishing, hunting and story-telling; after Tea Cake's impromptu feast, she tells him she'll kill him dead if he "classes her off" from a good time again; she turns her back on her money to take her place in the fields, thereby quelling concerns "that she thought herself too good to work like the rest of the women" (127); and she discovers the beauty of Bahaman drumming despite the scorn with which others regard it (133). After a season on the heterogeneous muck, Janie can answer the "color struck" Mrs. Turner's denunciation of dark-skinned Negroes and her support for a separate light-skinned class with color blind indifference, maintaining that the mixing of such racial "classes" "don't worry me atall" (136). Instead, Mrs. Turner's "groveling submission" to the idol of the material white body and its approximations is presented as a contemptible parody of true visionary consciousness (138). Janie's new "classless" identity is strengthened through her alliance with Tea Cake. Compared with Joe Starks' official and autocratic hold over the black community, Tea Cake's undisputed leadership on the muck is never formalized, but is instead based on democratic affections and shared activities. Even the jealous blows Tea Cake delivers to Janie to prove his "possession" are preceded and matched by those with which she favors him when she drives off the persistent Nunkie. The muck, then, emerges as a truly utopian, anti-hierarchical space in which Janie comes into her own as a folk heroine.

But the hurricane exposes the myriad fractures in the fantasy of what turns out to be an antediluvian world. The first and deepest of these fractures is racial, initiated by Tea Cake's low-rating of the Seminole's warnings of hurricane danger; by invoking instead the reliability and knowledge of the white bossman, Tea Cake reminds us that the muck is ultimately owned and governed by whites, bracketing and undermining his own democratic province. Significantly, the scene of hierarchical reversal accomplished through this "act of God" is prefaced by a visionary moment, suggesting that faith in a redemptive *material* sphere was after all misplaced: "The time was past for asking the whites folks what to look for through that door. Six eyes were questioning *God*.... They seemed to be staring at the dark, but their eyes were watching God" (151). As wind and water give "life to lots of things that folks think of as dead" and "death to so much that had been living" (151-2), the hurricane instigates a full-scale return of repressed hierarchical relations in the novel: compared with the moving images of inter-species harmony Hurston offers, with disaster inspiring snakes and wild animals to a temporary hilltop truce, she shows a bleaker picture of human segregation, in which "[w]hite people had preempted that point of elevation" (156) that offers safety. Tea Cake is not only coerced by whites into burying the dead but also, as he glibly observes, helping God enforce the Jim Crow law through segregated burial and the provision of coffins for whites corpses alone (163). The rabid dog's bite that Tea Cake sustains transforms him from a loving partner into a virtual animal himself, reversing the trend in the muck section of humanizing and elevating the folk. Janie, of course, is forced to kill the animal Tea Cake has become and with it, her dream of gender equality made flesh; this paves the way for the further exposure of gender divisions at the trial, where white women provide Janie with the sympathy so conspicuously lacking in the response of the black men. The men conclude, revealingly enough, upon her acquittal: "'Aw you know dem white mens wuzn't gointuh do nothin' tuh no woman dat look lak her'" (179). The final return of the repressed, then, is our confrontation with the species of value that has always fundamentally distinguished Janie from the folk—her mulatto features, and the social status they both signify and allow.

While *Their Eyes*, I am arguing, is thus unable to sustain an unwaveringly level gaze at the folk beyond temporary fantasy, it makes one further attempt to subvert hierarchical relations through its strategy of Janie's embodiment. As we saw in Hurston's placement and displacement of her body in relation to the "Spy-glass of anthropology" and its objectifying lens early on, and as we later observed about her evasion of the potential distortions endemic to textualization through her preference for cultural enactment, embodiment and its power served as a recurrent and important resource for Hurston. Although embodiment, too, risks the perils of objectification, those perils may be obviated by the body's potential to reassert itself as experiential subject. Yet another way to track Janie's development in the novel, then, is by observing the ways in which she attempts such a reassertion against the objectifying impulses of other characters, who typically deprive Janie of her coherence as a subject through a fragmenting and synecdochical gaze. From Nanny's reproach against Janie turning her body into a "spit cup" (19), to Joe's fetishization of her hair, and criticism of her "hanging rump" (74), to Tea Cake's loving regard for Janie's lips and eyes (99), up through the attention paid by the occupants of the Eatonville porch to her "pugnacious breasts" and "firm buttocks" (2), the community of the novel sees Janie consistently in parts. But Janie resists this fragmentary vision through her resolute attempts to reassert her bodily integrity. She responds to Joe's criticism of her rump, for example, by insisting "Stop mixin' up mah doings wid mah looks" (74), and concludes, as we have seen, by returning the same kind of objectifying gaze when she says, "When you pull down yo' britches, you look lak de change uh life." Her first act after Joe's funeral is to burn the head rags that signified Joe's definition of her as property and his ownership of her in parts, and to let down her hair (85). When Tea Cake literally jeopardizes her bodily integrity when he threatens her with his gun, she kills him and takes his "seeds" —meant for planting, but arguably a synecdoche for his body as well—with her. Janie responds to the anatomizing vision of the porch by redefining it as "Mouth-Almighty" (5).

But just as *Their Eyes*' evasion of hierarchy proves only temporarily sustainable, Janie's resistance to the objectifying gaze through bodily reassertion does not turn out to be especially long-lasting and effective either. The final moment of its efficacy comes in what Carby has called the "gauntlet" scene, in which Janie's progress down the street upon her return to Eatonville is marked by a veritable tribunal of witnesses on the porch, who at first "couldn't talk for lookin'" (2) at Janie. But "the porch" shortly finds its voice, its initial verbal reticence yielding to its articulation of the hierarchical standards that were momentarily submerged on the muck: "why don't she stay in her class?," they want to know, while the women hope that "she might fall to their level some day." Their language is also represented as a weapon—their questions are "burning statements" and their laughs are "killing tools"(2). Carby reads Janie's refusal to narrate her story publicly through "the directly told and shared oral tale" as exemplifying the division and antagonism between Janie as a species of intellectual and the porch as folk (Carby 82-4). I would agree that the novel draws attention to Janie's "superior" positioning here relative to the folk, as I have been suggesting that it has done really all along; but I would argue that Janie's refusal to speak, taken together with the violent terms in which the porch's willingness to speculatively (and falsely) interpret is rendered, suggests the novel's indictment and gradual withdrawal from textualization altogether, just as Janie's refusal to pause before the porch's gaze and her sequestration inside her house indicates her retreat from embodiment as a method of resistance as well. Granted, Janie tells her story to Pheoby and tries to include an interpretive apparatus along with it to guarantee proper "understandin'" (7), but she declines the job of conveying it to the community herself, instead retreating further into the privacy of the house and her "visions," and delegating the job of translation to her friend. It is at this point that Janie openly criticizes language as a substitute for experience when she argues that "talkin' don't amount tuh uh hill uh beans when yuh can't do nothin' else," and concludes with her most explicit endorsement yet of empiricism as the key to knowledge: "you got tuh *go* there tuh *know* there" (183).

But the place to which Janie embarks after expressing this bold epistemology is not out into the world in search of an empirical horizon, but up a flight of stairs carrying, like Diogenes, a lamp "like a spark of sun-stuff washing her face in fire," which spatially and symbolically constitutes her as the ultimate visionary subject, ascendant over the degraded material world below and lit up with visionary power. (Pheoby anticipated this visionary transformation and rebirth when she described how Janie looked once having gained her own back yard: "You looks like youse yo' own daughter" [4]). Of course, Janie's ascent is pedestalled upon materiality—she owns those stairs, after all—but reminders of that fact are nowhere in evidence. Janie, furthermore, seems to divide from her own materiality in this scene, particularly as a black body, when "[h]er shadow behind fell black and headlong down the stairs" (183); she gains the top of the stairs, then, as blackness drops to the bottom, so that she achieves both elevation and in a sense transparency. Janie is thus disembodied and dematerialized at the end of the novel, a state that allows her to transcend the difficulties and limitations of the material body altogether. She is now free—free to enjoy the "pictures of love and light against the wall" incarnating Tea Cake (184), and further, I am suggesting, she is free from the problems of hierarchy and embodiment that have dogged her footsteps as an aspiring, empirically constituted seer throughout her journey. That freedom has been purchased, however, through the very hierarchical divisions her new status as visionary conceals: Janie cuts loose not only from her blackness here, but also from the voluntary poverty and association with black collectivity which were part of her heterosexual "contract" with Tea Cake, in favor of a new identity as a single, middle class individual.

Significantly, Hurston employs imagery to describe Janie's visionary dominion that recalls and selectively modifies the Boasian anthropological project. *Their Eyes* ends: "She pulled in her horizon like a great fish-net. Pulled it from around the waist of the world and draped it over her shoulder. So much of life in its meshes! She called in her soul to come and see" (184). The horizon, revealed here as an unequivocally visionary figure, is at once fashioned into a tool of collection, sifting and selecting the materials of life to be brought in for meditation and analysis, and reclaimed in the service of defining the self as world. The first set of meanings suggests a revision of the participant-observer method through the mechanism of the second set: in other words, Janie will assuredly reconsider observed materials through a secondary stage of interpretation, but here, her interpretive lens seems specifically introspective and subjective, rather than empirical and objective. By reimagining the materials of Janie's life as a store of resources reserved for the uses of the sovereign self, Hurston thus uniquely yokes anthropological method to an idealist project by draining it of its empiricist assumptions.

III. Emerson and the Language of "Primitive" Artistry

It is tempting to view Janie's turn away from empirical observation, experience and the material body upon which they depend in favor of a dematerialized visionary posture as her—and Hurston's—precipitous flight from the African American folk she so equivocally represents in *Their Eyes*. But I want to suggest that this visionary turn is not only a turning away, through which, as Carby critiques it, the "discourse of the folk...is irrevocably displaced in the figuration of a discourse of individualized autonomy existing only for the pleasure of the self" (Carby 88). Through the visionary, I would argue, Hurston is also turning back to a Romantic discourse of language and self that enables her to redefine the "primitive" language of the folk as constitutive of a specifically artistic practice, one whose conceptual rewards apparently exceed the bounds of individual pleasure. Hurston's first flirtation with such a discourse goes back to "Characteristics of Negro Expression," in which she reproduces in her theory of the evolution of languages a symbolic paradigm popular in nineteenth-century Romanticism, sometimes referred to as the superceded theory of language (Baym, et al, 1002, n.3). Like a variety of eighteenth and nineteenth-century figures, from Vico and Shelley to Herder,[28] Ralph Waldo Emerson took up the question of the origins of language by sentimentalizing the "primitive," equating the language of "savages" with a poetic purity, affective power and an unmediated linkage to nature, the return to which would revivify the linguistic resources of the modern poet. I am interested here in the version of this paradigm articulated by Emerson in "Nature" (1836) for its uncannily numerous correspondences with Hurston's conceptual language—beginning with the origins of poetic language in "Characteristics," extending to the rhetorics of Universal Being and transcendence present in *Their Eyes*, and culminating in the novel's use of "thought pictures," particularly through its central figure, the horizon. If individually, the points of intersection between Hurston's and Emerson's concepts and language appear merely suggestive, cumulatively, they point irresistibly in a direction of discursive confluence. While it is impossible to know for certain whether or how widely Hurston actually read Emerson, juxtaposing the two writers on these shared issues, I am arguing, helps to expose a dimension of a discourse on primitivism and artistic authenticity, indisputably present in her work, whose historical sources otherwise are hidden from view. The constellation of primitivism, artistic authenticity, and individual possibility and transcendence epitomized by Emersonian thought, I am suggesting, was culturally and discursively available to Hurston, perhaps uniquely so as a student of anthropological discourses of the primitive. Hurston would not have been the first modernist writer to engage with such discourses equipped with only a limited awareness of their historical roots.[29]

There are, to be sure, ironies implicit in turning to Emerson to isolate one of Hurston's discursive resources. As readers attentive to Emerson's racial politics have noted, his notions of individual potential and transcendence did not extend to those of African origins, despite his eventual sympathy with abolitionism and his sporadically progressive racial views. As Cornel West has demonstrated through a reading of Emerson's journals and essays, Emerson evinced an early belief in a racial "scale of being" and its sometime corollary, racial obsolescence theory (which predicted the eventual extinction, like the dodo, of the "lesser" races), which persisted even into the late, canonical essay, "Fate" (37). Moreover, Emerson's conceptual program for self-expansion can equally be understood as a blueprint for a far more material program of imperialist expansion and conquest.[30] Such views, needless to say, would seem to make Emerson complicit with race "scientists" and other precursors of American anthropology's roots in racial determinism, and hardly an antidote to them. But to ignore Hurston's potential involvement with Emersonian discourse on such grounds is to presume her incapacity to occupy conflicting discursive locations on race, a presumption which even a cursory reading of "Characteristics" or *Tell My Horse*, to take only the most obvious examples, would dispute.

Just as Boasian anthropology offered Hurston a scientific discourse and method through which to reclaim the category of the primitive through a cultural relativism presuming equal complexity across cultural and racial differences, Emersonian Romanticism, as I will elaborate below, offers a theory and method of reclaiming the primitive as well; and arguably, the Emersonian narrative of artistic authenticity may have held more resonance for a writer like Hurston than Boas' cultural authenticity, since her commitments tended towards literature more consistently than toward social science. Interestingly, Emerson himself is often viewed as writing against an objectifying view of nature he ascribed to natural science, thus anticipating up to a point the difficulties Hurston would experience in relation to Boasian positivism.[31] Although I am not claiming that Hurston so self-consciously traded one looming white male figure for another as the basis for her own intellectual architecture, I am suggesting that Emersonian concepts function —however schematically in Hurston's piecemeal appropriation of them—as a temporary palliative to the problems that self-reflexivity and racial embodiment posed through her adoption of Boasian anthropological perspectives. Her appropriation of such concepts should not be construed, however, as obviating the real conflicts which the adoption of Emersonian notions of artistry would pose for Hurston as a black woman, but only as an imaginary solution to the myriad social contradictions she inhabited. As much as do Boas' anthropological methods, Emerson's primitivist aesthetics also depend on the suppression or transcendence of the body, though the body imagined to be capable of decorporeally merging with the All was neither female nor black. Nevertheless, disembodiment achieves a positive valence in Emerson through its linkage to Universal Being, a valence that necessarily overshadows its merely instrumental value in Boas as a means to objectivity; the disembodied seer at the basis of Emersonian thought, then, offered Hurston substantial payoffs in the form of artistic valorization and spiritual communion which together are the primary sources of that seer's appeal.

With such qualifications in mind, let me turn to Emerson's version of the superseding theory of language as he articulates it in his 1836 essay, "Nature":

> Every word which is used to express a moral or intellectual fact, if traced to its root, is found to be borrowed from some material appearance.... We say the *heart* to express emotion, the *head* to denote thought;

and *thought* and *emotion* are, in their turn, words borrowed from sensible things, and now appropriated to spiritual nature. Most of the process by which this transformation is made, is hidden from us in the remote time when language was framed; but the same tendency may be daily observed in children. Children and savages use only nouns or names of things, which they continually convert into verbs, and apply to analogous mental acts.... As we go back in history, language becomes more picturesque, until its infancy, when it is all poetry. (13-14)

Emerson's formulation prefigures Hurston's in surprising detail, describing the language of "children and savages" in the same terms in which she theorizes Negro hieroglyphics as tied to "sensible things" or objects; she even has a linguistic category in "Characteristics" entitled "Verbal Nouns" (177). Emerson's linguistic hierarchy, moreover, makes explicit what remains suggestive implication in Hurston—that "primitive" language is the language of poetry, conceived of as high art. Such a sublimation of "primitive" technique is doubly useful to Hurston, as it helps to frame Janie's thought-pictures of Tea Cake—the "pictures of love and light against the wall" through which he's made manifest in the novel's final images—specifically as forms of artistic expression, at the same time that it serves broadly to stamp Hurston's figural language in the novel with the seal of artistic prestige and purity.

Both Hurston and Emerson, furthermore, make use of an analogy between language and money to establish for their preferred linguistic practices a stable grounding in "verifiable" values, encompassed by the intimate linking of word and thing. For Emerson, corrupt language consists in language which has lost its "gold standard" of value in the world of objects and thus, the guarantee of its linkage with "natural facts":

When simplicity of character and the sovereignty of ideas is broken up by the prevalence of secondary desires.... new imagery ceases to be created, and old words are perverted to stand for things which are not; a paper currency is employed when there is no bullion in the vaults. (15-16)

One can read here Emerson's simultaneous anxiety to ground subjective and linguistic purity in the "objective" and stable value of bullion, and thereby to preserve its simplicity from the "perversions" of desire and abstraction; the poet's goal, as Emerson puts it later, should be to "pierce this rotten diction and fasten words again to visible things; so that picturesque language is... a commanding certificate" (16), a fully underwritten currency. This conception of a "picturesque language" with its guaranteed value finds its parallel in Hurston's celebration of barter in "primitive communities"; picturesque language likewise functions to secure an inherent linguistic value and meaning, ultimately expressed by the yoking together of word and thing in the condensed proximity of the hieroglyphic. We can observe numerous reworkings of this linguistic genealogy and standard of values in *Their Eyes*, in which Hurston's hieroglyphics, or "thought pictures" as they are called in the novel, serve as intermediary terms between the superseding theory of language and a transcendental model of visuality. Not only the culminating images of Janie's vision of Tea Cake in the novel's final scene, but also the earlier images of the horizon and pear tree, can be understood as exemplars of the "picturesque" language of hieroglyphics Hurston first described in "Characteristics"; only they are developed beyond the crude "crayon enlargements of life" (48) that characterized the folk expressions of "thought pictures" (personified by the porch "lying sessions") to a greater degree of refinement, which is measurable through their pronounced disembodiment. If words are signs of natural facts in Emerson, natural facts are themselves the symbols of particular spiritual phenomena (13), and the trajectory of thought-pictures in *Their Eyes* seems to participate in this means of authenticating artistry through the merger of the particular into the universal.

While the horizon and pear tree still derive part of their meaning from their presence in the phenomenal world of objects, Tea Cake has been liberated from that world as ghost or spirit. This privileging of dematerialization is consistent with another dimension of Emersonian thought which likewise imagines visionary possibility in a disembodied form. Thought-pictures "evolve" in the text apace with Janie's development in—and out of—her material body, such that the physicality of the pear tree matches Janie's sexually awakening body, while her ephemeral projections of Tea Cake mirror Janie's own incipient dematerialization. Such an evolution echoes the path charted for Emerson's poet; to recall the most famous lines of "Nature":

> Standing on the bare ground,—my head bathed by the blithe air, and uplifted into infinite space,—all mean egotism vanishes. I become a transparent eye-ball. I am nothing. I see all. The currents of the Universal Being circulate through me; I am part and particle of God. (6)

As Janie ascends the staircase at the end of *Their Eyes* and divides from her black "shadow," she comes to approximate the uplifted "transparent eye-ball" and its universal purview; she thereby recovers the position of universal subject lost when the objectifying visual medium of the photograph taught her she was "colored" in the white folks' back yard. She thus recalls Emerson's rhetoric of Universal Being in "Nature," part of a larger argument about the essential oneness of the natural world; as he puts it more directly later in the essay: "A leaf, a drop, a crystal, a moment of time is related to the whole, and partakes of the perfection of the whole. Each particle is a microcosm, and faithfully renders the likeness of the world" (22). Hurston echoes this conception in *Their Eyes*, at first negatively, when Janie is described as too uneducated to know that she is "the world and the heavens boiled down to a drop" (72); and later positively when, in the closing image, Janie takes the horizon from "the waist of the world" and drapes it over her own shoulders.

The image of the horizon itself is a recurring figure of visionary possibility in Emerson; as he puts it, in a phrase which draws the several parts of his theory together: "There is a property in the horizon which no man has but he whose eye can integrate all the parts, that is, the poet" (5). The visionary artist who can claim that property, then, is an individual rather than a collective force, one whose heightened powers of vision at once win him title to the horizon and must elevate him above the sights of the folk whose origins he may nonetheless claim. At the close of *Their Eyes*, Janie closely corresponds to this Emersonian vision of the poetic seer: she, too, has laid claim to her "property in the horizon," both in the visionary and material sense, however under-acknowledged the latter may be in the novel; she likewise owns the "eye [which] can integrate all the parts" since she herself now personifies Universal Being with its vision of interconnectedness; and finally she, and by extension Hurston, takes on the mantel of the poet, having distilled a "savage" picture language into the medium of art.

Yet, as is perhaps fitting in Hurston's chosen medium of artistic expression, the novel, Janie's "transcendent" position appears to be mitigated by its social and interpersonal construction; it is framed and circumscribed, that is, both by the very material encumbrances which have made it possible, and by the persistently hierarchical love relation that at once forms its motive and its chief substance of expression. That Janie cannot fully achieve the status of Emerson's poet—of "*he* whose eye can integrate all the parts" (my emphasis)—is furthermore suggested by her apparent confinement to her house, as emblem of the curtailed and feminized private and domestic sphere. Such a narrow, hemmed in version of her "property in the horizon" may remind us of the distinction Hurston's narrator draws in the novel's opening lines, when she suggests that, unlike men, women must restrict themselves to surveying exclusively imaginative horizons (1). Furthermore, Janie's "shadow," as the metaphor of blackness of which she attempts to divest herself in the final scene, is arguably not so easy to dispense with; certainly Emerson would not have regarded it so, but rather as an inescapably atavistic impediment. If we take the metaphor seriously, moreover, shadows are among those nagging consequences of embodiment from which we proverbially can never escape. Far from completely autonomous, then, Janie's transcendence more closely resembles what might be called an embedded individualism, or what Christopher Newfield has described as the conflict between the subject's constitution through external structures and its potential for autonomy—a pressing contradiction explored in Emerson's negotiations of the poet's imitative and inventive obligations, but which takes on added urgency in relation to the black woman artist who has worked to define herself, elsewhere, within that rubric.[32]

To the extent that she succeeds in burying the immediate historical and cultural consequences of Janie's materiality under a transcendentalist mantel, Hurston's manipulation of Emersonian tropes may be taken as a measure of her own ambivalence about representing and celebrating African American culture. Yet, her identification with that mantel is destabilized by her and Emerson's divergent relations to the term that joins their projects—namely, the primitive. Whereas Emerson understands the primitive nostalgically as a model and a means to preserve a language the purity of which will secure for his poet a transcendental merger, Hurston's relation to the term is at once less instrumental, more personal, and firmly anchored in the more immediate problem of reconceptualizing and reclaiming the artistic expression of the black community. These material interests so manifestly represented by African American bodies and community, including her own, bring to the surface a second irony entailed by Hurston's use of Emersonian tropes: beyond the fact that she functions by definition as a trespasser in Emersonian territory, as it were, her presence there works to expose the idealist limitations of a theory so blind to the situated nature of embodiment. Precisely because Janie can recast herself in the mold of Emersonian seer, in other words, Hurston is able to demonstrate the ways in which the transcendentalist ethos is an expression of cultural isolation and privilege, since the very availability of that identity is predicated upon Janie's physical and psychic detachment from her community through a financial independence that has been purchased, furthermore, through the exploitation of its labor.

Just as Hurston's construction of Janie as visionary operates reflexively as both an adoption and adaptation of Emersonian terms, her stylistic practices also refer to and revise Emerson's notions of poetic language. Hurston complicates Emerson's account of "primitive" artistry by assimilating the picturesque language of "children and savages" into the "high" cultural linguistic container of the novel; she thus historically telescopes, in Emerson's terms, the linguistic practices of early and advanced stages of cultural development into a hybridized simultaneity, effectively overturning them as discrete forms of evidence for an evolutionary model of culture. As a consequence of the new contexts in which these several Emersonian paradigms are pressed into service and the revisionary effects they entail, Hurston may be seen not simply as a writer retreating from the consequences of black embodiment, but equally as one advancing to reclaim some lost territory. She does so by actively appropriating a discourse whose spoils include a means of reorienting black female subjectivity to the center of aesthetic and visionary possibility, as well as situating it within the dominant trajectory of American literary history described and presided over by Emerson. Yet, we risk obscuring the underlying conflict between these alternatives if we overlook the ways in which the universality proffered by Emerson's poetic genealogy necessarily elides the specificity and materiality of the body, Hurston's revisionary efforts notwithstanding. Through Janie's transformation, then, Hurston accomplishes a reorientation of the visual economy, the outcome of which is equally distant from the objective and objectifying empirical observation of the orthodox anthropological gaze, and from the subjective revisions of that gaze Hurston made use of when she foregrounded herself as material participant in her ethnographies. Unlike her white, male modernist peers, who were content to explore the varieties and limits of subjective visuality left over from the collapse of objective forms, Hurston turns to a visionary model through which she attempts to redefine and revalue her art.

In a 1943 interview with the *New York World Telegram*, Hurston maintained: "I don't see life through the eyes of a Negro, but those of a person" (Clipping, qtd. in Hemenway 289). In the wake of her repositioning, through her character Janie, from spokeswoman of the folk to transcendent seer that she tentatively accomplished six years before in *Their Eyes*, Hurston's 1943 self-description needs to be understood as more than either a grand ahistorical evasion or the expression of a political conservatism widely seen as typical of her later years. Instead, we need to comprehend it as the outcome of a philosophical tradeoff—the casting off of a black, female body whose cultural meanings she could not control, even through the optical apparatus of science, in exchange for an artistic vision poised on the brink of a universal transparency, however much that alleged transparency was actually underpinned by a white male body, fixed but concealed like a watermark beneath its surface. Perhaps Hurston grasped the terms of that tradeoff when, in her autobiography, she recalls her affection for Odin, the hero of a Norse tale known from her childhood, who plucked out one eye in exchange for knowledge (*Dust Tracks* 39). The image anticipates in complex and disturbing ways the one-eyed seer in Ellison's *Invisible Man*.

Notes

[1] For a history of the ways the black female body was viewed as a site of atavistic sexual difference and excess, see Gilman.

[2] For an account of anthropology's roots in imperialism, and charges of its indifference to the exploitation of subject peoples, its use of knowledge to benefit whites, and its complicity as an instrument of white rule, see Willis, and Caulfield. In light of this institutional context, what critics beginning with Richard Wright have seen as Hurston's neglect of the issue of black's exploitation by whites can perhaps be understood as discipline-wide subordination of issues of exploitation to culture; see Caulfield, 184-5.

[3] Melville Herskovits later joined this company, but I am concerned here with the problematic positioning of the black and female gaze.

[4] Hurston's research on an indigenous subculture experienced as 'deviant' by some arguably places her project closer to sociology than social anthropology in key ways, and makes her version of the participant-observer method appear more mainstream; the naturalist method pioneered by the Chicago School of sociology in the 1920s and 30s, for example, placed less emphasis on objective study, and greater stress on the interaction between the observer and observed. But Hurston clearly allied herself with Boasian methods, as her request that he write the foreward to *Mules and Men* suggests. See Roberts.

[5] For a full discussion of the history of the participant-observer method in anthropology, see Clifford 1983.

[6] Marianna Torgovnick offers a compelling analogy for the gendering of civilized/savage relations in anthropology, comparing the mythic model of the Odysseus/Polyphemus relationship, in Homer's *Odyssey*, with the male anthropologist/native Other; see also Sontag.

[7] See Freud's account, for example, of the transmutations encompassed in the literal killing of the primal father by "savages" compared with the psychically contained Oedipus complex, in *Totem and Taboo* (1913), 140-151; and Stoddard.

[8] Kuper stresses the influence of German debates about Darwin versus Lamarck on Boas' thinking.

[9] Another Boas student, Otto Klineberg, whom Hurston assisted informally in the 1930s, published *Characteristics of the American Negro* in 1944, which set forth the same conclusions.

[10] For an extended discussion of Fry's 'primitivist aesthetics,' see Torgovnick, Chapter 4.

[11] As Szwed points out, Melville Herskovits was an exception to this trend, but his perspective was largely ignored at the time.

[12] James Clifford describes the allegorical dimension of the transformation of experience and oral expression into text, and its collusion with an "allegory of salvage" casting the lone ethnographer as the anguished custodian of a fragile, disappearing culture, in "On Ethnographic Allegory," Clifford and Marcus 112-13 Interestingly, Hurston herself is not exempt from such allegorizing impulses, sometimes depicting African American folklore as an endangered form requiring immediate transcription, while elsewhere suggesting that, far from dying out, it's a vital, and evolving art; see "Characteristics of Negro Expression," in Scott 180.

[14] For a discussion of the intricacies of the Mason/Hurston relationship, see Hemenway, Chapter 5.

[15] For accounts of Hurston's music collecting and of her intiation into Voodoo rites, see Mules and Men.

[16] This theory of linguistic 'development' is hardly original with Hurston, being a commonplace of Romantic thought from Emerson to Shelley. I'll have more to say about Hurston's debt to Romanticism at the end of the essay.

[17] The conceptual resemblance works, of course, both ways; as Pound's use of the Chinese ideogram indicates, there is plenty of room for an analysis of white modernist Orientalist and primitivist appropriation here, as well as black modernist assimiliation of 'high culture' aesthetic standards.

[18] Michael North offers such a deconstructive reading of a 'primitivist' moment in an earlier Hurston essay, "How It Feels To Be Colored Me," in which he interprets Hurston's employment of jungle imagery as a purely strategic opportunity for her to undercut its cultural meanings; such a reading, I would argue, suppresses Hurston complex attachments to such imagery, which I am arguing lead to competing rather than consistent motives and effects, and help explain her choice to borrow it at all. See North 178-9.

[19] That Hurston felt it necessary to confront the charge of black imitation of white culture seems especially ironic given Michael North's argument about the pervasive mimicry of black dialect by white writers in the dialect literature produced from the 1880s on. See North 21-2.

[20] Mules and Men went through a series of drafts and revisions before its ultimate publication; and the editorial interventions into Dust Tracks on a Road substantially excised Hurston's sharp political criticisms of U.S. foreign policy, of Anglo-Saxons' superiority complex, and more, transforming it into a nearly pandering, unreliable text. For detailed accounts of the publication histories of Hurston's texts, see Hemenway; to

my knowledge, the most detailed account of editorial intervention into Dust Tracks on a Road is Claudine Reynaud's in Smith and Watson.

[21] For recent, detailed readings of Hurston's ethnographies, see for example: Hernández; Wall's Women of the Harlem Renaissance; Dolby-Stahl; Sánchez-Eppler; and Boxwell.

[22] While I'm aiming to invoke some of the most readily available readings of the novel's trajectories here, this is intended neither as an exhaustive list, nor to dispute the many factors which complicate such trajectories' unidirectionality.

[23] The image of the horizon is clearly a resonant one for Hurston and she returns to it in praise of a favorite teacher as "a pilgrim to the horizon" in Dust Tracks, 107.

[24] Barbara Johnson similarly reads Hurston's discovery of her blackness in the Jacksonville section of her autobiography as a loss of identity in Dust Tracks, 68; see Johnson, 175.

[25] See also Mary Helen Washington, 241.

[26] I'm indebted to Gates' reading of this moment as an instance of synesthesia; see Gates, 202.

[27] Like the middle class Negroes of Hurston's essay, Joe too appears to distance himself from black entertainments he privately enjoys; for instance, he refuses to participate in the porch "lying sessions," but he laughs "his big heh, heh laugh" at them just the same (Their Eyes 51).

[28] A dominant model of historiography in Europe in the eighteenth and early nineteenth centuries conceived an elaborate analogy between the development of civilizations and the life cycles of man. An early and highly influential articulator of this idea is Giambattista Vico, for whom all nations pass cyclically through childhood to maturity, with each stage of their development being marked by a corresponding linguistic stage. Thus, poetry is portrayed as the definitive genre of primitive civilizations, tragic drama the genre of young adulthood, and non-fiction prose, the genre of civilizations in full maturity. Vico's model is cyclic, positing a return; the late eighteenth century adopted the model and altered it to reflect a linear pattern of growth. The notion of correspondences between linguistic, individual, and national growth was popular among German intellectuals such as Herder and Niebuhr; it was an assumption which gave rise to the discipline of philology. Among British poets of the late eighteenth and early nineteenth centuries, the belief that cultures in an early stage of growth spoke a more metaphorically vibrant language was a source of some dismay; it forms the basis upon which Thomas Love Peacock and Percy Bysshe Shelley carried out their famous (and partly ironic) debate upon the history and modern viability of poetry. Blake, Carlyle, and Macaulay all explored, modified, and felt the influence of Vico's "developmental" historical/linguistic paradigm. See Steiner 75-80; Said passim; and Ruth Roberts 63ff.

[29] For two convincing, book-length arguments on white modernists' seemingly unconscious deployments of nineteenth century discourses of the primitive, see, for example, Torgovnick; and North.

[30] For additional accounts of Emerson and race, see also Lee; and Nicoloff.

[31] See Whicher on Emerson's critique of natural science.

[32] Newfield explores the relative values of invention and imitation in Emerson's vision of the poet in terms which clearly have resonance for Hurston's anxieties about black artistry, as they are expressed, for instance, in "Characteristics"; see Newfield 43ff.

Works Cited

Awkward, Michael, ed. *New Essays on Zora Neale Hurston*. Cambridge: Cambridge University Press, 1990.

Baym, Nina, et al, eds. *The Norton Anthology of American Literature*, Vol. I, 4th edition. New York: W.W. Norton & Co., 1994.

Behar, Ruth and Deborah A. Gordon, eds. *Women Writing Culture*. Berkeley: University of California Press, 1995.

Boas, Franz. *The Mind of Primitive Man*. 1911. New York: The Macmillan Co., 1927.

———. "The Study of Geography." 1887. *Race, Language and Culture*. New York: The Macmillan Co., 1940.

Boxwell, D.A. "'Sis Cat' as Ethnographer: Self-Presentation and Self-Inscription in Zora Neale Hurston's *Mules and Men*." *African American Review* 26.4 (1992): 605-17.

Braithwaite, William Stanley. "The Negro in American Literature." Locke 29-46.

Carby, Hazel V. "The Politics of Fiction, Anthropology and the Folk: Zora Neale Hurston." Awkward 71-93.

Caulfield, Mina Davis. "Culture and Imperialism: Proposing a New Dialectic." Hymes 182-212.

Clifford, James. "On Ethnographic Allegory." *Writing Culture: The Poetics and Politics of Ethnography*. Eds. James Clifford and George E. Marcus. Berkeley: University of California Press, 1986.

———. "On Ethnographic Authority." *Representations* 1.2 (1983): 118-146.

Clipping, Douglas Gilbert. "When Negro Succeeds, South is Proud, Zora Hurston Says." *New York World Telegram*. Feb. 1, 1943.

Davie, Sharon. "Free Mules, Talking Buzzards, and Cracked Plates: The Politics of Dislocation in *Their Eyes Were Watching God*." *PMLA* 108.3 (1993): 446-459.

Dolby-Stahl, Sandra. "Literary Objectives: Hurston's Use of Personal Narrative in *Mules and Men*." *Western Folklore* 51 January (1992): 51-63.

Emerson, Ralph Waldo. *The Selected Writings of Ralph Waldo Emerson*. Ed. Brooks Atkinson. New York: The Modern Library, 1992.

Flint, F.S. "Imagisme," *Poetry I*. 6 March (1913): 198-200.

Freud, Sigmund. *Totem and Taboo*. 1913. Trans. James Strachey. New York & London: W.W. Norton & Co., 1950.

Fry, Roger. *Vision and Design*. New York: Brentano's, 1920.

Gates, Henry Louis Jr., ed. *"Race," Writing and Difference*. Chicago and London: University of Chicago Press, 1985.

———. *The Signifying Monkey*. New York and Oxford: Oxford University Press, 1988.

Gilman, Sander L. "Black Bodies, White Bodies: Toward an Iconography of Female Sexuality in Late Nineteenth-Century Art, Medicine, and Literature." Gates 223-261.

Gordon, Deborah. "The Politics of Ethnographic Authority: Race and Writing in the Ethnography of Margaret Mead and Zora Neale Hurston." Manganaro 146-162.

Hall, Stuart and Tony Jefferson, eds. *Resistance Through Rituals*. New York: Holmes & Meier Publishers, Inc., 1975.

Hemenway, Robert E. *Zora Neale Hurston: A Literary Biography*. Urbana and Chicago: University of Illinois Press, 1977.

Hernandez, Graciela. "Multiple Subjectivities and Strategic Positionality: Zora Neale Hurston's Experimental Ethnographies." Behar and Gordon 148-65.

Hurston, Zora Neale. "Characteristics of Negro Expression." 1934. Scott 175-187.

——. *Dust Tracks on the Road*. 1942. New York: Harper Perennial, 1991.

——. *Mules and Men*. 1935. New York: Harper Perennial, 1990.

——. *Their Eyes Were Watching God*. 1937. New York: Harper Perennial, 1990.

——. *Tell My Horse*. 1938. New York: Harper Perennial, 1990.

——. "What White Publishers Won't Print." Wall 953.

Hymes, Dell, ed. *Reinventing Anthropology*. New York: Pantheon Books, 1969.

Johnson, Barbara. *A World of Difference*. Baltimore and London: The Johns Hopkins University Press, 1987.

Klineberg, Otto. *Characteristics of the American Negro*. New York and London: Harper & Brothers Publishers, 1944.

Krupat, Arnold. "Irony in Anthropology: The Work of Franz Boas." Manganaro 133-145.

Kuper, Adam. *The Invention of Primitive Society*. London and New York: Routledge, 1988.

Lee, Kun Jong. "Ellison's *Invisible Man*: Emersonianism Revised." *PMLA* 107.2, (1992): 331-344.

Lévi-Strauss, Claude. *Structural Amthropology*. Translated by Claire Jacobson and Brooke Grundfest Schoepf. New York: Basic Books, 1963.

Locke, Alain, ed. *The New Negro*. 1925. New York: Atheneum, 1992.

Manganaro, Marc, ed. *Modernist Anthropology*. Princeton: Princeton University Press, 1990.

Newfield, Christopher. *The Emerson Effect*. Chicago & London: University of Chicago Press, 1996.

Nicoloff, Philip. *Emerson on Race and History*. New York: Columbia University Press, 1961.

North, Michael. *The Dialect of Modernism*. New York and Oxford: Oxford University Press, 1994.

Palyi, Melchior. *The Twilight of Gold, 1914-1936*. Chicago: Henry Regnery Co., 1972.

Pound, Ezra. "A Few Don'ts By an Imagiste." *Poetry* I. 6 (1913): 200-6.

Pucket, Niles Newbell. *Folk Beliefs of the Southern Negro*. Chapel Hill: University of North Carolina Press, 1926.

Reynaud, Claudine. "'Rubbing a Paragraph with a Soft Coth'? Muted Voices and Editorial Constraints in *Dust Tracks on the Road*." Smith and Watson 34-64.

Roberts, Brian. "Naturalistic Research Into Subcultures and Deviance." Hall and Jefferson 243-52.

Roberts, Ruth. *Arnold and God*. Berkeley: University of California Press, 1983.

Said, Edward W. *Beginnings: Intention and Method*. Baltimore: The Johns Hopkins University Press, 1975.

Sanchez-Eppler, Benigno. "Telling Anthropology: Zora Neale Hurston and Gilberto Freyre Disciplined in Their Field-Home-Work." *American Literary History*. 4.3 (1992): 464-488.

Scott, Bonnie Kime, ed. *The Gender of of Modernism*. Bloomington and Indianapolis: Indiana University Press, 1990.

Smith, Sidonie and Julie Watson, eds. *De/Colonizing the Subject*. Minneapolis: University of Minnesota Press, 1992.

Sontag, Susan. *Against Interpretation*. New York: Farrar, 1966.

Steiner, George. *After Babel*. London: Oxford University Press, 1975.

Stoddard, Lothrop. *The Rising Tide of Color*. New York: Charles Scribner's Sons, 1921.

Szwed, John F. "An American Anthropological Dilemma: The Politics of Afro-American Culture." Hymes 153-81.

Torgovnick, Marianna. *Gone Primitive: Savage Intellects, Modern Lives*. Chicago and London: University of Chicago Press, 1990.

Wall, Cheryl A., ed. *Zora Neale Hurston: Folklore, Memoirs, and Other Writings*. New York: Library of America, 1995.

——. *Women of the Harlem Renaissance*. Bloomington: Indiana University Press, 1995.

Washington, Mary Helen. *Invented Lives: Narratives of Black Women, 1860-1960*. New York: Anchor-Doubleday, 1988.

West, Cornel. *The American Evasion of Philosophy*. Madison: University of Wisconsin Press, 1989.

Whicher, Stephen E. *Freedom and Fate: An Inner Life of Ralph Waldo Emerson*. Philadelphia: University of Pennsylvania Press, 1953.

Willis, William S. "Skeletons in the Anthropological Closet." Hymes 121-52.

"Yes, Anyone with Half an Eye Could See That it Wasn't She": Helga Crane's Artistic Decolonization

Venetria Patton

In Nella Larsen's *Quicksand*, her heroine, Helga Crane is not only the subject of artistry, but also an artist. She is not an artist in the traditional sense like Axel Olsen, the Danish painter who paints her portrait; however, she, like Olsen, creates images for others to behold. According to Marilyn Elkins, the text of Helga's art is her artistically enhanced face and body (271). Elkins argues that Helga Crane tries to turn herself into an art object by enhancing her physical traits and arranging "her surroundings into an artful backdrop for her beauty" (265). However, as Olsen's portrait of Helga reveals, Helga is ultimately unsuccessful in her attempt to construct her own image.

Quicksand is in many ways the story of a frustrated artist. Helga's life clearly follows the three defining elements of the artist manqué: the young artist, whose socially determined identity prohibits her free artistic expression, is frustrated; the mature artist, who attempts to reconcile her artistic identity with a domestic one in a society that defines the two as antithetical, is unsuccessful; and the older artist, who has long ago renounced art in order to realize a life as wife and mother, lacks fulfillment (Rose 156).

A majority of the text focuses on Helga as the young, frustrated artist in Naxos, Harlem, and Denmark. Her frustration arises from society's insistence on constructing its own image of Helga while ignoring her own presentation of herself. Helga is in the dual position of being both "the producer and product of art" (Dittmar 144); however, others refuse to acknowledge her as an artist and see her only as an art object. This resistance to Helga as artist is a means of resisting Helga's subjectivity; she is not expected to create her own identity, but to be subjected to others' definitions. Due to the history of imperialism and the pervasiveness of colonial ideology, Helga is limited in her ability to construct an alternative to the "colonizer's" vision: the Western world has a history of empire building that leads to white privilege benefitting all whites, even those who are not seeking a colonial relationship with people of color. White privilege permeates Western culture, including Western art, and as a descendant of displaced Africans, Helga falls victim to the colonizing gaze.

The novel opens with a detailed description of Helga sitting in her dim room. The reader is told, "An observer would have thought her well fitted to that framing of light and shade" (2). The reader can picture Helga with "narrow, sloping shoulders and delicate, but well-turned, arms and legs"; "sharply cut face, with skin like yellow satin"; "dark eyes"; " pretty mouth"; "ears delicately chiseled, and ... curly blue-black hair" (Larsen 2). Ann Hostetler observes that "Larsen presents the narrator as painter in the verbal portrait that opens the novel, framing the subject of Helga Crane within a rarefied environment of carefully rendered and illuminated objects" (36). This initial portrayal of Helga is just the first of many constructions of Helga as an object to be viewed.

Although Helga is presented as a spectacle and readers are positioned as spectators, Larsen appears to question the quality of representation provided by the images. If the various pictures of Helga were simply mimetic representations, she would recognize herself in the images, but this is not the case. Pratibha Parmar notes that "[i]mages play a crucial role in defining and controlling the political and social power to which both individuals and marginalized groups have access" (qtd. in hooks 5). Thus Helga's resistance to her various framings is very much about her desire to define herself; she is responding to the colonizer's gaze and resisting it. Samia Nehrez asserts that "[d]ecolonization ... continues to be an act of confrontation with a hegemonic system of thought; it is hence a process of considerable historical and cultural liberation. As such decolonization becomes the contestation of all dominant forms and structures, whether they be linguistic, discursive, or ideological" (qtd. in hooks 1). Based on this definition of decolonization, it is clear that Helga's denial of her representations is her means of contesting ideological structures.

Helga is unable to recognize herself in others' representations of her because she is continually misread. It is clear that Helga does not belong at Naxos, "for it tolerated no innovations, no individualisms" (4). Helga spends a good deal of time planning her wardrobe, which suggests that she is conscious of the image she is creating, but her elaborate wardrobe is considered "queer," "odd," and even "indecent" by the Naxos faculty (18). Thus Helga's sense of artistry is at once a blessing and a curse. She receives attention, but not the kind desired. Helga is clearly trying to construct an image, but she is ultimately unable to control the way she is seen by others. This inability to govern her own image increases her dissatisfaction with Naxos. Her love of color does not coincide with the conservative atmosphere of Naxos: "Indeed, it was this craving, this urge for beauty which had helped to bring disfavor in Naxos—'pride' and 'vanity' her detractors called it" (6). Although Helga is not well received by the majority of her colleagues, she is told by Margaret, a fellow teacher, "'It's nice having you here, Helga. We all think so. Even the dead ones. We need a few decorations to brighten our sad lives'" (14). While Margaret clearly has good intentions, she has unwittingly called attention to Helga's status as object.

Margaret's remark indicates that Helga is not on equal footing with her colleagues; instead, she is viewed as a decoration, denied subjectivity, and relegated to object status. This is true even for those who like her, such as Margaret, and even for the person she is closest too—her fiancé, James Vayle. Initially James and Helga were both outsiders, which fostered their friendship, but after he is accepted by the Naxos community, James does not have the same need for Helga. She realizes that he no longer wishes to discuss the failings of Naxos because he is now part of it. Although James has less use for Helga's conversational skills, he still has an intense desire for her body. "The idea that she was in but one nameless way necessary to him filled her with a sensation amounting almost to shame. And yet his mute helplessness against that ancient appeal by which she held him pleased her and fed her vanity—gave her a feeling of power. At the same time she shrank away from it, subtly aware of possibilities she herself couldn't predict" (8). Helga is torn by conflicting emotions as she considers her sexual appeal. When confronted with her own sexuality, Helga cannot allow herself to even think about initiating any type of sexual activity. She is overcome by something akin to shame, but Helga's shame is joined with a degree of pleasure regarding the power she wields over him. This ambivalent response to her sexuality is later repeated in her meetings with Dr. Anderson.

Helga's conflicted response to her sexuality is similar to her feelings about being described as a decoration. She is in part thrilled by the attention she receives, but she also realizes that this is attention accorded to an outsider. She is a decoration or sex object, and in both cases, she is an outsider. This is as true for Margaret's innocuous comment as for the treatment she will receive in Denmark. Helga's attempts to enhance her physical beauty do not bring the desired results—she receives attention, but she is not accepted or taken seriously. As long as she is merely a curio, Helga is not a subject, but an object. She tries to construct an image, to express her subjectivity, but she is ultimately unable to control the way in which others see her, which is guided by the "colonizer's" vision, even if the viewer is not a colonizer. For example, Margaret's reference to Helga as a decoration and James' view of Helga's sexuality are both bound up in stereotypes about black women that result from the colonial past of slavery. These stereotypes will be discussed in more detail later, but it is important to remember that the colonized group is just as susceptible to internalizing the "colonizer's gaze" as the colonizer.

The misperceptions dominating Helga's life are symbolized in her conversation with Dr. Anderson about leaving Naxos. He almost convinces her to remain until he enrages her by calling her a lady. What Anderson meant as a compliment generates turmoil, shame, and anger for Helga. Marilyn Elkins explains that Helga's turmoil is in response to the juxtaposition of her sexual awakening with Anderson's labeling of her as a dignified, well bred lady. This description suggests that Helga should deny the sexual arousal she has just experienced. She risks losing Anderson's respect by responding to her passion (270). The passion, which Helga must repress, spills out in anger. She becomes so enraged that she cannot grasp his meaning. Helga responds by saying, "The joke is on you, Dr. Anderson. My father was a gambler who deserted my mother, a white immigrant. It is even uncertain that they were married" (Larsen 21). These comments are clearly meant to refute his conception of her as a lady.

In this context, Anderson's compliment becomes a means of objectification. He calls attention to the fact that society lumps women into one of two categories—lady or Jezebel. Jezebel, or the over-sexed black woman, is just one of the stereotypes which developed out of the institution of slavery. Jezebel was everything the Victorian lady was not—she was neither maternal, nor innocent. "Jezebel lived free of the social constraints that surrounded the sexuality of white women. She thus legitimated the wanton behavior of white men by proclaiming black women to be lusty wenches in whom sexual impulse overwhelmed all restraint" (Fox-Genovese 292). The Jezebel stereotype is clearly related to the stereotype of the sexually promiscuous slave. Rather than see her as victimized when raped by her master, the female slave was blamed: "her ability to survive degradation was her downfall. As victim she became the assailant, since her submission to repeated violations was not in line with the values of sentimental heroines who died rather than be abused" (Foster 131). Thus the female slave is associated with illicit sex and viewed with jealousy and loathing instead of sympathy.

Hazel Carby asserts in *Reconstructing Womanhood* that "[b]lack womanhood was polarized against white womanhood in the structure of the metaphoric system of female sexuality and taboo sexual practices" (32). Black women were excluded from the realm of true womanhood and regarded as everything true women were not. Although this view of black womanhood developed during slavery, freedom did not alter the way in which black women were perceived. Thus black women writers "had to define a womanhood which would not only address their exclusion from the ideology of true womanhood but, as a consequence of this exclusion, would also rescue their bodies from a persistent association with illicit sexuality" (32). Therefore black women writers were often in the position of defending black women's morality or displacing their sexuality (174).

Larsen attempts to negotiate these two dissatisfying options through Helga Crane. Although the terms, Jezebel and lady, are polar opposites, both are objectifying. Helga is denied subjectivity because "[s]he is not allowed to choose the terms and objects of sexual desire" (McDowell 148). Thus Helga's rage is in response to society's refusal to see her as an individual rather than a prefabricated type, whether it be lady or Jezebel. It is clear from Helga's manner of dress that she values her individuality and that she seeks to present herself according to her own taste and beliefs. Thus she chooses to dress in "rich greens, deep reds, in soft luxurious woolens, or heavy, clinging silks" while at Naxos rather than the drab navy blue, black, and brown worn by the other teachers (Larsen 18). Even while unemployed in Chicago, Helga dressed smartly in a tailored suit with matching "fawn-colored hat, and slim, brown oxfords, and ... a brown umbrella" (31). She even opposes the tastes of Harlem society by choosing to wear a "cobwebby black net [dress] touched with orange" that Anne considered "too *décolleté*, and too *outré*" (56). Each of these scenarios illustrates Helga's willingness to go against conventions in order to be true to her own sense of style.

However, Helga's attempts to construct her image are continually rebuffed by a society that prefers to pigeonhole her as a particular type. Thus her limited success in crafting her image has less to do with her failure to express herself than with the beliefs and values of those around her. The Naxos community with its repressive "Victorian" atmosphere does not allow for Helga's inventiveness. In fact, the community's attempt to mold Helga after their values is similar to its approach to educating its students. Helga describes Naxos as "a big knife with cruelly sharp edges ruthlessly cutting all to a pattern, the white man's pattern" (4). True to its name, an anagram for Saxon, Naxos sets out to enforce white ideals. The Naxos commitment to conformity to white ideals is akin to the pressure black women writers felt to repress the sexuality of black women. The Naxos community fears being judged negatively by any one individual's actions and thus all are forced to conform. As a result, the school enjoys and benefits from being recognized as "a show place in the black belt" (4). The school is frequently visited by famous white ministers who admonish them that "if all Negroes would only take a leaf out of the book of Naxos and conduct themselves in the manner of the Naxos products, there would be no race problem, because Naxos Negroes knew what was expected of them. They had good sense and they had good taste" (3). Ultimately, Naxos is both a product of and a tool of white supremacy.

Helga does not fit in at Naxos and rather than try to understand her differences, the community dismisses her. Because Helga does not have family, she is tolerated but not accepted. As far as Naxos and African American society are concerned, someone as marginal as Helga cannot afford to be different. Thus Helga's efforts at individualism bring censure or limited appreciation, but not understanding or acceptance.

Helga's dissatisfaction with Naxos leads her to try her luck in Harlem, but again she finds herself out of place. This sense of incompatibility is in part due to her biracial identity and in part a result of her inability to come to terms with her sexuality; however, these two different issues are ultimately related as sexuality is ultimately racialized. On their way to New York, Helga confides in Mrs. Hayes-Rore regarding her family history.

Mrs. Hayes-Rore thinks "the story, dealing as it did with race intermingling and possibly adultery, was beyond definite discussion. For among black people, as among white people, it is tacitly understood that these things are not mentioned—and therefore they do not exist" (39). Although Mrs. Hayes-Rore introduces Helga to Harlem society by putting her in touch with her well connected niece, she does admonish her not to mention her white relations to other blacks. Mrs. Hayes-Rore's response to what she views as the unseemliness of "race intermingling" shares at its root the same repulsion expressed my Mrs. Nilssen, Uncle Peter's new wife. Mrs. Nilssen's desire to deny any familial connection to Helga is driven by her own repulsion to "race intermingling." As she recalls in her later conversation with Mrs. Hayes-Rore, Helga understands and internalizes this reaction because "[s]he saw herself for an obscene sore in all their lives, at all costs to be hidden. She understood, even while she resented" (29). Helga is a living, breathing, enactment of a social taboo, and she cannot escape the stigma without giving up some aspect of her identity.

While in Harlem, Helga lives as a black woman and hides her connection to whites, but this secretive existence becomes stifling. She initially enjoys the isolation from the white world that Harlem provided: "No, not at all did she crave, from those pale and powerful people, awareness. Sinister folk, she considered them, who had stolen her birthright"(45). But she becomes discontented as she realizes her desire for something familiar but nameless. Helga is repulsed by her friends, particularly Anne with all her talk about race. She is annoyed by Anne's professed hatred for white people since Anne was so thoroughly assimilated.

In the midst of this inner turmoil, Helga meets Dr. Anderson again. The significance of this meeting is evident in Helga's physical response to the meeting: "A peculiar, not wholly disagreeable, quiver ran down her spine. She felt an odd little faintness. The blood rushed to her face" (49). She jeers at herself for being so moved, but she cannot help the sexual arousal that his presence triggers. During the cab ride home, she is aware "of a strange ill-defined emotion, a vague yearning rising within her" (50). The fact that this emotion is ill-defined is due to Helga's unwillingness to come to terms with her feelings. Rather than confront her emotions, Helga flees and attempts to avoid further meetings.

Helga's avoidance of Dr. Anderson is typical of her pattern of fleeing whenever she becomes uncomfortable. Just as she cannot come to terms with her sexuality, she cannot come to terms with her biracial identity. At first she thinks she can do without whites, but then comes a time "when the mere sight of the serene tan and brown faces about her stung her like a personal insult" (53). She is uncomfortable in the all black environments of Harlem and Naxos because she is expected to deny her affiliation with whites. In fact, she envies Audrey because she has "the assurance, the courage, so placidly to ignore racial barriers and give her attention to people" (62). Audrey mixes easily with whites and blacks without hiding her race. Although Audrey is described as almost alabaster, with "a skin of unusual color, a delicate, creamy hue, with golden tones," she is identified as black (60). The implication is that Audrey is biracial, but unlike Helga, she is comfortable with her biracial identity. This comfort with her racial identity is mirrored by her seeming comfort with her sexuality as well. She is described as a sensual woman who dances with pleasure and clings to Dr. Anderson. In fact, it is the sight of the two clinging figures that sends Helga fleeing from jealousy.

The next time the reader sees Helga she is onboard a ship sailing for Copenhagen. Initially, Helga had been content and happy in Harlem, but soon "[a] sensation of estrangement and isolation encompassed her" (Larsen 48). While in Harlem, Helga distances herself from whites, but this denial of part of her heritage becomes too much to bear. She decides to go to Copenhagen, "where there were no Negroes, no problems, no prejudice" (55). She imagines being "among approving and admiring people, where she would be appreciated, and under-stood" (57). Helga symbolizes her decision to leave Harlem with her clothes. She makes the decision to leave on the eve of a dinner party in her honor, so she decides to wear "that cobwebby black net touched with orange" of which Anne disapproved. She recalls "Anne's words: 'There's not enough of it, and what there is gives you the air of something about to fly,'... and she smiled as she decided that she would certainly wear the black net. For her it would be a symbol. She was about to fly" (56). Her decision to flee is in response to her feelings of being misunderstood and unappreciated.

Helga has begun a pattern in which she continually moves on to new scenes and locales in hopes of finding happiness and understanding, but despite new locations, she is continually dissatisfied. She is continually labeled by others, rather than taken on her own terms. The misperceptions which Helga experiences are epitomized by the painting of her portrait in Copenhagen. While Helga resists a number of caricatures of herself, her resistance is particularly evident in her reaction to Axel Olsen's portrait of her: "The picture—she had never quite... forgiven Olsen for that portrait. It wasn't she contended, herself at all, but some disgusting sensual creature with her features" (89). Olsen insists that his portrait depicts "the true Helga Crane" (88); however, Helga refuses to accept his representation of her. According to Pamela Barnett, "Helga Crane is Larsen's assertion of the always-mediated nature of representation—an assertion of the ideological content of supposedly pure aesthetic choices" (599). In other words, Helga asserts that Olsen's portrait has been corrupted by a world view which taints the way he sees and represents her. Sander Gilman argues that artistic representations consist of icons which represent rather than present the world: "[W]hen individuals are shown within a work of art ... the ideologically charged iconographic nature of the representation dominates." The individual represented synthesizes perceptions of the group to which the individual belongs. The viewer's attention is focused "on the relationship between the portrayed individual and the general qualities ascribed to the class" (223). In Helga's case, she serves as a representative of black womanhood, and thus Olsen's portrait is colored by his and society's perceptions of black women.

Despite Helga's revulsion toward the portrait, Olsen's portrait is not atypical. As a woman of African American descent, Helga is subject to stereotypes about African American women. Carby observes that due to the history of slavery, the black female body is associated with sexual licentiousness. Thus Olsen's portrait does not merely denote Helga's image, but also colors her image with the connotation of black women's sexual voraciousness. He presents Helga as a Jezebel. In fact, it is Helga's awareness of the Jezebel stereotype that feeds into her inability to see herself as a sexual being. Helga cannot imagine herself in a sexual context without taking on the extremes associated with the Jezebel image.

Thus the text is very much about Helga's attempt to come to terms with her sexuality, and the difficulty of this task is represented by Olsen's portrait and Helga's response. She must contend with the "colonizer's gaze" because it is this view to which dominant society subscribes. Helga flees to Denmark to avoid the racism of the United States, but in Denmark she merely finds a different form of racism. Here her difference is heightened and exoticized. Helga's aunt, Katrina Dahl, encourages Helga to emphasize racial difference through clothing. Helga is expected to dress in much brighter colors: "'You must have bright things to set off the color of your lovely brown skin. Striking things, exotic things. You must make an impression'" (Larsen 68). Fru Dahl justifies their different styles of dress by their different status: "'Oh, I'm an old married lady, and a Dane. But you, you're young. And you're a foreigner, and different'" (68). It is clear that the last unspecified difference is racial difference.

Fru Dahl has already decided to use Helga in the role of the exotic to aid her own social position: "In her own mind she had determined the role that Helga was to play in advancing the social fortunes of the Dahls of Copenhagen..." (68). She begins at once to deck Helga in outfits suitable for her position as an exhibit. Away from Harlem and the black community, Helga takes a different place in society; she "became a mere object for white consumption" (Carby 172).

Helga enjoys the attention that she receives in Denmark, but she is also troubled by its nature. In response to her aunt's comments about her clothing, "Helga began to wonder. She was dubious, too, and not a little resentful. Certainly she loved color with a passion that perhaps only Negroes and Gypsies know. But she had a deep faith in the perfection of her own taste, and no mind to be bedecked in flaunting flashy things" (Larsen 69). Although Fru Dahl dresses Helga the way she thinks young black women should dress, this does not line up with Helga's own taste. This discrepancy between Helga's taste and her aunt's perception of what it should be calls attention to the disparity between representations and the person presented. Fru Dahl believes that she is presenting "the true Helga Crane." What she is instead presenting is her idea of Helga. Thus Helga feels like "a veritable savage" (69) when her aunt dresses her. But then of course, this is the point, although Helga does not realize it yet.

"[S]he was being treated like an exotic object, admired only as a representative of the primitive and sensual" (Carby 169). This point becomes more and more apparent as time passes. In response to her treatment at coffee and dinner, "Helga herself felt like nothing so much as some new and strange species of pet dog being proudly exhibited" (Larsen 70). The other women respond to Helga as though she were some kind of curio: "True she was attractive, unusual, in an exotic, almost savage way, but she wasn't one of them. She didn't at all count" (70). Helga is seen only as an object; her subjectivity is erased—she does not matter. Thus Fru Dahl may erase Helga's identity and present her version of Helga because Helga's subjectivity is denied. She is not seen as a person in her own right, but as a representative of others' impression of blacks. In other words, Helga represents the stereotype of her class and is not seen as an individual. This is a case of "perceptual colonization": Helga is exploited by Fru Dahl as though she were a raw material to be formed as Fru Dahl imagines. This is not to say that there might not be some overlap between Fru Dahl's perception of Helga's taste and Helga's, but it is clear that Fru Dahl is manipulating Helga's image to fit her own ideas.

While the women gaze at Helga only to dismiss her, Olsen blatantly stares at her as though visually devouring her. "[H]e looked intently at her for what seemed to her an incredibly rude length of time..." (71). As he gazes appraisingly at her, he verbally inventories her features, "'Superb eyes ... color ... neck column ... yellow ... hair ... alive ... wonderful ...'" (71). This inventory of her features also operates as a means of dissection. Helga is viewed as so many parts rather than as a whole person. Significantly, Olsen's words are directed toward Fru Dahl, as he has nothing to say to Helga. Olsen's strange behavior clarifies

Helga's role: "Here she was a curiosity, a stunt, at which people came and gazed" (71).

But it is not that they were merely curious about natural differences between people, for Helga's difference was enhanced. Her natural differences did not sufficiently meet their preconceived notions about her racial difference. Her aunt had said Helga was different but just what she meant by that is unclear to Helga: "Did it mean that the difference was to be stressed, accented?" (72). It does if Helga is to be exhibited as a curio. Helga arrives at this realization during the shopping expedition for her portrait attire. Without even consulting her, the Dahls arrange to have her portrait painted and invite Olsen to select her attire. "The day was an exciting, not easily to be forgotten one. Definitely, too, it conveyed to Helga her exact status in her new environment. A decoration. A curio. A peacock" (73). Throughout the trip she was boldly stared at and commented upon by complete strangers.

At first Helga is disturbed by this kind of attention, but she becomes accustomed to it: "She was incited to make an impression, a voluptuous impression. She was incited to inflame attention and admiration. She was dressed for it, subtly schooled for it. And after a little while she gave herself up wholly to the fascinating business of being seen, gaped at, desired" (74). Helga does not mind being objectified when she thinks the gazes are merely admiration, but once she suspects how she is viewed she becomes incensed. This realization is crystallized by the painting of the portrait.

Having one's portrait painted is literally the ultimate objectifying experience. Helga's objectification, however, assumes specific racial and colonialist meaning. Her objectification begins with the discussion of the portrait. Much in contrast to the usual European practice of portrait painting in which a bourgeoisie subject contracts for a portrait, thus making the artist an employee, Olsen appraises Helga and makes arrangements with her relatives to paint her portrait without ever speaking to Helga, despite her ostensible bourgeois status. When she is told by an onlooker that Olsen intended to paint her and had come to see her, she is surprised, "'I'm sure you're mistaken. He didn't ask, didn't say anything about it'" (71).

Barnett observes that "Helga's consciousness of the objectifying transaction marks the artist-model relationship. Her agency is denied when she is not 'consulted personally'" (585). Olsen and the Dahls assume that Helga has nothing to say about the arrangements. They have taken upon themselves the role of her image construction and representation. Helga has been rendered passive as her identity is slowly recreated by others.

According to Barnett, "the idea of a painted portrait is generally objectifying; it is a genre that locates a human being as an object of the gaze and assumes the passivity of the rendered subject" (588). This objectifying experience is further complicated by the race, gender, and class dynamics in play during this particular portrait session. Helga, a poor black woman, is at the mercy of her privileged white male portrait painter. Olsen clearly has all of the power in this exchange of services. Helga does not merely model for Olsen; rather, Olsen creates his image of Helga. As he paints her portrait, it is clear that Olsen begins to confuse Helga with the image he is painting: "he had made, one morning, while holding his brush poised for a last, a very last stroke on the portrait, one admirably draped suggestion, speaking seemingly to the pictured face" (Larsen 84). Olsen's conflation of Helga and her image reveals that he cannot differentiate between the two. Either he actually believes that he has captured the real Helga on his canvas or he thinks of Helga as his creation. However, Helga maintains a sense of herself apart from her image and thus does not respond to his draped suggestion because she does not identify with her painted image. The reader is not provided with the exact wording of Olsen's suggestion, but is told that he was either implying marriage or something easier. Thus the direction of the suggestion to the image rather than Helga's person is significant. If Olsen has indeed implied a desire for a sexual relationship outside of the bounds of matrimony, this would clearly be a proposal to direct to the sexualized image on his canvas. Helga's confusion about Olsen's suggestion is linked to her sense of herself as a subject rather than a sexual object (Barnett 589). Helga's confusion is later clarified when Olsen actually proposes and asks why she ignored his earlier suggestion. Upon learning that she had been correct about his first insinuation, Helga becomes insulted and incensed. She then rejects his proposal and thus clearly indicates that she and the portrait are not one. Helga refuses to play the passive object for Olsen to manipulate. Her rejection of his proposal allows Helga to distance herself from the portrait and to refute her painted image.

Helga cannot forgive Olsen for the way he misrepresented her: "Helga may recognize her features in her portrait, but she does not recognize her self in this 'primitivized' depiction of her sexuality" (578). According to Barnett:

> Realist portraiture is impelled by principles of docu-mentation; portraits are painted to serve as artifacts of a particular person's presence or physiognomy. But Larsen's novel disrupts such notions of direct documentation. *Quicksand* suggests that portraiture, both verbal and visual, also reflects the symbolic resonances culturally assigned to the human body. (577)

Although it is not clear from the text that Olsen intended to create a realist portrait, Barnett's comments are still useful. Expressionism was one reigning school in the twenties, which sought to capture what was under the surface of the realist portrait. It seems that Olsen's portrait was probably expressionist, especially as Helga sees a "sensual creature" rather than herself when she looks at the portrait. An expressionist painting, one might say, would reveal Eurocentric cultural perceptions even more blatantly since it intends to depict what is "below the surface."[1] Larsen critiques the tradition of portraiture and its "pretensions of mimesis. Supposedly aesthetic renderings show traces of preexisting ideological basis; the white imagination's fantasy of the black woman's sexual voracious-ness lies below the surface of the portrait" (Barnett 578). Olsen's depiction of Helga as a sensual primitive being is not accidental but constructed: "The relationship between stereotypical icono-graphy and the construction of identity is highlighted by the fact that before painting the portrait, Axel Olsen decides to accompany Helga on a shopping trip" (585). He purposely chooses a wardrobe that will enhance his image of her as a sensuous exotic.

Although Helga rejects his depiction of her, Olsen insists that he has captured "the true Helga Crane" (Larsen 88). According to Elkins, Olsen's notion of truth encodes social and political agendas. His portrait poses Helga "as an inert and thus governable object of the male gaze..." (151). However, Olsen does not completely govern Helga's image, for the portrait actually presents a double image—"the Helga that is, and the Helga that Olsen wants to see" (Silverman 610). Thus the spectator is confronted with a "disgusting sensual creature" with [Helga's] features (Larsen 89). In other words, it is not that Helga is not sensual, but she is more than just a sensual creature. A truly realistic, mimetic representation of Helga would suggest her sensuality without distorting Helga's features.

Helga's battle with Olsen over "the true Helga Crane" is emblematic of the struggle for representation that Helga has fought throughout the text. "Through Helga, Larsen simultaneously shows the need for black women to create new forms of self-representation and the profound difficulty of the task" (Hostetler 44). Issues of gender and race come together to color the way in which Helga is viewed and represented by others. Although Danish involvement in colonialism did not rival that of Britain and France, the reception that Helga receives in Denmark is clearly attributed to the cultural power of images created by the colonialist ideology that pervaded European culture. The history of slavery and colonial relations between First and Third World countries has created a scenario in which the non-European body is exotified and eroticized. It is this colonial view of black women that makes it so difficult for Helga to come to terms with her sexuality. She cannot accept her sexuality because for her any hint of sexuality means that she is indeed the Jezebel of the colonial gaze. However, denying her sexuality is just as painful an option. Throughout the text, Helga responds to this predicament through her sense of artistry. She attempts to display herself in a manner that heightens her beauty without turning her into the oversexed Jezebel. She does not want to be limited by society's preconceived notions of her race and gender.

Thus when she sees her portrait, she does not find her image reflected there. Helga refers to the portrait image as "disgusting" and "sensual," while the Danish maid refers to the picture as "bad" and "wicked"(89). Their different reactions to the painting represent two different yet related traditions of representation. "The black representation—or actually lack of representation— of female sexuality is one that views sexuality as 'disgusting,' in some way defiling pure womanhood. The white representation of black female sexuality is one that designates it as 'wicked,' licentious, dangerous" (Barnett 588). Larsen, however, is satisfied with neither response. While Larsen does not wish for black sexuality to be categorized as "bad" or "wicked," she also refuses "to rescue black women through a reactionary portraiture of chaste, undesiring, safely married subjects" (580). For Larsen the response to a misrepresentation of black sexuality is not to repress or deny black sexuality, but to properly present it.

Thus, although Helga rejects Olsen's portrayal of her as licentious, she also rejects the opposite extreme of ladyhood as represented by Miss MacGooden, the dean of women at Naxos. As her name suggests, Miss MacGooden is the epitome of propriety. A lady, according to her standards, is not merely chaste, but completely unsexed. She remains an unmarried virgin because "[t]here were ... things in the matrimonial state that were of necessity entirely too repulsive for a lady of delicate and sensitive nature to submit to" (Larsen 12). Miss MacGooden responds to a history of sexual misrepresentation with sexual elision. However, "the repressive standards of the headmistress depend on an ideal of the exotic, decorative black woman; she has internalized the racist typology. The dean's impulse to repress is a reactionary response, a solution constrained by racist white vision" (Barnett 595). Thus Helga's refusal to follow Miss MacGooden's example is part of her refusal to be governed by white values. According to Barnett, Helga resists the idea of being a lady. "In fact, she is hostile to the designation and the repression it indicates.... [S]he accuses her colleagues of being prudish about sex, repressing individuality and beauty, and imitating white preoccupations with family and legitimacy" (593). By refusing to give into prudery developed in response to Victorian notions of rampant black sexuality, Helga refuses to internalize this racist ideology.

Although the portrait painting experience is based on the assumption of Helga's passivity, Helga rejects the role of passive model by denying the supposed truthfulness of the reproduction of her features. However, this critique is not merely a model's dissatisfaction, but the critique of another artist. Helga questions Olsen's skills and perceptions when she takes issue with his painting; however, her critique is ignored as Olsen assures her that he has captured "the true Helga Crane" (Larsen 88).

Olsen's rejection of Helga's denial, like Anderson's assertion of Helga's ladyhood, is part of Helga's socially determined identity. Helga's attempts at free artistic expression have been rebuffed which leads to Helga's frustration as a young artist. If we think of Helga as an artist who uses her body as her canvas, it is clear that her art has not been received on her terms. She attempts to create an illusion with her clothing, but instead of being seen as sophisticated or in some other positive manner, she is seen as a decoration, at best, or as a slut, at worst. Frustrated by the misunderstanding of her audience, Helga decides to try her hand at domesticity with Reverend Green. However, Helga does not completely reject her artistic impulse. She instead attempts to engage in an artistic domesticity by artfully arranging the domestic sphere.

After her marriage to Green, Helga returns with him to the tiny Alabama town where he is pastor of a church. She is enthusiastic about her new role as a preacher's wife and intends to aid her husband's parishioners: "She meant to subdue the cleanly scrubbed ugliness of her own surroundings to soft inoffensive beauty, and to help the other women to do likewise" (119). At first glance, this may seem in keeping with her socially determined identity, but I believe Helga is attempting to move beyond the traditional scope of the housewife's role. A homemaker is expected to keep a clean and pretty home, but Helga treats everything as an artistic tapestry. Helga's plans to artfully arrange her surroundings, however, are not well received: "When she went about to try to interest the women in what she considered more appropriate clothing and in inexpensive ways of improving their homes according to her ideas of beauty, she was met, always with smiling agreement and good-natured promises." But, "among themselves they talked with amusement, or with anger, of 'dat uppity, meddlin' No'the'nah'" (119). Thus once again, Helga's attempts at artistry are rebuffed and her intentions are misunderstood. Her actions might be perceived as middle class condescension, but I think Helga's previous experiences with middle class life both in Naxos and Harlem suggest that she too would be uncomfortable with traditional middle class values. Her actions, instead, should be seen as artistic endeavors.

While Helga's previous gestures of artistic expression left her frustrated as she was misunderstood by those around her in Naxos, Harlem, and Copenhagen, Helga is not merely frustrated in Alabama but forced to acknowledge her unsuccessfulness. Helga, the mature artist, realizes that her artistic identity and domestic identity cannot be reconciled in a society that deems the two as antithetical. Her domestic identity consumes her artistic identity, as she is used up by her children and domestic responsibilities: "So there was no time for the pursuit of beauty..." (124). This then marks her movement to the third stage of the artist manqué. Helga has become the older artist who has renounced art in favor of the domestic life of the wife and mother only to realize that these roles are unfulfilling.

Helga's lack of fulfillment in her domestic role is symbolized by her response to the birth of her fourth child. When the child "was held before her for maternal approval, she failed entirely to respond properly to this sop of consolation for the suffering and horror through which she had passed. There was from her no pleased, proud smile, no loving, possessive gesture, no manifestation of interest in the important matters of sex and weight" (127). Helga instead closes her eyes on the entire scene. For weeks Helga lays silent and listless as she hovers at the edge of unconsciousness. Helga eventually recovers physically, but mentally she will never be the same. Despite her resistance, Helga has lost the battle for self-representation, and she has been used up by her children (123). The last few pages of the text describe Helga's lethargy in the face of the tremendous demands of child birth and child rearing. The birth of her fourth child is particularly debilitating, and during this experience and its aftermath she loses all faith in God and humanity:

In her was born angry bitterness and an enormous
disgust. The cruel, unrelieved suffering had beaten down
her protective wall of artificial faith in the infinite
wisdom, in the mercy, of God. For had she not called in
her agony on Him? And He had not heard. Why?
Because, she knew now, He wasn't there. Didn't exist.
Into that yawning gap of unspeakable brutality had gone,
too, her belief in the miracle and wonder of life. Only
scorn, resentment, and hate remained—and ridicule. Life
wasn't a miracle, a wonder. It was, for Negroes at least,
only a great disappointment. Something to be got
through with as best one could. No one was interested in
them or helped them. God! Bah! And they were only a
nuisance to other people. (130)

WITH THIS VIEW OF GOD AND HUMANITY, IT IS
DIFFICULT TO IMAGINE THAT HELGA WILL BE ABLE TO
RECOVER HER ARTISTIC SENSIBILITY. I THINK HELGA
HAS GIVEN UP TRYING TO BATTLE THE "COLONIAL
GAZE" AND HAS SUCCUMBED TO SOCIETAL
DETERMINISM.

Helga is presented with a choice between two extremes:
Jezebel, as depicted in Olsen's portrait, and ladyhood, as
represented by Dr. Anderson's labeling of Helga as a well bred
lady. However, Helga rejects both extremes in an attempt to find
a more comfortable middle ground. This middle ground which
Helga seeks is womanhood—a womanhood which is neither
licentious nor sterile. Helga desires a womanhood comfortable
with sexuality. However, Helga's world does not appear to have
room for such a vision. She inhabits a world of black and white,
which has no need for gray.

This is the tragedy for Helga. The issues of race and
sexuality coalesce in the image of the tragic mulatta. Helga's
sense of being out of place amongst blacks and whites and
feeling like neither a savage nor a lady reveals the problems of
either/or categories. As a mulatta, Helga inhabits the border of
neither/nor. Helga does not fit the pre-established categories.
Larsen uses her existence to question these categories and to
open up ideas about race and sexuality. Her point is that Helga

does not and cannot fit into such a rigid society. Thus Larsen calls attention to the problems of a society which insists on labeling and restricting its members to categories of black and white with no room for gray.

Notes

[1] I credit Martin Japtok with these insightful comments during the editing process.

Works Cited

Barnett, Pamela. "My Picture of You Is, After All, the True Helga Crane": Portraiture and Identity in Nella Larsen's *Quicksand.*" *Signs* 20.31 (1995), 575-600.

Elkins, Marilyn. "Expatriate Afro-American Women as Exotics." *International Women's Writing: New Landscapes of Identity.* Eds. Anne E. Brown and Marjanne E. Goozé. Westport: Greenwood P, 1995. 264-73.

Dittmar, Linda. "When Privilege is no Protection: The Woman Artist in *Quicksand* and *The House of Mirth.*" *Writing the Woman Artist. Essays on Poetics, Politics, and Portraiture.* Ed. Suzanne W. Jones. Philadelphia: U of Pennsylvania P, 1991: 133-54.

Fox-Genovese. *Within the Plantation Household: Black and White Women of the Old South.* Chapel Hill: U on N. Carolina P, 1988.

Gilman, Sander L. "Black Bodies: White Bodies: Toward an Iconography of Female Sexuality in Late Nineteenth-Century Art, Medicine, and Literature." *"Race,"Writing, and Difference.* Ed. Henry Louis Gates, Jr. Chicago: U of Chicago P, 1986. 223-61.

hooks, bell. *Black Looks: Race and Representation.* Boston: South End P, 1993.

Hostetler, Ann E. "The Aesthetics of Race and Gender in Nella Larsen's *Quicksand.*" *PMLA* 105.1 (1990): 35-46.

Larsen, Nella. *Quicksand and Passing.* 1928 & 1929. Ed. Deborah McDowell. New Brunswick: Rutgers UP, 1986.

McDowell, Deborah E. "'That Nameless ... Shameful Impulse'" Sexuality in Nella Larsen's *Quicksand* and *Passing.*" *Studies in Black American Literature. Volume III: Black Feminist Criticism and Critical Theory.* Eds. Joe Weixlmann and Houston A. Baker, Jr. Greenwood: Penkevill Publishing, 1988. 139-67.

Rose, Jane Atteridge, "The Artist Manqué in the Fiction of Rebecca Harding Davis." *Writing the Woman Artist. Essays on Poetics, Politics, and Portraiture.* Ed. Suzanne W. Jones. Philadelphia: U of Pennsylvania P, 1991. 133-54.

Silverman, Brenda. "Nella Larsen's *Quicksand*: Untangling the Webs of Exoticism." *African American Review* 27.4 (1993): 599-614.

RECONTEXTUALIZING WOMEN'S HISTORY: URSA CORREGIDORA AS A "BLUES ARACHNE"

Tanya Monier

Françoise Lionnet has noted that Gayl Jones, like other contemporary female African and African-American novelists whose texts concern the post-colonial subject, incorporates and reconsiders "the negative mythic images of women (such as Medusa, Jezebel, Salome, the Furies, the Amazon, the madwoman, the hysteric, etc.)—which [she] exploit[s] and translate[s] into powerfully subversive fictions."[1] Scholars have carefully examined Jones' uncompromising treatment of the castrating Medusa figure, Eva, of *Eva's Man.*[2] However, their work overlooks the mythic subtext of her first novel, *Corregidora*, focusing instead on Jones' conscious use of blues expression both as a structural device that gives the novel a cohesive shape and as a tool that her novel's protagonist, Ursa, uses to reconcile herself with the past.

For this essay, I want to pull a previously unexamined name from the "etc." at the end of Lionnet's list of "monstrous" mythic women in order to examine the narrative pattern of *Corregidora* as a kind of storytelling web created by Ursa Corregidora, a new Arachne who reconstructs the web of her past and generates a new history through her art, singing the blues. The two versions of monolithic historical narrative that Ursa confronts—the official history of Brazilian slavery (which is itself an ellipsis) and her mothers' epic storytelling—make her feel equally oppressed; through her songs, she challenges herself to weave previously excluded "private histories" into her inherited web of memory.

Before I begin to analyze the ways in which Jones applies and reworks the Arachne myth in *Corregidora*, I will examine Ovid's version of the story in his *Metamorphoses*. Unlike later glosses such as *Bulfinch's Mythology*, Ovid's tale foregrounds issues—including class conflict and the excision of records of institutionalized sexual violence from official historical narratives—in ways that are similarly echoed by *Corregidora*. I do not want to imply that Jones' novel is simply a conscious translation of an ancient myth. Rather, I believe that Jones has masterfully incorporated elements of this myth into her blues novel; in doing so, she inverts complacent readings of "classical" knowledge, revising and perhaps completing Ovid's tale. The model of storytelling that emerges from Jones' work can be read as a potentially subversive language web that includes and connects elements that are usually excluded from historical narratives, especially the effects of violence on the black female body. Like Ovid's myth, Jones' novel forces the reader to re-examine these narratives from the perspective of the silenced subaltern.

I

Ovid, an icon of classical education, was a poet exiled to the Black Sea from Rome for writing poems that were evidently in "error."[3] The particular nature of this socially fatal error remains a mystery, but the pattern of Ovid's writing shows that he tended to walk the line between acceptable and acerbic satire; his mythological work frequently documents moments of resistance to authority and subsequent brutal, seemingly arbitrary restorations of "peace" that read uncomfortably like political fact. His *Metamorphoses* is a collection of stories that detail incidents of heavenly intervention in the lives of humans, resulting, as the title suggests, in humans' permanent transformation.

The myth of Arachne is particularly disturbing in its representation of swift, vicious "justice." Arachne is introduced as a poor, young Cretan who has "no distinction in her place of birth/ Or pedigree, only [a] special skill" at weaving remarkably lifelike images into her textiles.[4] Admirers wonder at how Arachne acquired her skill; but, the girl denies the possibility that Athena, the goddess of weaving, might have trained her because a "teacher so distinguished hurt her pride" (31). Publicly, she swears to challenge Athena herself to a weaving competition, and promises "should I / Lose, there is no forfeit that I would not pay" (33-34). Enraged, the goddess comes and reveals herself to the girl who "Blushe[s]" but has "no fear" of the situation because her "stupid heart" is set "on victory" (59-60, 66).

The two meet in competition to weave "real looking" representations of "ancient tales" (89). Athena's tapestry is a warning to Arachne about hubris; it showcases the gods in their formal glory at Athena's competition with Neptune that ended "the old dispute/About the name of Athens" (91-92). In each corner of the tapestry, Athena works images of other mortals who dared to deny or subvert the gods' authority, offering the girl images of their transformation as examples of heavenly "Victory" (91-125). Along the border of the golden-threaded tapestry runs a band of olive branches, symbol for herself and for "peace" (127-128).

Arachne's tapestry functions as an ironic but direct challenge to Athena's "official history" for she picks up the metamorphosis motif in Athena's text and inverts it. Where the corner images of Athena's tapestry show metamorphosis as an act of punishment from the gods, Arachne chooses mythic moments when male gods changed themselves into animals in order to satisfy their lusts. Europa—the founding mother of Crete, Arachne's home island—is shown being kidnapped by Zeus from her natal home, "cheated by the bull's disguise." Far from flattered by the god's attentions, "The girl was gazing at/ The shore she'd left and calling to her friends, / Seeming to dread the leaping billow's touch,/ Shrinking and drawing up her feet in fear" (129-134). Other mortal women are shown suffering the passionate expressions of Zeus, Neptune, Bacchus and Saturn in animal incarnations. Arachne's textile reveals famous seductions for what they are—unavenged incidents of rape, incest, and forced migration (130-160). Even the border design of the girl's tapestry is constructed to contradict the symbolic message of Athena's. Arachne weaves "A narrow band of ... flowers and clinging ivy intertwined" (169-170); taken in context, the border clearly represents the women's helplessness, like flowers bound and suffocated.

"Incensed at such/ Success" (164), Athena jealously rages at Arachne's skill, tears apart the girl's tapestry and strikes her repeatedly with her weaving shuttle. The girl "bravely" chooses to hang herself rather than "endure" punishment for her superior weaving (169-171). Out of a "pity" still driven by anger, Athena turns Arachne into a spider, warning her, "Live... but hang... and know/ You'll rue the future too: that penalty/ Your kind shall pay to all posterity" (172-174). The final lines of the myth present an image of Arachne, now all "slim fingers" and "belly," pulling her thread from her body to continue "pursu[ing] her former skill" (181-184).

This myth offers a curious moral: Shaking the political "web" at its edges makes the center tremble—but at what cost? A woman of low economic and legal status, literally from the margins of the empire, dares the goddess of the capital city (who is, significantly, the only known product of male birth) to produce "real looking" (i.e. truthful) representations of the founding moments of the gods' realm. Athena's rage is understandable, for Arachne's tapestry is a text that refutes all official catechisms; it calls "seduction" deception, "love" rape, and "victory" tragedy. Thus, in the interests of securing the hegemonic relations of power (represented by Athena's olive branches), Arachne must be contained before her subversive text finds an equally impassioned audience.

Rather than letting the girl kill herself—a final gesture of resistance for the powerless—Athena turns her into a spider, doomed to weave for eternity. Her punishment can now serve as a godly warning against impertinently stepping above one's social station, while proof of her counter-narrative is destroyed. Adam McKible sums up Walter Benjamin's points on such situations nicely: "The historical account given the greatest credence always belongs to the ruling culture. Thus, history is the Master narrative a dominant culture tells about itself. This narrative effaces as much contradiction as it can, destroying certain records, highlighting others, and creating heroes and villains generally convenient to it."[5]

Interestingly, the "doom" of every villainous rebel in Athena's tapestry is not death, which one might expect as a punishment for heresy: the gods execute the children of one, transform two into birds, and turn the last into a mountain (110-125). Land masses, animals and insects are parts of "Nature" which "Civilization" can ignore or mythologize while it landscapes, domesticates, or annihilates according to its needs and means.[6] Thus, Arachne-as-spider still weaves, but her actions are neutralized. Her weaving is no longer recognizable as a gesture of social defiance and righteousness but simply a natural or instinctual (and therefore negligible) part of her identity.

II

In the opening scenes of *Corregidora*, Ursa Corregidora, the protagonist and narrator, recalls how she miscarried a baby conceived in marital rape; the young blues singer is pushed down a flight of stairs outside the club where she sings by her jealous husband, Mutt Thomas. In the hospital, Ursa is also obliged (for unstated reasons) to have a hysterectomy. The novel's timeline spans the following two decades of Ursa's life as she slowly comes to reconcile herself with the childhood obligation laid on her by her foremothers, and, finally, with Mutt as well.

The Corregidora women train US-born Ursa to "bear witness" to their unavenged history by "making generations," having children to carry on the message in their blood and in unofficial oral history until Judgment Day when they can "hold up the evidence." The women conceive their oral history to be an uncompromising counternarrative that fills the gap in Brazilian history created by the "officials" who burned all slavery papers after its "pacific abolition" in 1888 (79). The Afro-Brazilian women's stories function as a myth of origins that they repeat in order "to know who they are";[7] their intertwining stories are drawn from the core of their rage over two generations of unavenged abuse at the hands of "evil" "Old man Corregidora, the Portuguese slave breeder and whoremonger" (9). Their storytelling does not spring from a collective unconscious of slavery and prostitution. Rather, it is a conscious collection of memories that, like official history, eliminates contradiction—in this case, the existence of their own physical and emotional desire—in order to streamline their counter-narrative: "as if the words repeated again and again could be a substitute for memory, were somehow more than memory. As if it were only the words that kept [their] anger" (11). Ursa comes to call these suppressed desires and frustrations "private history," and her goal is to incorporate her own and her mother's, which seem to have no place in the family stories.

The Corregidora women rely on certain assumptions to perpetuate their resistance. Most important is their belief that, while historical documents can be destroyed or falsified, as they witnessed in Brazil, memory—contained in the bodies of former slaves and their children—cannot lie; the experiences leaves an indelible mark on their bodies and minds.[8] To prepare the American born granddaughter, Ursa, to "bear witness" to the undocumented injustices of Brazilian slavery, three generations of Corregidora women "educate" her by reciting testimonials of slavery's monstrosities[9]: "My mother would work while my grandmother told me, then she'd come home and tell me. I'd go to school and come back and be told. When I was real little, Great Gram rocking me and talking" (101).

To the women, history is a story that can be told and retold until it overpowers and reshapes the lived experience of the listener.

> "...They burned all the documents, Ursa, but they didn't burn what they put in our minds. We got to burn out what they put in our minds, like you burn out a wound. Except we got to keep what we need to bear witness. That scar that's left to bear witness. We got to keep it as visible as our blood" (72).

This paradox is nicely summed up by Eduoard Glissant who states, "Myth anticipates history as much as it inevitably repeats the accidents it has glorified; that means it is in turn a producer of history."[10] In effect, the women's stories scar Ursa so that she comes to believe that relationships with men are all brutalizing, yet failure to bear children makes her less than a woman, and a traitor: "The important thing is making generations. Can't burn conscious, Ursa, and that's what makes the evidence. And that's what makes the verdict" (22). Though intended to record the experience of slavery, the stories are oppressive because they are applied, gospel-like, to tangentially related issues, especially heterosexual relationships. Thus, the Corregidora women's injunctions to bear children (preferably female) who can continue telling the story of their abuse are applied to the following generations' daily behavior in detrimental ways.

The Corregidora women do not consider the need for certain "rules" of historical representation such as translation or most accepted modes of situating a story in time. While this can be a liberating aspect of storytelling, the effect of these omissions is that the Corregidora stories become mythologized and internalized at once. This paradox is expressed by the women's inability to separate ritual retelling of sexualized violence from ritual reenactments of the same. Great Gram rubs five year old Ursa's thighs while she describes young slavemaster Corregidora as "a big strapping man": she then "catches herself" and pulls her hands away, but not before evidence of her own suppressed desire leaves its imprint in Ursa's memory (11). In another recalled story, Great Gram slaps Ursa when she questions: "You telling the truth, Great Gram?" (14). As if through osmosis, the mothers "squeeze," slap and rub the Corregidora story into Ursa until she "sings it back to them" (103).

Preserving and presenting versions of the past that resist official history is a worthwhile endeavor, whether in Athens, Greece, or Athens, Tennessee. But as Athena warned the transformed Arachne, generations suffer. Despite the women's efforts to create a coherent and unified counterhistory, the text of Ursa's heritage is loosely woven, filled with gaps, unmentionables. Ursa recollects a nightmare she had when married to Mutt that shows how she could not absorb her second

education without somehow translating it through her own
imagination and experiences:

> I dreamed that my belly was swollen and restless, and I
> lay without moving, gave birth without struggle, without
> feeling. But my eyes never turned to my feet. I never
> saw what squatted between my knees. But I felt the
> humming and beating of wings and claws in my thighs.
> And I felt a stiff penis inside of me. "Those who have
> fucked their daughters would not hesitate to fuck their
> mothers." Who are you? Who have I born? His hair was
> like white wings, and we were united at birth. (76-77)

Images within this sequence strongly echo another Greek myth,
Leda and the swan. Corregidora, though long dead, returns in
Ursa's dream to rape and impregnate her, disguised, like Zeus, as
a swan. Symbolically, Ursa is a second Leda, giving birth to
another generation that will continue to bear marks of a pain that
no longer has an immediate connection to it. Ursa's
hysterectomy is the crisis that marks the moment when her
connection to the Corregidora women's set web of resistance
begins to tear, putting her on the difficult road of self-
definition.[11] After she realizes that she is unable to pass her
mothers' story on to another generation of Corregidoras, she
focuses her efforts on passing the story on to her community
through her body by singing the blues.

Critics such as Hazel Carby have considered how women's
blues weaves tales of women's (often subversive) history
through physical expression;[12] that is to say, the blues singer's
body communicates as much as the lyrics that she sings. Like the
opera diva, the blues singer's voice proclaims, "A price has been
paid";[13] her own (often painful, sometimes violent) physical
experiences are an informal part of her training, and they are
applied to her art. As the expert singer shuttles back and forth
between refrain and verses, she layers seemingly unrelated
images or incidents; through her repetition "with a difference,"
meaning becomes clear. Thus, the act of singing the blues
conceptually corresponds to the act of weaving, for the blues
story, like the pattern of a textile, emerges through an act of
repetitive construction.

Ursa's dream sequences, internal monologues, and flashbacks also function as threads for weaving her blues text. In one of the most dense and telling flashback scenes, Sal, a waitress at Happy's Café, comments that Ursa could "pass" for Spanish (70). The moment triggers Ursa's angry retort, "I couldn't pass," and she instantly remember meeting Urban Jones, a pimp, who tried to pick up a seventeen-year-old Ursa during her only trip to a Northern city, Detroit. Like Athena in the myth of Arachne, Urban—as his name indicates—is a representative of the city, the geographical center of power; and Ursa, like Arachne, is a young woman with no power or status:

> "Come over here, baby." I went over to the car. He was a black man but he had two white girls in the back seat. One of them was barefoot and had her legs up on the seat. Another black man was sitting in front, leaning across the seat looking at me. The other man was out of the car, smiling, showing his gold tooth. "What's your name, baby?
>
> "Ursa."
>
> "My name's Urban, Urban Jones. They both kind of sound alike, don't they. *The Ur*." (70, my emphasis)

The pimp claims affiliation to her through the similarity of their names. Real currents of danger run through this seemingly innocuous exchange, for Urban's off-hand witticism about their names' shared phoneme draws the reader to recognize their encounter as a symbolic reenactment of the Corregidora Ur-narrative relationship of pimp and whore. Disturbing overtones of the Corregidora incest motif are notable in his repetition of the pet name, "baby." After establishing contact, Urban asks Ursa, "What are you?" (71). To her reply, "I'm an American." he retorts, "I know you a American.... But what nationality? You Spanish?" Ursa rejects this suggestion outright: "Naw" (71). Urban's questions confuse nationality and race, legal affiliation with genealogical filiation.[14] Ursa denies the connection to Corregidora, the "Spanish" (which is, in terms of street context, close enough to Portuguese) traits in her face and hair, a living text of forced miscegenation.

In this context, Ursa's "Naw" also answers the underlying question behind Urban's chatty interrogation—You a whore? The pimp repeatedly pressures Ursa to leave with him; her only way out of this situation is to insist that her "boyfriend wouldn't like it" (71). Ursa must give an appropriate answer to Urban's insistent questions about whether or not she has a boyfriend, clearly readable as a euphemism for "pimp." Upon recollection, Ursa admits she lied about the literal existence of this boyfriend, but at the deeper level, she told the truth. As a Corregidora, she was born and raised with the absent presence of a pimp and master.

Ironically, in order to avoid repeating the past (literally capture and coercion into prostitution), Ursa repeats Old Corregidora's own pattern of denial. Earlier in the novel, Great Gram recalls that Corregidora always became violently enraged when his whores told him he looked like an Indian, with "hair was so dark and greasy straight you could a swore he was a pure Indian, but if you even dare say something, he stick a poker up your ass, a hot coal poker" (23). Corregidora's violent reinscription of race and rank on the bodies of his slaves doubles as a denial of his own mixed blood, stemming from the centuries-long presence of the Moors in Iberia, and from intermarriage with Native Americans.

The other pimp's gold tooth also hints at a key element of the Ur-relationship, the economic exchange value of women's bodies which pimps and masters appropriate.[15] Ursa's memories echo with other images of this "gold": Old man Corregidora calls Great Gram (whose skin is, significantly, the same color as the coffee beans harvested from Corregidora's fields) "Dorita. Little gold piece. My best" (10); Mutt, too, tells Ursa, "Your pussy's a little gold piece, ain't it, Urs? My little gold piece" (60). Although the other women in Urban's car are white, in the Corregidora story of origins, gender outweighs race; Great Gram's stories imply that Corregidora's wife, too, was trapped by her husband's sexual and mental abuse, even as she vented her rage on the bodies of the other whores.

Part of Ursa's problem with untangling herself from her learned web of storytelling is that the stories' terms are interconnected, and as indicated by the names of the Corregidora women, contain each other. In Portuguese, *corregidore* means "colonial magistrate," "thus implying the extent of Corregidora's power over his slaves and their descendants and underscoring the legality of his brutality."[16] *Corregidora*, the chosen surname of Ursa's family, translates as "the chief magistrate's wife," which correctly conveys the fact that "well into the twentieth century... [these women] are all effectively his wives."[17] Similarly, all of the Corregidora women's first names are contained within that of their old master. Great Gram is "Dorita, my little gold piece," a name which explicitly links her body with commercial exchange. Ursa's mother is given the name Irene (41), which is Greek for "peace," but her husband, Martin, only calls her "Correy" (120). The title also includes the shadow of Corregidora's legal wife whose violent sexual demands rivaled her husband's and are so demonized in the women's stories that Ursa violently rejects even the possibility of continuing a friendship with Cat after discovering the lesbian relationship between her and young, bold Jeffy.

In the *Metamorphoses* myths, the gods' powerful interference in human lives result in physical change, such as changing a woman into a stork. In her novel, Gayl Jones removes the supernatural aspect, and symbolically shows the ways in which power transforms people. The considerable number of characters with animal names—Ursa, Tadpole, Mutt, Cat, Martin— indicates that some type of metamorphosis happens in their lives and personalities as a result of struggle against power. Ursa's name is significant when read as a pun. The Latin name meaning "little female bear" can be read as the beginning of the phrase most often repeated by the Corregidora women: "Little female, bear witness." Ursa is made (literally born) to bear witness to the atrocities performed upon her mother's line.[18] Like Ursa's light skin and straight hair, Mutt Thomas' name bears witness to the history of slavery and forced miscegenation in the United States. "Tadpole" McCormick, Ursa's second husband, takes his name from a childhood habit of spending time at local tadpole pools. But his name signifies two contrary forces in Ursa's life: a tadpole looks like a swimming sperm (Mutt declares "he's probably all dick," [157]), a link with the Corregidora women's reductive understanding of the male sex.[19] Yet, it is also possible to read Tadpole's name as a sign that he has potential to develop into a mature being. Unfortunately, he seems driven by the first element since he takes a young lover into their home after he becomes frustrated by Ursa's attitudes towards and reactions during sex.

Since Ursa gives too much importance to one version of the myth, she lets other opportunities for communication and union through storytelling pass. Catherine, or "Cat," seems to admit that she chose to pursue lesbian relationships as a frustrated response to the daily humiliation of working in the house of a racist sexual predator, but Ursa refuses to show any sympathy (64-66). Twenty years later, Jeffy tells Ursa that Cat no longer "feels like a woman" after a horrific accident at the factory where she worked literally scalped her (176-177). Although Ursa could use their similar feelings of loss as a place to open understanding between them again, she becomes angry, and calls Cat's reaction "lying" (176).

Likewise, Ursa's limited focus on the particular nature of her family's rage locks out possibilities of deep emotional and political understanding with her husbands. Mutt and Tadpole both offer brief stories from their own families that could be used by both as places to connect their stories with Ursa's, to share both the pain and the responsibility of the past and to work with it. Tadpole's brief anecdote about his grandmother, who was forced off of his grandfather's legally bought land because documents were missing when she went in to claim her rights, echoes the Brazilian injustice: "Anyway, they ain't nothing you can do when they tear pages out of the book and they ain't no record of it. They probably burned the pages" (78). Mutt is haunted by the fact that his grandmother, who was bought out of slavery by his grandfather, was later literally confiscated to pay off his grandfather's debt; bitterly ironic, Mutt notes that since her freedom was purchased, she was still someone's property (151). Instead, Ursa focuses on the gender rather than racial elements of abuse and re-enacts them in her relationships as if she is contained by the bounds of her name and the history it once represented: "because the way I was brought up, it was almost as if I was [them]" (151).

Before her hysterectomy, Ursa unquestioningly accepts the Corregidora women's stories as if they were a pattern on which to model her own disastrous relationships. She is not exactly a black widow figure, like Gram who literally lured Ursa's father into her room at the center of the old Corregidora house by revealing her naked body, then attacked him when she knew he was fascinated (131). Ursa also hesitates to fulfill her obligation by sacrificing her sense of self-determination and self-definition, unlike her mother who seems literally to channel the spirit of Ursa's Great Gram through her body when she recalls stories from the past: "I stared at her because she wasn't Mama now, she was Great Gram talking" (124). Despite her hesitations, though, Ursa carries on with the tradition of keeping the Corregidora name which indicates that she shares her foremothers' expectations of and reactions within male-female relationships.

Ursa's two husbands are pulled (and allow themselves to be pulled) into the role of Old Man Corregidora, widening the web and increasing the number of points in which she traps others and entangles herself. Ironically, Ursa is at her most miserable and self-deluded during her marriage to Tadpole when they live above Happy's Café. However, Ursa's self-metamorphosis (if you will) begins by experiencing moments of self-empowerment, such as opening new relationships with men, like Max, her boss at the second club she works at, the "Spider." When Ursa rebukes Max for acting like a seducer, he insists, "I didn't mean you no harm.... I wasn't trying to make you or nothing like that. I just..." (96). For the first time, Ursa reconsiders the situation as one which does not fit into her preset understanding of male-female relations: "... and then I was thinking perhaps he *wasn't* lying, perhaps he didn't want to make me, just wanted to be hugged and touched. I said nothing else" (96). At the Spider, Ursa slowly reclaims her own history and her mother's, recognizes the connections that bring her back to the center of abuse, and slowly moves past the center of entanglement.

After Arachne is turned into a spider, she is doomed to spin the same web pattern for eternity and have it be read as "instinct." Politically, her gestures are misunderstood, if not entirely ignored. A racialized version of this fate is evident in

Ursa's story about the Spider Web club. Ursa recalls that, as an adolescent, she overheard neighborhood men gossip at the dry goods store about the suicide of Miss Melrose, a local girl. The men, like the Corregidora women, are convinced that the girl killed herself over "some man" (135). The white police, they complain, won't do anything about the incident:

> "Somebody go down there and file a complaint they write it down, all right, while you standing there, but as soon as you leave, they say, 'Here, put it in the nigger file.' That mean they get to it if they can. And most times they can't. Naw, they don't say put it in the nigger file, they say put it in the nigger *woman* file, which mean they ain't gon never get to it." (135)

White officials have the authority to record history, but overlook (or throw away) records of violence done to black women; if they bother with the story at all, they write it off as the sad outcome of a failed romance. The black men, however, understand that the words "some man" do not signify "lover," but "rapist." The local men know they will not be able to persuade officials to recognize this injustice and help them, but a violent physical abuse of power must be answered with an analogous act of vengeance: "You heard about the shot heard round the world. They gon be some rumbling over here in Brackton when Mr. Melrose find that man" (135). Interestingly, the man's comment recontextualizes a line by Emerson commemorating the founding of the United States. Emerson's poem mythologizes the American Revolution as a call to the world for democracy and freedom; but here the Emerson quote is reconsidered as a gesture which avenges the rape and death of a black woman.[20]

Ursa recalls that several years passed before she learned the conclusion to the story of Mr. Melrose's revenge:

> "I learned from reading back papers in the school library that him and some other man got in a fight at the Spider Web—not the Spider   where I was to work later, but the old Spider Web that was long since torn down—and that he had either shot or knifed the man, the paper wasn't too sure which. But now Mr. Melrose was in jail,

and the police had claimed they still didn't know whether the man he had shot or knifed had had anything to do with his daughter." (144)

The old Spider Web is a place where people fall into set patterns of violence and vengeance, taking an "eye for an eye." Like myth, the Web just *is*, and outsiders can never know how or why it was made, just as the police (and "the paper") cannot understand the girl's suicide or father's revenge. This episode reinforces my analogy which likens the older Corregidora women's patterns of storytelling to the transformed Arachne: here, each generation is doomed to spin the same story of abuse through the body, "to make generations to carry on the saga of the brutality of man to woman, owner to property, master to slave."[21] And, in each case, those in power read the event as a natural or instinctual response that deserves punishment but not understanding.

Upon reflection, however, Ursa distinguishes between the Spider Web and the Spider, and makes a pointed aside that the Spider Web club was torn down, and is not the same club where she now sings. Destroying the building, of course, does not destroy the possibility of similar incidents happening elsewhere (say, Happy's Café). But, as the name indicates, the Spider Web represents a static site from which the creator, the spider itself, is absent; once the web is set, it tangles other creatures and (if not actively maintained) is slowly destroyed in the process. Likewise, for the Corregidora women, creativity ends with the birth of a girl-child; the storytelling education is a process of conservation and preservation. The Spider, on the other hand, does not refer to the product but the agent, the creator of patterns, whether new or old.

As a blues singer, Ursa reconsiders her relationship to her own body as a product and producer of both art and history—or, rather, history as art. A singer's power is located in her throat, or more specifically, in her vocal cords which are a particularly feminized part of the body, and symbolically stand in for the vagina.[22] As a slave and prostitute, Great Gram knew that buyers primarily wanted to examine a woman's genitalia while she stood on the auction block: "Tha's all they do to you, was feel up on you down between your legs see what kind of genitals you

had, either so you could breed well, or make a good whore"
(127). As Mutt sees it, at least, when Ursa sings at Happy's, she
is also "on the block": "I bet if I went over to one a those tables
and I asked them what they have and they would tell me the truth
about it, they'd say, 'Piece of tail, please,' and I asked them
'What tail' they say, 'That woman's standing right up there'"
(84). This could, in part, explain Mutt's compulsion to "sell"
Ursa to the crowd (159) and to pull her off the stage hours before
he pushes her down the stairs.

Mutt is correct in believing that there is something sexual
about Ursa's work. Singing before an audience creates a direct
connection between two or more bodies without touching—from
singer's mouth to listener's ear(s).[23] Ursa uses singing the blues
to position herself as the subject, rather than object, of narrative
and desire. Even before her miscarriage and hysterectomy, Ursa
works at turning her history of violence into "violent art,"[24]
shifting physical emphasis from womb to throat. Ursa has "a
hard kind of voice. The kind that can hurt you and make you still
want to listen" (96). After her hysterectomy, her singing acquires
a certain "strain." As Tadpole tells Ursa, it seems "like [your
voice] had sweat in it. Like you were pulling everything out of
yourself" (54). Singing functions as a sort of replacement for the
childbirth she would never experience; more, her method of
singing also resembles weaving because, like a re-politicized
Arachne, Ursa pulls strands of narrative from her memory
through her own body to "give witness the only way I can," a
compromise which happily achieves her personal edict,
"Everything said in the beginning must be said better than in the
beginning" (54).

Ursa's chosen mode of expression is not, however, embraced
by her mother, Irene, who sees singing as dangerous text
making, too close to public revelation: "Songs are devils. It's
your own destruction you're singing... unless your voice is raised
up to the glory of God" (53). Her reactions eerily echo Athena's
warning to Arachne against hubris. Irene likens singing the blues
to "the devil coming out of your own mouth" (146), an obscene
and punishable act. Even so, such comparisons can be read as a
process of exorcising the "devil" of Corregidora, and expressing
previously silenced private history—"I wanted a song that would

touch me, touch my life *and* theirs. A Portuguese song, but not a Portuguese song. A new world song. A song branded with the new world" (59).

Self-expression, especially the kind that locates self in political ways, always runs the danger of being misinterpreted, so holding on to old tales for perspective is essential. Ursa, like Arachne, is yet determined to weave her songs as representations of an unavenged truth: "But still I'll sing it as you talked it, your voice humming, sing about the Portuguese who fingered your genitals. His pussy" (53-54). Out of respect for her mothers, however, Ursa does not incorporate historical narrative in her songs. The blues does not require exacting and explicit recounting of events in its song lyrics. Even during her emotional and physical reunion with Mutt, Ursa can "explain it in blues, without words, the explanation somewhere behind the words. To explain what will always be there. Soot crying out of my eyes" (66).

III

According to Leslie Marmon Silko, oral expression, such as storytelling, is "something like a spiderweb" which is strong enough to "bring [formerly colonized peoples] together, despite great distances between cultures, despite great distances in time."[25] Gayl Jones' work successfully operates through what Carole Boyce Davies calls "critical relationality":

> Critical relationality is not interruptive or a series of interruptions (as in Marxism/feminism or race/class or gender/ethnicity formulations), nor does it embrace the hierarchy embedded in subalternization. Rather, it argues for the synchronic, multiply articulated discourses, which operate braid-like or web-like as a series of strands are woven.[26]

Linking threads of Ovid to Jones reworks our understanding of both, and opens new possibilities for survival and agency. While, traditionally, Ovid's myth has been appropriated and incorporated in the masculinist European tradition (and its reading has been conditioned by this fact), the myth's application in this novel demonstrates how myths propagated by the

dominant culture can be revised so as to undermine that very
tradition, or at least offer a radically different perspective on it.
Reciprocally, Jones' reading helps us to reread Ovid and see how
"narratives of resistance" constitute important, if often
overlooked, components in [hi]stories.

What the novel does for mythology is what Ursa does for
herself. "History still hurts" at the end of *Corregidora,*[27] but
Ursa has stopped thinking about herself as a doomed product of
history, instead recognizing herself as a maker of history; and in
the process, she becomes the first of the Corregidora women to
reconcile the reality of a sexual relationship with a man with her
history. The blues represents Ursa's compromise between the
injunctions to use oral history and to "make generations." The
text of her song can be written down and transmitted, but not
necessarily decoded: "If you speak a secret, you lose it; it
becomes public. But, if you sing the secret, you magically
manage to keep it private, for singing is a barricade of codes."[28]
Ursa is more cautious than her spiritual ancestor, Arachne, not
one to forfeit or endanger her voice and text for a single moment
of crushing victory.

Singing the blues sometimes creates a tense situation in which
the potential for violence lingers, but it is a way for Ursa to take
control of her sexuality and move it away from the sexualized
violence that characterize her stories. Ursa gradually moves from
accepting history as a closed pattern to recognizing it as an
ongoing activity, "a talent or a craft" (30) in which the focus
shifts from *making generations* to *generating*. Her web of song
need not follow the Corregidora women's pattern of binary
opposition; compromises *can* be made, and this is the core of
Ursa's ongoing quest to dismantle the old story web and build a
new one with herself at its center. As she well knows, "My veins
are centuries meeting" (46).

Notes

1   Lionnet, Françoise. "Geographies of Pain," *Callaloo* 16.1 (1993), 135.
2   see articles by Lionnet and Dixon.
3   Melville, A.D., Introduction to *Metamorphoses*, x. 1986.
4   Ovid, *Metamorphosis*. trans. A.D. Melville. (New York 1986), 121-125,
    (lines 10-11). All subsequent line citations will be inserted parenthetically.

[5] McKible, Adam. "'These Are the Facts of the Darky's History': Thinking History and Rethinking Names in Four African American Texts." *African American Review* 28.2 (1994), 230.

[6] see, for example, Annette Kolodny's *The Lay of the Land*

[7] Silko, 89.

[8] Clinton, Catherine. "Rape, memory and African-American Women" *History and Memory of African American Culture,* (New York, 1994), 205.

[9] Of education and oral history, Karen Fields states: "Education is about what we agree the young should carry in their minds: what schoolbook lessons and what non-schoolbook lessons they should receive, about where they stand in the world and what the world is made of." "What one Cannot Remember Mistakenly" *History and Memory in African-American Culture.* 160.

[10] Glissant, Eduoard. *Caribbean Discourse: Selected Essays,* 71.

[11] Perhaps here, I should play out one more pun; if Ursa's miscarriage is the fortunate tragedy that breaks the Corregidora women's pattern of birthing daughters of rape to carry the history of rape, then we must also read Ursa's hysterectomy as a "historectomy."

[12] see Hazel Carby, "It Just Be Dat Way Sometime: The Sexual Politics of Women's Blues." *Gender and Discourse: The Power of Talk,* eds Alexandra Todd and Sue Fisher (New Jersey, 1988), 227-242.

[13] Koestenbaum, Wayne. *The Queen's Throat.* (New York, 1993), 155. While I acknowledge the class differences between "high" opera and "low" blues, the cult of the diva carries over from genre to genre. Koestenbaum's text is extremely useful for making points about the importance of the blues singer's body as a text that is constantly under revision.

[14] See Edward Said, *The World, The Text, and The Critic,* (Cambridge, MA: Harvard, 1983), 18.

[15] It seems useful to point out again the significant presence of gold as a clear sign of wealth and power in both the myth and the novel.

[16] McKible, 234.

[17] McKible, 234

[18] Gottfried, Amy. "Angry Arts: Silence, Speech, and Song in Gayl Jones' *Corregidora,*" (*AAR* 1994), 560.

[19] Corregidora is repeatedly described as a "seaman. Naw, a sea captain" (23). While this shift obviously points to Corregidora's power as a ranking officer, would it be too much to say that Corregidora was also a semen?

[20] Perhaps the shot that started the American Revolution was fired at the 1770 Boston Massacre, basically a forgotten moment in history compared to the much more famous Boston Tea Party. The slaughtered mob was led by an ex-slave, Crispus Attucks.

[21] Harris, Janice. "Gayl Jones' *Corregidora,*" *Frontiers* 5.3 (1981), 2.

[22] Koestenbaum. larynx as "labia": 160; as alternatives for "our dreary genitals": 161.

[23] I'm playing with an old motif here. In *Hamlet,* the king has poison poured into his ear; Ursa's mothers poison her future relationships with men by pouring only stories of violence and abuse in her ear.

[24] Gottfried, 568.

[25] Silko, Leslie Marmom. "Language and Literature from a Pueblo Indian Perspective" *Critical Fictions*, ed. Philomena Mariani (Seattle, 1991), 83, 93.
    In a 1979 interview with Michael Harper, Gayl Jones made similar assertions about the power of storytelling: "'Storytelling' is a dynamic word, a process word [and it] suggests possibilities, many possibilities.... [S]torytelling is ... the kind of 'form' that can bring in everything—that can make movements between kinds of language and kinds of reality—dreams and memory also being kinds of reality."

[26] Davies, Carole Boyce. *Black Women, Writing and Identity: Migrations of the Subject* (New York, 1994), 56.

[27] McKible, 234.

[28] Koestenbaum, 157.

Works Cited

Benitez-Rojo, Antonio. The Repeating Island: The Caribbean and the Postmodern Perspective. *Trans. James Maraniss. Durham: Duke University Press, 1992.*

Bulfinch, Thomas. *Bulfinch's Mythology.* abridged by Edmund Fuller. New York: Dell Publishing. 1959.

Carby, Hazel "It Jus Be's Dat Way Sometime: The Sexual Politics of Women's Blues." *Gender and Discourse: The Power of Talk.* Eds. Alexandra Todd and Sue Fisher. New Jersey: Ablex, 1988. 227-242.

Davies, Carole Boyce. *Black Women, Writing and Identity: Migrations of the Subject.* New York: Routledge, 1994.

Dixon, Melvin. "Singing a Deep Song: Language as Evidence in the Novels of Gayl Jones." *Black Women Writers (1950-1980): A Critical Evaluation.* Ed. Mari Evans. New York: Anchor-Doubleday, 1984. 236-248.

Fabre, Genevieve and Robert O'Meally (Eds.) *History and Memory in African-American Culture.* New York: Oxford University Press, 1994.

Glissant, Edouard. *Caribbean Discourse: Selected Essays.* Trans. J. Michael Dash. Charlottesville: University Press of Virginia, 1992.

Gottfried, Amy. "Angry Arts: Silence, Speech, and Song in Gayl Jones's *Corregidora.*" *African American Review* 28.2 (Summer 1994): 559-570.

Harper, Michael. "Gayl Jones: an Interview." *Chant of Saints.* Chicago: University of Illinois Press, 1979. 352-375.

Harris, Janice. "Gayl Jones' *Corregidora.*" *Frontiers* 5.3 (1981): 1-5.

Jones, Gayl. *Corregidora.* Boston: Beacon Press, 1975.

Koestenbaum, Wayne. *The Queen's Throat: Opera,Homosexuality, and the Mystery of Desire.* New York: Vintage Books. 1993.

Kolodny, Annette. *The Lay of the Land: Metaphor as Experience and History in   American Life and Letters.* Chapel Hill: University of North Carolina Press, 1975.

Lionnet, Françoise. "Geographies of Pain: Captive Bodies and Violent Acts in the Fictions of Myriam Warner-Vieyra, Gayl Jones, and Bessie Head." *Callaloo* 16.1   (1993): 132-152.

McKible, Adam. "'These are the facts of the darky's history': Thinking History and Reading Names in Four African American Texts." *African American Review* 28.2 (1994): 223-235.

Ovid. *Metamorphosis*. Trans. A.D. Melville. New York: Oxford University Press, 1986.

Robinson, Amy. "It Takes One to Know One: Passing and Communities of Common Interest." *Critical Inquiry* 20 (Summer 1994): 715-736.

Silko, Leslie Marmon. "Language and Literature from a Pueblo IndianPerspective." *Critical Fictions*. Vol. 7. Ed. Philomena Mariani. Seattle: Bay Press, 1991. 83-93.

Tate, Claudia. "An Interview with Gayl Jones." *Black American Literature Forum* 13.4 (Winter 1979): 142-148.

——. "*Corregidora*: Ursa's Blues Medley." *Black American Literature Forum* 13.4 (Winter 1979): 139-141.

BREAKING CANONICAL CHAINS: GLORIA NAYLOR'S LINDEN HILLS

Tracey Thornton

In her novel *Linden Hills*, Gloria Naylor explores the difficulties for African Americans in carving out identities that do not rely on the Eurocentric paradigms of the dominant American culture and that instead, grow out of the shared and lived experiences of African Americans. At the same time that Naylor explores the construction of identities for her characters, she also explores the relationship between black women writers and the traditional canon. In doing so, Naylor encodes the oppression that black women writers have suffered as a discursive dilemma, that is, she consistently raises the problem of black women's relationship to power and discourse, offering a sustained critical look at the consequences of centuries of silence for African American women. Naylor addresses these issues in *Linden Hills* by decentering the metanarrative represented by Dante's *Inferno*, from which she borrows the structure of her novel, and by populating her novel not with caricatured characters from the inner city, but with affluent, successful people who struggle not to *achieve* the American dream (wealth, status, assimilation into the dominant culture), but to cope with the very consequences of achieving that dream. The dream, Naylor eventually shows us, is not one that has been created with people of color in mind.

In her exploration of the issues surrounding middle-class African Americans, Naylor continues the rich and varied tradition in African American literature of linking the cultural with the literary. *Linden Hills* allows a dense and multi-faceted view of the intersections between Naylor's own consciousness of agency as an African American female author and the multilayered consciousness of blacks in the diaspora, negotiating the many cultural, historical, and social matrices stemming from their positions as colonized subjects.

Naylor's novel offers us a view of an *Africentric, female-centered* interweaving of such broad concepts as spirituality, individual and communal constructions of subjectivity/identity, gender/sexual orientation, intertextuality and the ownership of ideas, and political/economic constructions of race and class. Naylor displaces an Anglo-American view of spirituality with its sights set on the rewards of heaven with a secular, terrestrial spirituality that is grounded not in a personal and individual communion with an all-knowing, all-seeing god but in a communion with the members of one's own community. She rejects the humanistic notion of a stable and fixed subject, depicting characters who have suffered because of their embrace of this ideal. Instead, Naylor offers up a notion of identity based upon the communal sharing of cultural traditions that allow the African American community to become a resource, a network for its own people.

In many ways, the struggles of her characters to cope with their historical otherness in America mirrors Naylor's own struggles to cope with her own status as a marginalized writer. Her clever weaving of the story of her characters around and within Dante's allegory demonstrates the tension between her and a literary tradition that has only recently acknowledged the efforts and vision of female writers of color. Naylor's reading of African American culture across these lines at all times resonates with her own position as a minority writer within (or outside of) a colonial literary tradition. This reading is most clearly demonstrated in the interweaving of the story of Willa Nedeed, the central female character in the novel, with those of the other characters. Willa's narrative, unlike the narratives of most of the characters in the novel, is not treated in a section of its own, but, instead, it is intermeshed with the histories of the other character's lives, creating a complex intertextuality that can be seen to symbolize Naylor's own position as a writer and cultural and discursive agent. Clearly, for Naylor, a history of African American people that omits the lives of African American women is an incomplete history, and what she offers in the novel is a reclaiming of these voices, a reclamation framed not only by Naylor's own literary position within a literary subculture, but also by the marginal position of her female characters, even within the African American community.

Naylor looks closely at the ways in which conceptualizations of physical characteristics, personal lifestyles, social relationships within/among communities, and especially the perversion of so called "natural" attributes by Eurocentric traditions of Christianity (utilized in rationalizations meant to perpetuate slavery) necessitate certain narrative strategies—such as resonances with Dante's *Inferno*. She analyzes the implications of the establishment of European Christian civilizations in the newly "discovered" parts of the Americas and how this establishment has fostered the subversion of entire cultural traditions (specifically, African American cultural traditions) and has also helped consolidate the unity of European cultural and religious dominance of these parts of the world. Naylor sees this dominance especially in the creation of cultural, social, and economic systems within the black community that alienate her own characters from their shared history. Naylor's characters can be seen actively participating in this alienation, from attempting to pass as white to adopting Eurocentric worship and funeral customs.

Indeed, Naylor's project, in many ways can be aligned with that of Afrocentric theorists, who attempt to remove African American cultural iconography from the "stasis of aggrandizement of Eurocentrism" (Asante 9) and relocate it within a framework that posits African Americans as human agents, able to effect change and receive support from within their own communities. However, instead of denying the complex relationship of peripheralized cultures to dominant culture or merely shifting centers from Europe to Africa, Afrocentrism views human beings as always participating in multiple cultural locations; thus, Afrocentrism does not negate Eurocentrism, but instead exposes those intersections where European practices (in education, in spirituality, culture, and social practices) meet specific cultural histories.

Naylor's novel is set in Linden Hills, a black, middle-class suburb whose inhabitants have turned away from their shared history and painful legacy toward the pursuit of the ever-elusive American dream, a dream laced with visions of executive offices and mansions on the hill. In their pursuit of this dream of acceptance and assimilation into the dominant culture, the residents of Linden Hills deny their deepest sense of who they are, their historical positions in the white world, and their own cultural legacies that encourage the formation of community. For some characters in the book, this assimilation involves an erasure of stereotypical, physical race markers, such as "bad hair," body odors, and distinctive clothing styles. Other characters deny cultural roots by anglicizing names, subverting the value of orality by privileging written discourse, and adopting European customs of communal interaction, such as mourning rituals. In our narrative journey through this neighborhood, we are confronted with the devastation wrought upon the inhabitants' lives by an all-consuming drive for material wealth and social status. Luther Nedeed, who lives at the bottom of Linden Hills, rules the community, driven by his hatred for whites and his desire to make Linden Hills "[a] wad of spit—a beautiful, black wad of spit right in the white eye of American, ... a jewel—an ebony jewel that reflected the soul of Wayne County but reflected it black" (Naylor 9).

Our journey through this neighborhood is guided by Willie Mason, a disenfranchised black poet who comes from Putney-Wayne, a lower-class neighborhood outside of Linden Hills, and his friend Lester, whose family lives on the outer edges of Linden Hills. Willie and Lester, in many ways, embody the conflict between white dominant culture and African tradition. While both are aspiring poets, Willie memorizes his poems, reciting them from memory, never writing them down. In fact, for Willie, the act of writing of his poetry down would in fact degrade its value. Lester, on the other hand, values the written word instead. Naylor appears to comment here on the relationship between literacy and black culture (a relationship that enjoys a long and problematic history from the privileging of orality in much of Africa to the prohibition of slave literacy in the antebellum south), and she also implies that Willie is more closely tied to his own roots than Lester, who enjoys the privileges of residence in Linden Hills.

As these two travel through Linden Hills doing odd jobs to earn money for Christmas, they (and we, as readers) are introduced to a cast of characters who have no connection to their own cultural history as black Americans. We are confronted by such characters as Maxwell Smyth, who has worked tirelessly to erase his own blackness and the stigma it holds in the white world into which he desperately wants to be accepted. Smyth, who is the highest ranking black executive at General Motors, pays for his professional advancement in the white corporate world with his racial identity. In order to make "his blackness ... disappear," he adopts strategies like spelling his name "Smyth," getting straight A's, never appearing to sweat or get cold, avoiding sex and its "erratic rhythms and temperature," and adopting a special diet and routine that allow him to control even his bowel habits so they become five-minute rituals finished off at the bidet" (Naylor 102-104). It is these physical characteristics and practices that, in Maxwell's mind, define the black community for him, and it is the absence of these things that set him apart from other members of his community. He readily adopts the myopic view of his own culture that a dominant white culture has taught him is inferior. According to Smyth, he is in "a race against the natural"—and he is "winning" (104). The "natural" for Smyth are those tell-tale features of blackness that would prevent him from being fully accepted into white society.

We also meet Laurel Dumont, the female counterpart to Maxwell Smyth. Laurel lives in the most exclusive section of Linden Hills and has already achieved the success that Smyth craves as a successful executive at IBM. However, while Smyth suppresses his physical and natural impulses to cloak his blackness, Laurel starves herself emotionally, cutting herself off from her family and her husband, who ultimately divorces her.

Laurel remains trapped in a "private valley" (224) where she "wrap[s] her soul around ... trivial things" (222). The divorce leaves Laurel alone to gather the fragments of her shattered and displaced self. It also leaves her homeless, as the policy in Linden Hills, as dictated by Luther Nedeed, is that since her husband's family is the original owner of their property, she must move out. She is unsuccessful in reclaiming the cultural traditions that might provide her with a real connection to the world, and she kills herself by diving into an empty swimming pool. Maxwell and Laurel's lives are examples of the type of emptiness that Linden Hills inhabitants feel as they deny their own roots that might provide them with fertile ground within which to plant their identities.

Luther Nedeed rules the residents of the exclusive Linden Hills neighborhood ruthlessly, spurred on by his maniacal hatred of a white-centered power structure. However, Luther selects his residents carefully, only choosing those "children of the parasites and outcasts from the South, who ... wanted nothing better than a way to forget and make the world forget their past" (10). Ironically, in his quest for independence from white society, Nedeed works from within the white capitalist system instead of challenging it. For Luther, the master's tools do not dismantle the master's house—only his own. He obtains a material success that costs him and his fellow residents their cultural connectedness, their shared history, and, in a sense their very color, for, as Luther says in the novel, "Empty goblets let through the most light ... [and] even a goblet filled with the darkest liquid will let through light—if it's diluted enough" (11, 13). People come from all over the nation, clambering to be allowed to live in the prestigious neighborhood, forgetting that "a magician's supreme art is not in transformation but in making things disappear" (12). Nedeed and his sons carefully court those who want to "forget what it meant to be black, because it meant working yourself to death just to stand still" (Naylor 16).

Catherine Ward's article "Gloria Naylor's *Linden Hills*: A Modern *Inferno*," details exactly how the structure of Dante's Hell and Naylor's black middle-class neighborhood are parallel. While the layout of the community is much like Dante's vision of Hell, only eight concentric drives cross Linden Hills. First

Crescent Drive through Fifth Crescent Drive correspond to Circles One through Five in Dante's upper Hell. Below upper Linden Hills lies a more exclusive section, the Tupelo Drive area, which corresponds to the City of Dis. As in the *Inferno*, in Linden Hills, up is down; the most prestigious lots are those lower down the hill. To gain one of these lots, all of the residents are forced to give up something—a part of their souls, ties with their past, ties with their community, their spiritual values, even their sense of who they are. Like Dante's lost souls, the people of Linden Hills live on a circle that is appropriate to their transgressions. At the center of Linden Hills is the house of Luther Needed, surrounded by a frozen lake (68-69).

As I read Ward's article and others exploring the relationship between Linden Hills and Dante's Hell, I find that not a single critic has explored what it meant that Naylor seemingly embraces a Eurocentric, male-centered text to send a message about the dangers of African Americans adopting white models and standards and ideals to form their own sense of self. If *Linden Hills* is indeed a critique of the black community's adoption of such Eurocentric paradigms, what does it mean that Naylor embraces Dante to write that critique?—especially given that Naylor has repeatedly faulted literary critics who locate their theoretical analyses of her work in a European framework, claiming that these critics, in stating that Naylor appropriates the white masters for her own purposes, give control of Naylor's art to those masters, thereby suggesting that a black female writer cannot artistically create narrative unless she employs the narrative form and techniques of the "great" Europeans (Hall 186).

However, if indeed we cannot view Naylor's obvious employment of Dante's *Inferno* as an attempt only to give voice to black experience in a literary tradition that has long silenced it, how might we explain the undeniable similarities between Dante's text and hers? What implications are there for this deliberate intertextuality? Naylor risks being accused of hypocrisy, of subordinating her word to the canonical discourses that have traditionally dominated, appropriated, or denied non-white and female voices. Is it subscription to these very paradigms that destroys her characters who live in Linden Hills?

Despite her detailed analysis of the parallel structures of Dante's *Inferno* and Naylor's *Linden Hills,* Ward fails to explore the implication of these parallels and in so doing posits Naylor as indebted to the canon for her own material. Ward's article subscribes to the notion that many critics examining African American literature hold, notions Michael Eric Dyson clarifies in a recent interview:

> No, only where we begin to write with a certain level of mastery and with those narrative patriarchal codes in place will we be able to exemplify our own specific form of mastery and intelligence, and then we will be in one sense entering the modern world and able to, in a very powerful way, show that we are worthy of participation in this American project of democracy and that we're worthy bearers of culture. (85)

Chekita Hall is one critic who deals with this tension between Naylor's use of Dante and her own position as a literary minority, though inadequately. Hall explains the tension by stating that it is the *reader's* and the *critic's* mistake to situate Naylor's books in a eurocentric paradigm in the first place, that it is the reader's will to situate all literature inside the already established tradition that draws the parallels between Naylor's work and Dante's. She goes on to say that it is an unwillingness to place Afro-American art forms within a black tradition that has denied black people a cultural expression (Hall 194). However, this explanation does not do justice to Naylor, nor to her black female consciousness, nor to her conscious use of Dante. While it may *seem* that Naylor is hypocritical in her adoption of Dante and other canonized masters, to assert this critique denies Naylor's own powerful voice and denies her knowledge of craft.

We might begin to arrive at a more nuanced understanding of Naylor's allusion to Dante by looking at Elaine Showalter's delineation of the three stages that literary "subcultures" go through in carving out a niche in the literary tradition: 1) imitation of the models of the dominant discourse; 2) protest against the morality and standards of those usages; and, 3) self discovery, or the reclamation of an authentic voice of the community (qtd. in Saunders 265). Naylor's *Linden Hills* is indicative of her mediation between the second and third stage—she relies on the physical topography of Dante's Hell, but the differences between Linden Hills and Dante's realm are telling and represent Naylor's protest of not only the paradigm within which Dante wrote, but also of his subject matter. Here, Naylor does not just "stand in for a larger narrative community, but inter[venes] with her own viewpoints about what constitutes authentic legitimate powerful black identity" (Olson 86).

Catherine Ward points out some of the differences between the two works: there are no heretics in Linden Hills because Naylor's sinners are at odds with themselves and not necessarily with God. Naylor also omits the vestibule of the neutrals, Dante's Circle One, and places her neutrals on First Crescent Drive. Neither is there a plateau for the virtuous unbaptized pagans in Naylor's novel. She considers Lester, her one pagan, as a neutral and places him in the first circle. Ward points out that Naylor may have made this choice because "heresy and failure to be baptized are offenses against belief, and Naylor is not concerned with belief as much as she is with choice" (Ward 69).

Ward's explanation points toward a reason Naylor may have had for borrowing from Dante in her novel—perhaps Naylor is making a statement about the traditions and practices of Europeanized Christianity and its inadequacy as a paradigm for framing black experience because it deprives African Americans of a meaningful relationship between themselves and their community. In other words, Naylor secularizes the tale—her characters don't sin against God, but against themselves; thus, her characters' morality is not a contract between them and a "white" god, but between them and their community, and most importantly, between them and their histories. In the novel, Lester's grandmother calls this true self "the mirror in your soul" (59). She iterates to Lester what seems to be the thrust of Naylor's message:

> Child, there's gonna come a time when you'll look at the world and not know what the blazes is going on ... And it can get confusing, trying to sort all that out, and you can lose yourself in other people's minds. You can

forget what you really want and believe. So you keep
that mirror and when it's crazy *outside*, you look inside
and you'll always know exactly where you are and what
you are. (59)

For Naylor, the importance of this mirror is evident, for herself
as a black female writer and for her characters. It must not only
reflect the individual, but it must also reflect the community
from which individual consciousness stems.

The narrative structure of Naylor's novel also offers some
insight into the complex relationship between Europeanized
religion and the African American experience. The novel is
divided into seven sections. Each section is titled with a date,
starting with December 19th. Each section represents one day
closer to the high Christian holiday of Christmas, a celebration
that marks the birth of Jesus Christ. Of course, for the inhabitants
of Linden Hills, this sacred time is marked by death, poverty,
and emptiness. There is little rejoicing, spiritual or otherwise,
going on in this neighborhood. By the end of the novel, it is clear
that for Naylor and her characters, the root of this despair is the
disconnection between the Linden Hills residents and their own
cultural practices.

This is evident as Willie Mason watches people at the
recently deceased Lycentia Parker's wake eating catered food
from a cold buffet. Willie remarks how different this wake is
from those he is accustomed to attending in his community. The
fact that no one at the wake brings food to the event surprises
Willie because "he knew that his family always fried chicken
and baked stuff for a wake" (136). Here, the occupants of Linden
Hills demonstrate their distance from their own cultural heritage.
Willie expresses this distance in a spontaneous poem:

> *This outpost, this douce, this dumb, this dead, in which*
> *We feast on human head, brought in on leaves,*
> *Crowned with the first, cold bud. On these we live.*
> *No longer on the ancient cake of seed,*
> The almond and deep fruit. This bitter meat
> Sustains us ... Who, then, are they, seated here?
> Is the table a mirror in which they sit and look?
> Are they men eating reflections of themselves? (139)

The traditional symbols of the Christian Last Supper are subverted here. The unleavened bread (the body of Christ) and the ritual cup of wine (the blood of Christ) are replaced by human heads and bitter meat, eaten by men who have lost touch with a tradition that is much more nourishing with its "ancient cake of seed."

While Naylor does indeed reject many of the meanings of Christian iconography and mythology, she does not imply that African Americans look towards an atheistic vision instead. Indeed, Naylor's novel highlights the complexity and importance of spirituality in the black community in her novel. That spirituality defies any simple and straightforward explanation due to its complex history within the formation of western (Christian) spirituality and its connection to the multiple locations and functions of African identity within western modernity (Jennings 1). For many African Americans, the spiritual is embedded in the temporal. There is a direct link between spirituality and social and ethical concerns with justice and freedom. This concern can be seen in many of the slave narratives of the nineteenth century and in more modern manifestations like Martin Luther King, Jr.'s passionate appeal to white oppressors to live up to the spiritual ideals they claim to embrace.

However, many historians and critics view certain Christian traditions, especially in the antebellum south, as derivgn from the faith of the master class. Religion for slaves, therefore, in some ways, was not a spiritually empowering paradigm but one more device used against them in their own oppression. Critic Paul Garon argues that even the black church, "in attempting to incorporate more 'civilizing' aspects of Christianity [the command to turn the other cheek, for example], has served the purposes of the ruling class by attempting to crush the spirit of revolt, replacing it with the doctrine of accommodation" (52). The religion offered to enslaved blacks then was the property of those who had dispossessed them and is therefore flawed and inadequate in providing what they seek—an identity that relies on its own history, its own voices, and its own struggles. As Malcolm X points out, Christian ideology places the realm of justice outside this world. That is to say, one gets what one deserves only after one is dead. Justice in the transcendent afterlife allegedly amends all of the inequities that can be found here on earth. Indeed, some historians have pointed out that it was precisely this belief—that though life might be horrible now, the pleasures of heave would provide relief—that appealed so strongly to the oppressed slaves of America.

The Christian religion promises a future of eternal reward for one's unbearable suffering on earth, and in doing so, Christianity, as it was administered by whites, helped to quell rebellion and dismiss the possibility of change. (While history tells the story of Nat Turner and Denmark Vesey, who chose to embrace a Christianity that demanded that they free themselves from the white master and seek vengeance for their own suffering, in fact, these leaders were not "reading" Christianity or the bible in the way that white slaveowners "read" them—my statements here are focused on the Europeanized, slaveholder version of Christianity.) Naylor implies in the novel that a religion that asks one to shoulder such an unjust and unwarranted penalty with meek acceptance is itself unjust, and praying to merely endure the severity of racist exclusion precludes blacks from moving towards radical reformation (Bell 15-16).

In fact, many self-named Christian slaveholders encouraged slaves to remain loyal to their masters on earth as a moral equivalent to being loyal to God. The Anglican church's "planter ethic" allowed planters to describe themselves as "God's overseers" to whom slaves owed absolute obedience. Mark Galli, in his article "Defeating the Conspiracy," notes that "the gospel that was presented to slaves by white owners was only a partial gospel [that preached] the message of salvation by grace, the joy of faith, and the hope of heaven [but that neglected] passages that said 'Break every yoke and let the oppressed go free'" (10). Furthermore, as Jon Butler points out in *Awash in a Sea of Faith: The Christianizing of America*, the "paternalism, violence, and sentimentalism" that the planter ethic engendered resulted in "African Spiritual Holocaust that forever destroyed traditional African religion systems as systems" (39). In the wake of this holocaust, slaves, says Butler, were left "remarkably bereft of traditional collective religious practices" (39).

It is the reclamation of these collective cultural practices that Naylor champions in her novel. For Naylor's characters, the Christian church exists as a system of white oppression, whereas the denial of the established church and the rejuvenation of a personal and communal religion become avenues in the route to freedom and the realization of a self rooted in communal awareness. Naylor and her characters create a new text of religiosity that stands at an opposite pole from white Christian practices and visions. Naylor's text expresses the divinity of the people and the Earth, not just of God and heaven. As Luther Nedeed questions in the novel, so does Naylor: "A white god? How could it be any color when it stripped the skin, sex, and soul of any who offered themselves at its altar before it decided to bless?" (17). Lester also echoes Nedeed's sentiments when he listens to Willie recall nostalgically how the members of Mt. Sinai Baptist in Linden Hills would hold Christmas parties every year for the poor children of Putney Wayne:

> I just had a hard time accepting all those things they [members of the congregation] were supposed to be doing in the name of God. The name of which God? The God of the U.S. Treasure if you look at this place. And you can hate me if you want, but I just can't get all choked up over some joker giving a kid a Tonka truck once a year when his garage is almost as large as my house. That's an LTD over there, Willie—did you notice? The only thing I can remember them telling my Jesus ever rode was a donkey. (155)

The dangers in wholesale adoption of established church practices are demonstrated in Naylor's telling of the story of Reverend Hollis, pastor of Mount Sinai Baptist Church in Linden Hills. Reverend Hollis lives on Tupelo Drive, the most exclusive section of Linden Hills. He is an alcoholic who longs for the spiritual experience of his younger days, when he would visit storefront churches in South Philadelphia to "sit in the back of reconverted candy stores with stained-glass cellophane peeling at the windows. Where, more often than not, the altar was a scarred wooden table with an oilskin cloth and plastic crucifix" (159). It was in these humble churches that "he could almost see the spirit racing back to front and back again ... [a] raw power [that] connected up with something in his center, where it transformed fear into fascination and mortality into meaning" (159).

These churches are directly contrasted with Mt. Sinai, where the wealthy inhabitants of Linden Hills worship. Mt. Sinai, according to Reverend Hollis, is a "cold church" whose members sit through his dry sermons "with the stilted patience that accompanies the beginning of a business meeting" and where he is nothing more than an "ambassador in chains" (162). And, in fact, Hollis comes to realize that though "any dictionary defined him as an agent of God," that he would be "hard-pressed to prove the existence that justified Mt. Sinai Baptist Church and the last thirty years of his life" (177). For Hollis, spirituality for African Americans was about "the power that was possible between people; together they created 'God'—so real and electrifying you could believe that once it was the voice that shook mountains" (177).

Naylor demonstrates in Hollis's story the cultural death that occurs when blacks seek redemption in a white, mercenary God. Clearly, Naylor's vision is not an atheistic one, but one that recognizes the hypocrisy of a white use of Christianity that could serve to justify both slavery and a class hierarchy that excludes minority members of its congregation. She rejects a spirituality rooted in a distorted Christian colonialist vision, and, instead, calls for a return to traditions that were subverted by slavery. Naylor's novel represents a reframing of white myths that deny African Americans an enriching cultural legacy that finds its meaning in the experiences of others in the community and their shared histories. Alice Walker calls this reclamation a decolonization of the spirit, a "crucial act of empowerment, one that might return reverence to the Earth" (30). As Walker points out, Christianity fought long and hard to deliver African slaves from a paganism that called for a primary spiritual relationship with Nature and the Earth. In fact, Walker goes on to say, "Millions of people were broken, physically and spiritually, literally destroyed, for nearly two millennia, as the orthodox Christian church 'saved' them from their traditional worship of the Great Mystery they perceived in Nature" (32).

For Naylor and her characters, legitimacy for the African American experience can only be found if spiritual freedom is tied to earthly freedom from symbols of the dominant culture, including a white God. Dante's version of Christianity must be replaced by a new religion, one that is able to see below the heavens to the earth to which African Americans are so closely tied. The writing of Naylor's text itself, which details the ultimate death of Luther Nedeed and the spiritual deprivation of the inhabitants of Linden Hills, signals a chance for the re-appropriation of religion on the terms of the black characters, not a revisiting of the repressive system of Christianity that has been forced upon them. Christianity, as represented through the white man's God, is not seen as a legitimate spiritual basis for these characters. Naylor's characters (and by extension, all blacks in the diaspora) must rewrite this religious text (literarily and spiritually) on the basis of personal revelation in order to further the redefinition at a communal level. For Naylor, the sanctity of the individual and the idea of self-realization through the new text is found in the community and through communal process. Here, and in her other novels, Naylor looks toward an Africentric paradigm, one that does not leave African Americans as "beggars at the table of a religion that sanctioned [their] destruction" (Walker 33).

In secularizing Dante's work, Naylor removes her novel from the paradigm that Dante's work grew out of—namely, European Christianity. She eschews this Christianity that was forced upon enslaved blacks in the early history of their existence on American soil. During that time, members of the white slavocracy viewed the embrace by slaves of their white god as a sign of white control. Religion for slaves, therefore, became not a spiritually empowering paradigm but one more device used by slaveholders to oppress them as well as another indication of the hypocrisy of the slaveowners who justified their own actions with a moral doctrine that they themselves did not practice. The religion offered to enslaved blacks, then, is the property of those who have dispossessed them and is therefore flawed and inadequate in providing what they seek—an identity that relies on its own history, its own voices, its own struggles. The Christian religion promised a future of eternal reward for one's unbearable suffering on earth, yet this history of imposed religion served, much to the white slave owner's relief, to weaken rebellion and dismiss the possibility of change. Through these nonaggressive doctrines of the Christian religion, African Americans were and are encouraged to accept the painful inequality they continue to experience.

Therefore, in appropriating Dante, Naylor does not attempt to insert the black voice into the canon; instead, by demonstrating the difference between the black man's earthly hell and the white man's spiritual one, she illustrates why such white paradigms cannot be used to delineate or provide a space for the pain, endurance, and everyday struggles of black people; for even though Nedeed seems to carve out such a space in the Linden Hills community, his own will to power over its inhabitants, which mirrors the oppression that whites engendered, prevents Linden Hills from being a space that is liberating or empowering for black people. In fact, as Luther Nedeed points out, "When men begin to claw men for the rights to a vacuum that stretches into eternity, then it becomes so painfully clear that the omnipresent, omnipotent, Almighty Divine is simply the *will* to possess" (Naylor 17).

For Naylor, the creation of African American subjectivity does not come from forgetting the past but in embracing it as a way to communal cohesiveness among black people, and it is this lack of community cohesion that leads to the downfall of many of her characters. Naylor reveals how the sense of self must connect with the struggle and history of Black people, thus allowing the self to heal from the knowledge of the cultural past. In fact, it is the very people that had "rooted themselves in the beliefs that Africa could be more than a word, slavery hadn't run its course [and that] there was salve in the blues" (Naylor 11) that Luther Nedeed does not want as residents of Linden Hills for it is these people that stand in the way of making Linden Hills a formidable force against white society—in Nedeed's mind, the only way he can turn Linden Hills into such a force is by encouraging a cultural amnesia that allows the residents of Linden Hills to believe that their painful history is behind them, not all around them.

In the same way that Naylor exposes "the inadequacies of forging an empowered sense of belonging through assimilating into larger society's wealthy capitalist system" (Bell 3) in her adoption and subversion of classical structures, she shows how the paradigm of white Christianity is also an inadequate vehicle for the formation of a black American identity. It is important to note that Naylor avoids making universal claims about the human condition in her novel. Instead, she particularizes the experience of African Americans. She in fact resists making universal claims, which Eurocentric texts are prone to make. Unfortunately, the universality claimed by these texts often exclude the very characters that Naylor seeks to draw for her readers—African Americans who are connected to their cultural heritage and to the communities where that heritage has been born. It is within the black community that Naylor finds redemption for her people, for it is there that blacks are able to firmly situate their own cultural matrix, breaking from the white literary tradition as well as a white religion which only sought to keep them oppressed. As Hortense Spillers wisely points out, "The very presence of a Black female literary tradition conscious of itself, challenges the traditional American canon, pointing out that it is a fable intended to encode and circumscribe an inner and licit circle of empowered texts" (251).

Works Cited

Asante, Molefi Kete. "Afrocentricity." *The Oxford Companion to African American Literature.* William Andrews, Frances Smith Foster, and Trudier Harris, Eds. New York: Oxford UP, 1999.

Bell, Rachel K. "Gloria Naylor: Quest for Place and Authentic Locations." Diss. San Diego State University, 1995.

Butler, Jon. *Awash in a Sea of Faith: Christianizing the American People.* Cambridge, Harvard UP, 1990.

Dyson, Eric Michael. Interview. *Race, Rhetoric, and the Postcolonial.* Gary A. Olson and Lynn Worsham, Eds. Albany: State University of New York Press, 1999.

Galli, Mark. "Defeating the Conspiracy." *Christian History.* 18.2 (1999): 10-11.

Garon, Paul. *Blues and the Poetic Spirit.* San Francisco: City Lights Books, 1996.

Hall, Chekita. "The Blues as a Paradigm of Cultural Resistance in the Works of Gloria Naylor." Diss. Bowling Green State U, 1995.

Naylor, Gloria. *Linden Hills.* New York: Penguin Books, 1986.

Olson, Gary A. and Lynn Worsham, Eds. *Race, Rhetoric, and the Postcolonial.* Albany: State University of New York Press, 1999.

Saunders, James Robert. "The Ornamentation of Ideas: Naylor's First Three Novels." In *Gloria Naylor: Critical Perspectives Past and Present.* Gates, Henry Louis and K.A. Appiah, eds. New York: Amistad Press, Inc., 1993.

Spillers, Hortense. "Black/Female/Critic." *Women's Review of Books* 2 (1985): 9-10.

Ward, Catherine. "Gloria Naylor's *Linden Hills*: A Modern *Inferno.*" *Contemporary Literature* 28 (1987):67-81.

Walker, Alice. "The Only Reason You Want to Get to Heaven is That You Have Been Driven Out of Your Mind." *The Humanist.* 57.5 (1997): 29-34.

II: CARIBBEAN WRITERS

"CAN'T LEAVE HOME WITHOUT IT": THE PARADOX OF MEMORY IN JAMAICA KINCAID'S *LUCY*[1]

Paulette Brown-Hinds

> My feet are (so to speak) in two worlds...
> When I left Antigua I thought I'm free of this! But I
> couldn't be free of it in my head...I would carry it around
> with me.
>
> Jamaica Kincaid

I

Jamaica Kincaid's writings of her Antiguan home read like a meditation on migration caught in the paradox of memory—the vacillation between remembering and forgetting. "Home" in her fiction, is a contested site, created and sustained in the realm of memory. Memory, grounded in the domestic ideals of home, family and the maternal, is inscribed in the personal—something that "belongs to you deeply" (33). In the collection *At The Bottom of the River* (1978), the idyllic and mystical Antigua is imagined from pre-colonial memory; *Annie John*'s (1983) rejection of a colonial education rooted in the recitation of

British history and literature confronts the amnesia of an African and Indian past virtually erased from History;[2] *Lucy* (1990) desires to forget her home in Antigua after her migration to the United States, but is plagued by the very memories she attempts to forget; and *The Autobiography of My Mother* (1996) remembers the forgotten foundations of new world culture through the semi-fictional/semi-autobiographical narrative of Xuela Caudette Richardson.

Kincaid's fictionalized home/space is consistently characterized as a place of exile, as with much of Black women's writing throughout the Diaspora.[3] And her own self-imposed exile[4] from Antigua, fictionally chronicled in *Lucy*, causes a dual alienation and estrangement from her homeland/place with both physical and spiritual dimensions. *Lucy*, Kincaid's only novel set outside the Caribbean, is embedded in a deep sense of homelessness and emerges not simply as a chronicling of the subject's physical movement—from the margin to the metropolitan center—but as a discernibly psychic or spiritual migration which constantly remembers/forgets and revisits "home." Consequently, we discover through her exilic fiction the psychic reality of placelessness—both literal and symbolic. Lucy's migration to the United States, I argue, is an attempt to break with the past, interrupt the ceaseless cycle of history, and create a rupture in the "seamless" narrative of colonialism. I contend that both Kincaid and her persona dramatis, Lucy, are searching for a discursive place within the paradoxical structure of memory and "new site" of America.[5]

Born Elaine Potter Richardson in Antigua in 1949, Kincaid entered the U.S. in the late 1960's at the age of seventeen when the flow of immigrants from the Caribbean to the United States reached its largest numbers.[6] As with much of Kincaid's fiction, Lucy's maneuverings in New York are based loosely on Kincaid's own experiences shortly after her arrival to America. Like many other Caribbean émigrés, Kincaid came to America in search of employment and like Lucy, Kincaid initially was employed as an *au pair* by a white upper middle-class family in New York. Lucy finds her new "home," which she shares with her employers—Lewis, Mariah and their four children—much like her old one: alienating. Paradoxically, Lucy's sense of place, the change in the landscape and geography, has very little effect on her sense of belonging. And her attempt to break with the past is initially expressed through scenic metaphors, one of the most tangible effects of migration. Lucy's first realization of her "new life" and dis/placement is physical, immediate, and intense, "like a flow of water dividing formerly dry and solid ground, creating two banks..."(5). She becomes, as Kincaid has noted in a different context, a botanist's dream, an exotic flower—uprooted, transformed (hybridized), and renamed.[7]

The new American environment also provides a structural framework for the novel. The narrative adopts a circular structure and is driven by seasonal changes—it begins in the winter on a "gray-black and cold" night and ends in the winter—something Lucy reminds us did not occur in Antigua when she says, "I was no longer in a tropical zone, and I felt cold inside and out, the first time such a sensation had come over me" (6). Lucy's feelings of placelessness—her longing to return to "a not very nice situation"—leaves her future uncertain: "If I had had to draw a picture of my future then, it would have been a large gray patch surrounded by black, blacker, blackest" (6). And it is in this space of uncertainty that Lucy's journey begins to take shape.

Consequently, when Lucy is jokingly referred to as the "Visitor" by her new employers, the impersonal moniker adds to her initial feelings of displacement and creates a boundary which serves as a reminder of her position in her new household. The narrator notes, "they said I seemed not to be a part of things, as if I didn't live in their house with them" (13). This appellation, which also functions as the chapter's title, is implicitly temporary in its very naming and seems to compel her home as well. While her new employer Lewis attempts to solidify this boundary by telling a story about his uncle who raised monkeys and became so used to them that he found it difficult to be around people, Lucy refuses to be cast as the "exotic stranger" while remaining outside the parameters of the family and maintaining her border position. When Lewis tells this story, Lucy's memory takes over as she recalls a significant dream. In the dream, a naked Lucy is being chased around the house by Lewis while his wife Mariah cheers, "Catch her, Lewis, catch her." Unlike the transplanted flower confined to the garden soil, Lucy freely runs around the yellow ground and escapes by falling into a snake pit, which is not actually an escape. It is, instead, a different type of entrapment because she is never truly free.

The color yellow, which is consistently tied to conquest and imperialism in Kincaid's fiction, links this domestic space to her colonial past in Antigua. The narrative is replete with yellow imagery: Mariah, Lewis and the girls are described as "six yellow-haired heads," the kitchen is decorated in various shades of pale yellow, and yellow daffodils dance across the pages of the novel. But, while Mariah and Lewis explain that Lucy should regard them as family, she feels at once enslaved and free in her new position and in their home which seems to also echo her dubious "escape" into the pit. She says, "the ceiling was very high and the walls went all the way up to the ceiling, enclosing the room like a box—a box in which cargo traveling a long way should be shipped" (7). The reference here to slavery and the forced migration known as the Middle Passage is unmistakable. Lucy is quite aware that her position as live-in nanny and her subsequent housing in the servant's quarters supersedes Lewis and Mariah's stated desire to make her "feel at home." It is clear that they would rather solidify her position as "Visitor" and outsider. Lucy is, however, able to "escape" the label in her telling of the dream at the dinner table by disrupting the domestic harmony that it—the table—represents.

While critics like Diane Simmons argue that this dream is about Lucy's evasion and Lewis and Mariah's desire to possess her (125), I would argue that it is also about Lucy's possession of them. She confesses, "I had meant by telling them my dream that I had taken them in, because only people who were very important to me had ever shown up in my dreams" (15). Lewis's telling of his story, which he uses against Lucy to exert his patriarchal power as male head of the household, is conquered by Lucy's remembrance of this shocking dream. Lucy inadvertently becomes the victor in this particular power play. She dismisses their psychoanalytic interpretation of her dream— "Dr. Freud for Visitor"—as they attempt to re-gain control of the situation. Her final words privilege her theory of the dream, "I did not know if they understood that" (15). However, she is left fluctuating between enslavement and freedom, possession and dispossession, home and exile, the past and the future.

II

As much of 20th century Afro-Caribbean women's writing, Kincaid addresses women's dual colonization through her fiction, but her interest in the confluence of sexual and colonial exploitation is further influenced by the experience of (im)migration. Lucy's attempt to permanently escape this dual colonization becomes (re)written in the unholy trinity memory/anger/despair: "I understand that I had memory, I had anger, I had despair" (134). For much of her anger and despair grows out of unceasing memories of an oppressive colonial identity which marks her not only as colonial subject in Antigua but also as exotic neo-colonial exile in America. Her colonial past and conditions of immigration to the United States not only point to her "difference" from white Americans, but from blacks as well. Lucy explains, "One day the maid who said she did not like me because of the way I talked told me she was sure I could not dance" (11). The maid's comments regarding Lucy's cultural and language "difference" is a small detail which hints at the vastly different histories experienced by black people throughout the Americas. These differences must be addressed, Abena Busia reminds us, if we are to offer meaningful analyses of the diasporic experience. Cultural differences are further illuminated by their personal music choices—the maid enjoys a R&B music group which seems to be modeled after the popular "Supremes" music trio, while Lucy enjoys the lyrics and rhythms of calypso. Lucy continues, "I could not join her and I told her why: the melodies of her song were so shallow, and the words, to me, were meaningless" (12). The two women are unable to reconcile their divergent histories, and the maid's presence virtually vanishes from the pages of the novel.

In her attempt to re-invent herself, Lucy believes she must forget her past. Upon her migration to the United States, Lucy experiences what Kamau Brathwaite calls "the trauma of forgetting" (or attempting to forget), a condition which befalls those who suffer "a tearing up from the roots" (33). I believe this "trauma" becomes particularly evident in Lucy's reaction to her mother's letters. Lucy's initial desire is to maintain contact with her mother: "I wrote home to say how lovely everything was...Everyone I wrote to said how nice it was to know that I was doing well" (10-11). But, when she writes to her mother describing her first ride on the subway, her mother responds with details about a horrible incident involving an immigrant girl—just like Lucy—who had her throat cut while she was a passenger on perhaps the same train Lucy frequently rides (20). The mother's desire to place Lucy within this narrative of fear is disrupted by Lucy's own memory of a similar incident in Antigua. She describes how a schoolmate became possessed by the Devil, "...and she would hear her as she cried out from the beatings by what possessed her. Eventually the girl had to cross the sea, where the Devil couldn't follow her because the Devil cannot walk over water" (21). The remembrance of the anecdote is suggestive of Lucy's own fear of the demons of colonialism symbolized by the letters. Through this symbolic connection, the Devil becomes a recurring motif and haunting symbol of colonialism. Lucy's belief in the "devil's" inability to cross the sea is similar to her belief that it is possible to forget her mother by refusing to accept any letters from home. In both instances, migration credulously offers freedom from oppression and oppressive memories.

Lucy refuses to be cast into another colonial scene and rejects the mother's "presence." The unopened letters which pile-up from family and friends become more like a burden. Lucy symbolically becomes the American literary figure Hester Prynne and the letters her Scarlet "A" as she "walks around with letters from my family and friends scorching my breasts" (20). Here the letters become symbolic of her colonial past and post-colonial relationship to Antigua instead of simply personal correspondence from family members and friends:

> The object of my life now was to put as much distance between myself and the events mentioned in the letter. Would I not be free to take everything just as it came and not see hundreds of years in every gesture, every word spoken, every face? (31)

Her desire to "forget" her mother is clearly connected to her desire to forget the colonial process: "I had come to feel that my mother's love for me was designed solely to make me into an echo of her..." (36).[8] Lucy's relationship with her mother and mother-country shares a preoccupation with domination. Kincaid explains: "I feel that, in particular, my own history is so much about domination; in fact we were called 'the dominion,' and all the colonies were 'the dominions'"(Perry 501). Lucy's personal history is also inextricably bound to Antigua's colonial history: "I had realized that the origin of my presence on the island—my ancestral history—was the result of a foul deed" (135). Lucy's lineage, like Kincaid's, is forged from the various cultures which came to inhabit her island home: African, Indian, and European. The foul deed, the dual atrocities of slavery and colonialism, devastated both the Africans who were uprooted, transported and enslaved, and the region's native population which was virtually exterminated by European settlers.

As a result of this insight, Lucy's rebellious nature, her desire to function outside the dominant system, asserts itself at an early age when her hatred for the descendants of Britain causes her to disrupt school choir practice. She explains, "I did not wish to sing 'Rule Britannia! Britannia, rule the waves; Britons never, never shall be slaves'" (135). As a descendant of Africans and Indians, she is well aware that in the distant past she would have been enslaved. While this act of non-participation symbolizes a small rebellion—"My action did not create a scandal; instead my choir mistress only wondered if all their efforts to civilize me over the years would come to nothing in the end" (135)—Lucy's disruptive behavior toward the "foul deed" (her colonial heritage), is not read by her mistress as an act of rebellion because in the mistress' eyes, the native is simply a beast which needs to be civilized.

When she learns that her mother named her after the fallen angel, Lucifer, Lucy at once feels "free." And, like Lucifer, who was exiled from heaven for plotting a heavenly war, Lucy begins to plan her separation from the mother and mother-country, a separation which she knows will never be complete. Her desire to escape her prison paradise is also tied to what she calls her "mother's betrayal." This betrayal—her mother's willingness to succumb to a system which offers black women limited spaces from which to function as well as to the mother-country's perpetuation of historical untruths—begins to sever the mother-daughter relationship.

If amnesia is one of the natural antagonists of meaningful historical knowledge (Kammen 688), then Lucy's forced forgetfulness leaves her balancing between an oppressive colonial past and an unknowable "post"-colonial future. What Lucy comes to realize, and actually has always realized, is that while she hates the circumstances of her birth and would like nothing more than to undo the irreversible sweep of history, she is inextricably bound to it:

> My past was my mother...I had spent so much time saying I did not want to be like my mother that I missed the whole story. I was not like my mother—I was my mother. And I could see now why, to the few feeble attempts I made to draw a line between us, her reply always was "You can run away, but you cannot escape the fact that I am your mother..." (90)

She learns she cannot escape her mother any more than she can her own colonial history. Antigua and her mother remain, instead, critical "sites of memory" (Nora 284).

Lucy's memories of colonialism cannot entirely be erased, only temporarily submerged to resurface at the mention of the sign, which is, in this case, daffodils. For instance, when Lucy is taken by Mariah in the Spring to see a garden of daffodils, Mariah comments on their beauty and simplicity revealing that they look as if they were made to "erase a complicated and unnecessary idea" (29). Because Lucy's colonial past remains present in her subconscious, her first and most immediate feeling is to destroy the flowers, cutting them down "[w]here they emerge from the ground" (29). Immediately—and unknowingly —she is cast into a colonial scene with Mariah when she discovers the beautiful flowers are daffodils. She asks Mariah, "'do you realize that at ten years of age I had to learn by heart a long poem about some flowers I would not see until I was nineteen?'" (30). The question is a consciously rhetorical one because it is clear that Mariah does know. Earlier Lucy had tried to convey to Mariah the devastating affects of a British colonial education on the psyche of the colonized by telling her why daffodils for her have come to symbolize terror and dread.[9]

Guilty of what Moira Ferguson calls "colonial complicity" (113), Mariah becomes a catalyst in the re-enactment of William Wordsworth's "I wander lonely like a cloud,"[10] the poem Lucy is forced to memorize and recite as a child about a yellow flower indigenous to Britain. For Wordsworth, the flower inspires bliss and pleasure: "A poet could not but be gay/In such jocund company/I gazed—and gazed—but little thought/What wealth the show to me had brought." Kincaid's daffodils, on the other hand, only inspire anger and despair. The daffodils represent more than Lucy's colonial past. Colonialism is, instead, inscribed within the structure of the narrative. Kincaid re-imagines Wordsworth's poem through her (re)telling of the incident, in a manner reminiscent of her revisions of Milton's *Paradise Lost* and Bronte's *Jane Eyre* in *Annie John*.[11] First, Lucy's feelings of alienation and isolation echo a typical Wordsworthian sentiment: while in a state of loneliness and detachment from her new social world, Lucy comes upon a natural event that shapes her future life. But unlike the poet, Lucy's encounter does not invoke a pleasurable memory. The way in which Kincaid presents the encounter mocks the poetic innocence of Wordsworth's un-expected surprise of "discovering" daffodils in the woods. In *Lucy*, Wordsworth's romantic notions are substituted with planned and calculated deception:

> Mariah took me to a garden, a place she described as among her favorites in the world. She covered my eyes with a handkerchief, and then, holding me by the hand, she walked me to a spot in a clearing. Then she removed the handkerchief and said, "Now look at this." (28)

Blindness functions as a controlling metaphor. Wordsworth's gaze and Lucy's obstructed vision operate within the same discursive space. In Kincaid's text, Wordworth's gaze becomes symbolic of the "colonial gaze" and Lucy is the reflection—the colonial subject who is the "imperfect image" of the British.[12] Her literal lack of vision mimics his symbolic colonial gaze. This directly challenges Wordsworth whose daffodils gain a type of perfection through the remembrance of the event.[13] In Wordsworth's poem, "the wealth" brought to the poet by the "spritely dance" of the daffodils has been interpreted as the ability to re-live that experience not only as a memory, but as an emotion. And while the memory of the event can spontaneously return to him to renew the emotion of the original experience with an added perfection, it only serves to remind Lucy of a colonial history of "imperfection."

Wordsworth's position at the center of the English literary canon is challenged as Kincaid privileges her own position from the "margins" of this literary empire, and in doing this she also changes the dynamic of history. History becomes not simply an ascending narrative with a beginning, middle, and end, but instead is told in the style of the African oral tradition which allows participants to add lines to the story. As Derek Walcott notes, "In an oral tradition the mode is simple, the response open-ended so that each new poet can add his lines to the form...based on the concept that the history of the tribe is endless" (11). Orality, in this sense, functions not as a counter-discourse to the colonial text, but in conjunction with it. Her story, then, is a communal remembering fusing both the African oral tradition and the European narrative of history. This fusion, a process Ngugi wa Thiong'o calls "orature," (Sander and Munro 48-49) acknowledges that literacy and orality have interactively produced one another over time. Through this process, Kincaid not only re-reads Wordsworth on her own terms, but re-writes the poem as well.

This scene is not just about the distant past which scripted Mariah as the colonizer and Lucy as the colonized. It is instead a telling reminder of how this narrative can be continuously re-written. Mariah exerts her control over Lucy in her position as employer, aligning Lucy's au pair status with that of slave or servant. Mariah's complicity with colonialism in this scene also takes on an active role, linking the past with the immediate present. In the end, Mariah is also unable to "see" her own position in this colonial narrative. Mariah's misguided attempts to empathize with her employee's history only serves further to alienate Lucy: "I was looking forward to telling you that I have

Indian blood in me." Lucy, who actually does have a Carib Indian grandmother, criticizes Mariah as one who feels that she can "own" history: "I could swear she says it as if she were announcing her possession of a trophy. How do you get to be the sort of victor who can claim to be the vanquished also?" (40-41). Like Mariah, Wordsworth's position in the narrative is decentralized, but it is clear that Kincaid astutely understands that her connection with Europe cannot be permanently erased or easily forgotten. Once Lucy attempts to forget the poem line by line, she dreams that she is being chased by bunches of yellow daffodils:

> I was being chased down a narrow cobbled street by bunches and bunches of those same daffodils that I had vowed to forget, and when finally I fell down from exhaustion they all piled on top of me, until I was buried deep underneath them and was never seen again. (18)

Lucy's attempt to escape the strictures of colonialism here parallels her former desire to escape her imperial present as the "Visitor." However, while she attempts to find a space from which to function in her new home, she instead finds herself smothered by the vivid memory of a British colonial past as the daffodils come alive against a European backdrop.

III

While Lucy's mother/country's domination initially spurs her migration to the United States and initiates her quest for "freedom," she discovers "freedom" is an elusive venture. When Mariah and Lewis separate, Mariah explains to Lucy that they are getting divorced. Mariah then exclaims that she feels free. Upon hearing this, Lucy thinks, "I meant to tell her not to bank on this 'free' feeling, that it would vanish like a magic trick" (128). Instead, she uses an analogy—a story about a ride she had taken to the country with her boyfriend, Paul. He spoke of great explorers who traveled in search of freedom as well as riches. For Paul, freedom is a universal ideal, "part of the whole human situation." While he revels in the ruins of an imperial past, the former home of a man who made his fortune from the sugar trade, Lucy sees the "dead animals" that had been trying to cross the road "when fast moving cars put a stop to them." Pointing out the animals to Paul she says, "On their way to freedom, some people find riches, some people find death" (129). Lucy understands that "freedom" is dependent upon a host of cultural, social, and economic variables, and that while she initially equated migration with "freedom" from the past, she now feels more "burdened" than free:

> When I finished telling Mariah this, she was silent for a while, and then she said, 'Why don't you forgive your mother for whatever it is you feel she has done? Why don't you just go home and tell her you forgive her?" (129)

But while Lucy cannot forget her mother/country's betrayal, she will also not forgive the "foul deeds" which obstruct her ability to return home.

The mother's betrayal also contributes to Lucy's anger and despair. Lucy explains that upon the birth of each son, Lucy's parents dream of the "important and influential" positions they might hold in society. Lucy's entire upbringing, on the other hand, focuses on her purity—her mother's goal to prevent her from "becoming a slut."[14] Upon hearing this Mariah is once again unable to "read" the situation, suggesting that Lucy read a book on "women in society." Lucy realizes that her/story could not be found in a generic book about women written by privileged white feminists who, like Mariah, are inclined to place all women into the same monolithic category.[15]

In the end, Mariah remains unable to discern the difference between her and Lucy's intertwining histories. As Elizabeth Spelman discusses in another context, white feminists typically ascertain two separate identities for black women, the racial and the gender, and conclude that the gender identity of black women is the same as their own. While they are both "women," their pasts have placed them in two separate and unequal positions—Mariah as the upper-middle class white housewife with a nanny and maid, and Lucy as the black immigrant nanny. While Mariah freely travels from winter home to summer estate, Lucy is practically homeless, only able to "imagine" home in her memories and dreams. In this sense, home is embodied in memory.

Autobiographically, *Lucy* also functions as an "internal migration,"[16] allowing Kincaid to revisit, recreate, and re-imagine her past experiences. Lucy's spiritual journey, her desire to escape the demons of her past while not forgetting important facets of her history, commences when she abandons her au pair position and begins to create her own future. She refuses to become a nurse, and instead turns to photography. When she receives an "urgent" letter from her mother, Lucy decides to purchase a camera. Subconsciously triggered by her forced forgetting of her past, Lucy's new purchase metaphorically becomes a way for her to control what she remembers and attempt to record what is forgotten.

Photographs are icons of collective memory, a way of recording eventful periods we wish to remember and share. Lucy's interest in photography is tied to her philosophy of history. Her photographs, like Kincaid's fiction, attempt to document domestic life.[17] Kincaid has explained elsewhere that she is essentially interested in domestic life and reduces "everything to a domestic situation" (Perry 136-37). Lucy, in turn, becomes fascinated with photographs of ordinary people doing ordinary things. And, her search for "freedom" causes her to attempt to control domestic memory by capturing them before they are forgotten.

Lucy's interest in photography also strikes a connection between textuality and visual imagery.[18] Both attempt to document history by crystallizing memory. "Documentation of necessity," according to bell hooks, "becomes an obsession for generations when the psychohistory of a people is marked by ongoing loss, when entire histories are denied, hidden, erased" (85). Lucy's position as "dramatic spectacle" in both colonial and psychoanalytic discourses is subverted by her decision to control the gaze.[19] Her interest in photography initially enables her to attempt to challenge the hegemony of the ghosts of colonialism that followed her across the sea. However, she finds this type of technology limiting as a mode of remembrance. Her obsession with taking pictures of people in transition—walking on the street—causes what she refers to as "printmaking difficulties." Once again, in her ability to feel "placed," Lucy and Kincaid's narratives converge as Lucy attempts to write herself in place.

The end of the narrative invokes the beginning as the cycle continues. It is once again winter, but this time Lucy is in her own home attempting to create her own life. Lucy Josephine Potter's exile, (we finally learn her complete name) becomes a "loophole of retreat"[20] in a decisive moment of ambivalence. In the final scene Lucy is alone in her apartment attempting to map out her future on the blank pages of her new journal. The yellow imagery of the previous chapters is absent, replaced with the symbol of American nationalism: the "blood red" cover of her journal, its "milky" white pages, and "beautiful" blue ink. Blindness returns as a controlling metaphor. Her lack of vision, obstructed by tears, figuratively returns her to the beginning of her journey evoking memories of the "gray patch" surrounded by varying degrees of blackness (6). Her future, once again, is completely bound up with her past. The past, we discover, is ever present—haunting, guiding, and something we carry around with us always.

Notes

[1]   Page numbers will be given parenthetically in the text. A version of this chapter was presented at the Pacific Ancient and Modern Language Association conference, Post-Colonial Women's Fiction panel at UC Irvine on November 15, 1996.

[2]   Here, I am defining history as colonial versions of history which begin with Christopher Columbus's discovery. For an interesting analysis of how these histories are constructed, see Franz Fanon. He states, "The colonizer makes history and knows that *he* [sic] is doing so. And because *he* constantly refers to the history of *his* metropolis, *he* clearly indicates that here *he* is the extension of that metropolis. The history that *he* writes is thus not the history of the country that *he* is plundering, but of *his* nation as it ravages, rapes, and starves others," p.36.

[3]   Carole Boyce-Davies addresses the many significations of home, homelessness, exile, and displacement in Black women's writings throughout the diaspora. I would argue that examples are numerous in writings by contemporary African-American women from Alice Walker's *The Color Purple* to Gloria Naylor's *Linden Hills* to the novels of Toni Morrison. Also see Farah Griffin.

[4]   This self-imposed exile became an informal ban from the island in 1985 after Kincaid made a return visit home which prompted the publication of *A Small Place*, her essay criticizing post-independent Antigua. See *A Small*

and Moira Ferguson, *Jamaica Kincaid: Where the Land Meets The Body,* pp. xii-xiii.

[5] Critics have discussed the significance of Kincaid's first fictional journey to the "new site"—the United States. Ferguson argues that Lucy stands in "the third scenario" (Stuart Hall), a non-binarist space of reflection. And Simmons argues that Lucy does not try to choose between two identities. I am interested, instead, in how Lucy psychologically negotiates the migration experience and how Kincaid negotiates the American literary landscape, pp. 120-34.

[6] Philip Kasinitz argues that in the decade between 1965-1975 the number of West Indians legally entering the United States surpassed migrants from the region during the previous seventy years combined, pp. 26-27.

[7] In her essay "Flowers of Evil," Kincaid explores the connection between conquest and botany: "The botanical garden reinforced for me how powerful were the people who had conquered me, they could bring to me the botany of the world they owned," p.158.

[8] While many critics have discussed the mother as both colonial and biological in Kincaid's fiction, Moira Ferguson offers the first extended critical study of the "doubled mother" concept.

[9] Throughout Caribbean literature, the daffodil has been a popular metaphor of colonial oppression. But Edwidge Danticat offers an interesting juxtaposition. In *Breath, Eyes, Memory,* the daffodil is symbolic of the resilience and strength of the colonized and enslaved people of Haiti, "They were really European flowers, French buds and stems, meant for colder climates. A long time ago, a French woman had brought them to Croix-des-Rosets and planted them there. A strain of daffodils had grown that could withstand the heat, but they were the color of pumpkins and golden summer squash, as though they had acquired a bronze tinge from the skin of the natives who had adopted them," p. 21.

[10] The poem is also commonly referred to as "The Daffodils."

[11] For post-colonial readings of Kincaid's fiction as revisions of colonial texts, see: Giovanni Covi, Craig Tapping, and Helen Tiffin.

[12] The daffodil is also the common name for any plant of the genus, Narcissus. Wordsworth's gaze here may be likened to that of the mythological character Narcissus who fell in love with his own image and was transformed into a flower.

[13] I must thank my colleague Martin Japtok for his insight on Wordsworth as well as the students in my Analysis of Poetry class at CSU San Bernardino (Fall 1997).

[14] For similar themes, also see Kincaid's "Girl" in *At The Bottom of the River.*

[15] Chandra Talpade Mohanty provides an excellent outline of the debate in western feminist discourse which constitutes "women" as a coherent group with identical interests and desires, regardless of class, ethnic or racial location." Also see Elizabeth Spelman.

[16] I discuss this concept more fully in an essay on the work of Paule Marshall. See my essay "In The Spirit: Dance As Healing Ritual in Paule Marshall's *Praisesong for the Widow.*"

[17] Kincaid's early interest in photography spurred her writing career. See her interview with Selwyn Cudjoe.

[18] This relationship is even more discernible in Kincaid's novel *Autobiography of My Mother*. In the novel, narrative time is marked by the development a photograph of the protagonist, Xuela Richardson.

[19] Gwen Bergner discusses the confluence of "woman as lack" in psychoanalytic discourse and the colonized as "not quite/not white" in colonial discourse as centered in the realm of the visual. Also see Homi Bhabha and Laura Mulvey.

[20] Harriet Jacobs (Linda Brent) refers to the space which she must conceal herself in as a "loophole of retreat," signifying a place of confinement as well as escape in *Incidents in the Life of a Slave Girl* , p. 117.

Works Cited

Bergner, Gwen. "Who is that Masked Woman? or The Role of Gender in Fanon's *Black Skin, White Masks* ." *PMLA* (January 1995): 75-88.

Bhabha, Homi. "The Other Question. Difference, Discrimination and the Discourse of Colonialism." *Literature, Politics and Theory.* Ed. Francis Barker, Peter Hulme, Margaret Iversen and Diana Loxley. London/New York: Methuen, 1986. 147-172.

Brathwaite, Kamau. "History, the Caribbean Writer and X/Self." *Crisis and Creativity in the New Literatures in English*. Ed. Geoffrey Davis and Hena Maes-Jelinek. Amsterdam: Rodopi Press, 1990. 23-45.

Brown-Hinds, Paulette. "In the Spirit: Dance as Healing Ritual in Paule Marshall's *Praisesong for the Widow*." *Religion and Literature.* Special Issue on Black Spirituality (Spring 1995): 107-117.

Busia, Abena. "Words Whispered over Voids: A Context for Black Women's Rebellious Voices of the African Diaspora." *Studies in Black American Literature III*. Eds. Houston Baker and Joe Weixlmann. Greenwood, FL: Penkevill Publishing Company, 1988. 1-41.

Covi, Giovanni. "Jamaica Kincaid and the Resistance to Canons." *Out of the Kumbla: Caribbean Women and Literature*. Eds. Carole Boyce Davies and Elaine Savory Fido. New Jersey: Africa World Press, 1990. 345-54.

Cudjoe, Selwyn. "Jamaica Kincaid and the Modernist Project: An Interview." *Caribbean Women Writers First International Conference.* Ed. Selwyn Cudjoe. Wellesley, MA: Calaloux Publications, 1990. 215-232.

Danticat, Edwidge. *Breath, Eyes, Memory.* New York: Soho Press, 1994.

Davies, Carole Boyce. *Black Women, Writing and Identity: Migrations of the Subject.* New York: Routledge, 1994.

Fanon, Franz. *The Wretched of the Earth.* New York: Grove Press, 1968.

Ferguson, Moira. *Jamaica Kincaid: Where the Land Meets the Body.* Charlottesville, VA: University Press of Virginia, 1994.

Griffin, Farah. *"Who Set You Flowin'"?: The African American Migration Narrative.* New York: Oxford University Press, 1995.

hooks, bell. "Black (and White) Snapshots." *Ms. Magazine* (September/October 1994): 82-87.

Jacobs, Harriet. *Incidents in the Life of a Slave Girl*. New York: Harcourt Brace Jovanovich, 1973.

Kammen, Michael. *Mystic Chords of Memory*. New York: Alfred A. Knopf, Inc., 1991.

Kasinitz, Philip. *Caribbean New York: Black Immigrants and the Politics of Race*. Ithaca, NY: Cornell University Press, 1992.

Kincaid, Jamaica. *A Small Place*. New York: Farrar, Strauss, Giroux, 1998.

——. *At The Bottom of the River*. New York: Farrar, Strauss, Giroux, 1978.

——. *Autobiography of My Mother*. New York: Farrar, Strauss, Giroux, 1996.

——. "In the Garden." *The New Yorker* (October 5, 1992): 154-59.

——. *Lucy*. New York: Farrar, Strauss, Giroux, 1990.

Mohanty, Chandra. "Under Western Eyes: Feminist Scholarship and Colonial Discourses." *Feminist Review* 30 (Fall 1988): 65-88.

Mulvey, Laura. *Visual and Other Pleasures*. Bloomington: Indiana University Press, 1989.

Naylor, Gloria. *Linden Hills*. New York: Ticknor & Fields, 1985.

Nora, Pierre. "Between Memory and History: Les Lieux de Memoire." *History and Memory in African-American Culture*. Eds. Genevieve Fabre and Robert O'Meally. New York: Oxford University Press, 1994, 284-300.

Perry, Donna. "Interview with Jamaica Kincaid." *Reading Black, Reading Feminist*. Ed. Henry L. Gates. New York: New American Library, 1990, 492-509.

Sander, Reinhard and Ian Munro. "Tolstoy in Africa: An Interview with Ngugi wa Thiongo." *Critical Perspectives on Ngugi wa Thiong'o*. Ed. GD Killam. Washington DC: Three Continents, 1984, 46-57.

Simmons, Diane. *Jamaica Kincaid*. New York: Twayne Publishers, 1994.

Spelman, Elizabeth. *Inessential Woman: Problems of Exclusion in Feminist Thought*. Boston: Beacon Press, 1988.

Tapping, Craig. "Children and History in the Caribbean Novel: George Lamming's *In the Castle of My Skin* and Jamaica Kincaid's *Annie John*." *Kunapipi* 9 (1989): 51-59.

Tiffin, Helen. "Decolonization and Audience: Erna Brodber's *Myal* and Jamaica Kincaid's *A Small Place*." *Span* 30 (1990): 27-38.

Walcott, Derek. "The Muse of History." *Is Massa Day Dead?* Ed. Orde Coombs. New York: Doubleday, 1974, 1-27.

Walker, Alice. *The Color Purple*. New York: Harcourt Brace Jovanovich, 1982.

REMAKING THE WOR(L)D: A POETICS OF RESISTANCE AND TRANSFORMATION IN MARLENE NOURBESE PHILIP'S *SHE TRIES HER TONGUE: HER SILENCE SOFTLY BREAKS*

Shara McCallum

Epilogue
I have crossed an ocean
I have lost my tongue
from the root of the old one
a new one has sprung

Grace Nichols
I is a Long Memoried Woman

Identifying the precise function of language as resistance is a task frequently undertaken and perhaps as frequently abandoned in frustration by readers and writers of Caribbean Literature. The fact of our language, that how we speak impacts who we are, has been bound up in the very notion of Caribbeanness from the emergence of such an identity, whether so named or not. The appearance of Creole languages, creolised[1] forms of culture and in turn identities is commonly viewed as historical evidence of African resistance to enslavement and attempts at erasure of culture by the Spanish, Dutch, English, and French who colonised the countries of the world now collectively known as the Caribbean. But can we extend this idea of historical resistance to present day writers who choose to employ Creole in their novels, stories, plays, and poems?

Creole has often received derogatory treatment. It is neither taught in schools nor used as a national language. Derisive terms are still frequently employed when describing the language, such as "broken" or "bad English" in the Anglophone Caribbean, all of which leads to the often stated view that opting to write in Creole is a choice informed by politics as well as aesthetics and is a form of resistance to cultural hegemony. West Indian writers such as Louise Bennett and Edward Kamau Brathwaite have been strong proponents of using Creole in written literature and not relegating it to second class status. It is thus traditional belief that their creative work, and that of others like them, serves to confront and disprove the (still) dominant idea of "good English."

In this essay I will explore to what extent Creole can serve as a "political" as well as an aesthetic signifier and to what extent it functions as resistance to the hegemony of Standard English. More so, I will investigate to what extent Creole has the ability to go beyond resistance and become transformative, that is, to what extent it is capable of redefining the world/self and our understanding of the same. Does a poetics of transformation, as well as a poetics of resistance, exist in Caribbean Literature and can it operate to radicalise the reader as well as the writer?

Another related and salient issue I will consider is the rendering of Creole on the written page and the truthfulness of that rendering. In their ground-breaking essay on the nature of Creoleness, "In Praise of Creoleness," Jean Bernabé, Patrick Chamoiseau, and Raphaël Confiant highlight the connectedness of culture and identity to language. They argue that in the initial production of literature from the Caribbean, there existed "a break, a gap, a deep ravine between a written expression pretending to be universalo-modern and traditional Creole orality enclosing a great part of our being. This nonintegration of oral tradition was one of the forms and one of the dimensions of our alienation" (897). Writing in Creole could (perhaps too) easily be seen as a way to bridge the divide, that chasm of self as understood through the "I" that speaks and the "I" we find speaking for us in the written literature coming out of the Caribbean. Yet such a solution, to write in the oral tradition, poses its own set of difficulties. As Edouard Glissant asserts in his essay "Free and Forced Poetics," "in the transition from spoken to written" word, much is lost and Creole is "vulgarised" (121). How then can Creole as written word function as a radicalising force and offer transformation for a disenfranchised people and tongue?

This question and the above stated idea of a transformative poetics provide the focal viewpoint from which I will discuss Afro-Trinidadian-Canadian writer Marlene Nourbese Philip's book of poems, *she tries her tongue: her silence softly breaks*, published in 1989, having won the Casa de las Americas Prize the preceding year. The opening section of Nourbese Philip's text centers on her retelling of the Proserpine-Ceres myth (known as Persephone-Demeter in Greek versions of the story) in which she updates the myth and situates it in the Caribbean. The practice of reenvisioning myths is common to contemporary poetry and is a tool ripe with possibility upon which other Caribbean writers such as Derek Walcott in his epic poem *Omeros* have capitalised. Nourbese Philip similarly uses this retold myth as a metaphor for the Caribbean and its history of slavery, colonisation, and resistance. Comprising the first section, the poems centred on this myth set the stage for the book's overriding concern with the inability of Standard English, as well as Creole as it has frequently been presented in written form, to convey Caribbean history and identity.

Nourbese Philip's original and experimental use of language in this section resonates throughout the book and responds to the "challenge" she sets forth in the book's prose introduction for the "African Caribbean writer who is at all sensitive to language and to the issues that language generates" (19). To answer this challenge, she employs linguistic and poetic strategies that disrupt and decentre Standard Written English in two ways. First, she employs what I call *content-based disruption*. Through semantics, through playing with multiple meanings of words and using double entendres, she challenges traditional interpretations rendered by Standard English and points out their logical inconsistencies. Second, she also uses what I term *formal disruption*, which includes her manipulation of grammar and syntax to convey new meanings not intended or reified in the lexicon of English imposed upon the African in the New World.

At times these disruptions and re-renderings of English erupt in Creole on the page. More frequently, she engages both Creole and Standard English, as well as the range between these ends of the linguistic spectrum found in the Caribbean. She enacts what she asserts in her introduction: "It is in *the continuum of expression* from standard to Caribbean English that the veracity of the experience lies" (18). Moreover, through her remoulding of language in these poems to create new meanings, Nourbese Philip unveils the power of language to define our understanding of reality and of the world. Importantly, she does so while refiguring "language in such a way that the historical realities are not erased or obliterated, so that English is revealed as the tainted tongue it truly is" (19). Delving into myth, religion, science, and the law, she turns the shaping power of the word back on itself. Thus she exposes the falseness of Eurocentric "truths" about the African woman in the Caribbean and uncovers real truths or, as she terms it, "the veracity of the experience."

The original myth of Proserpine and Ceres centres upon Ceres, the goddess of the earth, and her relationship to her daughter Proserpine. At the heart of this story is Proserpine's abduction by the god of the underworld; she is subsequently held there as his prisoner and forced to become his concubine/wife. Ceres, in grieving for her daughter, allows the earth to go to rot. Not until the other gods and goddesses prevail upon Jupiter is a compromise reached to prevent the utter devastation of the earth: Proserpine is allowed to return to her mother for half of each year and must remain in the underworld during the other half.

For the ancient Greeks and Romans, among several other purposes this myth served as an explanation of the seasons—

spring and summer signified by Ceres' happiness while with her daughter, fall and winter, her mourning. What many contemporary women poets have seen in this myth, however, is the parable of mother and daughter relations. The archetypal quality of the myth presents one explanation for why so many women poets' imaginations have been taken in by this story, why several contemporary women poets have even returned to it repeatedly in their poems. African American poet Rita Dove's 1995 book *Mother Love* is a book-length cycle of poems which all focus upon this story. Irish poet Eavan Boland has also retold this myth in a number of poems, spanning several books.

Nourbese Philip, beyond seeing the possibility for exploring the depths of mother and daughter relationships, is also attracted to the metaphor in this story in terms of the Caribbean: Proserpine is torn from Ceres in the same rape-like manner with which the African was torn from her homeland, her "mother" land, her "mother" tongue.[2] Moreover, beyond the metaphor of displacement and linguistic rape, the actuality of rape both for Proserpine and for the African woman enslaved in the New World resonates in Nourbese Philip's choice to retell this myth. Further, as Proserpine is forced to redefine her existence in this "underworld"—far from her mother and all that she has known—so too the African brought to the Caribbean and stripped of as much of her language and culture as the European coloniser could effect must find ways to survive and thrive in the face of extreme hostility and aggression. A great part of this survival, Nourbese Philip implies, relies upon Ceres and Proserpine's recognition and fostering of their interconnection and interdependence.

Their connection is restored to some extent in the original version of the tale when Ceres' grief over losing her daughter means that Proserpine must be returned to her mother for six months of each year to save the earth from withering and remaining in perpetual winter. Since a return to "Mother Africa" for the Caribbean person of African descent is not feasible at this point in history, Nourbese Philip captures the power of the myth by focusing instead upon Ceres and Proserpine's intense mourning and their search to find the "other." An important twist to this search is the fact that in Nourbese Philip's version the adopted daughter (i.e., the African who has now "adopted" the Caribbean as home) seeks her birth mother and vice versa. By shifting the focus of the myth from its resolution to its liminal potential and changing key elements of it, Nourbese Philip correctly portrays the state of Caribbean identity today as one that is sought and desired, one that continues to be negotiated, one that is creolised, in flux.

A key aspect of these poems for revealing the creolised or dialectic form of Caribbean identity is their overt conflation of the mother and the daughter. The idea of the "other" being the self—that mother and daughter are effectively two halves of the same self—is paramount in Nourbese Philip's rendering of the myth. In "Adoption Bureau," for example, Proserpine apparently goes seeking information about her mother. But as the poem unfolds, we realise she is equally trying to find herself. Looking for the "i-mage" of herself in the "racial memory" of her mother's language and body, she states, "Watch my talk-words stride,/like her smile the listening/breadth of my walk" and asks, "tell me, do/I smell like her? (29).[3] While she is without what would be considered actual memory of her mother due to a rift of time and space between them, "something" in her recognises her m/other, her almost forgotten but somehow and somewhat retained self: "I recognize the salt/sea the yet else and ...something/again knows sweet earth/the smell-like of *I and she*" (29, emphasis mine). The opening line of this poem prepares us for its lasting meaning: Proserpine has survived separation from her mother by retaining the thread between them, the "I and she" she "seeks" to know even more fully.

On her end, the mother, Ceres, echoes a similar state of connection to and disconnection from her daughter. In the poem, "Sightings," she describes the birth of her child in an inverted and telling fashion: "as I cracked from her shell—the surf of surge/the song of birth" (35, emphasis mine). We learn in "Search" that Ceres, like Proserpine, also feels "lost between She/ and I" (31). Another poem, "Clues," further reveals and confirms that Ceres conceives of her search for Proserpine as a twinned endeavour: "looking for me looking for she" (30). In order for Proserpine to find Ceres, Nourbese Philip suggests moreover that Ceres must also carry out the search: "she going find you, if you keep looking" (30).

Like Proserpine's, Ceres's redemption of their shared identity and the loss of that identity is rooted not only in the body they metaphorically share but also in their once shared language, now another source of their separation: "call and response in tongue and/ word that buck up in strange" (31). Nourbese Philip's extending the loss to include the mother "calling" and waiting for the daughter's "response" is significant for it asks us to reconsider all of the losses that come out of the Caribbean's history of enslavement, the middle passage, and colonisation.

Frequently in literature of the African Diaspora in the Americas, and in scholarship concerning that literature produced in the Americas, the loss or diminishment of cultural identity is considered one-directionally—that of Africans stolen from their homeland, their experienced grief, and the reconstruction of self they are forced to embark upon in a foreign land. In these poems, Nourbese Philip reminds us that we must broaden this loss to include the mother country, bereft of some of her children and also victim to similar exploitation and oppression, past and present. What she suggests is that the mother (country) is as dependent on the child, wherever that child may now be located in the world, for identity as is the child on the "mother." Hers is an interesting and a provocative response to Negritude and Afrocentric movements that look to Africa as the source or origin of "New World" African identity.

In contemporary literature, music, and art, there is much to support Nourbese Philip's suggestion here of dual and simultaneous influence or cross-pollination of culture. Reggae, coming out of Jamaica but influencing black (and white) music the world over, is one of the most pointed examples of this phenomenon. In the poem "Clues," Nourbese Philip specifically explores the idea of the African Diaspora as a source of fluid culture, wherein different geographic areas represent sites of culture that all influence and make up black identity. "Is pinch somebody pinch" the mother in search of her daughter in these series of poems and makes her see that "Stateside, England, Canada...the Black Bottom—Bathurst above Bloor, Oakwood and Englinton—even the suburbs them" all are possible places where the daughter might be found (30). Most of all, the mother is reminded that "she own and yours not up in together," that their destinies are intertwined (30).

Nourbese Philip retells this story then for its immediacy and relevance to the Caribbean in terms of symbolic content. Perhaps more importantly, however, she does so because of its ironic potential for deconstructing the English language and meaning connected to that language. The story of Proserpine and Ceres is rooted in European mythology, appropriated as such from the Greeks. Signifying not only upon the myth but upon the actual language in which it is rendered, she transforms something overtly European into that which is distinctly Caribbean. In a real sense, she uses both the language as well as the narrative of this European myth to upbraid itself.

Employing a syntax that deviates from Standard English and more closely approaches Creole is one of the ways she achieves such disruption. "Questions! Questions!," the first poem in the series, places us firmly in the Caribbean by beginning with the lines, "Where she, where she, where she/be, where she gone?" (28). Through anaphara and elimination of the verb, Nourbese Philip renders the rhythm of Caribbean speech on the page. Other lines in the same poem, such as "she friending fish" and "in the bay-blue morning she does wake," use particulars of Creole, specifically Trinidadian English with the repetition of "she" and use of "does," to recreate both the sound and meaning of the Caribbean language. In this instance those particulars include: inventiveness and improvisation as illustrated in the verbing of the noun "friend" and the use of "does" to imply an ongoing present not similarly captured by either the strict present, strict past, or participle forms of either of these tenses in Standard English. The demotic, as used by Nourbese Philip here, not only transforms the myth but also adds a layer of meaning that Standard English and the original version of the myth ironically can neither capture nor hold.

Most of the poems in this section rely upon Creole and jarring juxtapositions of words to create a breakdown of Standard English. "Dream Skins" and "Adoption Bureau Revisited," however, are two poems in this section which go beyond the aforementioned strategies and also begin to use the spacing of the words on the page to contribute to Nourbese Philip's goal of deconstructing the "master's tongue." The "field of the page," a term coined by US poet Charles Olson, is a poetic element that "experimental" poets, sometimes referred to as "language" poets, also make use of. In both cases, although I would argue with heightened impetus for black poets who engage in experimental writing, the goal is to ask the reader to question our traditional expectations of signification, of how the "sign" of language renders its meaning. In using the "white space" of the page, and I invoke this term with its obvious contextual irony, Nourbese Philip demands of the reader a more radical, improvisational, and performative reading of poetry, a reading which she insists upon more and more as the book progresses.

"Meditations on the Declension of Beauty by the Girl with the Flying Cheek-bones" is a poem that requires such a performative, radicalised reading from the reader. It is also one of the most powerful and successful poems in the book in terms of its ability to resist and transform negative images of the African through playing with how language is delivered, on the level of semantics as well as grammar and vocabulary. In this poem, Nourbese Philip challenges and disputes the "tainted" language that causes the speaker to question her own sense of worth each time she speaks or "breaks" her "silence." First, by exposing it as racist, Nourbese Philip tackles the aesthetic that has devalued African beauty. She then recasts that which has been deemed by the European colonisers as not-beautiful as beautiful: "Woman with the behind that drives men mad"; "woman with a nose broad/ as her strength"; "the man with the full-moon lips/ Carrying the midnight of colour/ split by the stars—a smile." While using words in Standard English, she reclaims them by conveying the power or "strength" of a "behind that drives men mad," the beauty in the image of full lips compared to the full moon.

On its own this poem would not be able to refute ingrained negative connotations of such images and words, however, had Nourbese Philip not already revealed the inherent ability of language to define reality and had she not previously reminded the reader of the Caribbean's historical relationship to language as one of oppression or suppression of an original tongue.

Throughout the poem, she repeats a series of phrases twisted and turned and strewn across the page to betray the violence of language in a Caribbean context. This gesture also requires the reader to follow and consider the physical movement of the words on the page in order to discern meaning, hence my previous suggestion that Nourbese Philip elicits from her readers a more active or "performative" engagement with the poem.

Through the repetition of the phrases, as well as her control of line breaks and spacing, she creates a visual and auditory image of the imposition of the coloniser's tongue. In doing so she raises, through form as well as content, the poignant question of how black men and women living within the confines of a language which is repressive can retain a cohesive sense of worth and self. Addressing the coloniser directly, again and again she asks:

> If not If not If
> Not
> If not in yours
> In whose
> In whose language
> Am I
> ...
> Beautiful

Using the "oppressor's tongue," Nourbese Philip forges new ways of looking at aesthetics and simultaneously "adorn[s] the word with [new] meaning" and "mourn[s] the meaning in loss"(49).

Audre Lorde, in her famous essay, "The Master's Tools Will Not Dismantle the Master's House," argues rather effectively that employing the language of the coloniser/oppressor only serves to reify the power of that language. Yet looking at Nourbese Philip's poems which insist upon conscious and reflective use of language, I think it is possible to see how, given the reality of the pervasiveness of English, one can in fact use the "corrupted" language to free oneself of its imposed meaning. In "Meditations," Nourbese Philip utilises syntactical shifts and manipulates semantics in order to render new ways of conceiving beauty. These two strategies, as I have noted elsewhere, are the prime ones employed throughout the book in "breaking" English in turn to "heal the word wounded" (21). And while these strategies are distinguishable they are also connected. Her attention to and understanding of that connection between how we speak—down to the ordering of our words— and what we mean to say, and what the spoken word conveys about us in turn, are what generate the powerful and original presentation of the Caribbean language in this book.

Similar to her representation of this demotic alongside Standard English, it is also Nourbese Philip's refusal to enter into either/or dichotomies that makes the poems in this book powerful, truthful representations of what it means not only to speak Creole but also to be Creole. In the poem "Dream-skins," the section "Afterbirth" may be read as a kind of linguistic and expressive Rosetta Stone for her poems and her approach to the question/problem of creolisation:

Afterbirth

> one breast
> white
> the other black
> headless
> in a womb-black night
> a choosing—
> one breast
> neither black
> nor white

Again, as discussed in previous poems, we see in "Afterbirth" her play with syntax and spacing of words on the page. The breath of the line is discernible through not only the line breaks, which add stress to certain words like "black" and "night," but also through the refusal of the words to stay pinned to a left margin. In addition, this poem, as with others we have seen, redefines denotative and connotative meanings of words. According to Nourbese Philip's rendering and contrary to common associations of these words, "night" and "black" are not to be feared. Both words are instead linked to "womb," a place of safety, of assurance. In this poem, moreover, we see Nourbese

Philip's refusal to couch identity in simplistic terms. Asserting ones *Caribbeanness* does not imply choosing Creole over Standard English or vice versa, nor does it insist on opting for "blackness" over "whiteness." Having linguistic and cultural access and ties to Africa, Europe, as well as Asia and Native America, is—Nourbese Philip tells us—what being Caribbean means.

In the section of poems entitled "Cyclamen Girl," she brings her penetrating gaze, her multiplicitous vision of the world and word to bear upon religion, particularly Christianity. In each of the poems in this series Nourbese Philip explodes the myth of religion and exposes Christianity as an institution that served and continues to serve European and patriarchal dominance. Moreover, Nourbese Philip demonstrates that this dominance occurs as a direct result of "The Word" having been imposed and still being imposed upon Africans and women.

In the Gospel of John 1:1, John says, "In the beginning was the Word, and the Word was with God, and the Word was God." This passage is perhaps most responsible for the traditional Christian interpretation of the sacredness of the divine "Word" and the belief that the "Word of God" is synonymous with God and with all existence. Further in the same passage is the assertion—"And the Word was made flesh, and dwelt among us, (and we beheld his glory, the glory as the only begotten of the Father,) full of grace and truth" (1:14). It is a statement akin to one of the central tenets of my argument regarding Nourbese Philip's exploration of the power of the spoken word, which is that when the word is spoken it becomes material and that the materiality of language is connected to the body, to the "flesh."

The question of what happens to the *body* of the African and the woman, though, when this language becomes distorted— when the word is manipulated to reify European and male domination—is at the heart of Nourbese Philip's critique of religion. The fact that Christian slaveholders sanctioned violence and acts of hatred against Africans and women is well known. The Salem Witch Trials, with the persecution of a Caribbean-born female slave, Tituba, alongside her white counterparts also accused of witchcraft and heresy, is one example of this kind of madness committed in the name of religion. Throughout the history of Christianity and slavery in the "New World," heinous acts have occurred in the name of "The Word," in the name of God. The perverted marriage between slavery and Christianity is one idea that Nourbese Philip focuses our attention upon in the "Cyclamen Girl" series of poems. Additionally, she prompts us to consider that continued repression of marginalised groups, notably women and gays, still occurs under the guise of "The Word of God."

Throughout "The Catechist," the first poem in the series, images of sexuality pervade: "Early-blooming brown legs..a stiff-petaled cyclamen/hot-housed...early bloomers in the heat of it all/with the lurking smell of early pregnancy" (38). Like the photograph that the poem refers to, the words convey a complex rendering of "negative" and "positive" space that the speaker is uncertain how to decipher. The girl's sexuality is set in relief to the overriding conservatism of the religion with its "confirmation dress crinolines stiff," suggesting eroticism, but more so constraint (38). Read in conjunction with its twin poem, "The Catechism," the contradiction is clear and clearly repressive: "the code of Victoria—no sex before marriage/no love after" (40). This code is particularly resonant for black women given the fact that the drive to assert one's purity and deny one's sexuality grows out of the need to refute ingrained, corrupted images of the black woman as lascivious and wanton in the European imagination.

The mixed images and impression of the black female subject as both in control of her body and erotic self and restrained by a male (European) order is what develops in the photograph "circa 1960" and in the present-day speaker's understanding of the image before her in "The Catechist." Throughout the poem, Nourbese Philip uses the denotations of English words to expose the paradox of the cyclamen girl's position. By invoking the word catechist, Nourbese Philip capitalises on the irony of the fact that the girl's faith is achieved through memorisation, in effect through forced speaking and learning. Cathecism is defined as the rules of Christianity and the instruction of those rules, through the asking of questions to elicit already established answers. As a frame for this young girl's inauguration into Catholicism, the word implies that the girl in the photograph is expected not only to learn the basic principles of the religion but more so to accept these tenets uncritically. Unlike the Cyclamen Girl—who appears conflicted about being a catechist (one who receives instruction) and who is "caught between/blurred images of/massa and master"—Nourbese Philip deciphers the predicament in her narration of the photograph and again critiques Christianity's connection to traces of colonial hegemonic power (38).

If there is any doubt as to Nourbese Philip's condemnation of Christianity as overwhelmingly repressive for the Caribbean woman of African descent, "Eucharist Contradictions" dispels it. Ensconced in the ritual of taking the Eucharist, the poem's central image reveals the destructive power of Christianity—its fracturing of identity for the black Caribbean woman. Returning to the metaphor of photography, of image-making, and the "cyclamen girl," Nourbese Philip connects the act of taking the host on the tongue to the severance of speech which accompanied the enslavement of Africans and therefore links the act to the denial of a unified identity for the Caribbean person: "with a speech sliced and spiced/into a variety of life and lies" she asserts that we are no longer able to "get-the-focus-right reality/of mulatto dougla niggerancoolie/that escaped the so-called truth of the shutter" (39).

So the "cyclamen girl," as much a representative of the Caribbean (woman) as Proserpine and Ceres, is left "in the glare of unanswered questions," standing in her "yellowed confirmation dress," and "curl[ing] like copra left to dry" (39). Rather than being a "confirmation" or affirmation of belief, taking the Eucharist is for the cylamen girl an act that throws her into further confusion. The description of her dress as "yellowed" and of the cyclamen girl herself as being like "copra," the dried white flesh of the coconut from which its oil is extracted, evince the fact that she is reaching the end of her belief. The closing image of the "brittle matrix of her coconut cocoon" emphasises that she is nearing the breaking point with her religion while also suggesting the possibility of a meta-morphosis of belief (39).

The cyclamen girl's transformation occurs in the last poem in the series, aptly titled "Epiphany," in which she "returns to her own," to "a land of shadows/Herring-boned with memory" and to "the great stone-bird mother" (45). This gesture suggests that redemption for the cyclamen girl and all like her is located in a maternal and possibly African or Native American religious order. Regardless of the specific referent of "the great stone-bird mother," what Nourbese Philip establishes in the images in this poem is clearly a non-European and non-male world and order. Moreover, she posits the idea that this world is in fact the one that belongs to the cyclamen girl as well as the one to which she belongs. This poem also reflects what I view as Nourbese Philip's desire not to leave "all cyclamen girls" in a place of destruction, where taking the Eucharist involves an act of self-mutilation: "with moon-caked madness/the waiting mouth/ crushes/the body bro-/ken for all cyclamen girls" (44).

Yet, the overall meaning of this poem resonates somewhat poorly for me. While it does achieve for the cyclamen girl a cohesive sense of self, the closing also unravells the tension between various self-definitions and the yoking together of different heritages and languages Noubese Philip achieves so beautifully and believably elsewhere in the book. For example, in an earlier poem in the series, "Transfiguration," the cyclamen girl is able by coming through the "circle of grief" to answer to all of her names: Aphrodite! Mary! Atebey! Orehu! Yemoja! Oshun! In so doing, the cyclamen girl comes to what I see as a truer reconciliation with her Catholic heritage, in the invocation of Mary, as well as with her other European foremothers (Aphrodite) and her African ones (Atebey, Orehu, Yemoja, Oshun). Her then constructed self is founded on the "transfiguration" or alteration of each identity—even those fraught with "contradictions"—rather than a dismissal of any one of them. It is also interesting to note that the word transfiguration is closely linked to the word convert. Rather than convert to Catholicism, Nourbese Philip implies that the cyclamen girl must convert Catholicism, make it a syncretic religion, in order for it to represent her reality. Through the cyclamen girl in "Transfigurations," Nourbese Philip portrays Caribbean identity as creolised, as based on multiple origins which, even when in conflict, are ever present and must be constantly negotiated.

In later portions of the book, Nourbese Philip continues to refer to simultaneous versions of a given "truth" and different levels of language. She does so to reveal competing versions of "history"—one in which Standard English (and European thought) is spoken to degrade the African and the other in which the African enacts the breakdown of Standard English to reveal the language itself as responsible for her/his degraded i-mage. While it is not as easy in the later sections of the book to pinpoint the Creole speech at work in the poems, the breakdown of Standard English and references to the destructive nature of that imposed tongue upon the psyche of the African Caribbean are still very clear. In earlier poems in the book, Nourbese Philip employs linguistic strategies that expose and unravel English as a "master tongue." In the latter portion of the book, language itself is not only the source of formal reconsideration and rerendering but becomes the subject of the poems themselves.

As does the title of the book, the titles of the poems/sections in the last portion of the book illustrate Nourbese Philip's interest in the relationship between linguistics and identity formation. "Discourse on the Logic of Language," "Universal Grammar," "The Question of Language is the Answer to Power," "Testimony Stoops to Mother Tongue," and "She Tries Her Tongue, Her Silence Softly Breaks" all reveal Nourbese Philip's concern with the ontological effects of language. As scholar Brenda Carr notes in her essay, "To 'Heal the Word Wounded': Agency and the Materiality of Language and Form in M. Nourbese Philip's *She Tries Her Tongue, Her Silence Softly Breaks*," "many of [Nourbese Philip's] sequence titles signal linguistic intervention as the dominant gesture of her text" (78).

In these sections, Nourbese Philip turns from redressing myth and critiquing religion and focuses her condemning gaze on another institution that has promoted (and to a lesser extent still promotes) racism and sexism in the name of logic, reason and truth: Science, and particularly the pursuit of scientific discovery in the 19th century. Through several poems, she explores the connection between science and the spoken word and considers the world of meaning that results from the false definitions of things in the name of science.

In "Discourse on the Logic of Language" for example, she exposes the racism practised as scientific advancement by "two learned nineteenth century doctors, the eponymous Doctors Wernicke and Boca," for whom "those parts of the brain chiefly responsible for speech are named" (57). That Dr. Boca "devoted much of his time to 'proving' that white males of the Caucasian race had larger brains than, and where therefore superior to, women, Blacks and other peoples of colour," sufficiently illustrates how a supposedly objective field of inquiry has often in fact been racist and sexist. In addition, as a counterpoint to this, Nourbese Philip inserts historical records, the "edicts" that concerned language and slavery, edicts that encouraged the stamping out of the "mother tongue" even so far as to cut out the physical tongue of the African. This scientific and historical "evidence," presented in an understated, factual, documentary-like fashion, undermines itself and reveals the horror of its own inhumanity, cruelty, and missed logic.

However, Nourbese Philip is not only interested in proving that science and the law conspired to annihilate language in the African brought to the New World and present(ed) the African as inhuman. She is also intent upon revealing how the African survived that willful dispossession of language and self. To show this, she provides, alongside these "scientific" and "historical" records, two simultaneous narratives from the perspective of the African, one in first-person, one in third-person, that further critique and ultimately undermine those "other" renderings of reality. The first-person account portrays the "foreign anguish" that is the English "language" or "l/anguish" for the African who has no "mother tongue," but Nourbese Philip refuses to only present a sense of lost language and identity. On the left margin running lengthwise down the page, a third-person narrator describes a mother with her newborn child. The mother is described as licking her child "clean of the creamy white substance covering its body," and then "blowing words—her words, her mother's words, those of her mother's mother, and all their mother's before—into her daughter's mouth" (56, 58).

While this image portrays what I see as a too-idyllic and even cliched notion of a matriarchal order, similar to the one represented in the poem "Epiphany," the child is nevertheless cocooned and saved by the "mother tongue," and the racial memory of her linguistic and bodily connection to the mother is preserved. As with Nourbese Philip's retelling of the Proserpine-Ceres myth, in the last series of poems in the book she again insists that we consider the umbilical cord and linguistic knowledge that has never been and is not fully severed.

But is the bond sufficient? And are the linguistic and poetic tactics Nourbese Philip's uses enough to make the claim that language in the Caribbean can sufficiently serve as resistance and transformation? The answer I would offer to these questions is a qualified yes. While it is difficult due to the vantage point from which we seek to understand Creole as a language to pinpoint its precise evolution, we can see evidence in the language to a "connection" to Africa. This connection can be seen in the retention of African-language rhythms in speech and the strong tendency of Creole to use metaphorical language, even if large amounts of vocabulary have been lost. Certainly these linkages support the notion that language is capable of being a form of resistance—in this instance, a resistance to the complete annihilation of a language and way of existing in and understanding the world.

When, as demonstrated in the poems in her book, the author is deeply aware of the force of language, both historically and presently, the potential for language to serve as resistance seems even more plausible and possible. By being cognisant of and in turn betraying how language actually imparts and creates meaning and by manipulating that same language to create new meanings and therefore new realities, Nourbese Philip gains power over the word. She ironically uses the same "tools" the "master" has imposed to fracture and degrade images of African Caribbean identity and fights against those oppressive images and evolves them into ones of pride and beauty.

I think it is also possible to say that she accounts for the deeper loss to which Glissant alludes when he asserts that the transition from Creole as spoken word to Creole as written word "vulgarises" the language. While Glissant states this, it is crucial to add that he posits this fact as due to certain "situations" associated with both forms of speech—"the written requires nonmovement...the oral, on the other hand, is inseparable from the movement of the body" (122). Nourbese Philip also acknowledges that the "challenge" is "to keep the deep structure, the movement, the kinetic energy, the tone and pitch, the slides and glissandos of the demotic within a tradition that is primarily page-bound" (23, emphasis mine).

Yet even while Glissant sees road blocks for the use of Creole, he has the foresight to state in the same essay that this "situation" is not interminable: "The word in the Caribbean will only survive as such, in a written form, if this earlier loss [of movement] finds expression" (121). He also concludes the essay on a note of optimism claiming that "Ethnopoetics belongs to the future" (134). Nourbese Philip's *she tries her tongue: her silence softly breaks* is undoubtedly a key part of that future of ethnopoetics Glissant envisioned, as well as helped to shape himself in his own writing.

While imperfect, as one might argue, since there is always some degree of loss in translation, Nourbese Philip's poems do capture the movement, cadence and rhythms of Creole speech on the page. Moreover, by simultaneously acknowledging the imperfection and misuse of language, she does this in a manner that also successfully approximates in written form the rebellious, resilient, fluid, and improvisational characteristics of the oral Caribbean demotic.

Through the use of a number of linguistic risks and the "challenge" she imposes upon herself, as well as through her storytelling/storymaking, Nourbese Philip translates the Caribbean language unto the page. She thus reveals how black women and all people of African descent in the Caribbean and throughout the Diaspora reenvision and recohere their identities in the face of the oppressive language that seeks to define them. And it is in so doing, and in the formal manner with which she portrays this situation, that Nourbese Philip's poetry moves from resisting the images inherent in that language to also transforming them for herself *and* the reader. She changes the reader's conception of the world, as any good literature will do, but I would argue that she also changes the reader's conception of how the world is created through the word. She alters the reader's expectations in the interaction between reading and forming meaning. Rather than highlighting her own beliefs alone, she forces those who engage, and I do mean engage, her poetry to experience how "truth" is created.

Carolyn Cooper, in her essay "'Noh Lickle Twang': an Introduction to the Poetry of Louise Bennett," identifies three stages in the development of Caribbean Poetry in English from 1900-1976. Those are Imitation (1900 to c. 1931); Introspection (1943-1958), and Experimentation (1962 to the present[4]), characterised according to the "mood of each phase" (318). Nourbese Philip's experimental poetry places her firmly in the last category and she adds significantly to that body of Caribbean poetry being written in English which explores new ways of defining what it means to be Caribbean through the language and gestures of a creolised self. Her poetry bridges the divide between theory and praxis and in so doing moves away from the sometimes static or stilted uses of Creole to define the Caribbean struggle for identity. She enacts a language in her poems that, like the people of the Caribbean who still reckon with speech as a source of identity, mediates the slippage between a "natural" and "forced" poetics.

Notes

[1] I might have easily chosen hybridised or syncretised versus "creolised" but intentionally use the latter to signify a particular theoretical framework that I employ throughout this essay.

[2] I think it would also be possible to make such a case for both Dove and Boland in terms of their relationship to "Mother Africa" and "Mother Ireland," respectively.

[3] Reference to "i-mage" comes from Nourbese Philip's introduction, in which she discusses the source of "anguish" over identity in terms of the Rastafarian use of the "I" versus the frequent lack of a meaningful and self-created image of the Caribbean person. "Racial memory" is the idea that memory of Africa, the middle passage, slavery, etc. is ingrained in the African in the "New World's" consciousness despite distance of time and space.

[4] The "present" is defined as the period of the 1960s and 1970s by Cooper. Still, I think the "third phase" is relevant to much Anglophone Caribbean poetry in today's present, twenty to thirty years later.

Works Cited

Bernabe, Jean, Patrick Chamoiseau and Raphael Confiant. "In Praise of Creoleness." *Callaloo* 13.4 (1990): 886-909.

Carr, Brenda. "To 'Heal the Word Wounded': Agency and the Materiality of Language and Form in M. Nourbese Philip's *She Tries Her Tongue, Her Silence Softly Breaks.*" *Studies in Canadian Literature/Etudes en Litterature* 19:1 (1994): 72-93.

Cooper, Carolyn. "Noh Lickle Twang: An Introduction to the Poetry of Louise Bennett." *World Literature Written in English* 17 (1978): 317-27.

Glissant, Edouard. "Free and Forced Poetics." *Caribbean Discourse*. University Press of Virginia: Richmond, 1992.

Lorde, Audre. "The Master's Tools Will Not Dismantle the Master's House." *Sister Outsider*. The Crossing Press: Freedom, CA., 1984.

Nourbese Philip, Marlene. *she tries her tongue: her silence softly breaks*. Ragweed Press: Charlottetown, 1989.

"BEYOND RECOGNITION": HERITAGE AND IDENTITY IN PAULE MARSHALL'S *THE CHOSEN PLACE, THE TIMELESS PEOPLE*

Joy M. Lynch

I

Authors depicting the conditions and ramifications of colonization have long been engaged in identifying and evoking the ambivalences contained in the concept of place. For these authors and their characters, "place" cannot be objectively rendered. Created from the interaction of histories and cultures, place is contained in language and so is embedded in the morality of human intercourse. Thus, we "make" land into "landscape" in the simple act of naming, revealing our anthropocentric impulse to qualify our surroundings based on their value for human use and consumption. We define a location as human property; we inhabit it and call it motherland, fatherland, native land, homeland. We categorize land to designate its potential productivity; it becomes highland, lowland, borderland, or outland. In nature, there is no "wasteland."

For many, however, place is a tangible reminder of difference, a locus of estrangement and displacement as lands and homelands are subject to colonizing influences, which often take the form of military, economic, cultural, and linguistic imperialism. Home ground sometimes overnight becomes foreign territory, foreign because named, owned, and made subject to another. For the displaced, the sense of "belonging" becomes disguised, concealed, or hidden behind the borrowed words, gestures, and silences that form the language of subjectivity. Place, then, becomes intimately implicated in the process of subjectivity, both in the continual dialectic between objects and signifiers, and between external pressures and internal desires. As a result, with colonization comes the threat of displacement and disembodiment.

In *The Chosen Place, The Timeless People*, Paule Marshall explores the history of slavery on a fictional Caribbean island and the contours of individuals as they are shaped by the colonizing of their land, culture, and history. The population of this island has inherited the economic, psychological and political by-products of being twice-colonized, first by the British colonial system and, more recently, by American economic interests. The traffic between nations—economic and racial—that constitutes imperialism results in a colonial condition reflected in individual identity. The tangible exterior conditions of imperialism stage many of the dynamics of connection and separation implicit in characters' behaviors towards themselves and others. The processes of human intimacy—power, submission, control, abandon, shame, pride, cruelty, generosity, fear, tenderness—mirror in specific ways the historical conditions that give them context.

Themselves "products" of a colonial condition, the characters of *The Chosen Place, The Timeless People* are not masters of their own bodies; their racialized bodies resist coherent identity, resulting in a "dis-integration" which may be resisted, accepted, or transformed. As the resultant racial, sexual, marital, and class borders intersect in the novel, historical forces become personalized, revealing the syncretic nature of multiple subjectivities created under the pressure of colonialism. Harriet and Saul, as visiting newcomers to the island, each are confronted by their implicit alignment with colonizing forces, but the protagonist Merle alone finds an appropriate identifying language for her self and her past, both in terms of the public history of Bourne Island and her personal history as identified with her British heritage.

In this essay, I will show how the crucial contestation between colonizing and colonized forces mark "place" in Marshall's novel. In other words, I explore how imperialistic influences exploit the Bourne Island landscape and how that landscape resists colonization in its ongoing return to a "native" state. I argue that the colonial encounter similarly marks the ways that bodies are created, defined, owned, and inhabited by the characters in the novel who, like the resisting landscape, silently refuse to incorporate modern technology and economic methods, the subjects that Saul Amron has been sent to investigate. I argue further that Merle, as both insider and outsider to the native population, carries a particular function in the novel: she exhibits in specific ways the material evidence of the conflict between colonizer and colonized on her body and, more importantly, in her subjectivity. Her language, with its alternating non-stop chatter and silences, replicates, indeed even incorporates, the silence held by a slavery-torn landscape and people. Through her sexual relations with Saul, Merle discovers a means to re-embody a pluralistic subjectivity by returning to the original "place" of the body, a metaphoric landscape through which to enact a healing process of unification, and thereby transforming the fragmentation of subjectivity caused by the colonial condition. Before turning one's attention to Merle, it is necessary first to recognize the violence committed against the landscape and its evidence on the bodies of the inhabitants of Bourne Island.

The novel describes the history of a people whose lives in the past few centuries have been defined by the many faces of colonization. It opens with a team of white American academic ethnographers and researchers from the Center for Applied Social Research (CASR), headed by Saul Amron, who have been assigned to investigate the daily world of an "underdeveloped" country whose inhabitants depend on near subsistence-level incomes from the growth of sugar cane and sugar by-products, industries that had developed during the days of plantation life. Despite their stated intention to assist in the development of alternative—or at least more efficient—methods of livelihood, CASR is partially funded by Kingsley and Sons, British entrepreneurs who own and run the local sugar processing plant and whose financial holdings would be compromised by any actual improvement in island economics. In other words, while Amron heads a research project intent on securing economic independence for the island, Kingsley and Sons own and operate the most profitable—and only—industry on the island. British and American monetary interests, then, are complicit in their efforts to bind present living conditions to a continuing dependency on foreign rule.

The landscape of Bourne Island contains the scars of the colonial past that has been enacted on its soil. The geography features the procession of history: images of land and landscape serve as a cultural matrix for the discovery, conquest and articulation of ethnic identity in the Caribbean. As much shaped by the prospects of colonial powers as the workers who strip its earth, the land intrudes into the novel like another character, at once a landscape and a human condition, a place of physical hardship and psychological dislocation. The colonizing process destroyed the land; the plantation industry ravaged the forests and despoiled the ecosystems for the production of sugar as it robbed the native inhabitants of their collective and individual self-determination. To the island peoples, "the physical geography has been, from pre-Hispanic times to the present, one of the dominant and inescapable influences on the pattern of life and society" (Knight 3).

The complex history of the land evokes a layered background for public and private lives. With American and British slavery insinuated into the interstices of the novel, the entangled drama of economic interests and multiple colonial histories unfolds in the private lives of the characters. The long struggle to dismantle imperialism, to overcome colonialism, and to create independent states in the Caribbean islands has produced uneven results, fragmenting ethnic communities, languages, and loyalties.

Having weathered centuries of exploitation, each character portrays some aspect of the slave past, their presence inevitably tied to the landscape of the past. Not only do the islanders suffer British or American exploitation, they also feel the pressures of their own hybrid politicians, whom they accuse of "auctioning" off their island "to the lowest bidder" (Marshall 209).

The many minor characters who inhabit the novel exhibit these processes of this history. Those in power drape their figures with the signifiers of culture and power; those who work are marked by the ravages of hard labor. Place, then, effects the psyche in ways that are replicated in the body. Description of place becomes subjective, as having "some personal meaning" (100). In internalized form, then, Bourne Island reveals the relationship of people to their pasts, their interiors, and their memories, and so it is emblematic of the "skin" of the novel, the liminal space where the collective memory of past exploitation (the "inside") meets the presence of present exploitation, the "outside." For instance, native legislators of mixed blood are plentiful in the novel. Suggesting V.S. Naipual's "mimic men," these middle-men "passed through the white prism" of their history, these intermediaries "were of a type, wearing English suits and drinking English rum" (53). The manager of the sugar cane fields, Pollard, "still held to the old ways" of making his "rounds" in "jodhpurs, polished boots, a cork hat and riding a piebald horse," calling to mind "some ghost who refused to keep to his grave even during the daytime" (53). Neocolonial dominance based on business interests is more fully encoded in the figure of Cane Vale's boss, Sir John, who costumes himself in keeping with his ancestral "place" in history. In safari dress to recall the imperialistic forces that "civilized" Bournehills, Sir John sports a khaki bush jacket with epaulets, shorts that cover his "old man's thighs [that] showed the pallor of the long London winter," and a pith helmet and swagger stick (220).

For the native population, the daily work on the island recalls the conditions of forced labor wearing out the will and starving the soul, aging them beyond their years. The process of cutting, gathering, tying and moving cane bales is an "unreality, a sense of something taking place long past" (161). The continued processes of sugar refining, a way of life transformed from plantation slavery to economic dependence on the white Western world, reflects the belief that "things are no different. The chains are still on" (210). Economic and capitalistic exploitation persists, despite the island's formal independence. For the workers in the fields, many of whom are still young, labor in the sugar-cane industry has "aged [them] beyond recognition"; the majority of them trudge through their days with the "same slightly turned up, fixed, flat stare that you find upon drawing back the lids of someone asleep or dead" (161-163). To these workers, the island is marked by "endless" fields of sugar cane, and they seem to live in a place made "timeless" out of its irrevocable past (13): "They continue to be, as their ancestors had been for hundreds of years, yoked to a system that literally works them to death while it steals the fruits of their labor" (Christian 113). Bournehills symbolizes "every place that had been wantonly used, its substance stripped away, and then abandoned" (100).

Yet despite the assault to its surface—by native workers stripping its fields at the behest of industry supervisors—the island landscape of Bournehills is unyielding in its resistance to domination. The land remains impenetrable, despite human efforts to contain it and "mark" it. The topography reflects an eternal life cycle beyond the pressures of imperialism, despite the Cane Vale owners' desire to harvest sugar for their profit. The hills trashed by sugar cane overproduction defeat the workers' efforts (and Cane Vale's profits) more often than not by returning to their wild "native" state.

Not even the symbols of Western civilization are able to mark their hold on the resisting landscape of Bourne Island. Corporate owners intent on gaining control over the landscape must build roads, which are crucial to the transport of sugar to processing plant to shipping docks. But more fundamentally, these transportation arteries enable infiltration by outside forces, thus confirming their power over the inscription of being, the making of landscape into "place." Thus, roads signify a pattern of coercion and containment historically implicated in the colonial enterprise. Yet the island's unrelenting insistence on returning to an ancient, primordial state, as if by some "natural will," turns roads into rivers of mud in the constant rains. The roads continually awash offer a visual paradigm for a wilderness and a people who resist attempts at colonization.

By analogy, the island people resist the penetration of superfluous modernization since they are unable to "become" colonized by the British and the Americans without accommodating themselves to western ideologies. Their bodies bear the marks of a colonial past; their faces are "eloquent of their life upon the ravaged land" (103). The boundary between native inhabitants and place is blurred, underscoring the metaphoric alignment between landscape and bodies that reveals the natives' unarticulated resistance to subjugation. The landscape, then, "enters" into the lives of the inhabitants, forming an "inhuman" aspect of community life in which the separation of human and inhuman, and past and present dissolves, beyond the kenning of outsiders. Old Aunt Leesy moves "in and among the shadows that stood like silent members of the household everywhere," "addressing" them while ignoring her returned nephew, Vere (27). With Vere back from the United States, life for Leesy is "in order" again, as if those born on the island remained in spirit, their bodily reunion with the land synchronic with their spirit's reunification with the body (27). As shadows are "peopled," so, too, the natives become shadows. Merle's cook, Carrington, becomes part of the landscape: she "could have been one of the massed shadows in the kitchen that had broken off and assumed human form.... [She] seemed less a person than a presence" (110). While to Merle, Carrington "goes with the house," her presence suggests a key to Merle's own identity: "You see, she was the last keep-miss of the man I'm to call father and the only one to bury him, so I guess she has as much right to the place as I do" (110-111).

II: The Landscape of the Body and the Embodiment of Landscape: Merle's Quest for Wholeness

While the native peoples have integrated the landscape and the scars of colonization into their present selves, Harriet, Saul, and Merle have yet to face the implications of their racialized perspectives on history. As each character engages with that landscape, he or she begins to remember and confront painful, hidden pasts—historical and personal—which have long been the sources of internal alienation. The landscape comes to "test" their characters, and each responds primally to his or her confrontation with the embattled land. Their struggles with a landscape that refuses to be contained—and so forgotten—reveal their inner beings and their relations to the "outside." For each, a subjective "map" of the island emerges which exposes his or her unacknowledged position within an imperialist and colonizing history. Place, then, becomes a location where the self and Other exchange, where political and personal selves intersect at the surface, where the defining lines of the collective body blur with the individual body. For example, outsiders imagine this native landscape to be "savage" and so inscribe it with their own personal darknesses. To Saul, who has yet to confront his guilt at his complicity in the death of his first wife, "these ragged hills ...could have been a troubled region within himself to which he had unwittingly returned" (100). To Harriet, whose body, with its unwrinkling linen drapery, exhibits sexuality shorn of sensuality and replaced with the desire to control, Bournehills is "some unexplored landscape having nothing to do with a physical place as such" (99).

Metaphorically aligned with the landscape, then, the human body provides a literal text on which the forces of colonization are frequently and directly written. It is commonplace that the visible presences of superficial variations of body, skin, and hair become inscribed by the dominant power as the signs of "otherness"—and as such, "absence" within its power structure. And so the body becomes both overdetermined and under-determined at the same time, the ever-present subject of both scrutiny and, paradoxically, of blindness. At the same time, the body, with its multiple openings, presents itself as a resilient surface which allows a penetrable and permeable borderland of identity, which carries in it the hazards of fragmentation and vulnerability, or the possibility of a resilient, multi-faceted, pluralistic subjectivity. In this way, a landscape whose resiliency mitigates the dominance of encroaching powers is reflected in the permeable body, whose psyche also resists domination: and so the resistance exhibited by the landscape is reflected in bodily and psychic resistances. If the body is a place on which the surface acts of exploitation are arrested, then the body becomes the means through which healing may take place, a healing which I argue is enacted in the sexual relations of Saul and Merle.

For Merle, the body exists both as a force in itself and as a reflection of the "landscape" of her psyche. It is in terms of her sensitivity to the landscape of Bourne Island that she *feels* her own existence. Her body, like her language, is "dis-integrated"; it signals confusion, paralysis, or disjointedness, a result of the contradictions inherent in an overinvestment in bodily form and surface (i.e., racialized skin) in the colonial regime. This external bodily fragmentation reflects a personal past that has been forgotten or submerged in order for her to create an apparent "seamless" present. Yet Merle's hybrid identity as *creole* also allows her the opportunity to explore the possibilities inherent in being "relative" to the fixed positions of inside and outside. Rather than allowing the fracturing of a unified identity to result in individual and cultural alienation, abandonment, or submission, Merle transforms the multiplicity of her subject positions and develops a resiliency that allows for a forgiveness of past transgressions and failures, and a hope for the future.

Like the landscape, Merle Kinbona has a "fluid" identity, one in continual process of inscription and reinscription by impulse and desire. At 40, middle-aged, and a product of both Caribbean and European heritages, Merle stands at the crossroads of her life, and her body is a visible link between and pointer to the burdens of racial and social instability reflective of the slave trade, the colonialism of the past, and the economic exploitation of the present.

Merle is a mass of contradictions, embracing a fluid ethics in response to the conflicts inherent in carrying within her the essences of both colonized and colonizers' pasts that have inscribed her personal history. She is haunted by a familial history she is reluctant to reveal—and which is known by her neighbors only in snippets and through local legend. As a descendant of an English plantation owner, Duncan Vaughn, and a West African native, Merle embodies directly the violent history of a slave past. When she was two years old, her father's white wife shot Merle's sixteen-year old black mother in front of her, a memory whose details and emotion she cannot recall. She is forever trying to name her mother's murderess, a loss of memory tied to the loss of voice she is constantly attempting to (re)cover and overcome with loquaciousness. Additionally, while Vaughn did not acknowledge officially her birth—a prospect which would damage his stature as a semi-official ruling progeny of the plantation elite—he nonetheless attempts to ease his guilt(?) by sending Merle to college in England. In so doing, he does not redress his wrong or eliminate his complicity in her illegitimacy, but only exacerbates—and paradoxically— highlights for Merle her confused identity. While she is in England, Merle becomes sexually involved with a British white woman, her benefactress who controls her life. Rebelling against the constraint, Merle severs her ties and meets Ketu, an African with whom she falls in love, marries and has a child. When the benefactress vindictively tells Ketu of their liaison, he responds by leaving Merle and returning to Africa with their child. With nowhere else to turn, Merle has returned to Bourne Island to attempt to resolve the personal losses in her life which at times overwhelm her and render her catatonic.

In her body, Merle exhibits the topographical ravages committed against the island and people: she "appeared to contain them all" (260). Her face, that "might have been sculpted by some bold and liberal Bantu hand," had been "despoiled . . in much the same way as the worn hills to be seen piled around her on all sides had been despoiled—stripped of their trees centuries ago, their substance taken" (5). She exhibits the fragmentation and alienation of the island people, such as Vere, Ferguson, Gwen, and Stinger, all worn down through the dynamics of racial subordination: her flesh, in its "slow, irreversible decline toward middle age" is beginning to "slacken and lose hold," even though her legs "were still those of a young woman" (4). Yet despite such self-division, Merle's face is "saved ... in part ... by the inner sunlight her eyes gave off. This said some vital center remained intact" (5).

While Merle's body shows the "despoiling" of these violent (hi)stories, her speech identifies most clearly the anxieties of self-colonization, revealing an identity buffeted by outside forces that have contained and (de)scribed her life. Despite her non-stop chatter that she wields like armor, she only reveals her own story in fragments throughout the novel, for she is as unable to face her personal loss as she is to contain it. Language implies a coercion of feeling into signification, yet even as it gives it form, language serves to contain emotion.

Merle compartmentalizes the past in order to control the fragments that are alienating both within and without. By categorizing and judging the experiences of her past, Merle reflects the self-condemnation of the policing spirit. When she repeats the story of witnessing her mother's murder to Saul, for example, she refers to herself condescendingly in the third person, "the little idiot of a child" who "would have at least remembered what the face behind the gun looked like" (338): "Even a half-wit like Seifert up at the almshouse would be able to point to his mother's murderer, I bet. Not me, though! Not your friend Merle! People say I was standing beside her body sucking my thumb like nothing had happened when they found her" (358). Her constant talking, thus, with its almost centrifugal pressure away from "meaningful" communication, serves as a reminder of her hybrid position. Merle "appear[s] to be trying ... to recovers something in herself that had been lost: the sense of herself as a woman perhaps. There was no telling" (5). She talks incessantly, compulsively, impulsively, in "a voice in a race against both time and itself" (173). Her talk is desperate, a "scarcely suppressed hysteria" (67), a "camouflage and a shield" (229), which she herself identifies as an indication of condition: "I'm a talker. Some people act, some think, some feel, but I talk, and if I was to ever stop that'd be the end of me" (65). Speech buffers her from intimacy with others, warding them off as she meets public hostilities head on. While she is silent about her private life, still she is outspoken about the politics of the island and the active remnants of colonialism.

While they are evidence of her dissolution, then, Merle's speech patterns nonetheless are, paradoxically, also key to her resistance and survival. For instance, her ability to move with ease between the many factions on the island earns her the disparaging label of "cultural broker," one whose allegiance to colonizer and colonized is ambiguous (118). And when faced with native island legislators' mealy-mouthed explanations for the harsh labor and economic conditions, Merle alone reminds them (uncomfortably) of their tenuous position as "mediator" between the natives and the American business interests.

Her language, then, often multiplies the meaning of the narrative, containing the multiplicity of both past and present, and serving to reinforce the image of the past carried forward as a relentless and inescapable "presence." In a scene in which Merle identifies the surrounding landscape as carrier of a brutal past, Merle explains the legend of Cuffee Ned and the uprising to another passenger in the car while they are on an excursion to "penetrate deeper into Bournehills" (103). Here, landscape *is* story: it bears the legends of past heroes when speech is silent and only physical placemarks remain. Merle directs, "Westminster Low Road dead ahead," while pointing to where the "dead hero's head" of Cuffee Ned had been exhibited on a tall spike (103). At the same time, she waves to Mr. Douglin, an old man working the fields, who returns the greeting with "empty holes that served as his eyes," a grim reminder of Cuffee Ned's head displayed on a wooden spike (103). As if unconciously recognizing the dim filter of the past through which the present is experienced, Merle swears "Oh, crime" as the car becomes engulfed, not in mud this time, but among the workers who do not stop their toil merely to let through a car. Her voice unwittingly breaks through silence and speaks a truth, of the "crime" of the slave past and the exploitation of laborers in the present, of workers as "abused" and "abandoned" as the landscape (100).

Further, although her body carries in it the intersection of cultures, and her speech keeps the "crimes" of her personal and the public histories at bay, it is in her silences, much more so than in her speech, that physical and emotional disintegration is made evident as an almost complete catatonia. As Melvin Rahming rightly observes, "her psychological suffering is so intense [bearing the full weight of the psychic malady of the Bournehills people] that she is given to recurring periods of total physical, emotional, and mental withdrawal—as if her consciousness of the economic and spiritual state of her people is too much for her" (131). When faced with her own insubstantiality compared to the weight of past "crimes"—either public or personal—she lapses into "long, frightening, cataleptic states during which she [is] more dead than alive" (398). Silence is the epitome of containment; it embodies experience without directing it into form. Yet silence also allows inner flight or displacement. During those times, she responds to no one, seeking the silent refuge of her home and garden: "It was as though she had fled completely the surface of herself for some place deep within where nothing could penetrate, leaving behind a numb spent face, a body which looked as if it had been thrown like a rag doll, its limbs all awry, on the bed and left there, and the dead eyes" (399). Her body "discarded," she has "retreated" to the "numb center" and is unable to be reached by others (399). Merle must accept contradictory truths in order to integrate this "disintegrated" body that portrays both the conflicts of her peoples and a tenuous existence in which open conflict is replaced with more subtle resistance. This healing takes place in her relationship with Saul and is evident in her sexual encounters with him, a healing which first takes the verbal form of storytelling.

In the final night of Carnival, with its atmosphere of exaggeration, spectacle and misrule, Merle tells the secret of her past to Saul, of her powerlessness at the hands of patroness and husband, in a "flat, expressionless voice" (327). She tells her tale behind the verbal defenses she has carried through her life: it is at first "obscure," filled with "long silences," "spoken too casually" in alternating "matter of fact" tones and "sharp cut-off hooks" (327). Her story is filled with self-denigration: she "fell in" with the crowd around the Patron, who spent money on "foolish people like [her]"; she was flattered "to have a rich Englishwoman" taking such an interest in "the good little brainwashed West Indian" that she was (328). Merle directly draws parallels between her own life and imperialistic, global forces: "During the time I lived [in England] I met people from every corner of the globe: India, Asia, Africa, Canada, Australia, Gibraltar, all over the place. The sun, you might say, never set on the little empire [her patroness] had going in her drawing room" (328). As she speaks, it is clear that Saul recedes from her vision, until she speaks only to herself, "staring through Saul into that other time" (334). The memory of the past brought out to light, with the presence of Saul alternately remembered and forgotten as she reaches back into silences, allows her to acknowledge to herself the complexities and the problems left unresolved in her sexual past. The pain that accompanies her revelations portrays the penetration of her past into her present so necessary to her eventual peace: "an old wound deep at her center that had never completely healed, but had, at least, remained dormant over the years, quiescent, had suddenly begun to lance her again" (334).

The intensity of that pain culminates in her memory of her husband and reveals the hidden chains of colonialism that control interiority as well as external life. Believing Merle's past to be a betrayal, Ketu had stopped sleeping with her altogether, "as though ... I stood for the worst that could happen to those of us who came to places like England and allowed ourselves to be corrupted. I wasn't Merle to him any longer, a person, his wife, the mother of his child, but the very thing he had tried to avoid all his years there" (334). Ketu's attitude shift about Merle from "beloved" to "thing" is internalized by Merle, whose relation to herself is likewise split: in the contradictory logic of the conflict of being both the victimizer and the victim, she is a "mistake" (334) and he is a "brute," her curses at him "giving off [the] venom" of her wound (336). The evocation of the history of feeling, of the process of her sorrow and Saul's witnessing of it, allows them the personal intimacy that informs their sexual relations.

Merle's sexual intimacies with Saul thus reflect the deeply rooted mistrust of the sexual intimacies that had devastated her in her past. Merle and Saul do not begin their conversation after Carnival intent on sexual intimacy. Yet their conversation evolves from distance—that of inquisitor and respondent—to verbal intimacy, with Merle losing the presence of here-and-now to move back through memory, through past, to the center of her pain and loss. But Merle is unable to unequivocally trust their closeness: to mask his racial lineage as Jewish, she aligns him with the Backra, a mixed people of the Canterbury district, an appellation that mutes his color and appeases her own mistrust of whites.[1] Caught in the web of multi-sited racial/colonial relations—between white and black sexual relations and the crossfire of those who, through sexual intimacy, "feel they still own you" (330)—Merle confronts the contradiction both within and without.

In order to break the cycle of self-colonization and self-alienation which has been formed by a sense of isolation from and mistrust of her intimates, Merle must develop a different *kind* of identity, one that will counter the alienating effects of a historically and personally ravaging past. Instead of preferring a singular, independent sense of selfhood, she must reconstruct her identity based on a collectivity, on subjectivity as formed consciously *in relationship* with others. One form of identity constructed in relationships is female bonding, much like the relationship Merle has with Gwen. Here the other is *not* Other, not opposite in gender or race. Rather, the other is contiguous and the relationship is not one of conquest but of collectivity, of a communion that breaks down boundaries, loosens distinct outlines, and merges individual and collective in order to explore the ambiguity of identity at the interface of subject with object/Other. Through this collectivism, a connection is created that does not threaten autonomy but preserves it.

Saul and Merle reach through to each other first in words: their respective positions with regard to each other blend, the recall of the past sparks the recall of the other's pain, and the boundary between self and other, like the one between the present and past, is blurred. More fully than in her relationship with Gwen, in her verbal and sexual intimacies forged with Saul, Merle begins to form a *new* subject, one who is plural and not unified, one who is ambiguous and embraces the plurality of her condition. Her sexuality, then, encompasses an acceptance of relativity which marks a transformation of colonial rule, a resisting of its static and defined purpose.

About their first night together, the last night of Carnival and the night that they reveal their secret histories, the novel is nearly silent, their conversation about sex at odds with their effusive talk that led them there. Saul initiates the connection by asking, "'Stay with me, Merle, for what's left of tonight,'" but Merle controls the contact with an intellectual barricade: "'On one condition ... That you don't make too much of it, meaning it goes no further than tonight'" (339). On the only other night discussed in the novel, Saul notes that Merle remains consciously guarded:

the "faint, self-absorbed, self-congratulatory smile he sometimes caught on her face at the height of their embrace said she knew her woman's power to move and delight, ... an unmistakable, almost frightening authority" (360). Both exchanges reveal the distance she creates and maintains to control another and herself, the response of the colonizer within. She admits to "using" Saul as her "new Juju man from Harley Street," a man she had turned to for hypnosis in order to try to recall the day of her mother's murder buried in her psyche (357). Her cynical claim that "people always do [use one another] in one way or another" reflects her being caught emotionally still by the lovers who "ruled" her for years, only now she will do the ruling (357).

Empowered through the release, a release both psychological and sexual, offered by her friendship with Saul, a friendship that does not mirror her earlier relationship to her patronness but one in which she is equally as or more powerful than her partner, Merle can now move from tale-telling of her past to actual embracing and redressing its ramifications in her present by replaying its terms of oppression and redrawing its outcome, as she does with Harriet. From the beginning of their acquaintance, Merle noted a primal sense within that Harriet touched: "Why if you don't put me in mind of someone I knew in England years ago" (71). But only at the end of the novel, when Harriet offers money to Merle to "buy" her out of Saul's life is Merle aware of again finding herself facing one whose assumption of racial and cultural superiority requires the complicity of her agreement. This time, Merle resists Harriet's (and by analogy, the Englishwoman's) rescripting of her life. Merle "search[es] intently for that other face hiding behind" Harriet's, suddenly giving "a violent start" as the past moves across the barrier of denial into the present: "and with a choked cry of fear, horror and dismay, her hand [came] up to fend off that other face which had at last, after all these months, revealed itself" (439). This time, rather than succumbing to the pressure of one with the apparent upper hand, Merle recognizes the power of the oppressed to refuse to comply, to resist the complicity that had haunted her for all of her life: she laughs, an "ugly anguished scream torn from the very top of her voice and as frighteningly empty and ironic as [a] huge gut laugh," in order to rid herself of "something dead" inside (439). This time, she knows her silence "can't be bought" (441). She tells Harriet that she will not leave the island at her bidding because "I don't like people ordering me about like I'm still the little colonial. I've had too much of that" (442). This challenge to her own part in her oppressive past, set in motion by the story she began with Saul, leads to the beginning of her recovery.

Having recovered the voice of her past, at the end of the novel, Merle notes a "marked change" in the voice of the Bournehills sea, as once again we are reminded that the exterior landscape reflects the interior character: the "roar of outrage" in the huge breakers had "lost some measure of its fury"—it flung itself with "something less than its usual hysteria" (461). Merle is more collected for having begun to "collect" her past: she is as decisive about her own life as she had been about the lives around her. This time she will leave in search of her husband and child in Africa. When Saul arrives to say goodbye, he is aware that she has removed the saint earrings and the heavy silver bracelets that had bound her wrists: she is "unburdened, restored to herself" (463). She no longer "whitens" her complexion with talcum powder "as though to mute her darkness," and her hair now stands "in a small rough forest around her face" (463). She returns to Africa to meet her past self, with the knowledge that "sometimes a person has to go back, really back—to have a sense, an understanding of all that's gone to make them—before they can go forward" (468). With Saul, Merle is able to find courage within, which allows her to confront her past and set in motion the healing process. The confrontation with her private past is significant in its public application: as Dorothy Denniston has pointed out, Merle reverses the route of the slave trade, returning to Africa via Trinidad, Brazil, Dakar, and finally to Kampala: "The reverse route serves to illustrate Marshall's artistic tracing of the black experience from the New World toward Africa ... [to a] personal cultural identity as African in its source, and it is in that naming (claiming) that [Marshall] posits both a self and a community" (Denniston 124-125). By confronting and realizing the confusions of her past, Merle transforms herself and learns to contain the competing internal forces of the colonizer and of the colonized which she inherited as daughter to a white plantation owner and a black mother.

The Chosen Place, The Timeless People makes clear the shaky foundation on which white Western power asserts itself over a native landscape and peoples. In his analysis of Paule Marshall's fiction, Lloyd Brown argues that the political and the personal are not separate themes, but interwoven subjects of her novels: "She analyzes power not only as the political goal of ethnic and feminist movements, but also as social and psychological phenomena which simultaneously affect racial and sexual roles, shape cultural traditions and mould the individual psyche" (Brown 159). I have explored but one aspect of this power—how our bodies carry a personal and a historical memory forward, and how our bodies may be the conduits through which our subjectivity is integral to the landscape which bears memory as well. Merle's intention to return to Africa at the end of the novel is not only a journey aiming at a repossession of African culture, history, and identity, as scholars have argued, but suggestive of the landscape itself, and the reintegration of that body of land lost in the middle passage. In Marshall's novel, corporeality—like landscape—is resilient, imaginative, fluid, adaptive, changing, and unencumbered. And as her ever-changing body evolves out of the constraints of colonization, Merle pieces together the cultures that had fragmented her voice and her body in her storytelling.

Notes

[1] Dorothy Denniston notes the similarity between "Backra" and "Buckra," a word commonly used by African American slaves to denote a person of Caucasian descent (Denniston 117).
My thanks to Martin Japtok, for his tireless enthusiasm and insightful suggestions in the writing of this paper.

Works Cited

Brown, Lloyd. "The Rhythms of Power in Paule Marshall's Fiction." In *Novel: A Forum in Fiction*, 7 (Winter 1974): 159-167.

Christian, Barbara. *Black Women Novelists: The Development of a Tradition, 1892-1976.* Westport: Greenwood Press, 1980.

Denniston, Dorothy Hamer. *The Fiction of Paule Marshall: Reconstructions of History, Culture, and Gender.* Knoxville: University of Tennessee Press, 1993.

Knight, Franklin W. *The Caribbean: The Genesis of a Fragmented Nationalism.* New York: Oxford University Press, 1990.

Marshall, Paule. *The Chosen Place, The Timeless People.* 1969. New York: Vintage Books, 1984.

Rahming, Melvin B. *The Evolution of the West Indian's Image in the Afro-American Novel.* New York: Associated Faculty Press, Inc. 1986.

RISING IN THE ASHES: READING *KRIK? KRAK!* AS A RESPONSE TO "CAN THE SUBALTERN SPEAK?"

Carmen Nge

I

In Edwidge Danticat's collection of short stories *Krik? Krak!*, a mother says to her daughter: "We know people by their stories" (185). "[T]heir stories" is ambiguous: it could mean the stories people tell or the stories told about them by others. While we might not know the storyteller, "we know" suggests that there is a community of listeners, an audience who will receive these stories. This community of listeners need not be homogenous, since stories are often open to multiple interpretation and different listeners will employ different interpretive strategies. In thinking about the interrelationship and interaction between stories, storytellers, and audience, I am interested in exploring the ways in which people deal with stories about suicide. Suicide is an act that frequently opens itself to multiple interpretations; people who hear about death by suicide conjecture about its causes and effects, and there is often an active audience working to find meaning in the death.

I became interested in suicide as act and metaphor after a discussion of Spivak's essay, "Can the Subaltern Speak?", which is now a seminal text that not only foregrounds some of the key issues in post-colonial studies but also constitutes a kind of "canonical" text in the field.[1] In the essay, Spivak mentions Bhuvaneswari Bhaduri, a young woman who is conflicted about whether or not to undertake the task of political assassination in the interests of Indian independence but decides to take her own life instead. Spivak chooses to include the story about Bhuvaneswari in order to emphasize her point that the subaltern cannot speak, a conclusion she reaches at the end of her essay. I was puzzled by Spivak's conclusion because I had read Bhuvaneswari's death as a moment of resistance and defiance, even if her family did not. Even though she died before ever having a chance to speak her mind, her act of suicide can be seen as an act that needs no speech.

In her astute reading of the tragic event, Spivak herself makes the point that Bhuvaneswari's choice to wait for the onset of her menstruation before committing suicide can be seen as an indirect contestation of and rebellion against sati. But because the latter's family (specifically the female members) did not impute anything positive to her action—they chose to see it as an act of desperation resulting from an unwanted pregnancy—Bhuvaneswari's death was seen as shameful and was subsequently dismissed. Since the subaltern herself could not speak and since her community refused to speak on her behalf and to tell her story, Spivak seems to imply that Bhuvaneswari's act is not an act of agency. I was troubled by the privileging of speech as agency; surely the subaltern's act of suicide in this specific instance can be deemed an act of agency, even in the absence of a discourse surrounding the event.[2]

In the context of sati, where the moment of a woman's public recognition and validation occurs in conjunction with her sanctioned suicide, what does it mean for a woman to reject such an ominous rite of passage? What happens when she hangs herself in her father's apartment in North Calcutta? In the case of Bhuvaneswari, who takes her own life not only as an unmarried woman but as a menstruating single woman, her suicide becomes an act of agency that transcends the structures of choice constructed for her both in the course of her life as well as at the funeral pyre. Bhuvaneswari's suicide can be read as a double move of resistance: she not only refuses to enact and embody the fruition of Hindu law, she also frustrates any attempt to associate her death with heterosexual sex and its concomitant result. By doing so, she not only refutes the primacy of religious prescription, she also annuls the fulfillment of the final component of the rite of marriage—death with her husband. Although she is coded "subaltern," Bhuvaneswari does not allow herself to be sublimated by her status as a woman; she refuses to be subjected to the kinds of discursive understanding of the publicly sanctioned suicide that occurs on the funeral pyre. She will not be viewed as a spectacle to be consumed by the audience, acting in a manner that is understandable to them. Bhuvaneswari will not be understood; her death is not marked by meaning, in fact, it elicits puzzlement—"[t]he suicide was a puzzle" (Spivak 103). She locates herself outside the discursive frame of sati and by so doing, eludes definition, comprehension, and confinement to the structure of meaning-making shared by her community.

Spivak, however, resists this reading of the suicide because for her, the tragedy of the story lies not in Bhuvaneswari's death but in the fact that her death has been dismissed and ignored by her family and community. Since no-one could (or was willing to) read the death as a rewriting of sati using the body as text, the women who knew Bhuvaneswari's story read it as the result of illicit love Chinyere Okafor.[3] What is crucial here, according to Spivak, is not only the hermeneutical project but the problematic of internalized gender that denies Bhuvaneswari recognition of the defiance and resistance inherent in her act. As a result of having internalized their own gender oppression, the women who had knowledge of the story could not imagine an alternative reading of Bhuvaneswari's suicide—one that would identify it as a "subaltern rewriting of the social text of sati-suicide" (Spivak 104)—except to presume that it had to do with her wish to conceal her love. As such, Bhuvaneswari's suicide will always be "unemphatic" (Spivak 104).

While I can fully comprehend the "unemphatic" nature of Bhuvaneswari's suicide, I find this entire discussion revealing because it underscores the primacy of the female intellectual in this debate of sati-suicide. Spivak concludes:

> The subaltern cannot speak. There is no virtue in global laundry lists with "woman" as a pious item. Representation has not withered away. The female intellectual as intellectual has a circumscribed task which she must not disown with a flourish. (104)

By recognizing the persistence of representation with regard to the subject of the subaltern, Spivak implies that the project of agency would reside in the female intellectual, whose job it is to excavate a reading and understanding of Bhuvaneswari's death in a manner that imbues it with agency rather than stigma. By positioning the female intellectual in the arena of representation, Spivak makes an interesting move—she is not only evoking a moment of speaking *for* but of a speaking *about*. As a writer and intellectual herself, she is undeniably speaking out against sati by speaking about Bhuvaneswari. Spivak clearly privileges speech with regards to subaltern agency because Bhuvaneswari's story must be spoken. Speech is intimately tied to transmission and legacy: that which is uttered and heard can be told and retold, and for an intellectual such as Spivak, the tracing of speech is also intimately tied to writing. Bhuvaneswari's story can not be ignored because it is now inscribed in Spivak's own text, to be read and re-read by many readers to come.

In "Signature Event Context," Jacques Derrida states:

> A written sign ... is ... a mark which remains, which is not exhausted in the present of its inscription, and which can give rise to an iteration both in the absence of and beyond the presence of the empirically determined subject who, in a given context, has emitted or produced it.[4]

Bhuvaneswari's act of suicide, or the performance of her death, is never a presence captured but a disappearance; what remains is its inscription, the written sign representing the act. The space of writing thus becomes a space for recognition and validation— the written text captures the trace of her death act for its readers; it is a space that resists elision. While I am not interested in doing away with this notion of writing as an enabling space in which act and memory can be fixed, I think that Spivak's own position as a female intellectual in this context is important. Spivak's claim that the subaltern cannot speak evidently opens up a space for Spivak herself to speak, if not about the subaltern, then certainly for her.[5]

Since an act is as much a sign imbued with meaning as any written text, why is Bhuvaneswari's act of taking her life subordinate to her ability to speak? Of course, since speech disappears at the moment of death, the irony is that all death acts are speechless; this is not to say that death acts are devoid of power and impact. On the contrary, they often elicit a wide range of responses and reactions. In this regard, the subaltern's inability to speak in the event of her death is inevitable; nevertheless, we cannot wholly read her speechlessness as a lack of agency. In "Cultural Theory, Colonial Texts: Reading Eyewitness Accounts of Widow Burning," Lata Mani underscores and deconstructs this misreading: "It is not merely women's words that serve as testimonials to their condition. Women also spoke through their actions" (398). What is interesting about this speech-act is the fact that it cannot be adequately captured, but only experienced; archival work attempts to excavate the act but, in effect, it can only excavate the act's inscriptions. What is done is irremediably lost and what remains to be unearthed is the traces of the act located in archival texts. In "Can the Subaltern Speak?," the archive is the focus of Spivak's deconstructive practices; in effect, it is Spivak's emphasis on discourse—the subaltern's ability to speak—that provides for and enables her own scholarship.

II

My engagement with Spivak brings me back to *Krik? Krak!*, a collection of stories that, coincidentally, grapples with the intersection of death, speech, and writing. I will focus on two stories in particular that foreground this discussion—"A Wall of Fire Rising" and "Children of the Sea"—and specifically examine the two figures who enact their deaths in the course of the narrative: Guy, the father of Little Guy and husband to Lili, who dreams of flying a hot-air balloon; and Célianne, the teenage mother on board a leaking vessel full of Haitian refugees. Both characters embrace death in the stories but the very manner of their deaths and the contexts that occasion them are decidedly different. Nonetheless, as readers, our experiences of their deaths are very much connected to our perception of them as written narrative. Like Bhuvaneswari, both Guy and Célianne become known to us because they have been written about; however, unlike Bhuvaneswari's, both Guy and Célianne's suicides retain meaning as points of resistance and agency, neither misinterpreted nor elided.

In his discussion of death in the work of Rilke, Maurice Blanchot states:

> To die an individual death, still oneself at the very last, to be an individual right up to the end, unique and undivided: this is the hard, central kernel which does not want to let itself be broken. One wants to die, but in one's own time and one's own way. One doesn't want to die just anybody's undistinguished death.[6]

In "A Wall of Fire Rising," Guy dies a decidedly unique and distinguishable death: he jumps out of a hot-air balloon. The scene of death in the story cannot be divorced from the flying of the hot-air balloon; if Guy had not managed to get the balloon up in the air, he would not have been able to die in the manner that he does. It is his ability to fly the balloon that inspires awe and amazement; in fact, neither Assad, the owner of the balloon, nor the factory foreman can fathom how such a feat could be accomplished:

> "He's further away than he seems," said young Assad. "I still don't understand. How did he get up there? You need a whole crew to fly these things."
>
> "I don't know," the foreman said. "One of my workers just came in saying there was a man flying above the factory."
>
> "But how the hell did he start it?" Young Assad was perplexed.
>
> "He just did it," the foreman said. (Danticat 77)

Assad is "perplexed" because Guy defies what he expects of the latrine-cleaning Haitian man, someone he deems to be intellectually subordinate to him. Guy's action is a further affront to the sugar-mill heir because presumably, he had to steal the hot-air balloon before he could actually fly it; thus, his act of flying is enabled by his act of theft—an act of conscious defiance of the laws of property and ownership.

This act of defiance is sanctioned and celebrated by the workers in the factory: "Many were clapping and cheering, calling out Guy's name. A few of the women were waving their head rags at the sky, shouting, 'Go! Beautiful, go!'" (Danticat 76). Their cries of encouragement signify their solidarity with him, a fellow worker like themselves who they had accepted even though he had often stood apart from them. Throughout the narrative, Guy is portrayed as someone who did not usually participate in the nightly rituals of the group; he and his family disliked the atmosphere of the nightly news event, and since they did not take part in the viewing, they were also left out of the storytelling that ensued after the news. These storytelling sessions are significant because they can be seen as a nightly ritual of resistance—the people would wait until the gendarme left before they began, "cursing the authorities under their breath" (Danticat 60). Despite Guy's non-involvement, there is no indication that the people in the community ostracize or criticize him and his family. In fact, what is interesting about Guy's suicide is that we can infer the likelihood that his story will be told and retold among the community of storytellers. Unlike Bhuvaneswari's death, which is regarded as a shameful event that must be rejected and forgotten, Guy's death is not likely to be similarly dismissed. The community will remember him as they get together for the nightly news watch near the sugar mill and its fenced-up field, the place that Guy had trespassed in order to get to the hot-air balloon. The space will remind them of his death and some of their stories will revolve around Guy and the symbolic meaning behind his actions. I am not suggesting that all these stories will be similar—no doubt different members of the community will have different interpretations of the events and, over time, the meaning and frequency of stories of Guy's death is also likely to change.

Although we will never know the content of these stories, it is undeniable that Guy's feat will go unsurpassed, etched in the memory of his community. His stealing and flying of the hot-air balloon and his subsequent death mark him as unique, someone who rightly stands apart; nonetheless, his standing apart does not mean that he stands alone. In an interesting way, the fire that enables the hot-air balloon to fly reminds us of the bonfires that the community builds for their nightly story-telling. Paper, among other things, is used to make these bonfires—"They made bonfires with dried sticks, corn husks, and paper" (Danticat 60); similarly, Guy also uses paper to illustrate how the hot-air balloon flies:

> Guy reached into his shirt pocket and pulled out a lighter and a crumpled piece of paper. He lit the paper until it burned to an ashy film. The burning paper floated in the night breeze for a while, landing in fragments on the grass.
>
> "Did you see that, Lili?" Guy asked with a flame in his eyes brighter than the lighter's. "Did you see how the paper floated when it was burned? This is how that balloon flies." (Danticat 62)

This image of fire connects Guy to the people in his community, a shared image that symbolizes their collective resistance. The title of this story, "A Wall of Fire Rising," very appropriately conveys this collective force; the community's defiance is like a wall of fire, formidable and consuming, and at the same time, it refuses to be stopped, for it rises and will not be contained.

In "Children of the Sea," Célianne's death, unlike Guy's, does not come as a surprise to us. Her death is not only a foreshadowing of the imminent death of everyone else on board the vessel, it is also inextricable from the systematic torture, enslavement, and killing of her people—a community intimately acquainted with death: "... i hate those soldiers, those macoutes, and all those people here who shoot guns. on our way to ville rose, we saw dogs licking two dead faces. one of them was a little boy who was lying on the side of the road with the sun in his dead open eyes" (Danticat 19). In such a context, no-one is able to escape death; in fact, after Célianne dies, the narrator, who is on board as well, recognizes only one path for himself—it is the path that leads to the bottom of the sea.

> I go to them now as though it was always meant to be, as though the very day that my mother birthed me, she had chosen me to live life eternal, among children of the deep blue sea, those who have escaped the chains of slavery to form a world beneath the heavens and the blood-drenched earth where you live. (Danticat 27)

The death that the narrator envisions is not a space of erasure but a profoundly historical space; it connects him to a larger corpus of souls, to a sense of continuity and an affirmation of memory. Perhaps it is this connection, this rejection of corporeality in favor of a communion of spirits that frees Célianne. Interestingly, like the children of the sea who are released from their servitude through their deaths, Bhuvaneswari is released from the chains of religion, marriage, and sati by her act of suicide. Célianne, like Bhuvaneswari, does not speak, she only dies; however, unlike Bhuvaneswari, her death does not remain an elision. It is not set apart, disconnected from the history of deaths that has claimed her ancestors; in fact, the narrator captures her story in his notebook in its entirety.

Danticat's use of a narrator figure in her story is strategic because he functions as a storyteller of sorts; at the end of the story, we know that he dies when the boat he is on capsizes, but without him we may never have known of Célianne's story. Her tale resonates throughout his notebook entries because it accurately captures the realization of everyone else's despair and futility onboard the boat. Inasmuch as the narrator writes about Célianne and, in a sense, speaks for her, she also speaks for him and all the rest of the people onboard. It is perhaps no coincidence that the narrator is asked to discard his notebook only after Célianne's death. His words not only capture the trace of Célianne's death, they also act as means for his own self-creation. The entries in the narrator's notebook might not be read by his lover—"I know you will probably never see this" (Danticat 27)—nonetheless they open up a space of living, a space for the imagination to preserve his own life as well as the life of Célianne and others on board the vessel.

Although Danticat leaves ambiguous the possibility that the narrator's notebook, or even he himself, will be salvaged, in a subsequent story, "Caroline's Wedding," she alludes to Célianne's death. The women in this story—Ma and Gracina—attend a special church service on Sunday in remembrance of refugees who had drowned, one of whom sounds remarkably like Célianne.

> "We make a special call today for a young woman whose name we don't know," the priest said after he had recited all the [other names]. "A young woman who was pregnant when she took a boat from Haiti and then later gave birth to her child on the boat. A few hours after the child was born, its precious life went out, like a candle in a storm, and the mother with her infant in her arms dived into the sea." (Danticat 167)

Even though the people at the service do not know the name of this woman, it does not matter; she, along with the rest of the named, will be remembered in the Haitian community. As much as the wedding preparations and celebrations are an important aspect of the Haitian-American community in "Caroline's Wedding," the memorial service is no less significant. In a sense, they are both about unions—Caroline's marriage to Eric is a union of the living, and the memorial church service is a union between the dead and the living. Even the words used to refer to Caroline's move away from her familial home are remarkably similar to the words used to refer to the dead: "We will miss [Caroline] greatly, but she will never be gone from us" (Danticat 207).

The allusion to Célianne's death, thus, allows us to entertain the possibility that the narrator's notebook may have indeed been salvaged and read by other characters in the various stories. As Gracina mentions in "Caroline's Wedding," "Ma says all Haitians know each other" (Danticat 169), and stories are easily transmitted among them; because Danticat uses the narrator's notebook entries in her own book, we as readers are also invited into this community of listeners and storytellers. The interaction between the narrator and his girlfriend reflects our own interaction with Danticat's text; in a sense, we participate in the perpetuation of these stories by reading and sharing them with other future readers. In her essay on *Krik? Krak!*, Ellen Kanner underscores this emphasis on the perpetuation of stories that resist the elision of people and their histories: "The author's deceptively artless stories are not of heroes but of survivors, of the impulse toward life amid death and the urge to write and to tell in order not to forget."[7] There are echoes of this sentiment in "A Wall of Fire Rising," through the voice of Little Guy, who will go on to tell his father's story and prevent its erasure. In the same way as the narrator's notebook entries in "Children of the Sea" act as a bridge of writing, Little Guy's recitation for his school play acts as a bridge of speaking:

> *A wall of fire is rising and in the ashes, I see the bones of my people. Not only those people whose dark hollow faces I see daily in the fields, but all those souls who have gone ahead to haunt my dreams....* The boy continued reciting his lines, his voice rising to a man's grieving roar. He kept his eyes closed, his fists balled at his side as he continued with his newest lines. *"There is so much sadness in the face of my people. I have called on their gods, now I call on our gods. I call on our young. I call on our old. I call on our mighty and the weak. I call on everyone and anyone so that we shall all let out one piercing cry that we may either live freely or we should die."* (Danticat 78-79)

Little Guy's recitation of the slave revolutionary Boukman's speech begins to take on a new resonance and meaning when placed within the context of his father's death. The lines he recites are connected to a history of bondage and a call for freedom. Guy's suicide and the circumstances that caused it necessitate a resuscitation of the spirit of Boukman and his rallying cry to his people. His cry does not discriminate— "everyone and anyone" can participate in the struggle for liberation—and he advocates for a collective conscience, for "one piercing cry."

The two stories, "Wall of Fire Rising" and "Children of the Sea," certainly resonate with the title of Danticat's book. The stories recognize the call and response tradition of storytelling and the sense of community that is tied to the experience of orality: "over the years when you have needed us, you have always cried "Krik?" and we have answered "Krak! and it has shown us that you have not forgotten us" (Danticat 224). However, in her text, Danticat also foregrounds the connection between speech and writing: "It was their whispers that pushed you, their murmurs over pots sizzling in your head. A thousand women urging you to speak through the blunt tip of your pencil" (Danticat 222). For Danticat the writer, her act of writing is a response to the "whispers" and "murmurs" and "urging" of her female ancestors. Evidently, the "Krak!" for Danticat does not have to be primarily a verbal response; it can also be a response in the form of written words. If her female ancestors told stories in order to transmit history and to ensure its survival, Danticat writes stories to fulfill the same function. For her, writing and speaking are one, both affirming and memorializing the women who came before for those who will come in the future: "And this was your testament to the way that these women lived and died and lived again" (Danticat 224). As such, the literal response to "Krik?"—the stories that are written down and contained in the 224 pages of Danticat's book—resists death. Danticat herself tells us that her stories in *Krik? Krak!* "are more of a collective biography" and that she "knows someone it happened to or might have happened to. It's a lot of people's stories."[8] In a sense, then, Danticat's storytelling is akin to Spivak's retelling of Bhuvaneswari's tale; both writers are drawing from actual events and by reinscribing them for a larger audience are able to affect their transmission to others, even to those beyond the original community of people involved with the event itself.

III

> Can I die? Have I the power to die? This question has no force except when all the escape routes have been rejected. It is when he concentrates exclusively upon himself in the certainty of his mortal condition that man's concern is to make death possible. (Blanchot 96)

In his formulation of the relationship between suicide and mortality, Blanchot's coupling of death with power is important because it denies the association of suicide with disempowerment. However, the kind of suicide he talks about is imbued with power and agency only when the one attempting it can no longer envision a meaningful existence. His statement echoes the words of Steve Biko: "You are either alive and proud or you are dead" (152). For Biko it is simple: if one cannot imagine being alive *and* proud—these two things necessarily operate together—then one must only consider death. For him, the way in which one chooses to die can be coded "political"; thus, one's death can become a political act.[9] If we are to conceive of death in this way, then Guy, Célianne, and Bhuvaneswari's suicides can be seen as political acts.

Guy's suicide can be read as a conscious act of interruption; through the enactment of his own death, he intervenes in his future and interrupts the transmission of the "poor struggling" image that he inherits from his father:

> "You know that question I asked you before," he said, "how a man is remembered after he's gone? I know the answer now. I know because I remember my father, who was a very poor struggling man all his life. I remember him as a man that I would never want to be." (Danticat 75)

Célianne's suicide can be read as an act of power precisely because she rejects the only escape route possible—throwing her dead baby overboard and waiting for her inevitable death—and refuses to rest her hopes on futile imaginings of salvation and freedom among the living. Finally, Bhuvaneswari's suicide can be read as an act of agency not only because she refuses to codify her death as resulting from heterosexual passion, but also because she chooses to abide by her own moral codes—she will not participate in a political assassination—even if it means revoking her responsibilities to her nation's liberation struggle.

None of the three suicides occur in a vacuum; they obviously impact the people who know or hear of Guy, Célianne, and Bhuvaneswari. It is neither the case that one suicide is able to transmit more meaning than the others, nor that one is an act of agency and the others are not; rather, it is how people perceive these suicides that differentiates them. For both Guy and Célianne, their deaths are linked to the living by virtue of their transmission as acts of resistance and continuity; they are narrated as history to remind their descendants of the pain and loss that had to be endured in the name of freedom as well as personal and political autonomy. For Bhuvaneswari, her death has been construed as an enigma—a shameful enigma that needs to be forgotten because it leaves too much room for interpretation and it resists attempts to give it a singular meaning. But is such an act ever really forgotten? Surely, the fact that Spivak was able to unearth the story is indicative of its persistence in communal memory; Bhuvaneswari certainly did not need to speak in order to be remembered. Otherwise, how would Spivak have even known to ask?

Notes

1 Bellamy, Elizabeth Jane and Sandhya Shetty. "Post-colonialism's Archive Fever." Center for Literary and Cultural Studies, Barker Center, Harvard University: December 7, 1998. Spivak herself was also present during this presentation/discussion.

2 Benita Parry levies a similar argument in her essay "Problems in Current Theories of Colonial Discourse," where she is critical of both Spivak and Bhabha for their lack of interest in either thinking outside the bounds of discourse or envisioning an opposition to colonialism and oppression that is not tied to the primacy of discursive practices. As a side note, I want to emphasize that I am not arguing for all suicide to be read as an act of agency and resistance.

3 It is significant that Spivak identifies the usage of the word 'love' because illicit love does not have to do with sex. Thus, Bhuvaneswari's rejection of heterosexual sex as a reason for her suicide remains intact, uncontested.

4 Derrida, Jacques. "Signature Event Context." Trans. Alan Bass. *Margins of Philosophy*. Chicago: University of Chicago Press, 1982: 317.

5 In her most recent book, *A Critique of Postcolonial Reason: Toward a History of the Vanishing Present* (Cambridge, MA: Harvard University Press, 1999: 309), Spivak actually acknowledges her own double complicity: her speaking about Bhuvaneswari has been read by others as a speaking for her, thereby enabling the subaltern's speech even after death; at the same time, Spivak herself is aware that her own decipherment of the suicide should by no means be regarded a sufficient representation of the voice of the subaltern herself. Once again, I see that the primacy of the event is still very much based on a preoccupation with speech and its relationship to an audience

[6] Blanchot, Maurice. *The Space of Literature*. Trans. Ann Smock. Lincoln: University of Nebraska Press, 1982: 122

[7] Quoted in Bloom, Harold. (Ed), *Caribbean Women Writers*. Philadelphia: Chelsea House Publishers, 1997.

[8] Sturgis, Ingrid. "Young Author Reclaims Haiti's Stories as Birthright." Excerpted in Bloom, Harold. (Ed), *Caribbean Women Writers*. Philadelphia: Chelsea House Publishers, 1997.

[9] I am interpreting 'political' here in its broadest sense, i.e. not only having to do with a resistance against the oppressor, but also having a kind of resonance that goes beyond the individual, personal experience so as to have an effect on more than just one person.

Works Cited

Biko, Steve. *I Write What I Like*. London: Heinemann, 1978.

Blanchot, Maurice. *The Space of Literature*. Trans. Ann Smock. Lincoln: University of Nebraska Press, 1982.

Bloom, Harold. (Ed), *Caribbean Women Writers*. Philadelphia: Chelsea House Publishers, 1997.

Danticat, Edwidge. *Krik? Krak!* New York: Vintage Books, 1996.

Derrida, Jacques. "Signature Event Context." Trans. Alan Bass. *Margins of Philosophy*. Chicago: University of Chicago Press, 1982

Mani, Lata. "Cultural Theory, Colonial Texts: Reading Eyewitness Accounts of Widow Burning." Lawrence Grossberg et. al. (Eds.). *Cultural Studies*. London: Routledge, 1992: 392-405.

Parry, Benita. "Problems in Current Theories of Colonial Discourse." Ashcroft et al. (Eds.). *The Post-colonial Studies Reader*. London: Routledge, 1995: 36-44.

Trinh T. Minh-ha. "Writing Postcoloniality and Feminism" Ashcroft et al. (Eds.). *The Post-colonial Studies Reader*. London: Routledge, 1995: 264-268.

Spivak, Gayatri Chakravorty. "Can the Subaltern Speak?" Williams, Patrick and Laura Chrisman (Eds.). *Colonial Discourse and Post-Colonial Theory: A Reader*. New York: Columbia University Press, 1994.

———. A Critique of Postcolonial Reason: Toward a History of the Vanishing Present. Cambridge, MA: Harvard University Press, 1999.

(RE-)WRITING THE MARGINALIZED BODY: GRACE NICHOLS'S *THE FAT BLACK WOMAN'S POEMS*[1]

Melissa Johnson

"Her libido is cosmic, just as her unconscious is worldwide."

HÉLÈNE CIXOUS, "THE LAUGH OF THE MEDUSA"

"In the act of eating, as we have said, the confines between the body and the world are overstepped by the body; it triumphs over the world, over its enemy, celebrates its victory, grows at the world's expense."

MIKHAIL M. BAKHTIN, RABELAIS AND HIS WORLD

The two quotations above describe quite aptly the character Grace Nichols created in *The Fat Black Woman's Poems* (1984). Grace Nichols is a young Guyanese poet who has lived in Sussex since 1977. *The Fat Black Woman's Poems* is her second collection of poetry, following the critically acclaimed collection

I is a long memoried woman, which received the Commonwealth Poetry Prize in 1983 and is excerpted as the concluding section of *The Fat Black Woman's Poems.* She has published two subsequent collections, *Lazy Thoughts of a Lazy Woman* (1989) and *Sunris* (1996). In "The Battle with Language," an essay written for the First International Conference of Caribbean Women Writers, Nichols reflects on the origins and the achievements of "The Fat Black Woman's Poems," the first section of the volume:

> Although *The Fat Black Women's [sic] Poems* came out of a sheer sense of fun of having a fat black woman doing exactly as she pleases, at the same time she brings into being a new image—one that questions the acceptance of the "thin" European model as the ideal figure of beauty. The Fat Black Woman is a universal figure, slipping from one situation to the other, taking a satirical, tongue-in-cheek look at the world. (287)

The poems are fun and funny, but they are also revolutionary. In writing about a fat, Black, Caribbean woman in Britain, Nichols writes the female body, as Cixous instructed in "The Laugh of the Medusa," in a transgressive, binary-defusing way, and the body she writes functions as the grotesque body as defined by Bakhtin in *Rabelais and His World.*[2] The fat black woman, defined and marginalized in terms of race, gender, size, and post-colonial status, becomes—through Nichols's satire and the lens of Cixous and Bakhtin—the Fat Black Woman, a powerful and hopeful figure. She reclaims the heritage and pride imperialism has attempted to deny her and the Caribbean people and at the same time celebrates a syncretic multi-cultural existence.

I realize that using the theoretical frameworks of white European theorists, such as Bakhtin and Cixous, to elucidate the work of a Black Caribbean writer has its dangers. Deborah McDowell addresses the question of critical methodology in "New Directions for Black Feminist Criticism" and concludes that she is in agreement with Annette Kolodony who writes it "'would be shortsighted'" to reject "'all the inherited tools of critical analysis because they are male and western'" (1144). Rather than simply imposing a methodology or methodologies

on a text, I do, as Gina Wisker instructs in the introduction to
Black Women's Writing, attempt to recognize "the diverse
'otherness'" of Nichols's text and to understand "as far as
possible" the contexts from which it evolved (6). At the same
time, I intend to always keep before me the dangers of
universalizing or homogenizing the post-colonial experience and
thus denying its cultural and social specificity, as well as the
threat of theoretical colonization.[3]

Although Nichols depicts the Fat Black Woman as culturally
and racially distinct, this distinctiveness is one of hybridization.[4]
A hybrid or cross-cultural identity is created by the many strands
of culture—African, Caribbean and European—which combine
to form the consciousness of The Fat Black Woman. The
exploration of the nature of that consciousness through Bakhtin's
conception of the carnivalesque in Rabelais is not merely a
theoretical exercise but relies upon the historical connections and
societal parallels that exist between Medieval and Renaissance
England and the Caribbean, particularly the rites of Carnival.

As Stallybrass and White observe in *The Politics and Poetics
of Transgression*, the most effective applications of Bakhtin
"focus upon cultures which still have a strong repertoire of
carnivalesque practices ... where the political difference between
the dominant and subordinate culture is particularly charged"
(11). This is certainly true of the Caribbean and is demonstrated
in Nunley and Bettelheim's beautiful and insightful *Caribbean
Festival Arts: Each and Every Bit of Difference*. In an analysis of
aesthetic sources they note: "Caribbean festivals embody an
aesthetic formally rooted in the early European, African and
Asian traditions brought to the West Indies between the fifteenth
and nineteenth centuries." Like the Fat Black Woman, Caribbean
Carnival is hybrid, encompassing not only the European tradition
Bakhtin discusses but also "the African sensibility of
masquerade" and the Asian or East-Indian aesthetic (35).

Although Carnivals or folk festivals have become much more
about aesthetics, tourism, and consumerism than about
sanctioned release and reversal as compared to the Medieval and
Renaissance festivals Bakhtin writes about, Carnival in the
Caribbean is politicized and expresses class struggle. Rex

Nettleford's conclusion to *Caribbean Festival Arts* makes this clear:

> But to the ordinary people, festival arts ... affirm the use of the mask, literally and metaphorically, in coming to terms or coping with an environment that has yet to work in their interest, a society that is yet to be mastered and controlled by them, despite the coming of Independence. The ambush of the society under the cover of masquerades in festival has been one way of attempting control, if only a temporary one. ... Many students of Caribbean society past and present see the festival as a temporary respite from a world of drudgery, hardship and toil, whether under slavery, during colonialism, or in post-Independence. ... To be a King or a Queen for a day or two may well speak to a deep aspiration for recognition and status that elude the denigrated African in exile, the alienated worker, the jobless citizen with little sense of hope otherwise. (194-196)

Caribbean Carnival, in addition to incorporating the hierarchical reversals and transgressions of Bakhtinian Carnival, is a temporary release from a history of imperialism, slavery and racism as well as from contemporary economic stratification. In the introduction to her new collection, *Sunris*, Nichols discusses her own experiences with Caribbean Carnival, Guyana-style, and with its music, calypso:

> As a child, carnival, steel, pan, calypso, in fact anything that came from the ordinary folk including the Creole language itself were despised and regarded as products of a low-class consciousness by the colonial powers that be .... But despite various repressive measures, which included the banning of the drum, carnival continued to flourish. (2)

Nichols goes on to quote David Cuffy, who interprets Carnival as "a deeply resonant anniversary from the bondage of colonial slavery; a journey of freedom as well as a mechanism of social release" (qtd. in Nichols 2). In her work, Nichols extends the limited temporal and geographic boundaries of Carnival by creating a permanent textual space for transgression and release. Rather than writing out of oppression, Nichols writes a space outside of oppression. She creates this space through her carnivalesque re-writing of the marginalized female body.

As Gabriele Griffin observes in "'Writing the Body': Reading Joan Riley, Grace Nichols and Ntozake Shange," "Nichols's poetry is, in many respects, the perfect example of an *écriture féminine*" (33),[5] a term created by Hélène Cixous and defined in "The Laugh of the Medusa" as follows:

> A feminine text cannot fail to be more than subversive.
> It is volcanic; as it is written it brings about an upheaval
> ... in order to smash everything, to shatter the framework
> of institutions, to blow up the law, to break up the
> "truth" with laughter. (1099)

The "truth" which "The Fat Black Woman's Poems" breaks up is that a fat, black, Caribbean woman in London is a victim of sexism, sizism, racism, and imperialism. Rather than focusing on the binaries of Male/Female, thin/fat (desirable/undesirable), white/black, and British/Caribbean (Colonizer/Colonized) and on her victimization through the repeated privileging of the first terms, Nichols's Fat Black Woman reduces marginalisation to a failed shopping trip, pities the Miss World contestants, and creates a space where beauty is redefined. Nichols does not merely flip the binaries, as Susheila Nasta points out in *Motherlands: Black Women's Writing from Africa, the Caribbean and South Asia*, (xvi) but instead presents a different perspective, or as she herself says in "The Battle with Language," creates a "world a little more to my own liking" (289). That world is reminiscent of Bakhtin's carnival, a "temporary liberation from the prevailing truth and from the established order" which marks "the suspension of all hierarchical rank, privileges, norms and prohibitions" (Bakhtin 10). When we enter this world through the poetry of Grace Nichols, we must check all Western patriarchal and philosophical baggage at the door.

"Beauty," the first poem in the collection, alerts the reader that he or she is entering a Caribbean landscape where stereotypes do not apply. The locale can be inferred from the references to "fields" (3), "hibiscus" (5), "the sun" (7) and the "sea," (13) as well as Nichols's origins in Guyana. "Beauty" defines beauty as "a fat black woman," lit up by the sun and embraced by the sea. For anyone who owns a television or has seen a fashion magazine, this is not the "norm" or ideal for beauty either in appearance or action. Nichols addresses this issue in an interview with Kwame Dawes. In exploring how "the past of colonial history" causes tension in her attempt to synthesize the disparate cultural strands from which she is writing—Caribbean, European, and African—Nichols says:

> The fact that, I mean, all of our cultural "things" were denigrated and looked down upon while the European "things" were the ones celebrated in every way, even in terms of physical beauty. So there is always going to be that tension because some of these things still exist even today. So some of your writing will be a kind of reaction against that, impacting against it and at other times there is synthesis. (5)

"Beauty" is a reaction against the European definition of beauty that was and is privileged. Nichols redefines beauty and exposes it as a cultural and social construct. In this poem beauty, as well as being fat and black, is active and dependent on inner satisfaction and communion with nature rather than passive and dependent on approval and/or desire from other humans:

> riding the waves
> drifting in happy oblivion
> while the sea turns back
> to hug her shape (11-14)

Beauty is defined as obliviousness to the narrow and psycho-logically destructive constructions of beauty imposed by European culture and society. This does not necessarily imply that the fat black woman is ignorant of these constructions. A decisive abrogation of them is clear in the concluding lines of "Looking at Miss World." After losing hope that "some Miss" will "uphold her name" (3-4) and becoming disgusted at the "hopeful despair" of the "slim aspirants" (7 and 6),

The fat black woman gets up
and pours some gin
toasting herself as a likely win. (17-19)

This abrogation of European standards signals "a return to the body which has been more than confiscated from her [woman], which has been turned into an uncanny stranger on display," much like the contestants in Miss World (Cixous 1093).

As well as celebrating the female body in a pan-erotic manner which dovetails nicely with the recommendations of Cixous, "Beauty" is also the first toe in the water of the "boundless ocean of grotesque bodily imagery" (Bakhtin, *Rabelais* 319) in the sequence. Bakhtin defines "grotesque" as a style with the "fundamental attributes" of "exaggeration, hyperbolism and excessiveness" (303) and the grotesque body as "a body in the act of becoming" (317) as well as being "cosmic and universal ... stress[ing] elements common to the entire cosmos: earth, water, fire air" and with the ability to "merge with various natural phenomena" including seas and islands (318). Cixous also equates *écriture féminine* and its practitioners with the sea: "we are ourselves sea, sand, coral, seaweed, beaches, tides, swimmers, children, waves.... More or less wavily sea, earth sky—what matter would rebuff us?" (1100). The Fat Black Woman is consistently identified with the sea and becomes larger, both bodily and symbolically, as the sequence continues.

"The Assertion" follows "Beauty" and continues to define the Fat Black Woman's universe, and reveals its subversive origins. This poem displays the hyperbolism and defecatory imagery of the grotesque—the Fat Black Woman is now "Heavy as a whale" (1) and "sits / on the golden stool" (4-5)—as well as the uncrowning trope of Carnival. The Fat Black Woman has seized power from the "white robed chiefs" (7) as her "birthright" (14) and "refuses to move" (6). This is a political act which confronts patriarchal power with physicality and laughter—"giving a fat black chuckle / showing her fat black toes" (16-17)—just as "laughter and the material bodily lower stratum" are an essential part of the transgressions of folk carnival (Bakhtin, *Rabelais* 82), and the "Laugh of the Medusa" is a manifesto for how "to become at will the taker and initiator, for her own right, in every symbolic system, in every political process" (1094). It is important to note that The Fat Black Woman speaks as well as laughs here—"This is my birthright" (14). Her usurpation of the golden stool and seizure of her birthright are expressed through the description of her body that precedes her declaration:

> the fat black woman's fingers
> are creased in gold
> body ringed in folds
> pulse beat at her throat (10-13)

Her body expresses her seizure of power in the rings on her fingers and the robe (like that of the chiefs) with which her body is "ringed in folds." Her assertion is based on her history, which the "resignation" of the chiefs validates. That history includes not only the Caribbean heritage expressed in "Beauty" but the West African origins revealed in the artifacts of this poem. As Rattray reveals in *Ashanti*, the golden stool is an Ashanti heirloom, which "was never to be sat upon" (290). The stool was believed to contain the "*sunsum* (soul or spirit) of the Ashanti nation" and any insults to it were cause for execution or war (289). By sitting upon the golden stool rather than the silver stool of the Ashanti Queen Mother, The Fat Black Woman inserts her story into the his-story of the Ashanti. This assertion goes unchallenged in the Carnival space created in the text: "the white robed chiefs / are resigned / in their postures of resignation" (7-9). Rather than merely displacing the chiefs by reversing the hierarchical postitions of King and Queen, man and woman, The Fat Black Woman brings her history and that of the Ashanti women from the margin to the center, without marginalising the chiefs who originally occupied that center. Their resignation conveys acceptance of the usurpation of their power, without which it could not be usurped. The Fat Black Woman, frustrated by marginalisation, continues to confront history and other abstractions with physicality and the grotesque in "Thoughts drifting through the fat black woman's head while having a full bubble bath."

In this poem, The Fat Black Woman has grown even larger— she equates herself with the sky, the sea and the waves—and contemplates confronting the abstractions of anthropology, history, theology and the "slimming industry" with her "steatopygous" body.[6] Through her appropriation of this term, which has been used to depict African people as evolutionarily less civilized, the Fat Black Woman undermines and unmasks the monoglossic nature of that supposition. By applying this term to the sky, sea, waves and herself, the Fat Black Woman places her "foot / on the head of anthropology" (5-6), "swig[s] [her] breasts / in the face of history" (7-8) and scrubs her "back / with the dogma of theology" (9-10), triumphing over "all that oppresses and restricts" (Bakhtin, *Rabelais* 92) by bringing it "to the material level, to the sphere of ... the body" (19). This action not only frees the Fat Black Woman from the anthropology that has studied and labelled her "racial" characteristics[7] as anomalous, the European history which marginalises and stigmatizes her as a Caribbean woman and the ancestor of slaves, the Christian theology which denigrated African gods, and the diet industry which insists her size is unacceptable and unattractive, but also heralds her discovery of the "impregnable language that will wreck partitions ... and rhetorics, regulations and codes" (Cixous 1097). This "language" is discovered in writing the body through an appropriated discourse and thus it deconstructs that discourse, revealing the gaps in its representation. It is a language of the grotesque body through which, Bakhtin says, "a new, concrete and realistic historic awareness" may be born from "the living sense that each man [or woman] belongs to the immortal people who create history" (367).

The Fat Black Women's cross-culturality, her various histories, become the focus in "The Fat Black Woman Goes Shopping," which presents the whole mosaic of the heritage of the Fat Black Woman and her connection to and isolation from that heritage:

THE FAT BLACK WOMAN CURSES IN SWAHILI/YORUBA

and nation language under her breathing
all this journeying and journeying (15-17)

The Fat Black Woman is from the Caribbean. This is evident in the Creole diction and syntax in this poem, as well as in her knowledge of Swahili, Yoruba, and nation language. Swahili is an Eastern and Central African language, Yoruba a Nigerian one, and nation language is a term coined by E.K. Brathwaite meaning "the distinctive native dialect of an Afro-Caribbean country" (Allsopp 400-401). This poem is a wonderful illustration of Bakhtin's concept of heteroglossia as discussed in *The Dialogic Imagination*, one aspect of which is "the internal stratification of any single national language into social dialects" (262). Bakhtin himself was doubtful that poetry could demonstrate heteroglossia: "The concept of many worlds of language, all equal in their ability to conceptualize and to be expressive, is organically denied to poetic style" (286). The comments that Nichols makes in the interview with Dawes on her own use of a continuum of language in her work belie these conclusions: "It's not really very, very intense Creole at times or very standard English; there are so many registers and mixtures which I like using and exploring" (2-3). Bakhtin does not deny the possibility of a dialogic poetry but argues it only exists in satiric and comic genres, which he classifies as "low" (287).[8]

Although *The Fat Black Woman's Poems* is certainly satiric, it is not "low" poetry except in its carnivalesque emphasis on the lower body. Bakhtin does not seem to have considered the use of dialects in poetry or the poetic technique of dramatic monologue, in which the speaker is not only removed from the poet and the poet's language, but also maintains a singular voice through which heteroglossia can be expressed "as an aspect of the word doing the depicting" (287).

Only two poems of the sequence, "Invitation" and "Thoughts drifting through the fat black woman's head while having a full bubble bath," are traditional dramatic monologues. They also exhibit heteroglossia in their use of Creole as well as in their appropriation of pop culture phrases—"Come up and see me sometime"—and the jargon of anthropology. The majority of "The Fat Black Woman's Poems" are not traditional dramatic monologues but they engender heteroglossia through their elision of the speech of The Fat Black Woman with that of the speaker/poet within the sequence and within individual poems as well as through their use of the Creole continuum. Both "The Fat Black Woman's Instructions to a Suitor" and "Small Questions Asked by the Fat Black Woman" can be read as poems quoting the Fat Black Woman and thus as a combination of her voice and the voice of the poet who attached the title and wrote the poem. "The Fat Black Woman Composes a Black Poem..." and "... And a Fat Poem" are presented as creations of the Fat Black Woman, who in this way becomes a distinctly separated voice from the speaker, although this complicates her relationship with the poet who has attached the titles.

This complication and elision of the voices and identities of the Fat Black Woman and the poet/speaker is most evident in "The Fat Black Woman Goes Shopping." The shared use of both Standard English and Creole and the lack of punctuation to differentiate The Fat Black Woman's speech from the text of the poem makes it difficult to separate the voices but clearly demonstrates the presence of more than one voice:

> Shopping in London winter
> is a real drag for the fat black woman
> going from store to store
> n search of accommodating clothes
> and de weather is so cold
>
> Look at the frozen thin mannequins
> fixing her with grin
> and de pretty face salesgals
> exchanging slimming glances
> thinking she don't notice
>
> Lord is aggravating (1-11)

This use of the Creole continuum, defined as "not simply an aggregation of discrete dialect forms but an overlapping of ways of speaking between which individual speakers may move with considerable ease," utilizes heteroglossia to express The Fat Black Woman's multiple heritages (Ashcroft, Griffiths and Tiffin 47). The combination of Nichols's use of Creole and the multilingualism that she attributes to The Fat Black Woman is a metonymic device for "insert[ing] the truth of culture into the text" by employing language use as a synecdoche for the cultural experience it signifies (Ashcroft et al. 52-53). When this device is understood, the "journeying and journeying" of line 17 can be seen to refer not only to the shopping trip but also to the Middle

Passage and the "exile" to Britain; the post-colonial Black British experience encompasses all of these journeys. This woman has come this far only to be sneered at by "salesgals" for her size. As stated earlier, this is the only representation in the sequence of The Fat Black Woman's marginalisation and ostensibly it is based only upon her size. By the end of the poem, she has laughed it off, making a joke at her own expense:

> The fat black woman could only conclude
> that when it come to fashion
> the choice is lean
>
> Nothing much beyond size 14 (18-21)

Representative of the grotesque and/or carnivalesque, in its use of the marketplace language of cursing and the ability to laugh at one's self, this poem also expresses the idea stated more explicitly in "Trap Evasions,"

> Refusing to be a model
> of her own affliction
> the fat black woman steers clear
> of circles that lead nowhere (1-4)

Rather than dwelling on the various isms of oppression, these poems push them to the margins, defining The Fat Black Woman in terms of power and strength rather than affliction.

"Invitation," which asserts The Fat Black Woman's control over her own body and defines her diffuse sexuality, reinforces this emphasis on strength and self-determination. This dramatic monologue is divided into two sections. In the first, The Fat Black Woman makes clear that she is aware of and comfortable with her fat, and does not need to be advised on it:

> If my fat
> was too much for me
> I would have told you
> I would have lost a stone or two
> . . . .
> But as it is
> I'm feeling fine
> feel no need

to change my lines (1-5, 13-16)

This section ends with an invitation to "Come up and see me sometime" (18). This phrase, made famous by Mae West, suggests an aggressive and healthy sexuality. The second section of the poem repeats the invitation, twice in the first two lines, and is followed by a description of The Fat Black Woman's charms which are identified with fruit, seals, the sea, and an exaggerated largeness. Like the grotesque body, her body "outgrows its own self" and becomes part of the world. The emphasis is on the lower body and the sexual organs while the second part of the poem focuses on one of "the main events in the life of the grotesque body ... copulation" (Bakhtin, *Rabelais* 317). This poem restores to The Fat Black Woman "her goods, her pleasures, her organs, her immense bodily territories" through the act of writing and celebrating that body (Cixous 1093).

In the seventeen poems which make up the series of "The Fat Black Woman's Poems," Grace Nichols writes the body of a Fat Black Woman and transforms that traditionally marginalized figure into a hybridized figure of subversion and empowerment which is indomitable, even in death. Like the grotesque body, the body of The Fat Black Woman is really two bodies; "one body offers its death, the other its birth" (Bakhtin, *Rabelais* 322) Although the Fat Black Woman imagines her funeral in "Tropical Death," the final poem of the collection, "Afterword" equates her with the "ancestral body, which is renewed in the next generation," an aspect of the grotesque as defined by Bakhtin (322). This poem prophesies the Fat Black Woman's joyful re-emergence from the forest:

> behold now the fat black woman
> who will come out of the forest
>
> when the last of her race
> is finally and utterly extinguished
>
> when the wind pushes back the last curtain
> of male white blindness (13-18)

The Fat Black Woman will emerge at some point in the future
and can be seen now. As Bakhtin defines it:

> One of the fundamental tendencies of the grotesque
> image of the body is to show two bodies in one: the one
> giving birth and dying, the other conceived, generated,
> and born. This is the pregnant and begetting body, or at
> least a body ready for conception and fertilization, the
> stress being laid on the phallus or the genital organs.
> (26)

The Fat Black Woman "will come out of the forest ... flaunting
waterpearls / in the bush of her thighs" (2, 5-6), an obvious
reference to sexual readiness, even though "the last of her race"
has already died. Just as the grotesque body cannot be degraded
and cannot die within the realm of carnival, The Fat Black
Woman will always return to "stake her claim again" (21).

Although empowering, funny and subversive, the transformation of the Fat Black Woman from a marginalized victim
into a triumphant survivor, like Bakhtin's Carnival, is temporary
and qualified. It exists only in the imagination and consciousness
of the Fat Black Woman and in these poems. Although the
poems create a textual space of transgression that will outlast the
temporal and geographic boundaries of Carnival, they must be
read for that space to exist. There are few enough readers for
poetry, and even fewer for Caribbean poetry, and even fewer
than that for Caribbean poetry by women, as Bruce Woodcock
observes:

> If we look at the history of women poets in the English-
> speaking Caribbean ... the situation is similarly one of
> marginalisation.... The women ... have only recently
> made inroads into what itself is a fairly new male literary
> domain. (56)

By writing about Nichols, I hope to encourage others to read her,
to make a space for the beauty and spirit of the Fat Black
Woman, the Long Memoried Woman and the Lazy Woman. As
Cixous insists and I want to believe:

> writing is precisely *the very possibility of change*, the
> space that can serve as a springboard for subversive

thought, the precursory movement of a transformation of social and cultural structures. (1093)

"The Fat Black Woman's Poems" are a hopeful and powerful vision of a new syncretic heritage and future that combines all the disparate strands of post-colonial culture. Nichols's reaction to the diaspora, racism and sexism is to satirize and combat marginalisation and oppression through the carnivalesque figure of The Fat Black Woman. It is an admirable response.

Notes

1   I would like to thank Ed Madden and Kwame Dawes for their guidance and feedback on this essay as it evolved.

2   I am following here in the footsteps of Evelyn O'Callaghan's *Woman Version* which utilizes the work of Cixous, Irigaray, and Bakhtin in reading Nichols's novel *Whole of the Morning Sky,* as well as Elizabeth Cullingford's Bakhtinian interpretation of another transgressive marginalized figure, Crazy Jane.

3   See Ashcroft, Griffiths and Tiffin's *The Empire Writes Back* for a more complete discussion of the dangers of universalizing. Surprisingly, as the quotation from Nichols above indicates, she herself interprets the Fat Black Woman as a universal figure. However, Nichols's conception of "universal" seems to be closer to Wilson Harris's concept of the cross-cultural explored in *The Womb of Space: The Cross-Cultural Imagination* than to the universal as an imposed cultural construct which privileges the European as the norm.
See Ketu Katrak's "Decolonizing Culture" on the need for theoretical models for postcolonial women's writing which recognize and perpetuate the social responsibility of the texts, without "appropriat[ing] 'third world' texts within an intellectual hegemony" (160).

4   "Hybridity" is the basis for one model used in post-colonial theory and informs the theories of Homi Bhabha, Wilson Harris, and Edward Brathwaite. It derives from "a consideration of the nature of post-colonial societies and the types of hybridization their various cultures have produced" (Ashcroft, Griffiths and Tiffin 34). Guyana, where Nichols was born and grew up, is perhaps the most hybrid country of the Caribbean due to its mixture of native Amerindians, Africans imported as slaves, East Indians, Chinese, Portuguese imported as indentured laborers, and the European descendants of the Dutch and English colonizers.

5   Griffin was referring specifically to what she sees as the "not purely cerebral" but performative appeal of *I Is a Long Memoried Woman* (33). The observation is perhaps more valid for *The Fat Black Woman's Poems.*

6   Steatopyga is defined by the OED as "A protuberance of the buttocks, due to an abnormal accumulation of fat in and behind the hips and thighs, found (more markedly in women than in men) as a racial characteristic of

certain peoples, esp. the Hottentots and Bushmen of South Africa." This term, although of Greek origin, was used to describe African people in 1822 by W.J. Burchell. Burchell was careful not to apply it as a generalized characteristic; later anthropologists, and Darwin, were not so discerning.

[7] By referring to "racial" characteristics or "racial" differences I do not mean essential or biological differences between the "races" but refer rather to those differences of morphology and phenotype that are and have been used to designate or categorize persons as belonging to specific races.

[8] For discussions of the applicability of heteroglossia to poetic works see Karen Simroth James's "On veult responce avoir: Pernette du Guillet's Dialogic Poetics" and David Richter's "Dialogism and Poetry."

Works Cited

Ashcroft, Bill, Gareth Griffiths and Helen Tiffin. *The Empire Writes Back: Theory and Practice in Post-colonial Literatures.* London: Routledge, 1989.

Allsopp, Richard, ed. *Dictionary of Caribbean English Usage.* New York: Oxford University Press, 1996.

Bakhtin, M.M. *The Dialogic Imagination: Four Essays.* Trans. Caryl Emerson and Michael Holquist. Austin: University of Texas Press, 1981.

——. *Rabelais and His World.* Trans. H. Iswolsky. Bloomington: Indiana University Press, 1984.

Cixous, Hélène. "The Laugh of the Medusa." Trans. Keith and Paula Cohen. *Signs* I (1976). Rpt. in Richter 1090-1102.

Cullingford, Elizabeth. "Crazy Jane and the Irish Episcopate." *Gender and History in Yeats's Love Poetry.* Cambridge: Cambridge University Press, 1993. 227-244.

Griffin, Gabriele. "'Writing the Body': Reading Joan Riley, Grace Nichols and Ntozake Shange." *Black Women's Writing.* Ed. Gina Wisker. New York: St. Martin's Press, 1993. 19-42.

Harris, Wilson. *The Womb of Space: The Cross-Cultural Imagination.* Westport, Connecticut: Greenwood Press. 1983.

James, Karen Simroth. *"On veult responce avoir: Pernette de Guillet's Dialogic Poetics."* *A Dialogue of Voices: Feminist Literary Theory and Bakhtin.* Eds. Karen Hohne and Helen Wussow. Minneapolis: University of Minnesota Press, 1994. 171-192.

Katrak, Ketu H. "Decolonizing Culture: Toward a Theory for Postcolonial Women's Texts." *Modern Fiction Studies.* 35.1 (1989) : 157-79.

McDowell, Deborah E. "New Directions for Black Feminist Criticism." *Black American Literature Forum* 14:4 (1980). Rpt. in Richter 1137-1146.

Nasta, Susheila. Introduction. *Motherlands: Black Women's Writing from Africa, the Caribbean and South Asia.* New Brunswick, New Jersey: Rutgers University Press, 1991. xiii-xxx.

Nichols, Grace. "Caribbean Writers Talk Yuh Talk: Interviews with Caribbean Poets." *Talk yuh Talk: Interviews with Caribbean Poets*. Kwame Dawes. Charlottesville: University of Virginia Press, 1998.

———. "The Battle with Language." *Caribbean Women Writers: Essays from the First International Conference*. Ed. Selwyn R. Cudjoe. Wellesley, Massachusetts: Calaloux Publications, 1990. 283-289.

———. *The Fat Black Woman's Poems*. London: Virago Press, 1984.

———. *Sunris*. London: Virago Press, 1996.

Nunley, John W. and Judith Betteheim. *Caribbean Festival Arts: Each and Every Bit of Difference*. Seattle: University of Washington Press, 1988.

O'Callaghan, Evelyn. *Woman Version: Theoretical Approaches to West Indian Fiction by Women*. New York: St. Martin's Press, 1993.

Rattray, Capt. R.S. *Ashanti*. Oxford: The Clarendon Press, 1923.

Richter, David, ed. *The Critical Tradition: Classic Texts and Contemporary Trends*. New York: St. Martin's Press, 1989.

———. "Dialogism and Poetry." *Studies in the Literary Imagination*. 23.1 (1990) : 9-27.

Stallybrass, Peter and Allon White. *The Politics and Poetics of Transgression*. Ithaca: Cornell UP, 1986.

"Steatopyga." *OED*. 2nd ed. 1989.

Wisker, Gina. "Introduction. Black and White: Voices, Writers and Readers." *Black Women's Writing*. New York: St. Martin's Press, 1993. 1-18.

Woodcock, Bruce. "'Long Memoried Women': Caribbean Women Poets." *Black Women's Writing*. New York: St. Martin's Press, 1993. 55-77.

III: AFRICAN WRITERS

Ramatoulaye's Letter: Cross-Cultural Reading Strategies & the Criticism of Mariama Ba's So Long a Letter

Merri Lisa Johnson

Rather than emphasizing the impossibilities of reading across man-made and, hence, fundamentally arbitrary lines, I posit that a willingness to acknowledge that race and gender are constructed can enable rather than disable provocative journeys.

Michael Awkward

I. Reading Lessons

Letters bridge large distances. For five years my grandmother has sent me a hand-written personal letter every week from Georgia to Ohio and later from Georgia to New York. The thin pages from my grandfather's retired doctor's practice arrive each Friday, filled with details from her homemaker life: gardens, weather, get-togethers. The distance they bridge is geographical, creating a connection between us to assuage our strange apartness—atypical for our family, all of whom live in Carroll

County or gravitate back there after a period of adventure or schooling. The distance bridged by Grandma's letters also spans an internal geography. I am not "laid out" the same way she is. Religion, sexuality, language: we have different desires in all these areas. Reading her weekly letters is like poring over the architecture of her soul, seeing where her frame mismatches with mine, and where it joins me again. This work of perceiving in the details clues to what matters to her gives me good practice in reading the texts of women who differ from me; I am able to see in her stories a lens on a world I do not share, yet wish to appreciate, to decipher and understand. Through her letters I received the lesson that interacting with other people and their texts requires an elasticity of perspective, an ability to dialect-switch, to hear the nuances of difference and sameness across cultural chasms marked by generation gaps (between me and Grandma) or wide oceans (between me, a white American critic, and the black African women authors I study). Letters (epistles and literature) bring us closer together, allow us opportunities to practice listening and responding to each other.

In reading the novels of African women, I engage in what Maria Lugones calls "playful 'world'-travelling."[1] As much as has been made of the differences between white women's feminism and the feminisms of women of color, I see connections between my dilemmas as a white woman and the dilemmas of African women. Similar issues of sexual colonization appear in their novels and my own writing. However, in the white Western critical interpretations of African women's novels I also find patterns of bias that distort this literature through projections of American women's desires, fears, and culturally-specific histories of oppression. Who am I to stand in judgment of these women critics? No one, really, just a reader of Grandma's letters-a woman who is as different from me as an African woman, and as much the same. Through her, I am seeking out a way to connect with another woman without requiring her to be like me, to recognize her as similar but separate from me, to widen my own psychological landscape by accomodating her value system as valid even as I choose a different one. I used to think she had failed as an independent woman because she willingly defers the television remote control to PaPa, because she majored in home economics and made a career of wifehood, because she lived to please a man, attended the local Methodist church and submitted to its patriarchal teachings, self-subordinating at every turn, or so it seemed. I still question whether her choices support a liberatory world for women, but I am learning not to judge her as failed by my standards, and instead to measure her by the standards she set for herself, by the degree of happiness she has achieved, by her effect on the people around her. In all these ways, she is a success, maybe even a feminist of sorts, though not my kind. This is my reading lesson: to allow difference to survive in my critical world, to allow for the possibility that I am neither at the center of feminism or the world, nor paradigmatic of women's social desires.[2] With this exercise in mind, I turn to a set of critical articles on Mariama Ba's epistolary novel, *So Long a Letter*.

II. Ramatoulaye's Letter

So Long a Letter formulates itself as a book-length letter from Ba's main character, Ramatoulaye, to her best friend, Aissatou, written during her forty-day confinement as a widow in Islamic Senegal. The letter provides a space in which Ramatoulaye can reflect on her experiences and choices as an African woman whose husband took a second wife (a common practice in Islamic cultures) and abandoned his first wife emotionally and financially (a less common practice) for a girl the age of their daughter. Ba explores the questions of polygamy, patriarchy, and female subjectivity in the contexts of African and United States cultures by juxtaposing Ramatoulaye's decision to stay with her husband despite his injurious behavior with Aissatou's decision to leave when faced earlier with similar circumstances. In writing this letter, Ramatoulaye develops an understanding of her own actions, her own desires, and the different but valid actions and desires of her absent friend, and through this exploration, Ba deals with the difficult entanglement of sexism and tradition without lapsing into oversimplified prescriptions of either feminism or nationalism for African women.

Ba thematizes writing in ways that suggest this letter should be considered a form of self-constitution and a method of revolution in gender identity for her African woman protagonist. In their introduction to *In Other Words: Writing as a Feminist*, Gail Chester and Sigrid Nielson describe writing in ways that illuminate the importance of Ba's use of the letter as a link between oral communities and arenas of political action: "Writing is essential to women's struggle for liberation from second-class status, poverty and enforced silence. Feminism, literacy and education for women are closely linked worldwide" (9). Describing the activist possibilities of writing, Chester and Nielson express a view that, when applied to Ba's novel, sheds a strongly positive light on Ramatoulaye as a writer:

> Learning to organize thoughts on paper, to express feelings, to respond to others, is an enormous extension of women's power. It allows for communication over time as well as distance.... Though feminist action takes place in groups, it starts with each woman's personal conviction. (17)

Ramatoulaye, in engaging in the act of writing, in appreciating the worth of her own voice, and in exploring freely the shapes of her own ideas even as they conflict with those of her cultural background, creates a space in which to discover her own "personal conviction," a discovery integral to feminist actions such as revising one's self-perception and one's relationship to the world.

In the essay, "Words are Weapons," (the title of which indicates again the relation of writing to revolution), Pratibha Parmar reiterates the position "that writing is a crucial form of action.... a powerful means of protest and change for subjugated people all over the world" (149). Parmar points to writing as a way of exploding systems of oppression: "While writing can not always be a substitute for action, words are nevertheless powerful weapons in the struggle against imprisonment, exclusion and invisibility" (149). These are precisely the struggles to which Ramatoulaye is subjected by her patriarchal culture and against which she writes. Her "ebb and tide of images" become a force that undergirds Ramatoulaye's sense of self-worth by confronting and cultivating her own "take" on reality. This view of writing is advanced with strength by

Chandra Mohanty, who asserts that "the very practice of remembering and rewriting leads to the formation of politicized consciousness and self-identity. Writing often becomes the context through which new political identities are forged. It becomes a space for struggle and contestation about reality itself" (34).

These statements could, however, apply to any oppressed group (African men included); what differentiates African women's thematic use of writing from men's is the framework out of and against which they write—men assert a black voice in a system that works to silence nationalist concerns, and women assert a black female voice in a system that would continue to subordinate their voices even in post-independence societies. Ba speaks of this coercion to silence: "In all cultures, the woman who demands or protests is devalued" (qtd. in Miller 271). In fact, Ba herself writes of the "special task" of "the woman writer in Africa" which she sees as the need to "overthrow the status quo which harms us," and she designates "literature as a non-violent but effective weapon" in this battle (qtd. In Miller 271-72). Parmar asserts the vital necessity for Black women to "become visible in ways we can control," and states that "writing is one way of doing this" (153) in a creative and subversive manner. Ramatoulaye's letter, her "prop," as she calls it, holds her up, makes her visible to herself-and more broadly to the world of African and Western readers in whose hands Ba places it.

Abena P. B. Busia, in her evocatively titled essay, "Words Whispered over Voids: A Context for Black Women's Rebellious Voices in the Novel of the African Diaspora," also subscribes to "the belief that [black women's]narratives can be transformational" as "a process of affirmation, to proclaim that selfhood, our very own, which has heretofore been 'othered'" (1). Ramatoulaye's letter contributes to such a project by invoking the image of woman-as-author in the context of a Senegalese culture that does not traditionally include such an image. As a "prop in [her] distress" (1), the letter Ramatoulaye writes acts both as therapy and non-violent weapon. The present "need to hear words whispered over voids, to learn what it is we must tell each other, despite the vagaries of our respective conditions, across the generations of time and the enormities of space" (2) to which Busia attends, speaks to a context in which voice is central and crucial, and in which conversation and listening are priorities.

The epistolary form of *So Long a Letter*, unusual in African literature,makes a gesture of communication among women in different cultures,specifically between the African woman writer and the woman reader in theUnited States.[3] Ramatoulaye begins:

I have received your letter. By way of reply, I am beginning this diary, my prop in my distress. Our long association has taught me that confiding in others allays pain.... The past is reborn, along with its procession of emotions. I close my eyes. Ebb and tide of feeling: heat and dazzlement, the woodfires, the sharp green mango, bitten into in turns, a delicacy in our greedy mouths. I close my eyes. Ebb and tide of images: drops of sweat beading your mother's ochre-coloured face as she emerges from the kitchen, the procession of young wet girls chattering on their way back from the springs. (1)

This sensual description of memory marks the letter as a conjure-space, where bodies are brought (back) together through the power of language. The novel closes before Ramatoulaye actually hands the letter over to Aissatou, leaving it structurally poised towards exchange. Mildred Mortimer, in her article on the narratee's role in this novel, reads "the act of writing as a process of disclosure that promotes discovery and ... clearly reinforces female bonding" (76). Christopher Miller similarly argues that although the "moment of closure remains outside the scope of the novel ... the symbolic act of handing over this text to a friend seems to reinforce the positive image of literature that Ba promotes: the text we are reading is a tangible sign of the link between the two women, and that link can lead to others" (289). The letter that comprises this novel functions as a literary device through which Ba mediates what Mortimer calls "the conflict between the patriarchal tradition that confines African women to domestic space and women's struggle to claim public space" (69); the letter bridges the distance between private and public space, representing Ramatoulaye's negotiation of the tension between women's bodies and patriarchal restrictions of motion, presence, and voice.

The novel invites a reading of letter-writing as a form of community building within Africa and among women at large, as the final note Ba sounds is one of hope for community, evoking a sense that the journey towards happiness is worth the risk of "hav[ing] to write you so long a letter" (89). Women emerging from shadows and green plants sprouting from dirty hummus represent a future of collective possibility through images of regeneration, awakening, and correspondence. In the gesture of writing this long letter, Ba strives to sort through the complicated issues facing Ramatoulaye and other similarly conflicted women by entering into a cross-cultural conversation about women's identities in relation to African and other national patriarchal traditions. The problems surrounding such an exchange loom large, from the effects of the United States marketplace on the African canon to the appropriation by Western feminists of African women's stories to exemplify Western literary theories[4]; nevertheless, the letter is here, in my hands and yours, and we must try to read it well. Ba criticism to date ranges from nuggets of startling insight to troublesome critical moves; by looking at these in detail, it is possible to pinpoint useful techniques of cross-cultural reading, and less useful ones as well.

Let me begin with the most effrontive example. I find it surprising that, as late as 1991, a critic could use constructions such as "universality" versus the merely "parochial" appeal in African literature without problematizing or at least qualifying them in some way, yet Glenn W. Fetzer employs that very contrast in his article on "Women's Search for Voice and the Problem of Knowing in the Novels of Mariama Ba." The point hardly needs to be made again that this equation of the culturally-specific and non-Western with the parochial, that is the small and less significant, as opposed to the "human" issues that "transcend" the "Third World" (31) is a racist social construction of reality. Fetzer proceeds to analyze the theme of "self-realization" in Ba's novels as it is "informed by the way [the characters] individually perceive reality" (33, my emphasis). While the reading touches on interesting aspects of the novel— epiphanic and defining moments in the lives of various women characters—it fails to contextualize Ba's characters perceptions of reality. Certainly African views of voice and knowledge and, most of all, of selfhood as primarily communal should influence any critical approach to these themes in an African novel. Indeed, because of the absence of this dimension, Fetzer's analysis remains very much on the surface of Ba's novels, looking solely to a Western feminist study "on epistemological development in women" (*Women's Ways of Knowing: The Development of Self, Voice and Mind,* edited by Mary Field Belenky, et al), as the interpretive context.

Fetzer posits this text as "instrumental in contextualizing the protagonists in Ba's novels" (34) without regard to the problem of translating cultural concepts from Western to African women's lives and texts. Although the conclusions drawn by this critic amount to nothing outrageously out of sync with the characters he analyzes—in fact, his reading of Ramatoulaye's letter as a therapeutic and consciousness-raising tool seems accurate and insightful—his remissness about cultural context nevertheless prevents a full assessment of the development he perceives, and his stagnation on the level of "individual experience" derails the political possibilities of Ba's narrative; pain and injustice remain simply matters of individual or "human" lives rather than appearing in the communal and structural light in which Ba casts them. The critique of cultural and religious customs such as Islamic standards of beauty or the institution of polygamy embedded and resisted in Ramatoulaye's "search for voice and problems of knowing" becomes in Fetzer's analysis bleached and neutered, Ba's culturally specific themes recuperated into a repertoire of "universal concepts" such as "love, happiness, choice, and self-expression" which are "common to all cultures" (41). The idea of liberating and affirming the "true selves" (40) of Ba's female characters would indeed be more meaningful if anchored in the real material circumstances which imprisoned and discounted these selves in the first place.

In addition to abstracting African women's novels into "universal" themes, another problem apparent in Ba criticism is the urge to judge the main character.[5] For example, critics frequently stumble over Ramatoulaye's decision not to leave her husband after he takes a second wife, a decision that marks her as a traditionalist, a victim to many Western readers, but

discussions of *So Long a Letter* that dwell on this question are
not only distorted by Western eyes that latch onto the
"aberrations" of "otherness," they are also willfully blind to the
facts of cultural constraints, the boundaries within which
Ramatoulaye's decisions had to be made. Asking whether she
was a weak or strong woman frames the discussion of this novel
in ways that divert critical attention from evaluating societal
superstructures within which characters are contained. This
question formed the boundaries of a discussion of *So Long a
Letter* in a graduate course on "The African Novel" in which I
participated. It also appears in published Ba criticism; Mildred
Mortimer notes that socio-political approaches to this novel form
a consensus "that Ramatoulaye, the heroine, is a victim of a
society that endorses and encourages polygamy, but [critics]
disagree as to whether she uses her energies heroically to
overcome obstacles or to reproach bitterly the patriarchal
structure" (69-70). The latter question disturbs me in its focus on
categorizing the individual as a good or bad role model, a gesture
that flirts with critical colonization by asking the character to
become who the reader needs her to be instead of examining the
story as a dramatization of problematic cultural conditions and
limited choices within those conditions. I am not convinced that,
as Mortimer asserts, "[t]he reader's task in this work is to
evaluate Ramatoulaye's inner journey" (70); rather, I am more
interested in the forces that shape that journey, "the tension
between enclosure and the outward journey" that, according to
Mortimer, characterizes women's experience of Senegalese
culture.

Hyper-attention to the individual makes me uncomfortable
because of its similarity to the destructive tendency in literary
criticism, noted by Elaine Neil Orr, to designate and dismiss
some women authors as *not feminist enough*.[6] *So Long a Letter* is
what Orr calls a "fictio[n] that invite[s] a feminist negotiating
criticism," a work that "appeals to actual and utopian worlds and
points of reference. They are generically and politically impure,
asking the reader to sympathize with characters' conventional as
well as progressive longings" (22-23). Recognizing
Ramatoulaye's negotiations of tradition and women's liberation
reveals her "canny movement within limits as well as expansion

of territory through crossings of antagonistic fields" (Orr ii). On a similar note, I concur with Christopher Miller's statement that "to say that [Ba] should have been more radical ... is to miss the essential point" which is that Ba "ends 'silence' and exclusion.... Those who wish for something more radical will not find it among Senegalese women novelists, at least not yet" (289). I would also underscore the concluding point in Irene Assiba D'Almeida's "The Concept of Choice in Mariama Ba's Fiction." Assessing the different choices made by the characters in *So Long a Letter* (Ramatoulaye's decision to stay with her husband, Aissatou's decision to leave hers), D'Almeida declares that

> what is important is that the choices have been made. For too long a time women have been denied to choose the course of their lives, even though choice is at the center of what gives significance to human existence. In this novel Mariama Ba shows clearly that women do have a deep consciousness of the options opened to them and that they are willing to make the choices that will make their lives more wholesome, no matter what the consequences might be. (171)

In fact, other critics consider Ba's purpose radical, and her subtlety strategic; Ella Brown describes *So Long a Letter* as "indirectly quite critical of the author's society," going on to note that the concluding idea-"life would be much happier in a society that gave greater consideration to the needs of women"-if it were "boldly stated, must be offensive." Instead, Brown asserts that Ba uses "a pious heroine who suffers" in order "to enlist the sympathy of readers," concluding that "[t]he indirection of the protest is suited to a society where women have so small a degree of freedom and can expect so little justice" (218). My point in bringing Brown's analysis to bear on the question of how best to analyze Ba's novel (and novels in general) is that characters' actions take on a different tone—one of negotiation, even liberation at times—when the critic considers the cultural and literary constraints within which these actions unfold.

This contextual analysis is important to any socially-relevant literary criticism because thinking which remains on the individual level obscures the way fiction reproduces and contests societal power structures through individual stories. This is not to say that characters are merely ideological ciphers, but that characters (like the real people who create them) are products of worlds driven by forces largely beyond their control, and that they don't have to be "exemplary" to be valuable.[7] This tendency to look for sameness not only oversimplifies responses to literature into evaluations of "good" and "bad" characters, it also imposes structures that may or may not be fitting for individual texts. Nina Baym's explanation of "Why I Don't Do Feminist Literary Theory" (subtitle to her article, "The Madwoman and Her Languages") illuminates the problems of cross-cultural reading by (inadvertently appropriative Western) women. She declares that if "you start with a theory of difference [between women's and men's texts], you can't see anything but" (284); I would add that the same goes for sameness: if you begin by assuming sameness, you can't see the difference.

In an article on African women's fiction, Florence Stratton imposes the structure of American feminist criticism as conceived by Sandra Gilbert and Susan Gubar in *The Madwoman in the Attic* on *So Long a Letter*, among other novels.[8] Her pursuit of "the shallow grave" she perceives in all women's writing is not oblivious to the need for "culturally specific" analyses (144); however, her choice of the archetypal critical model ultimately leads to the annexation of African texts to Western literature and a slight misreading of Ba's novel. As a "harrowing story of living burial" in which "female characters are enclosed in the restricted spheres of behavior of the stereotypes of a male tradition," Stratton's version of *So Long a Letter* enacts what Naomi Wolf calls "victim feminism" (I use the term cautiously, not wanting to replicate Wolf's haphazard theoretical bravado). Positing Ramatoulaye as a "sacrificial victim" (147), she renders invisible the images of joy and possibility created by Ba. "[T]he unhappiness of Ramatoulaye," writes Stratton, "is the result not only of her victimization by the male social order but also of her continuing complicity in the process" (159). This dual criticism has the same effect as the patriarchy Stratton opposes: by pronouncing *So Long a Letter* an epistle of powerlessness, Stratton disenfranchises the main character: "Ramatoulaye has been blinded, paralyzed, wasted-

disabled-by her conditioning.... Ba tells the story of the living death of every woman who is unable to break out of that conditioning. In effect, Ramatoulaye mourns her own demise" (166). This reading startles me with its overwhelmingly negative interpretation of Ba's character and letter. Stratton's focus on the "archetype" of the "shallow grave" obscures in her vision the very important utopian strands of this novel, in particular the image that counters the enclosures of female subjectivity, the emergence of women from their social graves, the blossoming with which Ba concludes. Her article models what happens when Western frames of reference are raised to the level of archetype and traced through the literature of non-Western cultures. We see things that are not necessarily there: the blemish is not on Ramatoulaye's life but on our faulty lens.

In addition to the selective insights of archetypal readings, the desires and fears of Western feminists further distort this literary letter. In particular, Western feminist perspectives on marriage, wifehood, and tradition influence Stratton's reading in such a way that Ramatoulaye is designated a priori a victim and a fool:

> Although she is a professional woman, Ramatoulaye skips with barely a glance over that aspect of her life, focusing instead almost exclusively on the domestic domain. It is in her housewifely role that she finds her primary identity, and she expends most of her human energy on excecuting that role to perfection. With a satisfaction that borders on the masochistic, she bears witness to her limitless devotion. (161)

I am able to hear the disdain in this passage because I share its Western feminist bias to an extent, having condescended to or at least distanced myself from my grandmother for years because of her decision to make wifehood her career; however, I wrestle with my own blindness in this area. The assertion that "Ramatoulaye seems to have sprung full-blown from the pages of studies such as Betty Friedan's *The Feminine Mystique*," that "[s]he makes a cult of domesticity and mounts (to borrow a phrase from Friedan) what sounds like 'a propaganda campaign to give women 'prestige' as housewives' by transforming the drudgery of daily domestic tasks into exalted professions" (161), reflects what has become a veritable phobia of marriage in Western feminism more than it accurately interprets Ramatoulaye's approach to housework or Ba's perspective on male-female relationships, which is far from separatist. Indeed, African feminism can be distinguished from much Western feminism by this divergence in matters of heterosexual love and family (Grimes 69). Further, Stratton's thesis precludes her from acknowledging Ramatoulaye's rejection of marriage in its oppressive forms, as when she refuses one of the suitors after her husband's death: "'You forget that I have a heart, a mind, that I am not an object to be passed from hand to hand. You don't know what marriage means to me: it is an act of faith and of love, the total surrender of oneself to the person one has *chosen* and who has chosen you.' (I emphasized the word *chosen*')" (58).

I prefer Gail Griffin's description of women's work to Stratton's; rather than judging it masochistic, Griffin sees it as hard, yes, but also transformative and powerful. Reflecting on Penelope, of Greek mythology, she writes:

> I was bound on a wheel, moving in a vicious and exhausting circle: washing dishes and clothes so they could be dirtied again, scrubbing floors to clear the way for more muddy boots, changing babies who promptly required changing again, cooking meals that quickly disappear, bearing children only to watch them die and then bearing new ones-doing women's work, which traditionally amounts to remaking and reordering their worlds daily, ensuring that life goes on against and through constant destruction. As it happens, that's the gods work too. (259)

Griffin chooses to posit women's work as sacred rather than mundane. The assumption Stratton makes in "The Shallow Grave" is that wifehood is necessarily destructive, that the home is necessarily a "domestic enclosure" which precludes productive introspection and personal growth. It often does, to be sure, but through Ramatoulaye's letter, if we read it carefully, and to the end, the home becomes a space of self-constitution, discovery, reinterpretation, housing many active gestures of imagination and world-building.[9] I don't know if I would go so far as to call the letter a "revolutionary script" as does Mildred Mortimer, but her assertion that "Ramatoulaye has learned to use enclosure as her refuge and writing as a means of communication to strengthen female bonding" (77) makes a welcome shift towards reading Ramatoulaye right.

Ba criticism brings many important feminists and philosophers to bear on *So Long a Letter*: Gilbert and Gubar, Cixous, Annis Pratt, Mary Belenky. Even Sartre makes an appearance. Few works, however, read Ba's fiction in terms of Black feminism. They would be more accurate if they did. Chikwenye Okonjo Ogunyemi provides a good example of what different stories emerge in literary criticism from this perspective. Ogunyemi explores womanism in Black women's novels, establishing it as the appropriate framework for these works of transformation and joy and providing a useful definition: "Black womanism is a philosophy that celebrates black roots, the ideals of black life, while giving a balanced presentation of black womandom.... This philosophy has a mandalic core: its aim is the dynamism of wholeness and self-healing that one sees in the positive, integrative endings of womanist novels" (240). Although Mariama Ba does not appear explicitly in her article, looking at the ending of *So Long a Letter* through the perspective of Ogunyemi's womanism reveals the importance of emphasizing its positive, utopian qualities. Ramatoulaye traverses painful circumstances and ends in a position of self-healing and community-building, achieving "the dynamism of wholeness."

Griffin, Mortimer, and Ogunyemi create lenses through which to view tradition as not inherently negative, a view essential to understanding African women's writing (important as well to a growing body of similar approaches in the United States). Abena P. B. Busia contributes to this developing paradigm as well in her important essay, "Words Whispered Over Voids." Busia's reading of *So Long a Letter* as primarily about "being nourished by roots in a changing world without becoming withered or bound by them" (27) offers a corrective to the critical one-sidedness cited above. Busia describes Ramatoulaye as "a heroine for whom the making of the modern state becomes also

the making of a modern woman who survives and lives in the
state and ... becomes a mistress of her words, and worlds" (29).
Adele King also offers glimpses of this more positive reading of
Ramatoulaye, writing that she "attempts to preserve the tradition
of the common bowl and the stability of the family" (180).

These are not negative or masochistic desires. I keep
returning to Grandma, who also preserves the common bowl
(although she requires our use of flatware, so the common bowl
operates partly as metaphor in her case); as a product of late
twentieth-century Western feminism, I think of her as I struggle
to overcome the kneejerk response to tradition and community I
was weaned on as an American feminist, to recognize their value
in African women's literature. King continues: "Rejecting those
traditions and customs that inhibit the natural expression of love
and respect forms the basis of Ba's morality, applicable to both
family and public life. Traditions are neither good nor bad in
themselves, but must be judged against higher moral standards"
(184). Ramatoulaye chooses African community as her
framework, working within it to make a more inhabitable space
for women.[10] Whether one agrees with Ramatoulaye's
traditionalism or not, her bravery is admirable: "Once more, I
was refusing the easy way because of my ideal. I went back to
my loneliness ... I wore it again, as one wears a familiar garment.
Its cut suited me well. I moved easily in it ... I wanted
'something else.' And this 'something else' was impossible
without the full agreement of my heart" (70). This integrity
characterizes Ramatoulaye as an important heroine for Africa
and for women.

The words of one African diaspora writer, the acclaimed Toni
Morrison, seem appropriate as an ending note since it was
through my desire to write about her work that I began studying
cross-cultural reading strategies:

> Critics of my work have often left something to be
> desired, in my mind, because they don't always evolve
> out of the culture, the world, the given quality out of
> which I write. Other kinds of structures are imposed on
> my works, and therefore they are either praised or
> dismissed on the basis of something that I have no
> interest in whatever, which is writing a novel according

to some structure that comes out of a different culture. I am trying very hard to use the characteristics of the art form that I know best, and to succeed or fail on those criteria rather than on some other criteria. I tend not to explain things very much, but I long for a critic who will know what I mean ... I am yearning for someone to see such things-to see what the structures are, what the moorings are, where the anchors are that support my writings. (407)

As a white Western critic, or as any critic, it is one's responsibility to do the work to discover the moorings.[11] In order to avoid a colonizing posture, we must be prepared to read the nuances in documents such as Ramatoulaye's letter—and to write back.

Notes

[1]   Lugones defines cross-cultural love relationships and reading practices in contrast to Western patriarchal configurations of culture and play, which are agonistic and competitive. Instead, she envisions "the playful attitude" as an "openness to surprise, openness to being a fool, openness to self-construction or reconstruction ... uncertainty, lack of self-importance, absence of rules or a not taking rules as sacred, a not worrying about competence and a lack of abandonment or resignation to a particular construction of oneself, others, and one's relation to them" (401). This attitude, when drawn on in the activity of "world"-travelling, creates an alternative to what Lugones perceives as a "racist or ethnocentric failure of love of White/Anglo women", offering "a loving way out" of the damaging phenomenon of "arrogant perception" (392). Such a philosophy of cross-racial and cross-cultural relationships can be applied in the study of literature with exhilarating results; it offers "a loving way out" of the tension surrounding the issue of white critics and black texts, not by bullying one's way through, not by invoking privilege, but by trying to see the world of the novel through the author's eyes. While I am aware of Carole Boyce Davies' critique of this concept, in which she speaks from her history of growing up as a child of the Caribbean, watching tourists turn "playful 'world' travelling" into an industry of racism and colonization, I find Lugones' work useful in attempting to read across the lines of race and nationhood.

[2]   Carla Kaplan encourages a critical turn relevant here from second-wave feminist desires for identification to third-wave negotiations of difference based on desire. She writes: "The integration of desire (which need not demand sameness) into a literary politics of identification (which does) allows for difference as well as sameness, for disidentification and conflict as well as collaboration and cure" (45). Kaplan creates a critical

framework she calls "the erotics of talk," in which attraction does not erase the other: "[F]oregrounding desire as part of the recuperative process mitigates against some of the more solipsistic, self-celebratory dangers of the recuperative paradigm. Insofar as the critic recuperating a woman's text identifies its heroine as herself, she rescues not another woman, but an aspect of her own being. If the other woman can only be seen—and saved—insofar as she represents a version of oneself, then perhaps we can only save, liberate, or help ourselves, one of the messages of nineties-style self-help ideology which I would be particularly loathe to see feminism adopt" (45). In this view, women critics would do better to desire women characters than to identify with them, a shift I have made with Grandma, in which I desire her, want her to exist in and of herself, rather than require her to be a version of me I can live with. "Desire," suggests Kaplan, "might allow us to listen to each other, through the mediation of the text, without assuming, as identification tends to do, that we already know what the other is saying" (40).

3   Christopher Miller is a useful source on literary trends in the African novel. His reading of *So Long a Letter* in particular sheds light on the meaning of this novel's epistolarity. One point Miller makes is the use of Aissatou, the narratee, as a double, or "fictive reader within the epistolary framework, [who] stands in the place of the real reader of the novel; her place in the West and specifically the United States makes of her an appropriate 'double' for many readers of *So Long a Letter*" (275).

4   I refer again to Miller, who treats the effect of the Western marketplace on the African canon in his chapter on Senegalese women writers (286-93).

5   Carole Boyce Davies argues against the "juridical mode" (*Moving Beyond Boundaries* 9) in the literary criticism of black women's writing.

6   Orr outlines "a negotiating feminist criticism" that "invites articulations of 'crossed' loyalties that nonetheless bring us closer to a nonsexist, nonhomophobic world." In this theory, Orr argues, "Readings that are merely oppositional ... only exacerbate the splits rather than putting them to use. Such readings call feminist only those practitioners who afford a politics of subversion. The Woman with the forked tongue, the bisexual, the dually aligned accomplice remains a suspicious character. She is not committed enough, not feminist or lesbian or postcolonial enough" (21). To suggest that Ramatoulaye is not "feminist enough," not "postcolonial enough," seems to me the height of critical arrogance and far too common among white Western critics of African women's novels and Ba's work in particular. While Orr's work refers to American women's fiction and American feminist literary criticism, her recent turn to African women's writing suggests her position might be equally well applied to both arenas.

7   Adele King conducts a balanced and attentive reading of Ba's moral universe as a blend of Western and African values; however, her statements about Ramatoulaye fall into the questionable pattern of looking for role models. King writes, "She is not an exemplary hero fighting to better her position in the world" (179), and further, "Ramatoulaye is no radical in national or in family politics" (182), finally concluding that "neither the conservative Ramatoulaye nor the westernized Aissatou is an

ideal" (183). But is reading literature necessarily best conducted by looking for ideals? My students recently dismissed Dorothy Allison's memoir, *Two or Three Things I Know for Sure*, because they saw Allison as a bad role model, an imperfect, a failed woman. This critical move collapses difference and demands of literature that it be less complex than it is, that it offer answers rather than posing hard and beautiful questions.

[8]   Elizabeth Abel notes "certain pervasive tendencies among white feminists, who have tended to read black women's texts through critical lenses that filter out the texts' embeddedness in black political and cultural traditions and that foreground instead their relation to the agendas of white feminism, which the texts alter, or prefigure, but ultimately reconfirm" (496).

[9]   Mortimer provides a more nuanced treatment of "enclosure" than Stratton, asserting that Ramatoulaye "reinterprets" the Islamic practice of "Le Mirasse" in which one makes "revelations of a deceased person's past so as to praise the individual"; her reinterpretation "allow[s] for the disclosure of Modou's financial and emotional treachery," an act of independent thinking and agency within limits on Ramatoulaye's part (71). Judith Fryer's *Felicitous Space: The Imaginative Structures of Edith Wharton and Willa Cather* also illuminates the possibility of reconceiving and reconfiguring the house as a space of growth rather than imprisonment.

[10]   Like Louise Yelin in her postcolonial feminist study of South African novelists, *From the Margins of Empire*, I am interested in exploring how the texts of contemporary "women invite us to explore what it means to choose a national identity ... In addressing issues of national affiliation, I examine the ways that [texts] represent their writers' relationship to dominant and oppositional (residual and emergent) national cultures and transnational political entities" (5).

[11]   Carole Boyce Davies and Anne Adams Graves assert that "[t]he failure of Western feminists to deal with issues that directly affect Black women and their tendency to sensationalize others create antagonisms" (10). I take their words as a challenge and an invitation to rectify this Western feminist solipsism, avoiding a criticism based on what Elizabeth Abel calls "white desires" (495).

Works Cited

Awkward, Michael. Negotiating Difference: Race, Gender, and the Politics of Positionality. *Chicago: U of Chicago P, 1995.*

Abel, Elizabeth. "Black Writing, White Reading: Race and the Politics of Feminist Interpretation." *Critical Inquiry* 19 (1993): 470-98.

Ba, Mariama. *So Long a Letter.* Trans. Modupe Bode Thomas. Oxford: Heinemann, 1981.

Baym, Nina. "The Madwoman and Her Languages: Why I Don't Do Feminist Literary Theory." *Feminisms: An Anthology of Literary Theory and Criticism.* Eds. Robyn R. Warhol and Diane Price Herndl. New Brunswick: Rutgers UP, 1997. 279-92.

Boyce Davies, Carole and Anne Adams Graves, eds. *Ngambika: Studies of Women in African Literature.* Trenton: Africa World P, 1986.

Boyce Davies, Carole. *Moving Beyond Boundaries: Black Women's Diasporas. Vol. 2.* Washington Square: New York UP, 1995.

Brown, Ella. "Reactions to Western Values as Reflected in African Novels." *Phylon* 48.3 (1987): 216-28.

Busia, Abena P. B. "Words Whispered over Voids: A Context for Black Women's Rebellious Voices in the Novel of the African Diaspora." *Studies in Black American Literature. Vol. 3. Black Feminist Criticism and Critical Theory.* Eds. Joe Weixlmann and Houston A. Baker, Jr. Greenwood: Penkevill, 1988. 1-41.

Chester, Gail and Sigrid Nielson, eds. *In Other Words: Writing as a Feminist.* London: Hutchinson, 1987.

D'Almeida, Irene Assiba. "The Concept of Choice in Mariama Ba's Fiction." Boyce Davies and Adams Graves 161-71.

Fetzer, Glenn W. "Women's Search for Voice and the Problem of Knowing in the Novels of Mariama Ba." *College Language Association* 35.1 (1991): 31-41.

Fryer, Judith. *Felicitous Space: The Imaginative Structures of Edith Wharton and Willa Cather.* Chapel Hill: U of North Carolina P, 1986.

Griffin, Gail. "Penelope's Web." *The Intimate Critique: Autobiographical Literary Criticism.* Eds. Diane Freedman, et al. Durham: Duke UP, 1993. 255-64.

Grimes, Dorothy. "Mariama Ba's *So Long a Letter* and Alice Walker's *In Search of Our Mother's Gardens*: A Senegalese and an African American Perspective on "Womanism." In *Global Perspectives on Teaching Literature: Shared Visions and Distinctive Visions.* Ed. Sandra Ward Lott, et al. Urbana: NCTE, 1993.

King, Adele. "The Personal and the Political in the Work of Mariama Ba." *Studies in Twentieth Century Literature* 18.2 (1994): 177-88.

Miller, Christopher. *Theories of Africans.* Chicago: U of Chicago P, 1990.

Mohanty, Chandra. "Cartographies of Struggle: Third World Women and the Politics of Feminism." In *Third World Women and the Politics of Feminism.* Eds. Chandra Mohanty, et al. Bloomington: Indiana UP, 1991.

Morrison, Toni. "An Interview with Toni Morrison." Nellie McKay. In *Toni Morrison: Critical Perspectives Past and Present.* Eds. Henry Louis Gates and K. A. Appiah. New York: Amistad, 1993. 396-411.

Mortimer, Mildred. "Enclosure/Disclosure in Mariama Ba's *Une si longue lettre.*" *French Review* 64.1 (1990): 69-78.

Ogunyemi, Chikwenye Okonjo. "Womanism: The Dynamics of the Contemporary Black Female Novel in English." In *Revising the Word and the World: Essays on Feminist Literary Criticism.* Ed. Veve A. Clark, et al. Chicago: U of Chicago P, 1979. 231-48.

Orr, Elaine Neil. *Subject to Negotiation: Reading Feminist Criticism and American Women's Fictions.* Charlottesville: UP of Virginia, 1997.

Parmar, Pratibha. "Words are Weapons." Chester 149-53.

Stratton, Florence. "The Shallow Grave: Archetypes of Female Experience in African Fiction." *Research in African Literatures* 19.1 (1988): 143-69.

Wolf, Naomi. *Fire with Fire: The New Female Power and How to Use It.* n.p., 1994

Yelin, Louise. *From the Margins of Empire: Christina Stead, Doris Lessing, Nadine Gordimer (Reading Women Writing)*. Ithaca: Cornell UP, 1998.

SELF-COLONIZATION, LONELINESS, AND RACIAL IDENTITY IN AMA ATA AIDOO'S *OUR SISTER KILLJOY OR REFLECTIONS FROM A BLACK-EYED SQUINT.*

James M. Ivory

"There is a kind of loneliness overseas which is truly bad. It comes with the cold wind blowing outside the window making the trees moan so. It is there in the artificial heat in the room which dried my skin and filled my sleep with nightmares."

Our Sister Killjoy 119

Ama Ata Aidoo was born in Ghana, which remained a colony under British rule until the year 1957. The subsequent impact of British rule on Ghana and Ghana's contemporary years as an independent and postcolonial nation fuel much of Aidoo's fiction. Aidoo's experimental prose and aggressive political ideologies concerning the relation between Ghana and the West continue to contribute to her reputation as a great writer. Prior to entering into a reading of Aidoo's novel, I wish to offer some definition for the term "self-colonization" as I use it in my essay. The term itself builds upon and in part appropriates the term "self-exile" found in Gay Wilentz's impressive reading of Aidoo's novel ("The Politics of Exile: Ama Ata Aidoo's *Our Sister Killjoy*"). Drawing on Terry Eagleton and George Lamming, she presents a thoughtful reading of *Our Sister Killjoy* as an example of a "politics of exile." While I have drawn on her work several times throughout my reading of Aidoo's novel, I suggest that my essay moves away from hers in one significant and important fashion. Wilentz's work is primarily an exploration of the sociological aspects of Aidoo's concerns. Wilentz writes that *Our Sister Killjoy* "is a relentless attack on the notions of exile as relief from the societal constraints of national development and freedom to live in a cultural environment suitable for creativity"(159). Though I find Wilentz's comments on exile accurate and compelling, her work focuses primarily on the surface, external, or sociological facets of Aidoo's narrative. However, introducing the term "self-colonization" adds and explores another dimension of Aidoo's novel: the psychological or, more specifically, the internalization of the postcolonial dialectic between colonizer and colonized. The term "self-colonization" refers to Aidoo's interest in and investigation of cognitive spaces which are symptomatic of the systematic destruction of cultures left behind by a history of colonization and neocolonialism. *Our Sister Killjoy* begins some time after Ghana's independence but nevertheless reveals a cultural collective consciousness which continues to erode the foundation of Ghana's contemporary cognitive landscapes.

Sissie, the novel's protagonist, is the reader's witness to this mélange of cultural erosion and is the central voice or consciousness in the story. Her sometimes disturbing and brazen honesty helps the reader become a witness to Sissie's journey from innocence to experience as she leaves Ghana to sojourn in both Germany and England, and as she returns to Ghana. Aidoo's title investigates Sissie's role in the narrative and raises important questions. First, who is the "our" in the title? Or better put, who or what does Sissie "belong to," and what does this idea of possession suggest? While Sissie's actual name is never revealed in the narrative, the name "killjoy" may be taken at its literal value as "one who destroys or lessens other people's enjoyment." Aidoo, through her novel, wishes to lessen the enjoyment of those from Ghana who have deserted their homeland—mainly men—and found Western capitalism an attractive alternative to building up their homeland. The second half of Aidoo's title—"Reflections from a Black-eyed Squint"— refers to a mental blindness concerning both the erosion that has been caused by those who have left and their inability to see through the rationales offered by the many who refuse to return home. The opening lines of the book read: "Things are working out/ towards their dazzling conclusions.../...so it is neither here nor there, what ticky-tackies we have saddled and surrounded ourselves with, *blocked our views, cluttered our brains*"(my emphasis 3-5). On the one hand, Sissie's squint suggests that what she sees is never clear or cognitively lucid; it is either too bright or too far away to be clearly in focus. Equally, the squint suggests the distance between what Sissie sees and where Sissie stands. The main issue I wish to highlight in these opening pages is that Aidoo emphasizes and reemphasizes her narrative as one that investigates internalized or cognitive spaces; her use of phrases like "emptied his head of everything"(6) and "mind-absorbing sport"(6) stresses this internalized dimension. Furthermore, Aidoo's narrative style—combining prose, poetry, and drama—and subjective narrator prove unsettling to readers, which parallels Sissie's unsettled mind and position.

For example, the identity of Aidoo's narrative consciousness adds to the emphasis on and complexity of these internalized and psychologically formative events. While Aidoo does not identify the narrator as a central figure within the narrative events, the narrator is not an objective or omniscient narrator with no opinions of regard and sympathies for the events as they unfold in the narrative. The narrator refers to characters in the story as "brothers and sisters," diminishing the gap between narrator-function and character function.

The narrator treats the characters as equals rather than from a "god-like" position. The voice of the narrator is one that expresses anger and disgust at what Sissie must witness; it is often difficult to determine a distinct line between Sissie's voice and the narrator's. Moreover, the narrator often yields her voice to allow other characters to speak in their voices, making the novel postmodern in its use of heteroglossia. The potential of and need for an independent voice becomes centralized in the final section, when Sissie takes over the narrative in her letter; Sissie's narrative control marks her move from an object position to a subject position. Sissie and "her" narrator have different roles but are dependent on each other. Aidoo's narrator's role is to establish and point out the historical background that foregrounds Sissie's journey and psychological development. For example, some of the earliest events in the narrative proper suggest that Sissie's role will be to observe and remark or reflect on some of the divisive political relations between Europe and Africa left by their dialectical pasts as colonizer and colonized. Moreover, the narrator has political insight that Sissie is incapable of early in the narrative; an early comment by the narator may serve as an example: "It is a long way to Europe. A cruel past, a funny present, a major desert or two, a sea, an ocean, several different languages apart, areoplanes bridge the sky" (8). The voice here, in its sardonic tone, foreshadows Sissie's trajectory.

Sissie's role thus is to gain experience. As we learn more about the narrator, "her" experiences have jaded her abilities to tell the story Sissie must tell; it is as if Aidoo herself is too close to tell this horrible story and removes herself two positions. But Sissie, as the least experienced, is even one place removed from the narrator; Sissie is used as an object of the narrative as she is "used" by others in the story. It is equally important to note, as Gay Wilentz points out, that Sissie does not choose to leave Ghana, but is selected "as a promising student and is given a scholarship to attend an international work-study program in Germany and to visit her colonial 'capital'—London"(162). However, while Sissie is surprised by this treatment, it is not this treatment that has the most profound impact on Sissie's mind and subsequent perceptions of her "brothers." It is her experience with her fellow countryman that greatly impacts her earliest impressions of the postcolonial voyage she is about to begin. The symbolic presence of an African named "Sammy"—who has assimilated a European cultural value system—affects her in a most profound way throughout her journey; the impact of this experience proves to have considerable psychological consequences.

While the narrative only describes in general or vague terms the events, food, and people of Sissie's first evening encountering Europe, the narrative recalls in more detail an encounter with "Sammy." I suggest that this signals both the importance of Sammy's internalized colonization as well as Sissie's own developing knowledge of self-colonization. Specifically, Sammy's significance lies in his willingness to be put on display for the benefit of Europeans. In many ways, and even in name, his role or performance echoes the negative portrayals of African Americans crystallized in the "Sambo" figure found in American cinematic and theatrical history. Aidoo emphasizes "Sammy's" inappropriate actions in the narrative by naming him as she does and by deriding his role-playing: "Sammy laughed all the time: even when there was nothing to laugh at. Or when she thought there was nothing to laugh at. And when he was not laughing loudly, he carried a somewhat permanent look of well-being on his face, supported by a *fixed smile*" (my emphasis, 9). The narrative voice concludes Sissie's encounter with Sammy with "Time was to bring her many many Sammys. And they always affected her in the same way"(9). While the Sammy figure introduces the central theme of "self-colonization," it barely penetrates the surface of Aidoo's observations on Ghana's cultural survival as it relates to a reductive collective consciousness—reductive in part due to its being fettered to a colonial "Ideal." As Chimalum Nwankwo writes in his article "The Feminist Impulse and Social Realism in Ama Ata Aidoo's *No Sweetness Here* and *Our Sister Killjoy*,"

> [T]he problems of the African woman are expressed as integral parts of the problems of colonial and post-colonial Africa. Aidoo's feminist concerns are not treated in isolation from Africa's political instability, the new master complex of the so-called elite, the atavistic problems of the rural African at the cross-roads of history, the fury and impotence of the radical African, the lure of the Western world, and so forth. Such

problems are all neatly slotted into a cultural matrix
often evoked successfully by the writer's rich personal
experience. (152)

These comments show that postcolonial issues often lie beneath
the surface of the problem. Therefore, it may be only through
unraveling the internalization of a (neo)colonial consciousness
that we can isolate the paralysis and pathologies of neocolonialism.

Aidoo's first steps in unraveling this (neo)colonial
consciousness is to start with the minds of those "gifted"
intellectuals who are blinded by the dazzling light of Europeans
promises and "utopias." Aidoo points out and condemns the
tendency of Ghana's most-promising intellectuals to leave
Ghana to be educated in the West (or the "been-tos" as they are
called), only to fail to return home to practice their newly-
acquired skills. Many refuse to return to their native land and
only wish to convince Europe of their worth: a worth often
associated with condemnations of the past. Later in the novel,
after Sissie has gained insight into this problem, she has a
conversation with one such intellectual, a "brilliant doctor" who
believes that his talents are better served by remaining in Europe.
He rationalizes this matter in two ways; the first involves the
available funds for practice and research in Europe versus
Ghana, a claim Sissie does not deny but still refutes later on. The
doctor states the following about medical practice in Ghana:
"Sister, there are no facilities at home to provide someone like
me with the congenial atmosphere in which to work. And that's a
fact! Where are the funds? You may not be aware of it but to
equip a first class research set-up for me would swallow the
annual budget of the Ministry of Health...No, let me stay here a
while" (128). The doctor's remarks align him with an earlier
"Sammy" ("Time was to bring her many many Sammys"(9)),
albeit the doctor proves a more formidable "adversary" for
Sissie.

For Aidoo, "Sammy's" and the doctor's ideas are a continual
reminder that, as in the time of Ghanian slave forts, important
resources (the intellectuals) are still being exported as a result of
a neocolonial campaign. One might specifically identify or
define this "campaign" as "Sammy" has already: a concerted

effort to convince the former-colonized world that Europe is rehearsal for paradise and to succeed there is to find true success.

The second part of the doctor's rationale for remaining presses this point: that work or value must be seen and evaluated (validated?) through a European cultural lens: "...But you can see how by remaining here someone like me serves a very useful purpose in educating them to recognise our worth...?"(129). However, this is where Aidoo draws a line and begins to refute the doctor's materialistic, self-serving, and myopic argument. While she concurs that the economic conditions are not equal in Ghana—as it is a developing nation—she also argues that worth and "value" do not and should not be definable by English currency or Europeanized values:

> But they have always known how much we are worth. They have always known that, My Brother, and a whole lot more. They may not consider it necessary to openly admit it...that's another matter. They probably know it is strategically unwise to. You see...My Brother, if we are not careful, we would burn out our brawn and brains trying to prove what you describe as 'our worth' and we won't get a flicker of recognition from those cold blue eyes. And anyway who are they?...So please come home, My Brother. (129-30)

Sissie's words are emotionally stirring and reveal her love and concern for a developing homeland that lacks the financial clout of the European world.

However, this financial "shortcoming" may be diminished by a closeness between humans, a closeness that Aidoo suggests is lacking in Europe:

> Come to our people. They are the only ones who need to know how much we are worth. The rewards would not be much. Hardly anything. For every successful surgery, they would hail you as a miracle worker. Because their faith will not be in the knives you wield but in your hands; in your touch...Once in a year; some man of means will come to give you thanks, with a sheep. Or a goat. Sometimes they may even make a subtle hint that you marry their beautiful daughter. (130)

Moreover, Sissie's comments tell us much about Aidoo's concerns and fears about the fragmentation or erosion of the Ghana "family"; this in part explains her use of the terms of endearment like "brother" and "sister" or "Sissie." Wilentz writes, "Unlike other exiles who have lost that sense of identity that comes from belonging to a community, Sissie becomes the eyes of her community, reporting on those lost ones who have forgotten maternal, familial and community ties, and squinting at these men—young and old—who refuse to return home to face national realities and rebuild their countries" (162).

And while, externally, the colonial memory and suffering lie at the heart of some of this erosion, internally, the both literal and symbolic African Mother has suffered damage inflicted on and by her children as well. In the following passage, we find one of those moments where the text blurs whether the thoughts rendered are the product of Sissie's more experienced conscience or the narrator's:

> Of course she has suffered, the African mother. Allah, how she has suffered. How much and for how long? Just look at what's been happening to her children over the last couple of hundred years.... Mother woke up to forced labor and thinly-veiled slavery on colonial plantations.... Later on, her sons were conscripted into imperial armies.... And now look at those for whom she's been scrimping, saving and mortgaging her dignity in order to send to school nearby, or abroad. Look at them returning with grandchildren whom she can't communicate with, because they speak only English, French, Portuguese or even German.... (123)

While this passage deals primarily with the role and abuse of the mother figure, one can equally see how the abuse moves out to fragment the cohesive bonds of a familial structure. We see bothers and sons separated and destroyed both physically and mentally by the geopolitical conflicts of other nations. Furthermore, in the oppressive Diaspora of slavery, more bonds are destroyed. And eventually, Aidoo points to imperialized Westernized education as another institutionalized form responsible for the disruption of basic communications among family members. As representative of sisterhood and potential motherhood, Aidoo employs Sissie's consciousness as a warning to others. Or as Wilentz accurately points out: "It is no mistake that Sissie is female; she is the representative of all the mothers and sisters and daughters who have been left behind on this illusive search for artistic, political, cultural, and perhaps even sexual freedom"(162).

Up to this point, I have been attempting to clarify the frame that Aidoo uses to support her narrative end game on the dangers of neocolonialism: both self-colonization and exile. However, from this point on, I wish to look more carefully at the collage or montage that makes up the portrait that Sissie is witness to that takes her from her rather passive "puzzlement" at the novel's inception to her brazen condemnation of her lover and others like him who choose to remain in Europe; she refuses to mail her final letter to him by the conclusion and seems to have become indifferent to the situation of her "been-to" brothers.

The story itself is broken into four parts: Part One—"Into a Bad Dream"—recounts Sissie's reflections on being chosen for the trip to Europe and concludes with her arriving in Germany. Part Two—"The Plums"—tells of Sissie's sojourn in Germany and her friendship with Marija, a lonely German wife and mother. Part Three—"From Our Sister Killjoy"—narrates Sissie's period in England. And, finally, Part Four—"A Love Letter"—examines the self-exiled African, including her lover to whom she refuses to mail her letter in a final act of defiance.

The last part of "Into a Bad Dream" serves to show how Sissie (or anyone) loses racial innocence, while at the same time awakening her to how the emphasis on individual and cultural differences can serve as a justification of colonialism and of continuing neo-colonial influence on other lands. This "awakening" is most pronounced when Sissie encounters her first Germans on German soil:

> Suddenly, she realized a woman was telling a young girl who must have been her daughter:
>
> 'Ja, das Schwartze Mädchen.'

From the little German that she had been advised to
study for the trip, she knew that 'das Schwartze
Mädchen.' meant 'black girl' ." (12).

Sissie's "awakening" results in an anger toward those who have
objectified her; however, immediately, her response will result in
a cycle of fear and anger toward the concept of "otherness": "For
the rest of her life, she was to regret this moment when she was
made to notice differences in human colouring" (12-13).

While Sissie regrets her response to this earliest form of her
racial objectification, the sense of isolation she feels as a result
announces one of Aidoo's central themes: that the existing
loneliness in Europe results directly from its involvement in an
imperial enterprise. To represent this theme of isolation visually,
Aidoo uses one word each on the final three pages of the first
section; these words (all questions) segue into questions about
loneliness and human relations: "Where/ When /How"(14-16),
respectively. Furthermore, this sense of isolation, which is
endemic to mental self-colonization, is made even more
profound when we realize that the three lines that precede these
isolated words refer to god-like power. Humans' desire for god-
like power is often the motivation behind the psychology of
imperialist expansion, yet to be god-like is to be lonely in a
human world: "Power to decide / Who is to live, / Who is to
die," (13). Yet again, Aidoo suggests how strong a motivating
factor the wish for power is in the (neo)colonial enterprise.

Expanding on her theme of loneliness, Aidoo begins the next
section, "The Plums," by introducing Marija, whose loneliness
becomes a metaphor for Europe's "abnormal climate," both
atmospherically and culturally. Marija seems to have become a
victim of this climate. The first meeting between Marija and
Sissie occurs in a round sentry post overlooking a castle. I would
suggest that both the sentry post and castle symbolize Aidoo's
theme of isolation, linking it to an oppressive and colonizing
past: "She [Marija] was a young mother pushing her baby in a
pram. Later she would tell Sissie that she did this quite often.
She would come and stand where Sissie stood, in the round
sentry post, and look at the town and the river" (19). As the old
village wall "speaks" of the days of "Our Sovereign Lord and
Master" (19), the theme of the continuity of past and present is

brought to bear upon their encounter. Marija's ancestors, presumably, once were bound in subjection to some lord just as the ancestors of those subjected wished to rule in lordship over other lands. Marija's routine and repetitive behavior of returning to this sentry post develops a paralytic repetition that is suggestive of meaningless activity meant to occupy her emptiness or loneliness. At the same time, returning to this seat of power hints at her being stuck in a historical "feedback loop," unable to free herself from the logic of domination.

Moreover, the sentry post and the subsequent history of the castle continue to reveal abuses of those in power but also point to the isolated loneliness of the sovereign lord; here, "sovereign" suggests power above others, while equally suggesting the loneliness which accompanies such power (echoing my earlier comments on god-like power). The symbolic replacement of the history of the lonely sovereign lord (the former castle) with young people (the current youth hostel) who visit as part of Sissie's program reveals other facets of this Westernizing programming. Symbolizing an effort to distance itself from its unattractive history, the castle's transformation to a youth hostel shows Western civilization's efforts of presenting Europe as a cultural paradise to the so-called "Third World" by "erasing" traces of the past. The former seat of power now serves as splendid backdrop for travelling international youth.

In the first section prior to Sissie's journey, Sammy, who has attempted to "erase" his past, provides Sissie with the European party line:

> Sammy had obviously been to their country before and seemed to have stayed for a long time. He was very anxious to get her to realize one big fact. That she was unbelievably lucky to have been chosen for the trip. And that, somehow, going to Europe was altogether more like a dress rehearsal for a journey to paradise. (9)

Directly contradicting this view of a European nirvana, Sissie's observes in Germany a world in which she finds an apparent cultural degradation illustrated by a breakdown of family. For example, we never meet Marija's husband Adolf; he is never at home. Furthermore, the naming of both father and son "Adolf" is equally disquieting and pregnant in its possibilities. In one case, while Sissie and Marija are out walking, the narrative consciousness describes their inner conflicts as part of Germany's dark past: "They walked on. Along the main thoroughfare of the town. Now their inner joys gone, too aware of the sad ways of man" (48). A graphic division later in these lines is marked by the line and question "And Our Sister?" further emphasizing the marked loneliness of these two women; they are together, but their individual histories, defined by oppression, insist that they be divided. Furthermore, the history evoking Hitler and his Nietzschean dream of the Aryan superman is framed by listed singular nouns, ending with a reference to the Führer, indicating his isolation and again paralleling my earlier remarks on sovereign lordship and god-like power. Aidoo then moves from the lonely and historically degrading position of Hitler to a historical vector pointing to Marija's growing infant son Adolf. Little Adolf's name recalls the naming of his father and the other "father," Hitler, while also evoking the absence of these fathers.

Little Adolf's absence after this meditation—he does not appear again in the narrative—stresses the historical separation and loneliness of these two women; Sissie notices that Marija's son "Little Adolf" had not been with them: "Sissie was silent. Thinking that she did not know about babies. But then wasn't Marija too often by herself anyway?"(49). Moving from the ghostly patriarchy to the absent sons of the patriarchy, the family inevitably fragments into its lonely components rather than becoming an emotionally binding and supportive structure.

Most profoundly, Marija's extreme loneliness and the erosion of the family are revealed through Marija's desperate but sympathetic sexual embrace of Sissie. As Wilentz rightly observes, "For Sissie, her comprehension of the emptiness of this isolated woman's life is exacerbated by Marija's attempt to reach out to her sexually. And, although this section may be problematic for some feminist scholars, it is evident that Aidoo—however sympathetically—sees this attempt at a lesbian relationship as a perversion of womanlove and part of the degeneration of European family life"(164). One sees that Marija's embrace is nothing more than symptomatic of the loneliness that neocolonialism breeds. Marija literally and emotionally needs someone to hold on to, while combatting the forces that comprise some of the darkest history of empire, alluded to by her husband's and son's name:

> Sissie felt Marija's cold fingers on her breast. The fingers of Marija's hand touched the skin of Sissie's breast while her other hand groped round and round Sissie's midriff, searching for something to hold on to. It was the left hand that woke her up to the reality of Marija's embrace. The warmth of her tears on her neck. The hotness of her lips against hers. (64)

There is, of course, considerable irony in the fact that Marija, symbolically and innocently linked to the imperialism and racism of Germany's past, seeks solace in the embrace of an African woman. But the anti-patriarchal and anti-racist potential of this scene (or its "exoticizing" and objectifying potential) are less explored than a set of contrasts set up immediately following this scene. In her reaction, we see Aidoo drawing a distinct line between human closeness or intimacy in Africa and human distance or loneliness in Germany:

> Sissie thought of home. To the time when she was a child in the village. Of how she always liked to be sleeping in the bedchamber when it rained, her body completely-wrapped-up in one of her mother's akatado-cloths while her mother herself pounded fufu in the anteroom which also served as a kitchen. Oo, to be wrapped up in mother's cloth while it rained. Every time it rained. (64)

Sissie's immediate response to and thoughts about Marija's actions make it abundantly clear that Aidoo's agenda is to explore corrupted womanlove and not to espouse anti-lesbian. In opposition to Marija's emotional starvation and desire, Sissie follows this awkward moment with a "thought of home." In Sissie's thoughts, we find a clear division between the land of the victim to empire (Sissie's) and the land of the victimizer (Marija's). The repetition of the word "wrapped," meaning being embraced by womanlove, in Sissie's recollection is directly opposed to Marija's "searching for something to hold on to." In other words, we see that Sissie's memories turn from the loneliness and desperation of this fragmented / fragmenting European family towards the closeness of her African family and womanlove.

Moreover, the image of rain (or the raindrop) in Sissie's memory further reinforces Marija's loneliness by pointing forward to Marija's reaction to this awkward moment: a single, lonely tear:

> Marija was crying silently. There was a tear streaming out of one of her eyes. The tear was coming out of the left eye only. The right eye was completely dry. Sissie felt pain at the sight of that one tear. That forever tear out of one eye. Suddenly Sissie knew. She saw it once and was never to forget it. She saw against the background of the thick smoke that was like a rain cloud over the chimneys of Europe,
>
> > L
> > O
> > N
> > E
> > L
> > I
> > N
> > E
> > S
> > S
>
> Forever falling like a tear out of a woman's eye.
>
> (65)

This image of the teardrop is even more powerful in that the word "loneliness," written in capitals, is vertically positioned on the page with each letter of the word occupying one line and poetically falling like Marija's tear down the left-hand side of the page. One might simply conclude the discussion of this section by assuming that Aidoo's primary interest is to reveal the cold loneliness she associates with Europe; however, this limited reading would hardly account for some of the complexities connected to Sissie's character and development as well as the title of the section itself, which, as one will recall, is "The Plums."

Aidoo introduces the plums as a source of personal and gluttonous temptation for Sissie. Interestingly, "plums," an anagram for the word "slump," prove to be Sissie's personal challenge while on European soil. "The Plums" develops a temptation that Sissie must overcome herself not to become a willing "victim" of self-colonization. Sissie's desire for these foreign fruits appears to be her undoing:

> It was midsummer and the fruit stalls were overflowing. She decided that being fruits, she liked them all, although her two loves were going to be pears and plums. And on those two *she gorged herself*. So she had good reason to feel fascinated by the character of Marija's plums. They were of a size, sheen and succulence she had not encountered anywhere else in those foreign lands. (my emphasis, 39)

Aidoo suggests that Sissie's overindulgence in these fruits develops in part due to their foreign character. And while Sissie will later criticize those "been-tos" who refuse to return home, here, she experiences the allure of foreignness. Interestingly, Aidoo develops this allure in reference to a fruit, something edible, suggesting that the desire may be even deeper than a cultural surface reading may account for. Furthermore, Aidoo points to even earlier and more unsettling origins for this temptation. Just as some of the earliest missionaries were also the earliest colonizers, Aidoo points to an origin and a tree, which indicate both a temptation and Sissie's subsequent, although temporary, "fall": "So she sat, our Sister, her tongue caressing the plump berries with skin-colour almost like her own, while Marija told her how she had selected them specially for her, off the single tree in the garden"(40). Certainly, the single and isolated tree points the reader to the Biblical tree of knowledge. Sissie's reaction to or desire for these fruits, which are identified with her own body (and maybe hint at her self-objectification, her acting out Marija's desire) allows us to witness her vulnerability.

However, Aidoo's eventual treatment of Sissie is much more interested in human relations than in religious issues. Sara Chetin, in her article "Reading from a Distance: Ama Ata Aidoo's *Our Sister Killjoy*," convincingly suggests that "Sissy [sic] is initially seduced by the overabundance and novelty of the food, particularly the plums, which represent her desire to experience a new world"(153); the world, I would add here, of the colonizer. However, it is not only the food that seduces Sissie: we see from the earlier example and in other moments in the story that Marija uses food as a form of seduction; "seduction" in this case gestures back toward Marija's embrace, noting her pathological loneliness.

Well before Marija attempts to sexually embrace Sissie, Sissie reveals that she has thought of an imaginary relationship between them that places Sissie in the position of her "self-colonized" brothers whom she will later unequivocally condemn. Aidoo repositions Sissie's consciousness within the context of a temptation similar to that of her "been-to brothers": "That was a game. A game in which one day, she became so absorbed, *she forgot* who she was, and the fact that she was a woman. *In her imagination,* she was one of these black boys in one of these involvements with white girls in Europe" (61, my emphasis). In this passage, Aidoo draws a connection between Sissie's uncontrollable desire for foreign fruits seen in the manner that she gorges herself and the imagined uncontrollable desire of her African brothers for white or foreign women. Furthermore, Aidoo's use of words like "delicious" and "savoured" emphasizes the connection between culinary desire and sexual desire:

> Sissie had thought, while they walked in the park, of what a *delicious* love affair she and Marija would have had if one of them had been a man. Especially if she, Sissie, had been a man. She had imagined and *savoured* the tears, their anguish at knowing that their love was doomed (my emphasis, 61).

As is evident here, Aidoo's emphasis continues to be on Sissie's mind. Sissie's honest efforts of adapting to and adopting Marija's lifestyle reveal what may be one of the earliest stages of self-colonization. While this example shows us how Sissie too is vulnerable to the temptations of self-colonization, she is not tempted for long. After her own musings about this imagined relationship, Sissie comes back to reality; she is shocked by her vulnerability to this mythic paradise: "Struck by some of the stories she had heard, she shivered, absolutely horrified"(61). And while Marija continues to tempt Sissie with food, her attempts can now only fail. Sara Chetin considers the cultural dialectic between Marija's advance and Sissie's rejection:

> Aidoo explores the cultural differences through the use of food and the women's misreadings of each other's concept of hospitality. Food, that universal symbol of sharing and nourishment, is also a symbol of hospitality turned sterile and unnatural. (152-53)

We see Sissie's first reactions to her changing relationship to food immediately following Marija's attempt to embrace her sexually. After the scene of the embrace, Sissie and Marija return to the kitchen. Importantly, the scene of the embrace takes place in Marija's and Adolf's sterile bedroom. The images associated with their bedroom prove to be in opposition to a private space reserved for intimacy and procreation: "Sissie could not associate her with the deserted looking chamber or its simple funereal elegance"(63). The bedroom's "desertedness" and its association with death in "funereal" prove that the bedroom's style opposes its expected function.

After Marija's and Sissie's return to the kitchen, their food starts to reflect the same sterility and literal coldness (death) associated with the bed chamber:

> Sissie would always puzzle over it. Cold food. Even after she had taught her tongue to accept them, she could never understand why people ate cold food. To eat ordinary cooked food that has gone cold without bothering to heat it is unpleasant enough. But to actually chill food in order to eat it was totally beyond her understanding, In the end, she decided it had something to do with white skins, corn-silk hair and very cold weather" (68).

Following this moment, both Sissie and Marija appear to lose their appetites. However, not just their appetites have been lost. Sissie's puzzlement over the cold food links its coldness with Aidoo's ideas on human relations in the colonizers' home; there is something about the pervasive loneliness (exhibited by Marija), the cold weather, and the cold food which equate to a human condition similar to symbolic death. Later in the final section, Sissie reflects on this idea:

> O, yes, everybody gets lonely some time or other. After all, if we look closer into ourselves, shall we not admit that the warmth from other people comes so sweet to us when it comes, because we always carry with us the knowledge of the cold loneliness of death? (119)

This cold, eventually leading to symbolic or actual death, stands as a monument to the enterprise of empire and those who would willingly subject themselves to its colonial whims; it is this symbolic death that Sissie manages to escape at the conclusion of "The Plums." And while Sissie escapes Germany with a brown bag from Marija filled with "sandwiches of liver sausages, a few pastries, a slab of cheese, and some plums"(82), she nevertheless encounters a similar cold and sterile atmosphere in England—"her colonial home"(my emphasis, 85). In the subsequent section, Aidoo investigates the theme of loneliness in the context of England and her ill-fated "been-to brothers" who have failed to escape the temptation she encountered in Germany with Marija and "her fruits."

In the third and penultimate section, "From Our Sister Killjoy," Sissie notices the high number of Diaspora blacks in England and that "[e]very man claimed that he was a student and so did every woman"(85-6). However, it is Sissie's response to the incongruent relationship between "her people" and the combative English climate that conveys Aidoo's theme of coldness and loneliness. Sissie witnesses the literal cold in the required additional clothes to survive in England's harsh climate; the ill-fitting, worn, and synthetic clothes further reveal England's sterile and economically unwelcoming environment:

> Above all, what hurt our sister as she stood on the pavements of London and watched her people was how

badly dressed they were. They were all poorly clothed. The women especially were pitiful. She saw women who at home would have been dignified matrons as well as young attractive girls looking ridiculous in a motley of fabrics and colours. Unused to the cold and thoroughly inefficient at dealing with it, they smothered their bodies in raiments of diverse lengths, hues and quality—in a desperate effort to keep warm. (88-9)

And the idea of being poorly clothed connects to just being poor: "For she knew from one quick composite vision that in a cold land, poverty shows as nowhere else"(89). Again, we see Aidoo developing economic concerns; these concerns come to impact the lives of those living in England as much as anything might. The often empty promises of advances and economic security drive many to continue in this life of cold and loneliness, which seems similar to Marija's life. Moreover, there are other important parallels to Sissie's sojourn through Germany.

While in Germany, Sissie witnesses the result of an internalized cold in the form of Marija's loneliness. In London, she witnesses a more fatally internalized cold in Kunle's self-colonization. As Sissie nears the end of her journey, she encounters more "sophisticated" and articulate "Sammys," the first of whom is Kunle. Kunle, an African, is "practically a Londoner, having lived in that city for seven years"(95). Through Sissie's reflections, we realize that Kunle has begun to internalize the beliefs and ideologies of the colonizer at the expense of his native home and culture. More importantly, Kunle represents another "Sammy": "The consciousness that shapes African experience abroad takes the form of Kunle in this chapter, another 'Sammy' who defends 'science' without grasping a moral sense of his own history as witnessed by his justification of the Christian doctor who used a South African Black man's heart to save a white man"(Chetin 156). However, it is not just "science" with which Aidoo grapples; we learn that, for Kunle and other Africans in London, the subject of heart transplantation has supplanted more immediately relevant homeland concerns: "As it turned out, uppermost in all their minds was not the war in Nigeria" but this South African heart transplantation (95). From that point, Aidoo uses the ideas of transplantation to point out Kunle's self-colonization.

The story of the transplantation makes literal what may be figuratively so in the "been-to": his heart is extracted and placed with the confines or context of a foreign body (politic). "[T]he Dying White Man had received the heart of a coloured man who had collapsed on the beach and... the young coloured man has allegedly failed to respond to any efforts at resuscitation and therefore his heart had been removed from his chest" (95). Aidoo's capitalization of "White Man" and her conspiracy-laden use of "allegedly" reveal the political aspects of this story lying beneath its "innocuous scientific benefits" that Kunle focuses on. In his position that "that Christian Doctor is a *Scientist*," Kunle fails to accept or is unable to notice the politicization of science in the developing world (my emphasis, 98); his "heart" has "been cleaned out of his chest"(95). The reference here is to the dying white man's heart; however, later events depicting Kunle's death associate him with that dying white man's heart. Kunle's heart has been replaced in the context of his colonial home and he now sees an Anglicized version of the world. Furthermore, Wilentz points out that

> Kunle, caught up in his identification with the dominant culture's "advances," has no comprehension of the irony of his own comments. For Sissie, Kunle not only represents the "been-to" who values the colonizer's world more than his own, he also represents the "been-to" who comes home with an exile's consciousness to complain and exploit rather than help build the nation. His identification with the culture of his exile makes him unable to confront the political realities at home. (167)

Additionally, Aidoo emphasizes the "heart transplantation" as a metaphor for Kunle's self-colonization in his tragic and ironic death. Since the heart symbolically functions as the seat of emotions, Kunle's automobile accident after his return and his heart's consumption in flames counter the cold climate and distance of London and Kunle's cold distance and blindness to the racial politics of the Christian Doctor's "heart trans-plantation." In depicting Kunle's automobile accident, Aidoo emphasizes both his conceit, having internalized and identified with the colonizer (if he had been driving, instead of a chauffeur, maybe the accident would have been avoidable), and his heart, the seat of emotions, empathy, and sympathy; in his case, his emotions have been supplanted and consumed by an Anglicized model:

> The flames had
> Swallowed it [his heart] up.
> Poor Kunle
> > Poor Christian Doctor
> > What waste
> > What utter waste.
> For it certainly would have gladdened Kunle's heart to find itself in the hands of the Christian Doctor. (107-08)

The image of Kunle's unconsumed heart in the hands of the Christian Doctor sarcastically highlights how his heart is in the hands of European ideas and ideals. Aidoo uses this image of the burning heart as a transition to the final section. In that section, the heart comes to stand for the love that one might feel for oneself or another. But what Sissie learns is that even a passionate love cannot overcome the lacuna neo-colonialism leaves between her and her "been-to brothers."

In the opening of the final section, entitled "A Love Letter," Aidoo explores love. However, this is not the love between a man and woman; it is the love of language, or what we might call the love between the writer and her craft. While it proves difficult to determine always where the writer wishes the reader to see her characters as surrogates for herself, I would strongly argue that Sissie's remarks about language reflect Aidoo's personal frustrations at expressing herself and her ideas within the confines of the colonizer's tongue. Sissie's remarks point directly to Aidoo's efforts to write in a less conventional prose style. For example, Sissie explores the very nature of the English language—itself shackled to the ideas, beliefs, and representations of Empire, and she wonders if it is ever possible to express oneself without that imperialistic presence always being there. In the letter to her lover, she writes about those limitations:

My Precious Something,
First of all, there is this language. This
language.

Yes, I remember promising you that I was going to
try and be positive about everything. Since you
reminded me that the negative is so corrosive. You even
went on to give me an illustration of what you meant
with an example from Medicine. That negativism is
malign, like cancer. It chokes all life within its reach as
it grows... I nodded agreement, my eyes lighting up at
how professionally clear you always are. But I
remember too that when I attempted to grasp your point
better by suggesting a political parallel, that negativism
then must be like the expansion of western civilization
in modern times, because it chokes all life and even
eliminates whole races of people in its path of growth,
you said, laughing:
"There you go again, Sissie, you are so serious."
(112)

This passage contextualizes the ideas Aidoo expresses in this
section. First, the personal and intimate address of the letter
suggests an intimate relationship to not only the unnamed lover
but to a language she may love but finds herself frustrated and
restrained by because of its colonial history. Equally, the lover's
scientifically-expressed ideas, linking him to Kunle, reveal his
efforts at suppressing her expression, just as the language of the
colonizer suppresses her. And it is precisely the manner in which
language is used that Aidoo concerns herself with in this section.
While Sissie works to express herself to her lover, an effort she
finally abandons, her "been-to brothers" attempt to use language
to deny their responsibilities to home and maintain their
privileged positions within their colonizer's home.

What Sissie ultimately learns about the language of the
colonizer is that it is used as a borrowed tool by all her African
"brothers" to offer excuses—and sometimes ridiculous excuses
—for not returning home: "For that is also the tragedy—trying to
explain their decisions not to go home. So many versions and
each one more pathetic and less convincing than the one
before"(121). In one example, a young man suggests that it is

unfair for him to return home because of economic hardships awaiting him due to his social position; he comes from a matrilineal family rather than a patrilineal one. The response of his friends, one of derision, reveals Aidoo's humor as well as her sense that the language of the colonizer often sounds ridiculous in the mouths of the colonized. Another example of the extent to which some will go to justify their decision to stay in the metropolis includes the rather humorous problem of facial hair:

> He is approaching thirty but he still can't grow a beard.
> A family trait. He feels such shame. So he has decided to
> have a hair graft on his chin. It is a very expensive
> operation, he declared. He is therefore staying to work
> for a little extra money to get it done. Then he would
> have to wait a year or so while the scars from the surgery
> healed and he also learnt to feel at ease with this new
> and permanent beard.... (124)

Not surprisingly, Aidoo uses an example that defines the problem as one primarily associated with men; it is mostly men who travel to the European "paradise" with desires never to return home, like "Sammy" and Kunle. Through these both humorous and serious encounters, we can see both Sissie's sad disbelief and Aidoo's anger at these "been-to's" rationalizations of their desertion of their homes in a language which was never theirs. While Aidoo works through and investigates the colonizer's language's inability to serve as an adequate vehicle of expression, sadly, in Aidoo's homeland, many wish not to listen because Aidoo's voice is female.

Ama Ata Aidoo, in her novel *Our Sister Killjoy, or Reflections from a Black-eyed Squint,* boldly makes many controversial—yet compelling—statements regarding the erosion of culture that is the legacy of the neocolonial nightmare. And while Aidoo has her critics who attempt to detract from her work, especially African men, her work remains an important contribution to postcolonial literature. Some have condemned her work as "too angry"; it seems that this complaint may be attributable to yet another form of oppression: gender oppression.

"In a speech, 'Unwelcome Pals and Decorative Slaves,' Aidoo refers to the attitude of her involvement in political issues, expressed in a meeting on national development: '[Some Professors] shouted that I am not fit to speak on public matters. That I should leave politics and such to those [men] most qualified to handle it'. Later in the speech, she comments: 'I am convinced that if Killjoy or anything like it had been written by a man, as we say in these parts, no one would have been able to sleep a wink these couple of years'" (qtd. in Wilentz 159-60).

In this anecdote, we see exemplified the divisive politics that manage to separate peoples not only in a global context but also on a local level. And while her novel has generated a number of polemics concerning the relationship of the colonizer to the colonized, of man to woman, of rich to poor, Aidoo offers no prescriptive measures by which to alter or heal these volatile relationships. However, this would certainly be asking too much of her short novel.

Nonetheless, even without providing any answers or solutions (for there may be none), she still calls out to the reader and demands that each of us employ our voices to speak out. Ironically, Aidoo ends her novel with Sissie choosing to speak out by "not speaking." Sissie ends her journey with her return to Africa. Sissie's refusal to mail her love letter is a final and rebellious act which robs the novel of its chance for hope; we are left with the despair that her final spiteful reaction to her "been-to" brothers is one of apathy: "Then she decided she didn't care anyway"(134). Aidoo's final move robs the novel of hope or "kills joy." And while this may be a harsh reality to accept, symptomatic of the postcolonial condition, the novel's final gesture should remind us of Sissie's earlier parallelism between colonialism and a cancerous growth. However, maybe Aidoo did indeed mail her "letter" in the form of this brilliant and experimental novel. And in her work, she challenges us all to resist the global oppression of colonialism in its many forms, especially when it begins to grow like a cancerous tumor within the very heart and soul.

Works Cited

Chetin, Sara. "Reading from a Distance: Ama Ata Aidoo's *Our Sister Killjoy*." *Black Women's Writing*." Ed. Gina Wisker. New York: St.Martin's Press, 1993.

Cooper, Brenda. "*Chaiba the Algerian* versus *Our Sister Killjoy*: The Case for a Materialist Black Aesthetic." *English in Africa* 12.2. (1985):21-51.

Korang, Kwaku Larbi. "Ama Ata Aidoo's Voyage Out: Mapping the Coordinates of Modernity and African Selfhood in *Our Sister Killjoy*. *Kunapipi* 14.3 (1992): 50-61.

Nwankwo, Chimalum. "The Feminist Impulse and Social Realism in Ama Ata Aidoo's *No Sweetness Here* and *Our Sister Killjoy*." *Nagambika. Studies of Women in African Literature*. Ed. Carole Boyce Davies and Anne Adams Graves. Trenton: African World Press, Inc., 1986.

Opara, Chimo. "Clothing as Iconography: Examples of Bâ, Aidoo and Emecheta." *Feminism & Black Women's Creative Writing: Theory. Practice. Criticism*. Ed. Aduke Adebayo. Agodi: AMD Publishers. 1996.

Owusu, Kofi. "Canons Under Siege: Blackness, Femaleness, and Ama Ata Aidoo's *Our Sister Killjoy.* " *Callaloo: A Journal of African-American and African Arts and Letters* 13.2 (1990): 341-63.

Wilentz, Gay. "The Politics of Exile: Ama Ata Aidoo's *Our Sister Killjoy*." *Studies in Twentieth Century Literature*. 15.1 (1991): 159-73.

WOMEN'S UTOPIC IMPULSES IN BUCHI EMECHETA'S *DESTINATION BIAFRA*

Su Fang Ng

At the heart of any vision of political transformation, of political revolution, is always the utopic impulse, whether conceived of as an attempt to return to an idealized past or as a movement that looks forward to a new millenium. Insofar as the field we know as post-colonialism attempts to recover a past history, culture and heritage free of European influence or to institute a future without the sway of European control, it participates in a utopic move. Even if we are careful not to idealize the past, to critique European colonization as invasive already implies a prior wholeness. For that reason, post-colonial critics are increasingly interrogating the "post" in post-colonialism: they question whether it truly signifies a going beyond or past the colonial, arguing that we are still very much in a (neo-)colonial world and that the expanding influence of the United States is a new cultural imperialism.[1] The trend toward skepticism suggests that the post-colonial project as a whole is going through a crisis of faith regarding its original utopic impetus: the belief in the possibility of a future without an unsettling European presence.

This skepticism has even led some critics to all but abandon the post-colonial project when they argue, perhaps rightly so, that history is always about unequal power relations and colonization, European or otherwise.

Interestingly, even skepticism contains at its core a utopic strain because the critique of the post-colonial as inadequate since freedom from our colonial past is not yet achieved, or perhaps even cannot be achieved, demands a purer and more authentic "post-colonial" than history can provide. Rather than to dismiss summarily the utopic strain in post-colonialism as illusionary by claiming that imperialism has always existed, and not just the European variety, as critics from both within and without post-colonial studies have done, I propose that it is important to account for the utopic vision in this highly contentious field.

I want to examine the post-colonial utopia by reading Buchi Emecheta's political novel *Destination Biafra* (1983), which in part is a study of Nigeria's transition from colony to independent state. The protagonist of the novel is one of the new rising generation of Western-educated intelligentsia: Debbie Ogedemgbe, the idealistic Oxford-educated daughter of a venal politician, joins the army in her desire to contribute to the reconstruction of Nigeria into an independent nation. She finds the task difficult: not only is decolonization marred from the beginning by the corruption of the political leaders, but also the military coup that ensues is likewise infected by the lust for power and the divisiveness of the military leaders. The novel chronicles events during the civil war that results from the conflict between the military leaders of Igbos, Yorubas, and Hausa over possession of the oil-wells in eastern Nigeria, an Igbo stronghold. Although a good part of the novel follows the fortunes of the country's leaders, characters who act in the sphere of high politics—that is, in central government where decisions have a national impact and even an international dimension—Debbie Ogedemgbe is the emotional and ethical heart of the novel. Debbie straddles both the public sphere of high politics through her family connections and the private space of ordinary Nigerians by sharing their suffering in the civil war that irrevocably changes their lives. The novel shows that the leaders and politicians are divorced from the concerns of the people they purport to represent. The disjunction between the two spheres becomes an important lesson for Debbie's political education. While Debbie does not accomplish much that is concrete—for instance she fails as a peacemaker between the military leaders of the two opposing sides—her maturation in the experience of the civil war stands as a testimony of hope for a new Nigeria.

Emecheta suggests that the Biafran, or civil, war during the years 1967-70 is part of Nigeria's growing pains. In her novel, she insists on the integral role of utopia and utopic vision in the decolonization project. The utopic longing is embodied in Debbie, but rather than dismissing that utopic longing as simply an impossible desire for a improbably perfect place of post-colonial political and social reforms, through Debbie, the novel interrogates the possibility for a post-colonial nation. Utopia, it seems to me, gets us to the center of post-colonial studies and of the post-colonial condition. In *Destination Biafra*, the utopic longing for the post-colonial nation is unachievable at the present time, but it is only with such ideals that true decolonization can happen. Otherwise, newly-independent nations lapse into cynicism and find themselves betraying the aims of decolonization.

In his survey of literary treatments of the Biafran war, Willfried F. Feuser divides the literature into three kinds: witness literature; poetry and drama; and fictionalized history and parables of the absurd. Although Buchi Emecheta's *Destination Biafra* (1983) is not included in Feuser's survey, it clearly fits in his category of fictional history. Moreover, in his reading of realistic historical fiction of the war, Feuser notes an "ardent desire for a better tomorrow, a superior because more human social organization" (141) in some of the fiction, a trait that Emecheta's novel shares. Although herself an Igbo, Emecheta makes the heroine of her fiction, Debbie, a minority Itsekiri, not a member of any of the three major ethnic groups. In her foreword, Emecheta credits reading Wole Soyinka's *The Man Died* (1972) for giving her a sense of the suffering of non-Igbos, which led to her creation of a woman "who is neither Igbo nor Yoruba nor Hausa, but simply a Nigerian" (viii). Even before the novel itself begins, Emecheta has taken pains to prepare the reader to think in utopic terms, to hope for "a better tomorrow," in Feuser's words, with her detribalized heroine-citizen representing the vanguard of a renewed, harmonious Nigeria. Despite the absence of any large-scale transformation of Nigeria into a post-colonial utopia, there is nonetheless hope and possibility in the new generation who are beginning, like Debbie, to think of themselves as Nigerian citizens rather than primarily as members of particular ethnic groups. In *Destination Biafra*, utopia is modified to mean the creation of a national identity free from ethnic loyalties and biases.

Although, with its overt political subject, this novel concerns itself with public matters in the way that her earlier novels do not, it can still be read as a continuation of Emecheta's earlier preoccupations with the more private problem of female autonomy in such novels as *Second-Class Citizen* (1975), *The Bride Price* (1976), and *The Joys of Motherhood* (1979). Nancy Topping Bazin reads Emecheta as a feminist or at least an emerging feminist. Yakini Kemp, however, identifies a romantic vision in *The Bride Price* and argues that the "women characters affirm their belief that romantic love has a foremost place in their emotional outlook" (15), suggesting that Emecheta's vision may not be feminist after all. On the other hand, Susan Z. Andrade, like Bazin, puts Emecheta within a women's writing tradition, arguing that in her novelization of the 1929 Igbo Women's War or Aba Riots, *The Joys of Motherhood*, Emecheta engages in a dialogue with her literary predecessor, Flora Nwapa, whose *Efuru* (1966) deals with similar issues of women's place in Nigerian society. Whether or not we classify Emecheta as a feminist, there is no denying that her work consistently revolves around women. In *Destination Biafra*, there is a strong link between the private and the public spheres. This is because utopia is reformulated in the end to mean a new nationalist consciousness, and the novel focuses on the ordeals of its female protagonist Debbie who attempts to live out her ideals of a united Nigeria. Indeed, it is only private citizens beginning to see themselves as Nigerian rather than Igbo, Yoruba or Hausa who can bring about national unity. And in the novel, it is the women who turn out to be these private citizens.

However, Chimalum Nwankwo criticizes Emecheta, arguing that her depiction of women in Nigerian society is not entirely accurate: Emecheta, says Nwankwo, does not take into account women's complicity in the oppression of women. If Nwankwo is right, Emecheta's vision can be said to be utopic in the sense that her novel idealizes women. But, in *Destination Biafra*, Emecheta does acknowledge the complicity of her heroine Debbie in a massacre of Igbos. Debbie leads a band of twenty soldiers to imprison a group of Igbo soldiers, whom they humiliate and finally murder. Debbie doesn't lose the reader's sympathy, at least not for long, because she has suffered from witnessing the torture and death of her father in the military coup. Later, she is raped by Nigerian soldiers as she tries to bring about peace by acting as a go-between and messenger between Abosi and Momoh. Although Debbie may have participated in violent acts or may have simply been naive, the end she envisions is a laudable one. Even if her dreams of a utopia never materialize, by the end of the novel Debbie constructs for herself a detribalized national identity that offers hope for the future.

Initially, however, Debbie wants to believe in the idea of a pure nation free from all the mistakes of the corrupt politicians, including her own father, who would sell pieces of their own country to European nations for private profit. She is thus taken in by the idea of Biafra, the region that secedes from Western Nigeria. Led by Chijioke Abosi and made up mostly of Igbos, Biafra claims to be truly independent and uninfluenced by Europeans. Debbie believes in Biafra more strongly than even the truest Igbo patriot: "I have a feeling that this is going to be the real fight for Independence. What we've had up till now was a sham—the Europeans leaving but putting greedy 'yesmen' in the government. Now the young men are fighting for our real freedom, and Biafra may hold the key to that freedom" (114). However, the narrator and characters in the book act as a dissonant, dissenting voice contradicting Debbie. Immediately after Debbie's statement claiming Biafra as the move toward real independence quoted above, the narrator undercuts it in the sentence that follows: "As the conversation grew more idealistic ... " (114). Moreover, Debbie's friend Babs replies, "All this is fine in theory but in reality sounds like a dream" (114). In fact,

of all the main characters, the only believer in the utopic Biafra
is Debbie herself.

A Biafra characterized as an ideal, a theory, and a dream is
hardly a solid foundation on which to build a new order. But
Debbie persists in her belief: she explains, "Biafra seems rather
symbolic to me. The ideal that we should all aim to achieve: a
nation that has been detribalized, a nation where wealth will be
equally distributed ... But it's early days yet" (122). Here, she
suggests that she understands Biafra as a symbol, not reality, but
it is an ideal that for her will translate into reality in the future.
While Debbie sees the future of Nigeria symbolized in Biafra—
the patriotic Biafrans are what she thinks the Nigerians ought to
be—the young Nigerian soldiers newly recruited to fight against
the secession of Biafra think of themselves as the "real
Nigerians" (148). With these two conflicting representations, the
war becomes formulated in terms of questions of authenticity as
both Biafrans and Nigerians argue that they are the true
decolonized nation. Whom do we believe? In this instance, it is
quite easy to dismiss the young soldiers' claim to be the "real
Nigerians." We are apt to understand authenticity as constructed,
and in fact, we see the narrative demonstrate the construction of
authentic Nigerianness by undercutting Debbie's utopian ideas
and the nationalist rhetoric of both leaders.[2] When Nigeria
retakes Ore and Benin from the Biafrans, Abosi is unwilling to
protect the Western Igbos now vulnerable to persecution from
the Nigerians. An old politician, Ozimba asks in anger, "Are
they not Biafrans then? We've been telling them they are—isn't
that why they fought for the cause?" (173). Unconcerned, Abosi
replies:

> "[W]e'll solve their problems after the war is over. But
> we cannot afford now to claim that Biafra is only for us
> Igbos. A great part of our mineral resources is in areas
> where the ethnic language is not really Igbo ... We'll sort
> out those boundaries later ... Meanwhile, Biafra stands
> for freedom, freedom for the persecuted Easterners, most
> of whom are Igbos." (173)

Abosi is only interested in retaining control over the oil resources. He keeps the definition of Biafra contingent, depending on how it will serve his political ambitions.

Abosi manipulates the definition of Biafra so that it appears as a powerful representation of a utopic homeland for the newly-independent Igbos. Attracted to that representation, Debbie braves a dangerous journey across a warring state to convey a message from the leader of the opposing side, Saka Momoh, asking Abosi to come to some kind of compromise. When her mother suggests that Debbie wants to go to the East to seduce Abosi, she rejects the insinuation: "I am going there because of his ideas. I don't believe this is the right time to fight for the concept of Biafra" (153). Although, at this point, Debbie finds that it is more urgent to stop the war, she still believes in the idea of Biafra as a utopia. She is still idealistic, even in her characterization of the war itself:

It is not a war between Abosi and Momoh. This is our war. It is the people's war. Our very first war of freedom. Momoh and Abosi started the purge, to wash the country of corruption and exploitation. Now there is a danger of the two men putting their self-interest foremost. If that is the case, the war will be taken out of their control and put into the hands of responsible leaders who will see the purge through and restore to us a new clean Nigeria. That is why I am going to Abosi, to warn him not to let himself be carried away by personal ambition to such a degree that he forgets his original aim. (153)

Debbie, we are not surprised to learn, given her military ambitions, sees violence as a necessary prelude to utopia. The war is a purge in order to make way for utopia. And she conceives of utopia here as a democracy: it is a "people's war." She only worries that the leaders may have strayed from what she thinks are their original pure intentions to rid the state of corruption, not knowing that they have been self-interested from the very start.

Her mother berates Debbie for her naiveté about the nature of corruption:

Go to the Biafra of your dreams, and when you get there you'll find ordinary people. Not angels, just people. And where there are people there will be corruption and

exploitation. You can't change human nature. But
maybe we all need our Biafras to keep us going. I only
hope you don't get too disappointed with yours when
you find it. (153)

Her mother suggests that Biafra has become an inspiration, a
vision, for Debbie. She also suggests that ideals, though
impossible to achieve, are necessary for human survival. The
human need for symbols may also explain the power of the
utopic representation of the uncorrupted, ethical country of
Biafra for both Abosi's constituents and for the readers of
Emecheta's novel because finally neither the voice of reason and
pragmatic politics nor Debbie's voice of undaunted hope can
silence one another. Two equal voices in the text create
something of a dialogic effect or are akin to the doubled
impression one gets from superimposed pictures. While the
narrator undercuts the rhetoric of nationalism by pointing to its
idealism, Debbie's claim is equally compelling because it is
utopic. The novel does not sanction Debbie's utopic vision, but
her earnestness is attractive. In the course of the novel, the
utopian dream becomes further and further undermined, but still
Debbie's earnestness allows for some limited changes. As I will
discuss later, women in the novel begin to take greater control of
their lives, while the men are creating a debacle with the civil
war.

   Her utopian vision leads Debbie to believe in the possibility
of an active role for women in high politics, so she applies to
join the army before the coup. But Emecheta's narrative suggests
otherwise and does not hold out high hopes for women's
involvement in traditional political roles. It requires the death of
her father, a wealthy Nigerian with political connections, for
Debbie to enter politics through the army. No woman had joined
the army before her, and her father certainly would have opposed
it if he were alive. In addition, it also takes her father's political
connections and her Oxford education for her to join the army.
Even when she is ostensibly allowed entry into the sphere of
high politics, she only becomes the messenger for male military
leaders turned politicians. As a woman, she would raise little
suspicion and no one need ever know that Momoh tried to
negotiate with Abosi if it came to naught. Even this attempt to

insert a woman into the sphere of high politics fails. Debbie only manages to complete her mission near the end of the book when the war has proceeded too far for a compromise and, in fact, Debbie spends most of her time trying to get to war-stricken Biafra in the company of women and young children. Her flight into the jungle removes her from the centers of power whose decisions affect those who flee. Debbie's role seems a marginal one when the male leaders are making monumental decisions that kill thousands and she keeps getting thwarted in her mission. Thus, Debbie is ineffectual as an actor in the sphere of high politics. Although, theoretically, she has access to the leaders of the warring sides, practically Debbie is isolated in the field.

Debbie's other attempt to act as a political leader occurs when she orders a group of Igbo soldiers to be killed. But she appears ridiculous because her victims cannot take a woman seriously as a military officer: the Igbo men are "bemused" and they find themselves "staring at Debbie Ogedemgbe and her small group with undisguised amusement as if to say, 'Whatever you do, however much you are armed and in command now, you are still a woman'" (75). Moreover, it is a moment of disgrace; the action is part of the beginning of the civil war: "While those officers were agonizing and dying little by little in their airless one-room prison, the country was plunged into the kind of bloodbath it has never seen before" (78).

Yet, it can also be argued that most of the novel's other moments of political action, as conventionally understood, are moments of disgrace. The first general elections in independent Nigeria at the start of the novel are a travesty: the future prime minister is selected beforehand by the British colonial officers so that Britain maintains control over the country's natural resources even after independence. The results of the elections disappoint the Igbo supporters of the popular Dr Ozimba, who is given the token post of president despite all his work to bring about independence. Colonel John Nwokolo, an Igbo who is assigned to keep watch on Ozimba after the elections in case he starts an uprising, complains bitterly, "It is not an election but a time bomb. It will explode soon, you mark my words. How many of us are going to sit on our backsides and let this happen? Mallam Nguru Kano the first Nigerian Prime Minister indeed!

This result is like playing *Hamlet* without the prince. Can you imagine a Nigerian government without the great Dr Ozimba?" (25). The military coup that follows is also flawed. Although the plan is to kill the leading politicians of the three major ethnic groups in order to eliminate corruption, somehow "not a single top Igbo politician had been killed" (63), apparently because Ozimba is in the United Kingdom for medical care and his deputy Eze is in hiding. This incomplete coup arouses the suspicion that it is an Igbo plot. Far from serving to unite Nigerians, instead it incites further ethnic divisions.

Moreover, we find the soldiers in the jungle acting unilaterally, not really heeding instructions from above. The common soldiers are out of the control of the political leaders. Even though Debbie has been personally instructed by the leader of West Nigeria, Saka Momoh, to carry an important message into enemy territory, none of the Nigerian soldiers nor civilians believe that she is a soldier herself. Indeed, Debbie's mission suffers a major setback when she is gang-raped by a group of Nigerian soldiers: "She [Debbie] wanted nothing but to lie there, to dream and die in her dreams. To get up and start living again after the experiences of the past night was going to be a Herculean task" (128). Debbie just about loses all hope at this point but for her mother's care. Debbie protests that she is a Nigerian soldier, not a Biafran, but the soldiers refuse to believe her. Her mother Stella, understanding the inflexible nature of ethnic divisions better than Debbie, insists that they say that Debbie was raped by Igbo soldiers because no one would believe the truth: "'I know they weren't Igbos!' Stella Ogedemgbe exclaimed. 'But you're not going to go about telling people you were assaulted by federal forces? No one would believe it. For your name's sake, that must be the story, though the less you refer to it the better'" (152). To what extent, then, are the political decisions made in the so-called center of power truly effective anyway?

That is the question Emecheta asks. Emecheta suggests that high politics may be cut off from reality. When she finally reaches Abosi, Debbie finds that Abosi's rhetoric has overpowered him: Debbie says, "That man intends to fight to the last. He still thinks he can win. He's living in a dream world"

(232). She makes the same judgment about Abosi that her mother has made of her. The difference between Abosi and Debbie, however, is that she knows that her dream is a dream though she would insist that it is a realizable dream; it simply isn't the right time for the fulfillment of it. Abosi, on the other hand, refuses to be honest about what can or cannot be achieved at the present time. Finally, we discover he is also dishonest about his motivations for leading the secession.

Almost as a counterpoint to her protagonist Debbie's unflagging hope for utopia, throughout the novel, Emecheta proposes the possibility of utopia and then abandons it or calls it into question. First, the military coup in *Destination Biafra* results from army leaders' utopic vision of a Nigeria free of corrupt Westernized politicians. Tired of the quarrels between politicians that lead to fighting between their bands of supporters, the army officers argue that "The best thing would be to have a completely new set of people [to govern the country]" (57). The officers decide that "The only sure solution must be for all the politicians ... to be killed" (58). Apart from the dubious use of violence, the coup is marred also by the realities of tribal conflict among the army officers. As it turns out, none of the Igbo politicians are murdered and the head of the military is, suspiciously, an Igbo man. Tribal conflict exists even before the coup is proposed. Saka Momoh, who later becomes the leader of Nigeria when the easterners secede, is dissatisfied with what he perceives as nepotism within the army: Momoh points out that Brigadier Onyemere, who leads the coup and the police state after the coup, "was choosing only officers from his own [Igbo] tribe" (52). Moreover, the hostility between Momoh and Chijioke Abosi, who becomes the leader of the seceded Biafra, also stems from class differences: Momoh "had never bothered to hide his hatred for him [Abosi], believing whatever evidence he heard that Abosi regarded soldiering as a rich man's sport" (52). Unable to defuse these conflicts with his advocacy of a united Nigeria, Onyemere is murdered. Onyemere's death suggests that the utopia that is a united Nigeria may not be viable, at least not at that particular historical point.

The death of Onyemere divides the country into two: the Igbos in the east led by Abosi and the Yorubas and Hausa and others in the west and south led by Momoh. Acting upon the shrewd thinking of his advisers, Abosi allows Momoh to be the titular head of Nigeria so long as he governs, and therefore controls, the oil-rich region in the east, traditionally the stronghold of the Igbos. Momoh, leader of the opposing West Nigeria, rather naively agrees to this at the peace talks at Abusi. The English waste no time in alerting Momoh to the financial consequence of giving East Nigeria autonomy. Realizing his mistake, Momoh, disregarding prior agreements, divides Nigeria into twelve states in order to weaken the unity of East Nigeria. At that point, Abosi declares Biafra's secession from Nigeria: "Now we have no choice but to fight for our right to live as a nation" (99). Biafra is created as a response to the dirty dealing by Momoh, incited by the British. Biafra as Igbo homeland is proposed as an alternative to a united Nigeria, but it also fails as a utopia. Abosi's claim that the war is the Igbos' fight to live as a nation is bolstered by the strong tribal feelings of the various ethnic groups and also by the fact that after Biafra declares secession, the Igbos who happen to live outside the East are persecuted and massacred in large numbers. Abosi's claim, then, is a form of the post-colonial utopia: the claim for the right to live independent of colonizing influences. Nonetheless, political circumstances do not allow for Biafra to exist peacefully. Control of Biafra fundamentally means control of the rich oil-wells of the East, and foreign powers including Britain, France, China, and Russia are eager to supply firearms to keep the war going in hopes of ensuring regular supplies of petroleum in the future. Both Abosi and Momoh too prefer to sacrifice their people for the oil. In the end, like the military coup, Biafra is a utopia tainted by the greed motivating the actions of all involved.

While there is no utopia, Emecheta suggests that the social sphere of women may be more efficacious in achieving political transformation. At least women have a clear vision. They are more honest. At the end of the book, Elina Eze, the wife of one of the Biafran politicians, says to her husband, "Wasn't the oil the reason for all this mess in the first place?" (240). But her husband refuses to admit it: "Is that what you are going to tell your children and granchildren [sic], that we men plunged our nation into chaos because of oil?" (240). He remains hypocritical and blind to the bitter end, even when he has lost everything. Emecheta's narrator confirms Elina's perception: "Pity for the shortsightedness of her husband and his sex came over Elina" (240). Later, Emecheta comments:

> Her husband [Eze] still stared into the distance, seeing the Biafra of his dreams which would be the richest land for black people, where he would be so wealthy that he would not know what to do with the money, where he would be so powerful that Europeans from all over the world would come to seek his friendship.... (240)

Eze, in his last hour, still dreams of power. His dream of Biafra starkly contrasts with Debbie's idealized one. His dream of inverting colonial relations is simply that, an inversion, not a transformation. Eze is still trapped in the logic of colonialism, just like the other wealthy Nigerians who send their children abroad in order to boast that their child is a been-to. Again, as one of the characters who represents the sphere of high politics, Eze does not inspire confidence in the ability of politicians to govern fairly, nor in the possibility of achieving Debbie's ideal through high politics. Nor does Eze inspire confidence that Nigeria will be truly independent.

This contrast between men blinded by avarice and women who are able to acknowledge the truth suggests that the issue of independence in the novel is not merely the problem of cutting Nigeria's colonial ties to Britain. Decolonization is also linked to women gaining independence from male dominance. Emecheta understands oppressive patriarchy as a disease of colonization:

> In the distant past in that part of Africa women were treated almost as men's equals, but with the arrival of colonialism their frail claim to equality had been taken away. Now, with the coming of independence, young women like these [Oxford-educated Babs and Debbie] were determined to play their part in the new nation; and this in turn was making the army boys more brutal to unlucky women caught in any helpless situation. (113)

The identification of patriarchy with imperialism is not complete, though. Emecheta is careful to temper her insistence on the link between the two with modifiers such as "almost" and "frail" in the passage just quoted.

Moreover, Emecheta seems to regard western culture as a source of power for the Nigerian women: her heroine, Debbie, received her education at Oxford and it is that education that, Emecheta implies, forms her into a nationalist. Debbie tells her corrupt father: "Oh, Papa, look what they did in the Congo. Look at how the illiterate soldiers in Ethiopia helped restore Selassie to his throne. Now educated men are going into the army for the love of defending their country" (38-39). As an educated woman, Debbie too wants to join the army for nationalistic reasons though her society understands the purpose of education to be to make her the embodiment of the perfect daughter: "That was what most fathers wanted: a daughter who not only was a been-to [one who has been overseas] but who could talk and behave like a European" (43). Although society would have praised her patriotism if she had been a man, because she is a woman she only appears foolish and foolhardy as her experience of derision and abuse when she enlists shows. The Nigerian soldiers who eventually rape her only laugh at her when she claims to be a soldier herself, accusing her of being a Biafran:

> This [her claim to be a Nigerian soldier] was greeted with laughter. The leader looked derisively at the crumpled man on the ground, then at Ignatius, and asked in undisguised mockery, "What is this? A battle fought by women? Is that how you intend to maintain your so-called invincible Biafra, eh?' (125)

It seems that it is Western education that allows women to break conventions. Juliana, who is Abosi's unorthodox new bride, is a barrister, having been educated at the London School of Economics and Gray's Inn, and a thirty-two-year-old divorceé with a young daughter who, in the British fashion, calls her "Mum" at the wedding of her second marriage. Similarly unorthodox, Debbie has had an English education and an English lover, Alan Grey, both of which give her the necessary access to the British media and the ability to publicize the terrible ravages of the Biafran war to the Western world later in the novel in order to solicit aid from the Red Cross.

The war itself serves as a catalyst for women to break out of their traditional, conventional roles. Women gain more authority as the novel progresses. At the start of the novel, women are portrayed as powerless. This is most clearly seen in the voting process of the first elections. The right to vote is a right that grants citizens the opportunity to participate in government. But here, people are forcibly taken to vote and they are coerced into voting for whomever dragged them to the polling booths; women are especially terrified by the whole process: "Their wives screamed in terror, not knowing what was happening" (19). At the same time, women are demonized in the popular imagination as the worst culprits of inequitable voting, paid to hide ballots in their clothing: "These women, it was said, had rigged votes. They were said to have had about a hundred ballot papers each, nicely tied in their enormous lappa cloths, and to have simply poured them into the ballot boxes" (20). But Hausa women, because they are Muslim, are not even allowed to vote by their men: the future Hausa prime minister Nguru Kano condescends to the British diplomats who question this Hausa practice, "In England, you had democracy for years before your women were allowed to vote? I presume this is so?" (11). When women attempt to break rules, they are punished. For instance, Madam Osajofo carries on an illicit gin trade, trying to circumvent the ban on local alcohol that only profits the politicians who get a cut on the imports, but she repeatedly gets caught and sent to prison. When Debbie's mother tells her father, the major beneficiary of the alcohol laws, that Madam Osajofo is in prison, he asks, "What was she caught doing this time?" and the reply is "Oh, the same thing, her illicit gin trade" (29). Madam Osajofo may be enterprising—she pretends to be in mourning and hides her illicit gin in the coffin—but in the end a group of children recognize her and she is sentenced eight years with most of her property confiscated.

But even upper-class women are not much better off, though they live in luxury, for they are dominated by their husbands: "To Nigerians, in marriage the male partner was superior and the female must be subservient, obedient, quiet to the point of passivity" (42). The wives of the rich become their husbands' status symbols: at the post-elections state banquet, "There was such a big show of wealth and the women came in the latest lace designs. Stella Ogedemgbe and her newly qualified daughter [Debbie] wore shoes heavily decorated with real gold" (39). In fact, rivalry between men can come to a head over women's clothing. When the wives of both Odumosu, the leader of the opposition, and his former friend, Durosaro, who succeeded Odumosu as leader of the Yoruba party, wear the same expensive lace dress to church, Odumosu, humiliated by his failure to win the post of prime minister, takes the coincidence as a personal insult: he fumes, "I bet that treacherous thief knew it [that Odumosu would not become prime minister] all along. I bet he is laughing at us. Now his wife has the audacity to wear the same outfit as my wife" (33). These women are viewed as no more than extensions of their husbands.

But the war gains women a greater control of their own lives, if only because their men are now dead. Toward the end of the novel, as the war worsens, the wives of politicians take matters into their own hands when their husbands prove ineffectual. These wives get together and smuggle their sons out of the country to safety:

> Luckily, the two women's sons [the sons of Mrs Ozimba and Mrs Eze, wives of leading Biafran politicians] listened to their mothers, and left Biafra along with the list of goods and bags of Biafran money. They wrote to their fathers soon afterwards to say that they were safe, and Dr Eze and Dr Ozimba both shook their heads and remarked, 'These women, what they can do.' When the second sons left, and Abosi began to be suspicious, Dr Eze claimed that his two sons had suddenly disappeared. This caused panic inside the cabinet for it was thought that enemies had infiltrated, abducting the sons of the top men. But both Eze and Ozimba slept better, and meanwhile their wives carried on a very lucrative trade [smuggling men out]. (216)

The women are acting in their self-interest, but they are able to do so because they refuse to believe Biafran propaganda. Mrs Ozimba's husband is furious with her because she confuses him with her criticisms of Biafra when he is trying to avoid being made a scapegoat: he argues, "You have to be strong and loyal. This is war and you are the wife of one of the people's leaders. You must have faith.... Even if our news is biased, it is our duty to try to believe it and make others believe" (215). Her husband's response provokes Mrs Ozimba's own anger: "As she looked at her husband, fury swelled her throat, making her look momentarily as ugly as a toad. Many, many things which she would have liked to tell this man forced themselves back into her belly like a lump of vomit that would not come out" (215). She is frustrated because she cannot persuade her husband to think of ways of saving their sons. Because her husband proves to be stubborn, she turns instead to her women friends.

Together with Mrs Eze, Mrs Ozimba sets up a trade smuggling men out of Biafra with the help of Stella Ogedemgbe on the Nigerian side: in a letter, Mrs Ogedemgbe "urged the wives [Mrs Ozimba and Mrs Eze] to remember that the only thing their politician husbands gave them was their names. And because she was Mrs Ogedemgbe she could send them food through the creeks via the Mid-Western towns. She would accept Biafran money, and that way they could get a business going" (216). Stella Ogedemgbe's argument that the wives owe no loyalty to their husbands is a radical departure from the traditional role of women as obedient and passive. This cabal of women is one women's community that has learnt through the hard lessons of the war not to rely on men. Even if their actions are not ethical, they have at least taken a step toward independence. And their actions have political consequences, even if they only ape the corrupt dealings of their husbands in the pre-war years.

The transformation of these wives through the experience of war cannot be underestimated. A prominent example is Debbie's own mother, Stella Ogedemgbe. When Stella is first introduced in the novel, she is the embodiment of the pampered wife of a rich man: she appears, "looking immaculately beautiful as usual" (27) and "sweeping a jewelled arm in the air with abandon" (28). Her highly independent daughter Debbie does not consider her marriage an appropriate model: "She [Debbie] could never agree to a marriage like theirs [her parents'], in which the two partners were never equal" (44). But when Debbie and Stella are stopped and harassed by Nigerian soldiers, Stella retains her dignity despite being stripped of her clothes, and for once Debbie feels proud of her mother: "she could not fail to admire her mother's courage" (127). Indeed, because her mother stands up to the soldiers, they escape death: "She admired her mother, who could use her tongue to move the hardest of men. Those attacking soldiers would surely have killed her but for the fact that, even in their vile drunkenness, they feared Stella Ogedemgbe's tongue" (129). Stella helps Debbie recover from being raped by the soldiers, saving her life:

> She [Debbie] was grateful for having her mother around. Her mother had nursed, talked, prayed, then bullied, telling her daughter to put it [the rape] all behind her, that she could still lead a perfectly normal life—this from a woman who for years had pretended to be so frail and dependent that tying her own headscarf was a big task. All that show of dependence just to keep alive her marriage and to feed her husband's ego; and to think she had played that charade for over twenty-five years!" (150)

Debbie learns then of her mother's true strength. It is the brutal war taking the life of her husband and the honor of her daughter that frees Stella from her prison of dependency. Yet, there are some things that do not change. Stella still holds conventional values, and she wants Debbie to get married: Stella advises Debbie, "'Why don't you stay here and get married? In marriage you'd have all the protection you need and no one would dare refer to what has happened [the rape] again.... An unmarried woman is never respected, Debbie. You know that. It is a man's world here'" (152). Stella seems to forget that having a husband, and a powerful one at that, had not protected her. Nonetheless, even though she may be working toward a conventional goal, Stella shows independence by taking action in trying to shape people's perception of her daughter: "I'm going to build a new image for you. After a few years, people will forget; and, with your dead father's name and money, the right man will soon come along" (152).

Although the politicians' wives do not become entirely new persons, they have made some advances. Stella may not be the sort of independent woman that her daughter is, but she has changed. The wives realize that they can shape their own futures. But if the novel shows that women can act and not just be acted upon, the politicians' wives are not the model that the novel urges its readers to imitate. The woman serving as a positive model who truly becomes a political actor in the service of her country, according to her ideals and ethics, is Debbie, and I shall conclude this essay by returning to her. But first I briefly consider the two examples of women banding together to survive who do come close to becoming political actors: the women in the border zone between Biafra and Nigeria, and the women and children with whom Debbie escapes Nigerian soldiers.

The group of Igbo women refugees and Debbie bond as a result of their harrowing experience hiding from soldiers in the jungle. Debbie joins these refugees when she pretends to be Igbo in order to find a way to enter Biafra to complete her mission. She and a crowd of Igbos are herded into lorries, but on the way to Biafra the men are taken out and murdered. Only the women and children are allowed to continue on the journey. Later the driver is shot by Biafran soldiers and the lorry disabled. The women have to finish the journey by foot without the protection of the Biafran soldiers who refuse to slow down to accommodate the women and children. The experience teaches the women refugees that they do not need to depend on men. When one of the younger women, Dorothy, laments the death of her husband and brothers, wishing to die as well, the older woman Uzoma Madako boxes her right ear and reprimands her, "What type of Igbo woman are you? Which bush community did you come from? What unlucky woman raised you as a daughter? Since when have men helped us look after children? Have you not old people in your cluster of homesteads, to do their job of bringing up the younger ones" (203). Uzoma, working hard to encourage the women not to feel sorry for themselves, is a very different person from who she was before. Like Stella Ogedemgbe, Uzoma changed from her husband's passive appendage to an independent woman who pushes the others to press onward despite themselves:

> Again Debbie marvelled at the resources of women. She
> had seen Uzoma Madako with her husband in Benin,
> seen the way she sat, her head resting passively on a pole
> that supported one of the sheds at the motor park;
> Debbie had seen the way she lifted her eyes as if they
> were so weighty, had heard the way she spoke in a
> whisper. And now look at the same woman, a few days
> after the death of her husband, she had the courage to
> slap another woman, to tell another woman to stop
> indulging in self-pity. (203)

In learning to survive in the jungle, the women learn about their
own strengths and their capacity to act for themselves.

But there are only a few in this group of women, and the
community they form is a transient one. The women disperse
once they reach Biafra. A more permanent community of women
is one in the border region between Nigeria and Biafra. Unlike
the group of refugees, this community is more like a polity. They
have organized themselves so they can go on living their lives,
refusing alliance either with Biafra or with Nigeria. As one
woman from the border declares:

> Yes, we became tired of being in the middle. Your
> Biafran soldiers killed our men and raped our girls,
> because you accused us of harbouring enemy soldiers,
> then Nigerian soldiers would accuse us of the same thing
> even though we are innocent. There was nobody to
> protect us, so we formed our own militia. (218)

Although their militia appears to be made up of men, these
people from the border who have in effect formed their own state
are mostly women: "Nearly all the five hundred or so women
hiding here in the bush had lost someone dear" (219).

The novel gives women far more prominence than men. Men
are relegated to the background, and because they are not given
the same powerful rhetoric as the women, they are
indistinguishable as characters. The women, in contrast, are
vocal about their disillusionment. They have seen their husbands
and sons killed. Abosi has had their leader, Nwokolo, whom one
woman calls, "our man from this part" (218), killed as a
scapegoat. This community of women, having lost their men and

their male leader, having had both the states of Nigeria and Biafra fail them, now seize political self-determination for themselves. Even with male soldiers of their own, the women do not shy from using physical violence to protect themselves: the Biafran soldiers encounter "women who were in a makeshift market in the bush, all armed with clubs, prepared to kill a soldier before being killed themselves" (218). The women's act of forming their own state has none of the superficial trappings of independence, for it is a matter of survival for these women. Debbie comments, "These people here have suffered more than you in the East will ever imagine. The real war is being fought here" (220).

Again and again, it is the people in the margins—Debbie's band of women fleeing the soldiers, the wives of politicians making escape plans as they watch their husbands dig themselves deeper and deeper into a hole, the border people caught in the middle—who understand the truth of the war, and because they are less complicit or because they suffer more, they are quite ready to be brutally honest. Emecheta depicts these women in the margins, removed from the sphere of high politics, as living the "real war," and in a novel where politics is war and war politics, she also claims that the community of women from the border is where real politics is.

It is through her encounters with these myriad possibilities of being a Nigerian citizen—some positive, many not—that Debbie comes to modify her notions of utopia. But before the novel ends, she becomes even more disillusioned with Biafra. She discovers that real politics, or the kind of politics she desires—a utopian politics free of corruption—is not to be had in Biafra. It shocks her to find that even the ordinary ferry man who can take her to Biafra must be bribed: "To think that all this ballyhoo started because people thought our politicians were corrupt and accused them of taking bribes. An ideal place where righteousness would rule, where there would be no bribery, was to be created, and that place would be Biafra ... And now even the canoe man asks for a dash" (223). But Debbie is not completely disillusioned with the idea of utopia. She merely postpones bringing utopia into being: "I still believe in what Biafra stands for; that's the only way I can accept the brutal killing of my father, and the deaths of Ngbechi, Dot and her baby [the women and children with whom she traveled in the jungle] and all those innocent nuns [who had offered them sanctuary]" (224). Debbie's words confirm her mother's suspicions that Debbie needs the idea of Biafra to keep her going. Even if the other reality, the utopia that Debbie imagines, cannot be realized, it is not pointless.

The episode with the ferry man is not Debbie's worst disappointment. When the Nigerians begin the attack on Biafra itself, Debbie goes back to Biafra on her second mission to convince Abosi to surrender. But when she gets there, Abosi has fled with his cars and family. Debbie wonders, "Where was Abosi, the symbol of Biafra?" (243). At this point, Debbie is in the same position as the border women who have lost their male leader. The male figure that Debbie has depended upon now proves to have feet of clay:

> Was her love for Nigeria greater than her admiration and suppressed love for this man? Her feelings were mixed. Let her find him first. He owed her—he owed all of those who had believed in him, in his burning zeal, in his ideal—an explanation. (243)

Abosi's flight is the final disillusionment. Debbie laments, "To be so betrayed, by the very symbol of Biafra!" (243-44). The most devastating treachery is when the symbol of a symbol is found to be lacking. Debbie had pinned all her hopes on Abosi's good intentions, but now she finds that there is nothing to prop up the symbol.

In the novel, Debbie traces a journey, both geographical and symbolic, from west to east (from Yoruba West to Igboland). The journey to the east traditionally symbolizes enlightenment, and indeed, as she gets closer and closer to the Igbo heartland Debbie becomes more and more aware of the sham of Biafra.[3] Abosi's betrayal, one imagines, would lead Debbie finally to repudiate the possibility of a political utopia since even the very core of Biafra is rotten. On the contrary, she is not disillusioned about the concept of Biafra itself. When her English lover, Alan Grey, offers her escape from war-torn Nigeria through marriage to him, she replies:

> I see now that Abosi and his like are still colonized.
> They need to be decolonized. I am not like him, a black
> white man; I am a woman and a woman of Africa. I am a
> daughter of Nigeria and if she is in shame, I shall stay
> and mourn with her in shame. No, I am not ready yet to
> become the wife of an exploiter of my nation. (245)

The moment of her greatest awareness of hypocrisy, when she
witnesses Abosi fleeing the country, is the moment when her
rhetoric of nationalism achieves its highest pitch. At the moment
of greatest shame, she declares full independence from Britain:
"Africa will never again stoop to being your wife; to meet you
on an equal basis, like companions, yes, but never again to be
your slave" (245). Her nationalist rhetoric is also a rhetoric of the
post-colonial utopia free of European domination. It is a brave
rhetoric, considering the rampant corruption we have seen so far
in the sphere of high politics. However, Debbie makes a gender
distinction in that outburst: though the men of Africa may be
"still colonized," Africa's women are striking out for the
independence of their country. The community of women at the
border bears out her contention that women are the true
decolonized citizens of Africa, and they make true, albeit in a
limited way, her utopian hope. The women carry on the legacy
of their foremothers who struck out for their rights in the 1929
Women's War when the colonial government threatened to tax
women, though it was customary for women not to be taxed.
Indeed, Emecheta herself alludes to this past history when she
titles the chapter in which the border women appear "Women's
War."

However, Debbie does not convince Alan Grey: "But the silly
woman had refused his help. That was the trouble with these
blacks. Give them some education and they quoted it all back at
you, as if the education was made for them in the first place....
That's life ... Nigeria will learn one day. See how long it has
taken us" (245-46). This attitude is only to be expected from
Alan, who has shown himself to be very pragmatic about
politics; in fact, though initially he appears to be sympathetic to
the Nigerians, Alan proves to be mainly concerned with securing
British interests in Africa. What is unexpected is that the narrator
seems to confirm Alan's view; the last sentence of the novel is:

"He was right, it was all a part of life" (246). Is Emecheta asserting that greed and the abuse of power is ubiquitous? Is Emecheta finally unremittingly cynical?

There are several answers to this question. Alan is right in that the civil war is part of a learning process for Nigeria. The lesson, however, is not the pragmatic, instrumental politics that Alan himself practices, but that true independence requires leaders and a people who are not materially dependent on the West. A mere form of democracy is not enough, as we see in the rigged elections at the start of the novel. The other answer is that there simply is no pastoral Ur-world. Prior to colonization, the ethnic groups were as divided as they are at the time of the novel. When Debbie says, "I want Nigeria to be one as we have always been" (166), she is laughed at. And she realizes the falsehood of her statement: "Nigeria was only one nation as a result of administrative balkanization by British and French powers" (166). Her only argument is that "for over half a century Nigeria had been one nation" (166). Debbie's argument, then, takes the recent history of imperialism into account. Her utopia becomes less and less of an idealized place, less of a no-place, and takes on a more solid aspect. The women she meets shows her what can be done and what the limits are: that people can form a political community, but that achieving national unity will take a long time; however, to give up working toward unity would be to give in to a colonized mentality and to corruption.

Though the novel makes it clear from the start that the war is about oil rather than solely about the Igbos' noble desire for independence as a newly decolonized people, Emecheta's Biafra nonetheless remains an attractive utopia, managing to evade the taint of oil even when Emecheta calls the utopic vision into question. This attraction can be attributed to the unflagging optimism of the heroine-protagonist of the book, Debbie, because for all our realism we need visionaries, which is what Debbie is. Biafra as utopia, or perhaps the idea of utopia itself, remains appealing despite the numerous times Emecheta undercuts the possibility of utopia, because of the close association of utopia with Debbie herself. Even if utopia is not to be found, Debbie stays a believer, and hence, utopia prevails in her. By the end of the novel, utopia becomes transformed. No longer a move to recuperate native wholeness or an idealized world, utopia instead becomes a faith in the possibility for genuine political action, and that action must be at the grass-roots level where people are forced to defend their very lives.

Emecheta uses this concept of utopia to suggest in her book that true independence is possible for both the colonial subject and the female subject in patriarchy. At the end, Debbie repudiates not only the British colonizer in the person of Alan, but also the African patriarch in the person of Abosi. Emecheta suggests that African women can act politically without men, white or black. If she has been maybe too enamored of the romance plot in *The Bride Price*, in *Destination Biafra* the romance plot is thoroughly emptied out. This later novel is a fully feminist text. Finally, Emecheta's modified utopia is one that gets us out of the impasse of having to choose between an undesirable instrumental politics and an illusionary pre- or post-colonial purity that does not exist. Emecheta's utopia offers us a productive direction toward which we can theorize the post-colonial.

Notes

[1]

In an interview with Robert Young, Gayatri Spivak says, "I find the word postcolonialism totally bogus" (224). She elaborates: "more economic and less territorial: this is neocolonialism, and in fact neocolonialism is like radiation—you feel it less like you don't see it—you feel like you're independent" (221). Others who question the term are Ella Shohat in "Notes on the Post-Colonial" and Graham Huggan in "Postcolonialism and its Discontents." Masao Miyoshi argues in "A Borderless World? From Colonialism to Transnationalism and the Decline of the Nation-State" that "colonialism is even more active now in the form of transnational corporatism" (728). At the same time that post-colonial critics are questioning our true separation from the colonial masters, critics from the center are criticizing the post-colonial project: Michael Holquist writes, "Stereotyping is a universal strategy for seizing the other," (460) showing that the so-called colonialism occurs even in a text like F. Scott Fitzgerald's *The Great Gatsby*. But Holquist's contention, I would argue, suffers from a lack of historical context.

[2]

In his article, Willfried F. Feuser quotes Dr. Nnamdi Azikiwe, the former president of the National Council of Nigeria and the Cameroons (N.C.N.C.), an Igbo party, whose nationalist rhetoric sounds very much like the kind Emecheta ironizes in her book: "It would appear that the God of Africa has created the Ibo [a variant spelling] nation to lead the children

of Africa from the bondage of the ages ... The Ibo nation cannot shirk its
responsibility from its manifest destiny" (114).

3   The symbolism is European, and Emecheta works within the European
genre of the novel. In fact, the novel can be viewed as a *Bildungsroman* of
the political maturation of Debbie Ogedemgbe.

Works Cited

Andrade, Susan Z. "Rewriting History, Motherhood, and Rebellion: Naming an
    African Women's History Literary Tradition." *African Languages and
    Cultures* 3 (1990): 149-65.
Bazin, Nancy Topping. "Feminist Perspectives in African Fiction: Bessie Head
    and Buchi Emecheta." *Black Scholar* 17.2 (1986): 34-40.
——. "Venturing into Feminist Consciousness: Bessie Head and Buchi
    Emecheta." *The Tragic Life: Bessie Head and Literature in Southern
    Africa*, ed. Cecil Abrahams. Trenton: Africa World Press, 1990. 45-58.
——. "Weight of Custom, Signs of Change: Feminism in the Literature of
    African Women." *World Literature Written in English* 25 (1985): 183-
    197.
Emecheta, Buchi. *Destination Biafra*. Oxford: Heinemann, 1982.
Feuser, Wilfried F. "Anomy and Beyond: Nigeria's Civil War in Literature."
    Présence Africaine: Revue Culturelle du Monde Noir 137/138 (1986):
    113-51.
Holquist, Michael. "Stereotyping in Autobiography and Historiography:
    Colonialism in *The Great Gatsby*." *Poetics Today* 9 (1988): 453-72.
Huggan, Graham. "Postcolonialism and its Discontents." *Transition: An
    International Review* 62 (1993): 130-35.
Kemp, Yakini. "Romantic Love and the Individual in Novels by Mariama Bâ,
    Buchi Emecheta and Bessie Head." *Obsidian II: Black Literature in
    Review* 3.3 (1988): 1-16.
Miyoshi, Masao. "A Borderless World? From Colonialism to Transnationalism
    and the Decline of the Nation-State." *Critical Inquiry* 19 (1993): 726-51.
Nwankwo, Chimalum. "Emecheta's Social Vision: Fantasy or Reality?"
    Ufahamu: Journal of the African Activist Association 17 (1988): 35-44.
Shohat, Ella. "Notes on the Post-Colonial." *Social Text* 31/32 (1992): 99-113.
Soyinka, Wole. *The Man Died: Prison Notes of Wole Soyinka*. London: Rex
    Collings, 1972.
Spivak, Gayatri Chakravorty. "Neocolonialism and the Secret Agent of
    Knowledge," interview with Robert Young. *Oxford Literary Review*
    (1991): 220-51.

"LOOSE OR DECENT, I DON'T KNOW": SPACE, SELF, AND NATION IN TSITSI DANGAREMBGA'S *NERVOUS CONDITIONS*

Jennifer Poulos Nesbitt

Late in Tsitsi Dangarembga's first novel, *Nervous Conditions* (1988), the protagonist Tambudzai (Tambu) admits that her opportunity to pursue a Western-style education will forever alter her relationship with home:

> I was to take another step upwards in the direction of my freedom. Another step away from the flies, the smells, the fields and the rags; from stomachs which were seldom full, from dirt and disease, from my father's abject obeisance to Babamukuru and my mother's chronic lethargy. Also from the Nyamarira that I loved. (*NC* 183)

Tambu, the narrator of *Nervous Conditions*, is about to enter the Sacred Heart convent school, where she will, paradoxically, both encounter the full force of racism and develop skills that may help her evade "the weight of womanhood" (*NC* 16) as it is experienced at her impoverished homestead. Despite her understanding of the disadvantages of life on the homestead, Tambu's lament has a curiously nostalgic tone that is heightened by the longing in the last sentence. She attaches her positive feelings about home to the river Nyamarira, free of the "dirt and disease" found on the homestead itself, balancing her litany of filth and failure with a short sentence fragment. In the following pages, I attempt to account for the weight Tambu lays on Nyamarira. For this passage, freighted with allusions to race, gender, and class in colonial Rhodesia, is about far more than leaving home.

In *Nervous Conditions*, the river Nyamarira is a site where subjects are both gendered and colonized. For Tambu, the river is a source of pleasure, but a pleasure deeply disciplined by both gender codes and colonial domination. Tambu's psychological attachment to the river thus fades into nostalgia as she becomes aware that the river participates in constructing gendered and colonized subjects. Nyamarira both organizes space through gender and enforces "natural" gender roles, and, further, reflects the organization of space by colonialism. Layered together, "the poverty of blackness on one side [colonialism] and the weight of womanhood on the other" (*NC* 16) stultify the lives of Shona women.

But Tambu's resistance to the formation of gendered, colonized subjects also destabilizes the meanings attached to the river, for the circuit of meaning that organizes gender and colonization also constructs the meaning of space. Indira Karamcheti's assertion about so-called Third World women writers holds true for the narrator of *Nervous Conditions*: "anatomy and geography are equally destiny" (126). The space Tambu occupies and moves through defines her as inexorably as her sex. Combatting that "destiny" is a treacherous project, especially since entitlement to the land is crucial in the battle against colonial power, and women are often considered embodiments of the home-*land*. Tambu's resistance to the circuit of representation that connects land claims and gender roles can easily be read as a betrayal of anti-colonial nationalist politics. In attempting to understand the role of the river Nyamarira in perpetuating the creation of gendered subjects, we begin to see the disturbance caused by Tambu's resistance to gender norms as crucial to a developing nationalist politics.

Nervous Conditions is the first part of a female *bildungsroman*, set in 1968 Rhodesia, just before the Zimbabwean guerrilla war for independence intensified. Tambu's adolescence occurs in the proverbial calm-before-the-storm: Though we hear of the rebels' actions occasionally during *Nervous Conditions*, national events are ancillary to the plot. Such events do establish, however, an implicit parallel between the twinned stories of a girl and a new nation coming of age. According to Tambu, her story is actually multiple because she chronicles the lives of several women in her family, some of whom "escape" the frustrating gender codes that prevail in Shona society (*NC* 1). Although this multiple focus refracts Tambu's success against other, perhaps failed, narratives, Tambu's escape through education is central to the novel. She draws from the stories of other women to navigate a Scylla and Charybdis created by the intersection of patriarchal customs and paternalist Western colonialism.

Scholarship on *Nervous Conditions* has primarily considered the psychology of gender and colonization, particularly as it relates to the various eating disorders in the novel (see Bahri, Creamer, McWilliams). Here, I take a different route—that of geography—to discuss the ways Tambu's resistance to patriarchy threatens a fundamental part of nation-building: the claim to land. For, as Edward Said comments briefly in *Culture and Imperialism*, "the main battle in imperialism is over land, of course" (xii-xiii). His call for a carefully-nuanced study of art "in the global, earthly context" rests on the claim that

> Everything about human history is rooted in the earth, which has meant that we must think about habitation, but it has also meant that people have planned to *have* more territory and therefore must do something about its indigenous residents. At some very basic level, imperialism means thinking about, settling on, controlling land that you do not possess, that is distant, that is lived on and owned by others. (7)

Imperialism, personified in *Nervous Conditions* as the white colonists who control Rhodesia, has altered the connection of the indigenous Shona to the land. For the Shona, colonial politics means spatial dislocation and impoverishment. Tambu's family homestead is "so stony and barren that the wizards [whites] would not use it" (*NC* 18), according to her grandmother; that is the only reason the Shona are allowed to farm it. Conditions on the homestead reflect the fall in the family fortunes: the farming chores are difficult, the "squalor was brutal" (*NC* 7), and both furniture and buildings are dilapidated. Although this squalor partially reflects the laziness of Tambu's father, the overall poverty is part and parcel of the spatial inequalities of colonialism.

Given the overdetermined meanings of the homestead, Tambu understandably focuses her "love" of home on Nyamarira, thus avoiding an attachment to lands saturated with restrictive meanings. But her evasion fails because it is based on the assumption that some spaces are devoid of such "affiliations" (Said 7). Tambu's initial position is that of Said, who attempts to distinguish between the land and the land's meaning:

> The main battle in imperialism is over land, of course; but when it came to who owned the land, who had the right to settle and work on it, who kept it going, who won it back, and who now plans its future—these issues were reflected, contested, and even for a time decided in narrative. (xii-xiii)

Dangarembga's novel shows conclusively that distinctions between "land, of course," and its role in signifying practices, cannot be made. Whether "real" or fictional, the land is always marked, producing and circulating meaning. As Henri Lefebrve claims in *The Production of Space*, space is both "a *product* to be used" and "a *means of production*" (83, emphasis original); it cannot be placed in a domain anterior to human meaning-making, and it is a site where meaning is negotiated. To claim a prior, natural state of the land merely creates a loophole through which to sustain "true" claims to land.

Invoking truth in relation to land raises questions of essentialism that have annoyed feminists and, more recently, feminist geographers because such essentialisms often mask limiting notions of women's subjectivity and agency. Both feminists and feminist geographers argue that space is organized by/organizes gender, and perpetuates patriarchy. Virginia Woolf's *A Room of One's Own* (1928) demonstrated with her famous example of the beadle on the college lawn that space is strictly demarcated by gender, and that the spaces themselves help produce these discriminations (5-6). More recently, feminist geographers like Doreen Massey and Gillian Rose have amplified Woolf's point, arguing that ideas about space and mobility are strongly marked by gender in conjunction with other factors, such as class, race, and global economic organization. Rose, in *Feminism and Geography*, argues that "transparent space" (159) implies something like Said's "land, of course": a vision of space as a fully knowable, natural object. Feminism, she states, "through its awareness of the politics of the everyday, [has] always had a very keen awareness of the intersection of space and power—and knowledge" (142). To avoid complicity with masterful notions of space, Rose proposes the concept of a "paradoxical space" "imagined in order to articulate a troubled relation to the hegemonic discourses of masculinism" (159). Rose, then, destabilizes the idea of space as fundamentally *there to be known* in order to resist the often sexist assumptions that ground this notion.

Massey claims that "space is socially constituted" (265) and also argues that space circulates meaning rather than simply providing a ground for human signifying practices. Massey finds that "the social and the spatial are inseparable and that the spatial form of the social has causal effectivity" (255). Massey's speculations about the idea of "home" are an example of the implications of her argument particularly germane to this paper:

It is interesting to note how frequently the characterization of place as home comes from those who have left, and it would be fascinating to explore how often this characterization is framed around those who—perforce—stayed behind; and how often the former was male, and the latter female. (166-167)

The association of the home, and by extension the homeland, with woman makes Third World women who resist such gender roles politically dangerous. Partha Chatterjee, for example, elaborates on the crucial role Bengali women played in securing "home" (*ghar*) as a site from which to launch a nationalist politics. Representing a never-colonized "inner, essential identity," women preserved a national culture until men could master Western ways "in order to ultimately overthrow the colonizer" (121). Similarly, the Zimbabwean nationalist movement's claim to their land rested on "going back to our roots" (Wilkinson 193), and these roots, Dangarembga bitterly writes, designate "the supreme honor roll qualification" for a woman as "Bride of the Year" ("This Year, Next Year" 43). The idea of the homeland is saturated with gender, and thus the maintenance of patriarchy is closely implicated in nationalist aims. When Karamcheti states that "women writers from the Third World do not pretend to claim virgin territory for literary representation but instead move to retake ground already heavily appropriated by the same (neo)colonial powers that have appropriated their physical land" (130), the net draws even tighter: patriarchy and colonialism weave a representational web that is difficult to unknot without running afoul of national loyalty.

Nervous Conditions situates the potential for Tambu to have a plotline—in the narrative and the geographical sense—in a gap that temporarily opens in the patriarchal succession. The narrator, an older Tambu looking back on her adolescence, announces, "I was not sorry when my brother died" (*NC* 1). Her animus rests on her brother's nonchalant enjoyment of male privilege. She views his specific behaviors—for instance, sending his younger sister running two miles to the bus stop for luggage he is quite capable of carrying himself—as manifestations of a general system: "in reality he was doing no more than behave, perhaps extremely, in the expected manner. The needs and sensibilities of the women in my family were not considered a priority, or even legitimate" (*NC* 12). Nhamo's death allows Tambu, quite literally, to take his place at a missionary school run by her uncle, and creates a narrative space in which women's stories emerge. At the end of the novel, Tambu reiterates that "the story I have told here, is my own story, the story of four women whom I loved, and our men" (*NC* 204). The men in *Nervous Conditions*, though exerting a powerful pull in the novel, have been decentered in order to reveal the stories of the women.

The mastery of space and mobility are important components of Nhamo's privilege. When Tambu worries that Nhamo has insufficient study time, her brother repulses her interference in his affairs with the remark, "I should know. I go to school. You go nowhere" (*NC* 21). He gets to *go*, and Tambu must stay at home, all "Because you are a girl" (*NC* 21), as Nhamo explains. Nhamo also uses his male privilege to make his sisters move at his will, as seen above, in order "to demonstrate to us and to himself that he had the power" (*NC* 10). His position exemplifies what Doreen Massey calls "power geometry." She uses this term to indicate the different levels of control subjects have over space, and she argues that the power level of one subject can weaken the potential power of another (3-4). In this case, Nhamo's ability to move balances Tambu's immobility; only when he disappears can she gain greater control over her place. Tambu acutely perceives the injustice of a power geometry that relies on arbitrary differences like gender to determine actions and agency. What she does not consciously realize early in the novel is the extent to which space participates in both the formation and perpetuation of power geometry. Her actions resist power geometry without articulating it as politics; Tambu is not fully aware of the implications of her actions. As Heidi Creamer points out, "the informed narrator shows how Tambu's previous understandings of her actions might have been naive, but that not all her actions were naive" (351).

Tambu's gradual understanding of the complicity of the river Nyamarira illustrates aptly her growing awareness. Tambu initially describes Nyamarira as Eden: "The river, the trees, the fruit and the fields. This is how it was in the beginning." Even in this prelapsarian state, however, gender roles matter. As children, Tambu and her friends "could play where [they] pleased" in the river without reference to gender, and they preferred the "deeper, cooler, more interesting pools." "But," the narrator warns, "the women had their own spot for bathing and the men their own too." Both pleasure and mobility at the river are limited by future gender proprieties; the girls are "apprehensive about growing so big that [they] would have to wash...with the women." The women's place to wash is "shallow...the rocks were lower and flatter...sensibly architectured for doing the laundry." Womanhood involves learning to prefer a less pleasurable bathing spot because it is convenient for domestic chores. The river participates in constructing gendered subjects and perpetuates patriarchal law (*NC* 3).

Dangarembga layers the spatial politics of colonialism atop pre-existing divisions of space along gender lines. The arrival and power of the colonial administration appears as changes in pedestrian traffic and river use, and the colonists are first seen as spatial intruders. They construct District Council Houses "to enable administration of [the] area" (*NC* 3). The government buildings, now "less than a mile away from the places where [they] washed," produce a doubled system of surveillance. Now, "all the inhabitants" of the village pass the washing place to go to the government offices, the bars, or the bus stop because the Council Houses have drawn the social and economic activity of the neighborhood into the colonists' orbit. Traditional bathing sites must be "relegated to further up the river" to preserve "decency." (*NC* 4) Although *decency* can be construed here as hiding nakedness, it also may indicate a desire to hide daily tribal business from the government's critical eyes. This displacement repeats the history of dislocation Tambu learned from her grandmother because the new bathing places are, by implication, less pleasant than the old. The inhabitants of the village suffer a diminution of pleasure in the river due to colonial intrusion, and by inference the women lose more. "Swim[ming] blissfully...in the old deep places" becomes a doubly illicit pleasure for Tambu, who now breaks both gender and race codes to swim there (*NC* 4).

These codes circulate meaning through space to bodies and back to space, so that even rebellion against the codes is articulated in terms that reify them. When Tambu and her friends, alone at the river, are freed from the observation of their elders, they make fun of "decency": "when we felt dangerous we raised false alarms for the sensual fun of it, shouting that a lascivious male was leering at us from the ridge" (*NC* 134). Their role-play enacts the realities of the gender system. At the

river, Tambu says, the leering male could be either black or
white; either way, as with Susanna at the bath, the girls' decency
could be compromised. Although they "act out" against these
strictures of decency, their ideas of pleasure and danger already
mirror patriarchal authority.

The passage from *Nervous Conditions* with which I began
this paper—"And also the Nyamarira that I loved" (183)—
strikes the reader oddly when it occurs because Tambu has not
mentioned the river as a site of pleasure or nostalgia for many
pages. The addition of Nyamarira to a litany of filth becomes
even stranger because it precedes a scene that clearly
demonstrates the river's role in maintaining the power geometry
of patriarchy compounded by colonialism. The scene in question
involves the reinstitution of the patriarchal and colonial order on
the homestead through the bathing of Tambu's mother. This
bathing guarantees both the mother's survival and Tambu's
escape, but it also ends the mother's rebellion against patriarchy
and the "Englishness" (*NC* 202)—her way of designating
colonialism—she accuses of collaborating to kill her children.
Her submission to these forces, with Tambu's complicity, turns
the mother's story into the story of "entrapment" Tambu
foreshadowed at the beginning of the novel (*NC* 1).

Tambu's escape requires that she subconsciously recognize
how gender codes trap her mother. As Tambu records the story
of her mother, she acquires barely articulated knowledge of the
forces ranged against her ambitions, and her capacity to act
complicitly with them. If only as a passive observer, Tambu
recognizes her mother's rebellion for what it is, and does nothing
to prevent her mother's reinscription within patriarchal norms.
After learning that Tambu's uncle and father will allow her to
attend the convent school, her mother refuses to eat and, more
significantly, ceases caring for her infant son Dambudzo,
successor to the prized Nhamo. "I knew what was worrying my
mother," says Tambu. "A medium could not help whereas I
could, by not going to Sacred Heart. But this was asking too
much of me..." (*NC* 184). If the mother were to die, male
relatives would force Tambu to abandon her education. As the
eldest daughter, Tambu would replace her mother as caretaker of

Dambudzo, and be consigned to maintaining and perpetuating male privilege in the form of the sole male heir.

Tambu's aunt, Lucia, saves her from this fate by using the Nyamarira to evoke "natural" maternal feelings on the part of Tambu's mother. This passage is worth quoting at length:

> "Sisi," she [Lucia] threatened, wading calf-high through the water and depositing Dumbudzo [sic] on a boulder, "watch me. I am putting him on this rock and leaving him there, right in the middle, in the middle of the river. If he slips into the water because you do nothing to save him then you will truly go mad, because this time you will be guilty." Dambudzo, because the rock was warm and smooth and because the water sparkled prettily at its edges, thought it was a jolly game. He gurgled at Lucia and crawled to the edge to splash. Babies are clever and do not crawl over edges, but mothers are anxious nevertheless.
>
> "Lucia," my mother said, "Lucia, why are you doing this? Why? Why do you bother me? Why don't you just let me die?" And removing her dress she waded out to the rock to wash herself and her son. While mother was washing, Lucia washed my mother's dress for her, so that when my mother and Dambudzo were clean, they were forced to sit in the sun until the dress dried. Now, unlike a physical ailment of which everyone is told, an illness of this nature is kept quiet and secret, and so when other women came to wash or to draw water they saw my mother and Lucia and Dambudzo leisurely waiting for their clothes to dry, which is a normal sight at Nyamarira. In addition, they were all very pleased to see Lucia and so they were very lively and gay when they came over to greet my mother and Lucia....It was all very good medicine. (*NC* 185)

Lucia's "rescue" of Tambu's mother, which Tambu calls "shock treatment" (*NC* 185), exemplifies the contradictions inherent in Tambu's relationship with the river. Life equals patriarchal domination, compounded by colonization, for Tambu's mother. First, Lucia forces the mother to act on maternal instincts—

"mothers are anxious nevertheless"—which the narrator views as a trap: "Babies are clever..." The verbs in the passage, *threatened* and *forced*, underline the narrator's perception of the coercion involved.

The second paragraph combines the approving gaze of "other women" with a conspiracy of silence about "an illness of this nature" to confirm the disciplinary nature of bathing at the river. The secrecy surrounding the mother's rebellion makes her defeat invisible. When other women see the trio "leisurely waiting for their clothes to dry," they only register it as "normal." The disciplining of the mother is a non-event. Instead, the women react normally to normal behavior, reintegrating the mother into the patriarchal order by "laughing over how Dambudzo had grown, what a handsome young man he was becoming" (*NC* 185). The river appears as a site of pleasure, as the phrases "warm and smooth," "sparkled prettily," and "lively and gay" indicate, but it is clearly a site of profound anguish for the mother: "Why don't you just let me die?" The narrator's final comment, that "it was all very good medicine," drips the acid of irony on the facts of the mother's "recovery."

To indicate her discomfort with and ambivalence toward this "good medicine," Tambu narrates the passage with great distance. It is not clear whether she directly witnessed the event, or whether she reports actions told to her by others. Present or not, however, Tambu's complicity in sacrificing her mother for her own benefit is clear. When Tambu leaves home preparatory to attending convent school, her connection to the river seems to lose force as a matter of course. But in that brief statement, "Also from the Nyamarira that I loved," Tambu encapsulates her awakening realization of the conflict between a nostalgic love for the land and a recognition of the power relationships it perpetuates.

Tambu's loss of Nyamarira as an affective connection to home impinges on the question of the role of gender in nationalism, and consolidates her discussion of decency as it is performed at the river. When Tambu attributes to "decency" (*NC* 4) the changes wrought on the river-space by the colonial presence, she notes that "all the inhabitants of the dozen or so homesteads that made up our village" (*NC* 3) cross the river to conduct business with the government. The neutral term *inhabitants* does not discriminate; Tambu gives no indication which inhabitants' gazes would be impertinent. The role of "other women" in the scene above shows that women's gazes are appropriate; their gazes are, in fact, extremely pertinent, because they normalize—confirm the decency of—the mother's behavior. Women policing women is "a normal sight at Nyamarira" (*NC* 185), and it is against this cultural order, sanctioned within colonialism, that Tambu rebels.

Tambu, as a woman leaving home, navigates a different course through colonialism and patriarchy than either her Anglicized uncle Babamukuru or her brother, who was to follow in his footsteps (*NC* 15). The two men pursue Western-style education in order to help the family regain some of the prosperity colonization ruined, and to maintain the patriarchal order. Babamukuru went to the mission "to prepare...for life in their [the colonists'] world" (*NC* 19). As Tambu's cousin Nyasha says bitingly, her father is "a good boy, a good munt" (*NC* 200), toadying to colonial powers to perpetuate what cultural "traditions and expectations and authority" (*NC* 190) he can given the situation. Nyasha—who spent her formative years in England—sees the sexism involved in this strategy: men, even as they adapt to Western ways to survive, expect women to retain traditional values. Nyasha notes that crucial to this tradition is "all the things about boys and men and being decent and indecent and good and bad" (*NC* 190). Western influence— whether perceived as an improving or destructive force—should not extend to women because women embody the Shona's cultural origins. The men layer Western sexism atop pre-existing values and force women into the role of culture preserver.

Tambu's pursuit of education upends rather than furthers these cultural goals. Her cultural value, according to her uncle, can be harmed by too much Western influence: "I have observed from my own daughter's behavior," says Babamukuru, "that it is not a good thing for a young girl to associate too much with these white people" (*NC* 180). Education might unfit Tambu for marriage with "a decent man" who can install her in "a decent home" (*NC* 180). Decency is preserved as long as Tambu remains in her proper place—at home. Babamukuru here uses a version of Chatterjee's argument about the role of women as signs of national culture under colonialism. Men, Chatterjee argues, must adapt to "the new conditions outside the home" brought by colonialism so that they can both fulfill their role as men and learn the tools with which to dismantle the master's house (130). Women, representing the "inner sanctum" of culture embodied in the home (Chatterjee 121), must advance only as far down the educational path as to make them better wives and mothers (*NC* 180; Chatterjee 128-129). Although Babamukuru's arguments are not cast in overtly nationalist terms, they align with the vision propagated by the Zimbabwean nationalists of "going back to our roots."

Only when Tambu's aunt Maiguru analyzes the tyranny of the word *decent* as it is used against women does Babamukuru relent and allow Tambu to accept the scholarship. Maiguru undermines Babamukuru's use of decency by invoking its opposite, *looseness*:

> People were prejudiced against educated women. Prejudiced. That's why they said we weren't decent.... I don't know what people mean by a loose woman— sometimes she is someone who walks the streets, sometimes she is an educated woman, sometimes she is a successful man's daughter or she is simply beautiful. Loose or decent, I don't know. (*NC* 181)

Loose is a pejorative term used to denigrate any exceptional woman who challenges male primacy. Etymologically, *loose* connotes unrestrained mobility. To oppose this term to *decent* implies that, although decency has no spatial connotation, "go[ing] nowhere" is a positive value that guarantees womanly propriety. The spatial implications of *loose* and the moral implications of *decent* fuse in a knot of signification that makes mobility in women a sign of licentiousness. Maiguru also rips the mask from Babamukuru's use of *decency* as a contrast between races, and reveals the patriarchal authority operating beneath his concern for Shona tradition: "when we went to South Africa, everybody was saying that we, the [educated] women, were loose. It wasn't a question of associating with this race or that race at that time" (*NC* 181). She repeats her husband's verb choice, *associate* (see above), to reveal the sexism behind constraints placed on women in the name of culture. Her analysis of decency unties the representational knot with which Babamukuru has nearly trapped Tambu, and gives Tambu the skills to read the meanings circulating through the bathing scene she will narrate in the forthcoming pages.

Tambu's story is a sophisticated critique of the connections between space, self, and nation that work so inexorably on the women in *Nervous Conditions*. The stakes Dangarembga plays with—"land, of course"—are high because the narrative highlights the production of sexual difference in national subjects—the citizens of a new nation—as integral to territorial claims. Dangarembga's brief comment on the colonists' vision of the land and people they rule, filtered through the naïve consciousness of young Tambu, usefully concludes this discussion: "They thought he [Babamukuru] was a good boy, cultivatable, in the way that land is, to yield harvests that sustain the cultivator" (*NC* 19). The colonists' view the land as material, but the land, no less than the person, is never prior to human history. The brutality of the colonists' simile lies in its failure to ascribe meaning to either the person or the land. What Dangarembga does in *Nervous Conditions* is to unearth the multiple levels on which such blindness functions to create and perpetuate power geometries. In the liminal space before Zimbabwean independence, Dangarembga shows that land, and claims to the land, are intimately bound up with understandings of gender, making what seems a small matter—Tambu's struggle to be educated—reveal plotlines suppressed in the name of nationalism.

The struggle brings together feminism and nationalism to reveal that the nostalgia inherent in nationalist claims renders women's role in nationalist politics dangerous and complicated. The meaning of feminism here encompasses both the worldwide struggle by women for self-determination, and a perhaps insidious form of Westernization. Exploiting the gap produced between the Shona's gender roles and a patriarchal colonialism by this double meaning, Tambu escapes what is, for her, a stifling home. But her embrace of the "English," despite her promise never to "forget" her roots (*NC* 188), positions her between cultures; her vulnerability to the double standard outlined by Maiguru remains. The impending war for Zimbabwe's independence gives this vulnerability deeper resonance. Writing of the wars in the former Yugoslavia, Loretta Stec attributes the brutal treatment of women during that war to "narratives that nostalgically link the subordination of women with definitions of nationhood" (155). If "the submission of women to men is a precondition to the resistance of one nation or people to the invasion, colonization or oppression of another" (Stec 151), then the place of women as cultural preservers is deeply implicated in originary claims to land. The meaning of the nation circulates amongst these signifying sites, making love for the land a conflicted emotion for women seeking self-determination, particularly at times of national upheaval. Tambu's desire for education can be labeled both "Western" and "feminist." Either term oversimplifies the matter; both are problematic for Zimbabwean nationalism because women's role is integral to cultural, and therefore territorial, claims. Tambu's conflicted response to Nyamarira crystallizes the difficulty of negotiating these powerful representational categories, and specifies the particular consequences of the impasse between feminism and nationalism.

Notes

[1]   Hereafter referred to parenthetically in the text as *NC*.

[2]   See Aegerter for a fuller discussion of Dangarembga's use of a narrative style that balances between "individual biography and historical contextuality and community" (231). Flockemann also notes that Third World women authors use a "dual focus" to avoid being coopted by a Western *bildungsroman* model that emphasizes the individual (38).

[3]   In taking this perspective, I am extending Sam A. Adewoye's argument that the issue of land is central to both the African novel and an African aesthetics. Based on his claim that the traditional African worldview advocates "the inseparability of man from the land" (xii), Adewoye states three major roles the land plays in writing by male African authors: connection to the ancestors, metaphysical continuity, and socio-economic survival. Dangarembga's novel participates in these traditions, but complicates them by suggesting that their maintenance requires an overdetermination of gender roles.

[4]   As Dangarembga further noted in a 1991 interview with Kirsten Holst Petersen, " the gender problem is always second to the national question" (347).

5   Dangarembga's presentation of the Zimbabwean situation differs from Chatterjee's discussion of Bengal in that Zimbabwean nationalism does not appear, according to her narrative, to offer women a new role. Her perspective is confirmed in various interviews (see Wilkinson and Petersen). Chatterjee, on the other hand, argues that male Indian nationalists incorporated a vision of women's emancipation into a "new patriarchy" that "conferred upon women the honor of a new social responsibility, and by associating the task of female emancipation with the historical goal of sovereign nationhood, bound them to a new, and yet entirely legitimate, subordination" (130). Indian women of the middle class were to be modern but not Western, preserving culture without the "barbarous" practices abhorred by Western colonizers (119). In *Nervous Conditions*, women are generally not offered an enlightened patriarchy.

6   The boy's ability to usurp the girl's plot literally occurs earlier in the novel. Tambu, deprived of schooling because her father has insufficient funds to send both her and her brother, decides to raise maize and fund her own education. She sows her crop on her grandmother's, now her mother's, "plot" of land and it grows into a "fine little crop." As the crop ripens, "they began to disappear." Tambu later discovers her brother has been stealing the maize and giving it away to his schoolfriends. (*NC* 19-23).

7   One of the many reasons Tambu's uncle has given for not sending Tambu off to Sacred Heart, even though she has a scholarship, is the necessity of providing for Dambudzo: "there is now the small boy at home. Every month I put away a little bit, a very little bit, a very little bit every month, so that when he is of school-going age everything will be provided for. As you know, he is the only boy in your family, so he must be provided for" (*NC* 180).

8   The *Oxford English Dictionary* traces *decent* to the Latin verb *decere*, "to become, to be fitting," and none of the definitions specify mobility or stasis as necessary to decency (397). *Loose* is a derivative of *lease*, which has the original meaning of "land 'let alone,' not filled" (954). The first definition for *loose* is given as "unbound, unattached" (997).

Works Cited

Adewoye, Sam A. *The Concept of Land in the African Novel*. Ibadan: Evans Brothers (Nigeria Publishers) Limited, 1989.

Aegerter, Lindsay Pentolfe. "A Dialectic of Autonomy and Community: Tsitsi Dangarembga's *Nervous Conditions*." *Tulsa Studies in Women's Literature* 15.2 (Fall 1996): 231-240.

Bahri, Deepika. "Disembodying The Corpus: Postcolonial Pathology in Tsitsi Dangarembga's *Nervous Conditions*." *Postmodern Culture* 5.1 (1994): 26 pars. Online. Internet. 15 Sept. 1997.

Chatterjee, Partha. *The Nation and Its Fragments*. Princeton: Princeton UP, 1993.

Creamer, Heidi. "An Apple for the Teacher? Femininity, Coloniality, and Food in *Nervous Conditions*." *Kunapipi* 16.1 (1994): 349-360.

Dangarembga, Tsitsi. *Nervous Conditions*. Seattle: Seal Press, 1988.

——. "This Year, Next Year..." *The Women's Review of Books* 8.10-11 (July 1991): 43-44.

Flockemann, Miki. "'Not-Quite Insiders and Not-Quite Outsiders': The 'Process of Womanhood' in *Beka Lamb, Nervous Conditions*, and *Daughters of the Twilight*." *Journal of Commonwealth Literature* 27.1 (Autumn 1991): 37-47.

Karamcheti, Indira. "The Geographics of Marginality: Place and Textuality in Simone Schwarz-Bart and Anita Desai." *Reconfigured Spheres: Feminist Explorations of Literary Space*. Eds. Margaret R. Higonnet and Joan Templeton. Amherst: U of Massachusetts Press, 1994.

Lefebvre, Henri. *The Production of Space*. Oxford: Blackwell, 1991.

Massey, Doreen. *Space, Place, and Gender*. Minneapolis: U of Minnesota Press, 1994.

McWilliams, Sally. "Tsitsi Dangarembga's *Nervous Conditions*: At the Crossroads of Feminism and Post-colonialism." *World Literature Written in English* 31.1 (Spring 1991): 103-112.

Petersen, Kirsten Holst. "Between Gender, Race and History: Kirsten Holst Petersen Interviews Tsitsi Dangarembga." *Kunapipi* 16.1 (1994): 345-348.

Rose, Gillian. *Feminism and Geography*. Minneapolis: U of Minnesota Press, 1993.

Said, Edward. *Culture and Imperialism*. New York: Vintage, 1993.

Stec, Loretta. "Female Sacrifice: Gender and Nostalgic Nationalism in Rebecca West's *Black Lamb and Grey Falcon*." *Narratives of Nostalgia, Gender and Nationalism*. Ed. Jean Pickering and Suzanne Kehde. New York: New York UP, 1997. 138-158.

Thomas, Sue. "Killing the Hysteric in the Colonized's House: Tsitsi Dangarembga's *Nervous Conditions*." *The Journal of Commonwealth Literature* 27.1 (Autumn 1991): 26-36.

Wilkinson, Jane, ed. "Tsitsi Dangarembga." Interview (1989). *Talking with African Writers: Interviews with African Poets, Playwrights & Novelists*. Portsmouth, NH: Heinemann Educational Books Inc., 1992. 189-198.

Woolf, Virginia. *A Room of One's Own*. New York: Harcourt Brace & Jovanovich, 1929.

LOCATION AND SEPARATENESS OF HEROINES IN AFRICAN AND AFRICAN-AMERICAN DRAMA—A STUDY OF HILDA KUPER'S *A WITCH IN MY HEART* AND LORRAINE HANSBERRY'S *A RAISIN IN THE SUN*

Chinyere Okafor

Set in a traditional homestead of Swaziland in the thirties, Hilda Kuper's *A Witch in My Heart*[1] seems to contrast sharply with Lorraine Hansberry's *A Raisin in the Sun,*[2] which is set in the modern American city of Chicago in the fifties, because their dramatic actions are differentiated by social background and geographical location. An in-depth analysis, however, reveals that the divergence is greatly overshadowed by the plays' intersection in several areas, such as the subordination of women, the marginalization of Africans by white colonialists and racists, as well as the constancy of struggle as a means of liberation. These correspondences connect with the central issue of this essay—gender, particularly the influence of a woman's location on the feeling of separateness generated by her subordination.

The terms "separateness" or "separation" are used here to delineate the feeling of remoteness from the mainstream, which is male. "Separateness" may be compared to what Trinh Minh-Ha refers to as the philosophy of "differentiation" utilized by the apartheid regime in South Africa (265). It also has a psychological resemblance to the alienation felt by the colonized from the political system of the colonizer. Separateness as an idea often uses physical difference (sex) as pretext for gender differentiation that assumes male as the standard, thereby relegating the female to a substandard and inferior position. This generates the feeling of separateness. It is dependent on the location or position of the woman from which she negotiates the structures of her society. The plays offer two spaces, the natal and marital, as basic locations of a woman. There is an inevitable link between space as a physical and psychological environment and the opportunities open for a woman's development and empowerment.

D. E. S. Maxwell's ideas about language and place throw more light on the notion of location. He examines the relationship between language and setting and sees location and displacement as "major concerns of all post-colonial peoples" (Ashcroft, Griffiths, Tiffin 24) because of the influence of the indigenous setting on the colonizing language and the consequent disjunction this creates in the process of communication. This emphasis on the influence of setting or place in language is germane to the discussion of location in this essay. Just as Maxwell sees the influence of place (landscape, indigenous language) on the colonizer's language imported to a colonized space, this essay looks at the influence of a new environment as physical and psychological space on the separateness which a woman feels when she transfers from a natal to a patrilocal marital abode. Relocation is not just a physical action but a process of redefinition and adjustment by the transported woman who re-forms her identity. According to Carol Boyce Davies, "re-negotiation of identities is fundamental to migration" (3).[3]

Gender has a forceful presence in the plays because of the insights of the playwrights as women, a strong uniting factor that, in this case, overshadows the fact of their being white and black. Born of white parents in Zimbabwe, Kuper has done a lot of anthropological work on Swazi social and political life. Born in Chicago of African-American parentage, Hansberry is one of the most celebrated playwrights in contemporary America. Their sensitivity as women influences their articulation of a gendered perspective through female protagonists, Bigwapi of *Witch* and Beneatha of *Raisin*. Both operate in societies where gender represents important divisions that have social, economic, and political consequences. The fact that men and women are made to do different things and are treated differently separates and genders them (Graddol and Swann 8), that is, apportions their spaces on a gender basis. Thus, sex sets men and women apart on a horizontal (physical) basis that surreptitiously becomes the beginning of genderation, and through the existence of a vertical ladder that places women on the lower level. Viewed spirally, women are in a peripheral position removed from the male gender that operates in the center. On the vertical and spiral levels, women feel separated, confined, and restricted to the bottom or the periphery, that is, outside the mainstream of action, whether it be political, as in the decision-making body of the family, or social and economic, as in the availability of opportunities.

The heroines of the two plays are on the lower and peripheral segments due to their location or relocation as insiders or outsiders in the homes where they operate. The insider/outsider position is here assigned from the point of view of patriarchal societies where marriage is patrilocal. Women are therefore in two basic positions: in the natal or parental home, where they operate as daughters/insiders, and in the marital abode, where they struggle as wives/outsiders without the full status accorded daughters and sons of the marital household. As spatial environment, the marital abode inhibits a woman's (as wife) potentialities because of the environmental adjustments she has to make in adapting and re-forming her identity. The formation of a new identity often involves re-naming through a husband and, in some cases, children. In pre-colonial Swaziland, as in some other traditional African societies, a married woman retains her father's name (see Arua and Engelbrecht),[4] while in Euro-American societal structure, she usually adopts her husband's family name[5] and through it forms a new identity that obliterates her former socio-political identity which she enjoyed in her parental home (Smith 38). The plays show that whether a woman retains her natal name as LaHlope of *Witch* or adopts the marital name as Ruth and Lena of *Raisin*, she also accepts new roles and relationships that put her in a separate and subordinate position. She is not a first-class member of the marital abode where she is subjected to the rules of the new family.[6] Ruth of *Raisin* and the wives of *Witch* accept a patriarchal agenda. This acceptance may appear surprising when we situate the plays in their historical contexts.

Raisin is set in the Chicago of the fifties, a period when African-American women had begun to tackle gender subordination and when black emancipation was building the volcanoes that erupted in the sixties. The black and gender emancipatory fervor of the period that forms the atmosphere of *Raisin* might make it appear a little ambitious to compare the play to *Witch*, which is set in a traditional Swazi homestead where the suppression of women by the patriarchal structure and that of black Africans by the colonialists had not yet yielded a sustained collective emancipatory struggle. Yet, the colonial dimension of *Witch* with its class structure is a point of intersection with *Raisin*, which has a strong class and racial dimension. However, the strongest point of convergence for the plays is gender. An examination of the women characters in the natal and marital settings reveals certain correspondences that outweigh (even while relating to) the historical circumstances of the play. Patriarchy, which was still part of African-American life in the fifties, yields elements and patterns similar to traditional Swazi ones. In the patriarchal set-up of both plays, for example, the privileging of sons is depicted covertly in *Raisin* and overtly in *Witch*. Both support the sociological theory of patriarchal privileging which states that sons occupy a higher position in families than daughters, whose places are marked by subordination (see Bosmaijan and Coryell). Men are centered as heirs of family wealth and as "direct link" to the patrilineal ancestors (Derman 22). This is the main reason why a Swazi man can marry another woman to beget a son for the family so that that son can inherit and link up with the ancestors (Bren 109), a practice that finds a parallel in traditional Igboland (Nigeria). The centering of men within the families parallels the situation in the wider society where women occupy a subordinate position. As daughters of the society, women are marginalized. They feel the separateness common to all daughters. The feeling of separateness is, however, heightened when a woman relocates as wife in patrilocal marriages. In the marital abode, another level of separateness is added to the original one lived as daughter inferior to sons in home and society.

The plot of *Raisin* focuses on the separateness that a woman can experience as daughter with the status of insider in the parental home. The play outlines the dreams of the members of the Younger family for upward mobility, and the struggles of the daughter, Beneatha, to develop without the constraints of subordination. The family would like the daughter to marry into a rich family, so they encourage her to date George from the well-to-do Murchison family. The matriarch, Lena, dreams of joining the propertied class while the son, Walter, dreams of becoming wealthy like his employer and Beneatha envisions becoming a doctor. All these dreams depend on the ten thousand dollars insurance benefit from Walter and Beneatha's father's death. Walter wants to use the money because for him, "money is life" (73), but the mother disburses it according to her wishes. She buys a house in a white neighborhood for thirty-five hundred dollars and gives Walter three thousand to deposit in the bank for Beneatha's school fees and thirty-five hundred dollars for himself. Walter looses his and Beneatha's money in a dubious business transaction, thereby shattering his dream and Beneatha's hopes of training as a doctor. In her despair, Beneatha loses the zeal to struggle on and declares, "Me, I am nothing" (132); eventually, she overcomes her despair and links up with a man from the African continent. The white community resists having blacks as neighbors and offers the family a bribe to prevent them from moving in; however, they reject the bribe.

Thus, the play ends on a hopeful note of what one might call "racial" self-assertion.

The daughter of the house, Beneatha, is an insider in her parental home where she suffers one level of separation that is common to all women as daughters: she fights the oppressive structures of her parental environment. For her, becoming a doctor is the center of her dreams and the center of the medical profession, but that center is regarded as the prerogative of men; in a fit of anger, her brother Walter defines woman's place in the medical profession: "Who the hell told you you had to be a doctor? If you're so crazy 'bout messing 'round with sick people—then go be a nurse like other women—or just get married and be quiet" (20). This calls to mind a similar prescription which the heroine Jet resists in Alexis De Veaux's *The Tapestry*. Like Jet, who insists on training as a lawyer in order to engage social injustices, Beneatha will not accept a space in the periphery as dictated to her. In a manner reminiscent of Mariama's fight in Rebecca Njau's *The Scar*, she engages the barriers of separation keeping her from the center. Mariama uses initiation ceremony and its laceration of women's genitals as a springboard to advocate the emanicpation of women and declares her intention in the struggle:

> I want them to free themselves from slavery
> I want them to respect their bodies and minds
> I want them to break away the chains. (116)

Unlike Mariama, whose fight encompasses all women, Beneatha struggles primarily for her own development. Operating in a highly individualistic society, Beneatha fights for her individual development. She relentlessly challenges the barriers that separate her from her goals. She indulges in hobbies such as horse riding and guitar-playing that are supposed to be the special preserve of men. She discusses ideas and plans her strategies.

Much of the conflict of *Raisin* revolves around Beneatha's love and marriage. She rejects the traditional dictum that prescribes marriage as her lot and affirms that she will make her own choice of a spouse if she ever decides to marry. Her family is disappointed by her attitude because she is expected to marry

the well-to-do George, but he is shallow and cannot match the
intelligence of the spirited heroine. Her failure to comply with
the expectation of her family makes her appear odd. "That pretty
rich thing? Honey, I knew you was odd," her sister-in-law, Ruth,
tells her in reaction to her rejection of George (34). Her rejection
of George is based on his inability to accept her personality,
which he sees as non-conformist. He dislikes her intellectualism
which, he disdainfully tells her, is unbecoming for a woman: "As
for myself, I want a nice—(Groping)—simple—(Thoughful)—
sophisticated girl... not a poet—O.K?" (88-89). George's view is
similar to that of Jet's boyfriend, Axis, who is not interested in
her pursuit of a law degree and tells her that, " I like a woman
who knows how to be a woman/for a man/knows what to do to
keep him" (160). The prescription of what a women's life is to
be becomes an obstacle that destroys Jet's relationship with
Axis. Similarly, Beneatha's relationship with George is
destroyed by the barrier of subordination and she finally decides
that she cannot cope with George's superficiality.

Asagai, the Nigerian student, provides a contrast to George
because he does not condescend to Beneatha. He captures her
attention with his interest in the "dynamics and dialectics of
revolution... and the continuity of human struggle" (Baraka 15).
Moreover, he admires her and encourages her sociopolitical
aspirations. When she appears to be losing hope because of her
brother's blunder, he rekindles her determination to struggle and
become a doctor. As an outsider in American society, Asagai
does not see medicine as gendered. Coming from a traditional
Yoruba society that sees healing as a gift which the gods can
bestow on anybody irrespective of gender, Asagai has no
problems with Beneatha's calling. His support and admiration no
doubt influence her in her partiality to him as a future husband
instead of the antagonistic George.

Beneatha's struggle is not limited to the politics of gender.
She also interrogates racial and cultural politics as obstacles in
her relationships and in life in general. She ignores the mockery
of her boyfriend, George, who sneers at her political
consciousness and questions the place of African-Americans in
the racist American world. Her interrogation of race, culture, and
gender stems from the triple exclusion she suffers as daughter of

a patriarchal, racist, and classist society. As a woman, she is separated from the mainstream dominated by men. As an African-American, she is separated from the mainstream American culture and center of action dominated by whites such as those in the white community who resist her family's entry into their fold. In a land where middle and upper class money and property are the standard (Davies 30), she is substandard. She tackles these barriers of separation and, as a result, exposes the confusions, frustrations, and obstacles encountered by women who try to redefine their boundaries. The focus of her struggle, however, is gender, because gendered space is her immediate environment from which she interrogates other boundaries. Her struggle therefore presages the advent of black nationalism and the "black women's liberation movement" (Rich 24).

Tensions arising from the conflict generated by Beneatha's struggle are lessend by the sisterly bonding and support of the women in her home, especially her mother, Lena, who is the matriarch. Her parental space is supportive because the head of the household, Lena, is not subordinate to a patriarch. Although she sometimes tries to maintain the standards established by the dead patriarch, she nevertheless has a free hand in running her family. It is an advantage which her son, Walter, would like to appropriate, because he expects to be privileged as a son. His expectations of privilege emanate from the weakening patriarchal background of the play. Lena exercises her power without equivocation. She is sometimes authoritarian and once uses violence (a slap) to force her daughter to conform to the rules of the house, yet her actions indicate that she loves her family and tries to treat the members fairly. She is able to understand her daughter's nature and gives her the support necessary for her development. She accepts and indulges Beneatha's experimentation with hobbies even though they are expensive and are regarded as men's hobbies. The sensitive question of marriage is not allowed to become a source of tension, since the women understand that the twenty-year-old heroine should have time to grow.

The physical and psychological space of her parental home enables the young heroine to experiment, make mistakes, and push on with the backing of the women of her natal home, who are familiar with the separateness she fights. Her political ideas, especially regarding her African roots, are also appreciated by the matriarch who goes out of her way to be gracious to her daughter's new friend from the continent. In this manner, the supportive environment of the natal home makes possible a favorable intersection of gender and politics which is conducive to the heroine's intellectual growth. One suspects that this kind of unconditional home support will decrease if the heroine marries and takes up abode in Africa as proposed in the play, because she would operate from a marital base in a setting where she is an outsider who has to adapt to the new rules of the patrilocal abode.[8]

Problems of dislocation are a reality that a wife faces in a patriarchal setting. It is this reality that problematizes Bigwapi's life in *Witch* because she fails to fulfill the main obligation of her marital abode, which is motherhood. *Witch* focuses on continuity, which is one of the most important issues in traditional African households. Although a woman is linked to a single sexual partner who is her husband, she is regarded as the wife of the family because her incorporation into the family affects the family as a whole. In socio-economic terms, for example, Bigwapi's *loboola* (bride wealth) is paid from the family's cattle kraal, and the child she begets belongs to the family and carries the family's name into the next generation. A woman is expected to follow the path that was constructed before she was incorporated into the family, the path followed by other wives before her, the path of submission and motherhood. Failure to subscribe to this prescribed life causes problems for the heroine, Bigwapi. The main dramatic conflict is introduced in the first scene when Ntamo, the patriarchal head of the homestead and biological father of Sikova, Bigwapi's husband, complains about Bigwapi's barrenness and alludes to the wastage of cows used for her *loboola* and for paying healers for "curing" her inability to conceive: "She should be grateful that we keep her here at all and don't return her whence she came and use the cattle we gave for her to marry one who would fill our huts with life" (3).

Thus, although the conflict centers on childlessness, the reason for the family's antagonism is partly economic. Bigwapi's husband Sikova spends money to procure her and the family blames her for the lack of money urgently needed for colonial taxation. Ntamo complains that the cattle kraal "is empty paying medicine-men brought by our son to cure her" (3). Arguing for the need to find money urgently, Sikova says, "... for each wife I must pay 10 shillings cash and thirty five shillings for my own head. If I have not the money I will be kicked into gaol... Father I will sell myself. Money is needed at our home..." (16-17). The lack of money which led to conflict in *Raisin* therefore finds a parallel in *Witch*, and while the conflict of *Raisin* hinges on the socio-economic advancement of the family, that of *Witch* rests on childlessness and continuity of the homestead; yet both are linked to colonial and neo-colonial exploitation of Africans by a white minority in Swaziland and a white majority in the U.S. The colonial presence has an impact on the heroine's plight by draining the family resources and making her take the blame. Bigwapi's supposed impoverishment of the family and her inability to fulfil the main role of a wife is considered a failure which creates another level of separateness—she feels excluded from the group of "fulfilled wives," outsiders in a periphal position who have performed their role. The matriarch, Nabosikova, whose name is derived from that of her son, Sikova, has fulfilled her obligation to the household by bearing a son by whose name she is called. Her name, a combination of "mother of" (*nabo*) and her son's name, indicates the importance of the role of mother—it defines her. The first wife has a daughter, the third is expecting a child, but Bigwapi is childless. This is a serious problem in an environment that measures woman's importance by motherhood.

The issue of childlessness is dramatized within the atmosphere of colonial exploitation as the people surrounding Bigwapi complain about the arrogance of the whites, the seizure of their fertile lands, and heavy taxation. Their distressed reaction to poverty, misfortune, and disease involves a belief in witchcraft. In the shadow of economic depression, Bigwapi's childlessness is an added burden on the family. It plants a deep sadness that overwhelms the heroine and generates reactions that complicate her feelings of separateness and subordination. Her plight separates her from the fulfilled womenfolk, and the anger in her heart makes her voice her yearnings in a negative manner. For example, she consoles her co-wife whose baby is ill by reminding her that she could have more if the child dies: "Why do you weep? You can bear others" (11). This consolation is seen as coming from a "dark heart," the heart of a witch (11). She is suspected of wishing others ill and actually causing evil by witchcraft.

Bigwapi suffers three levels of separateness. On the first level, she is subordinated like every woman on the basis of gender. On the second level, she experiences the exclusion and separation shared by all the wives, including her mother-in-law, who is the matriarch of the family. Their separateness is characterized by their peripheral position as outsiders in the marital household. It bars them from the source of decision-making power and also binds them as a subordinated group. Childlessness, however, deprives the heroine of this bonding and creates her third level of separation, which is both physical and psychological. She avoids the others and feels different from them. Yet, she yearns for their company and sometimes reaches out to them, but, in fear, they exclude her. For example, during a spell of stormy weather that makes the matriarch protect the insider and granddaughter Tekani, who is afraid, Bigwapi, the childless and suspicious outsider, is rejected. Her offer of help is refused and she is barred from entering the maternity chamber. In frustration, she voices her agony, which she believes is deeper than the labor pain experienced by the third wife:

> All right—I will go. How gladly would I have that pain. I would not cry but shout with joy. That little wife does not know what suffering is. To watch all women nurse their babies while my arms are empty. To have no daughter to work beside me in the fields, no son to eat the cattle of my hut. To have no son's wives to serve me in my old age, no home where I am mother. That is suffering! There is no pain where there is fullness—only where there is nothing, nothing, nothing. (37-38)

Such is the depth of pain that marks the third level of Bigwapi's separateness. Ironically, the same level is also marked by the joy of love she shares with her husband. That love is a major factor in widening the gulf of separation (both physical and psychological) between her and the other wives, who envy her and suspect her of using magical powers to procure such love. However, the fact of her childlessness makes that love distasteful in the eyes of many. For the patriarch, Ntamo, that love is destructive for the home because "A Home is built by respect, and strength, and truth in self... but where the ancient laws are thrown aside and a man thinks only of his desires, the home is weak, and witches strike to kill" (3). For the co-wives, it is an unnatural love that deprives them of their husband's company. For the mother-in-law, it is a love that thwarts her ability to see that her son shares his love between the wives. She complains that "his desires I cannot divide...his heart pushes him where I cannot guide" (3-4).

Unlike in *Raisin*, where the heroine's love is encouraged, the love between Bigwapi and her husband is scorned because it has not produced a child. It creates a barrier between the heroine and her in-laws. Her plight draws her close to her husband who vouches to sell himself to earn money for her cure: "On your account I will go to work—not here. Here there is no money" (14). Impoverished by the colonial system which caused the people to loose two thirds of their land to European settlers, the people augment their income by selling their labor to colonial property owners and by working in their farms or in the mines of South Africa. Many loose their lives under the dangerous working conditions in Johannesburg, reputed to be a place of death and "gold."[9] This is why both the antagonists (in-laws) and the protagonist (Bigwapi) unite in attempting to persuade Sikova not to work in the mines, a venture which they see as suicidal. In her bid to prevent him from going to Johannesburg, she accedes to his parents' plan to have him marry her little sister, Lomusa, so that she can have children on her behalf. Intent on her getting her heart's desire, he refuses. Sikova's sacrificial venture to Johannesburg and Bigwapi's selfless offer to share her husband with her sister show the extent they can go to see each other happy.

Hilda Kuper's knowledge of Swazi life based on her research and on her association with Swazis enabled her to see the other side of the companionship and sisterly bonding of wives in the polygamous household and to depict its intrigues, jealousies, and pains. She portrays women and men as victims of patriarchy, but wives as the foremost victims. For patriarchal continuity, for example, Sikova has to accept other women as wives even though they do not excite the kind of burning desire and selfless love he feels for Bigwapi. He explains the contradiction of his polygamous life to Bigwapi by asserting that she is the only woman who gives him joy. The other two wives were brought into the family to assure its continuity. He further reassures Bigwapi of her central place in his heart:

> I am a ripe man now and know myself. For me you will have no equal... you and I are one. I have no need for others to rejoice my body. If I take girls, it is not for joy, but to increase the home. That is why, should the little LaHlope have a son, we can all be thankful. (14)

This love, however, makes Bigwapi an object of hatred. In the absence of her husband, she becomes lonely and afraid. She is accused of killing the newborn baby by witchcraft and is sent back to her parents. But Bigwapi does not give up. She believes in her love and returns to claim Sikova when he comes back from Johannesburg. The traditional dictate of Sikova's father is pitted against the bond between the couple, and patriarchal authority wins as Sikova accepts the traditional pronouncement that banishes Bigwapi from the homestead. At the same time, he cannot dwell in the homestead that is full of pain without her, so he rejects his homestead and returns to the hostile city. In a last desperate bid to fight for her love, Bigwapi offers to go with him, but he also rejects her. Through this act, Sikova fails to liberate himself from cultural bondage as does his counterpart, Muwezi, in Elvania Zimiru's *Family Spear*. Here, the son, Muwezi, feels thwarted by tradition when his father performs the traditional duty of "digging the ground first," that is, deflowering his son's bride. The father sees colonial presence as an evil that is eroding traditional culture, so he makes a concerted effort to restore tradition, an act which ironically thwarts tradition by making it loose its links with continuity. Muwezi is a symbol of the continuity of the family, but he cuts his links with tradition by abandoning the homestead with his bride. While the tyranny of tradition makes his love for his bride stronger, it alienates Bigwapi and Sikova from one another. The strength of Sikova's love, however, compels Sikova to abandon the setting that is hostile to that love. It is a cowardly choice that offends both parties: the father and uncles who represent power in the family, and his lover-wife, who is disempowered in the periphery. The tussle between her and her father-in-law over Sikova's loyalty is her last chance to grab power and take control of her life, which she sees as irretrievably bound to the life of her husband. Her husband's failure to unite with her in the fight is a blow to the heroine.

Sikova suffers a serious dilemma due to Bigwapi's rejection by his father which is like a rejection of himself because of his declared oneness with Bigwapi: "you and I are one" (14). This compels him to abandon his birth place because it—the people living there—dismisses Bigwapi. This, in turn, is tragic for the homestead for it has lost its "only living fruit" (3) Although their love is thwarted by patriarchal domination, failure of Sikova to fight with and for the heroine elicits a curse from her:

> I will be with you in your fears and your loneliness, and you will remember me in everything you desire. My words will pursue you, and the memory of the things we did together, for I am your home. (67)

Rather than fight the patriarchal authority that has problematized his "home," he chooses the path of exile by banishing himself to the city, which, in turn, is an environment dominated by colonialism and racism. His choice of the evil of colonialism over the tyranny of patriarchy perhaps makes a statement about the severity of tradition and the urgency of the need to tackle it. This lends support to Ngugi's notion of "No cultural liberation without women's liberation," which conflicts with the idea of shelving women's liberation while pursuing African liberation as proposed in Felix Mnthali's poem, "Letter to a Feminist Friend" (Peterson 252-253). The plots of *Witch* and *Family Spear* show that African emancipation is connected with women's emancipation, and both impact one another. The rejection of the homestead by the male heirs marks the beginning of the end of traditional patriarchy in both *Witch* and *Family Spear*. The male heirs' choice of colonial cities may suggest that traditional patriarchy is worse than colonial domination. However, one must observe that none of the heirs indicate any knowledge of the impact of colonialism on traditional patriarchy, and any comparison of the two structures must recognize that impact. The feminist tenor of the plays and their depiction of the dual evils of patriarchy and colonialism demonstrate a simultaneous awareness of feminist and anti-colonialist concerns. This connection makes it impossible to try and separate these concerns in order to shelve one and engage the other.

The tragic ending of *Witch* contrasts sharply with that of *Raisin*, which ends on a hopeful note for the family, as members are moving to a better neighborhood and the heroine pursues her dream of becoming a doctor. Her bonding with Asagai is also a symbol of hope for the heroine's socio-cultural growth. The two plays are similar in their depiction of the support the natal family provides for its daughters. Beneatha's rejection of George in preference for Asagai parallels Bigwapi's rejection of her fiance in preference for Sikova whom she met at the king's festival. According to tradition, the natal family had mapped out Bigwapi's life by choosing a bridegroom for her and expecting her to marry him when she came of age. The family, however, understands her free spirit and is able to accommodate her yearnings when she falls in love with another man. This might be embarassing for her family, but because of the special place she enjoys as a daughter of the homestead, the family frees her from her former fiance, thereby making it possible for her to marry the man of her choice. Her status as insider in her father's homestead enables her to achieve her heart's desire.

Thus, the play portrays the natal home as a supportive environment for women. It is a place where a woman deals with the social and political powers she is born into and which she grows up to understand. Although not a son, she is an insider who knows how to deal with those who know her from birth and understand her nature as well as the need for flexibility in supporting her development. This kind of situation changes when a woman relocates to a marital abode where she is incorporated into another power structure, changing her status to that of an outsider. Her relegation to an outsider position is akin but not equal to that of a colonized male, who suffers one degree of separateness and marginalization by the colonizer, while the woman in an outsider position is doubly separated: first, as a woman, in her natal home, and, secondly and more severely, through her relocation to a marital abode.

In patrilocal marriages such as depicted in both plays, men never lose the power base that is familiar to them from their birth because they do not dislocate. They remain and operate within the same familiar family after marriage and therefore neither suffer the confusion of dislocation nor lose direct support of the natal family. When there is a change in the power structure, such as when the father dies in *Raisin*, and the power shifts to another person, a son may feel uncomfortable with the new head of the family, but the whole structure of uncles, aunts, and relations in which he operates remains unchanged, and so does his status as insider. This is Walter's situation in *Raisin*. The change in the headship of the family causes problems for Walter, who feels disempowered because a woman is heading the family and is expected to make financial decisions. But because the new head is his mother who understands his nature and yearnings, she tries to salvage his ego by giving him the opportunity to use part of the money as he pleases. He blunders, yet his mother asks Beneatha to forgive and love him. In addition, she gives him another opportunity to restore his ego by letting him act as a leader in the negotiation with the racist neighbor-to-be, Mr. Lindner.

Women appreciate the problems created by the experience of marital dislocation that is peculiar to them in societies where marriage is patrilocal. Such problems include acceptance or the lack thereof, relations with mothers-in-law, co-wives in a polygamous home, new rules, adaptation, and re-definition of self. It is the strength of this understanding that binds women, whether young or old, in a patriarchal setting. Thus, although an elder who has contributed to the growth of her marital home as mother, grandmother, and manager, Nabosikova in *Witch* exercises her matriarchal duties according to the rules laid down by the family before her arrival. As an outsider, she is unable to modify the rules of the family. Because she only carries out her duties as laid down by tradition, she is unable to help the heroine when the latter is faced with a tragic option because of her own position on the periphery of power. Her feeling of separateness is articulated in female comradeship to the heroine when she laments that every woman has a witch in her heart. She is using witchcraft as a symbol of the pain of separation, the burden and secret yearning and desire a woman carries in her heart, often stifled because of her subordination and disempowerment.

Witch's mother in law, unlike Lena of *Raisin*, is not empowered because power is vested in the patriarch, her husband, who wields it with traditional authority. She accepts the traditional status quo and makes no attempt to interrogate the forces of subordination. Her stance is therefore different from that of her daughter-in-law, the heroine, who engages the forces of her triple separation, and from that of the widowed Lena, who is able to make decisions and control her family of three generations. It also differs from that of her counterparts in some other African plays. In Zirimu's *African Spear*, for example, Debya, the mother-in-law, finds it difficult to change a traditional custom that breeds conflict and thwarts young lovers. She, however, tries to end this custom through her son by advising him to ignore it and leave the homestead with his bride in order to subvert the father's intention to perform the custom. In Aidoo's *Dilemma of a Ghost*, Esi Kom, the mother-in-law, is able to take control through her authority as matriarch and reach out to the African-American wife, Eulalie, when she realizes her son's complicity in the conflict generated by her supposed barrenness. She accepts the outsider Eulalie and ignores her son, Ato: "'Come my child' (And with that ESI KOM supports ALALIA through the door that leads into the old house. ATO merely stares after them... He looks bewildered and lost...)" (52). Female solidarity and an empowered mother-in-law also occur in Onyeaka Onyekuba's *Sons for My Son*. Here, the mother-in-law, Enyidie, is able to swallow her pride and proffer a hand of friendship to Ndidi, her childless daughter-in-law, whom she had earlier antagonized.

Daughters-in-law find themselves in particularly trying circumstances in the plays discussed here and have to negotiate various degrees or levels of separation. Bigwapi's dignity lies in her strength of character shown through her interrogation of these levels of separation. She is comparable to Anowa of Aidoo's *Anowa*, who also fights three levels of separation as daughter, wife, and childless woman. As daughter, Anowa fights to get her family to accept the choice of Kofi Ako as husband. As wife, she fights the forces that debase her sense of morality and dignity as a woman, wife, and member of a changing world. Her opposition to her husband's trade in slaves and her marginalization by her husband complicate a plot that ends in tragedy. Although both Anowa's and Bigwapi's lives end tragically, the reader is enriched by their predicaments, the complexity of their characters, and the constancy of their struggles. Bigwapi emerges as a resilient and complex character whose presence overshadows others in her world. In a chronologically structured sequence of events, the playwright depicts an intricate pattern of relationships, within and across gender, which entangels the protagonist as she attempts to define her space and finally ends in catastrophe.

Both Bigwapi and Beneatha are intelligent, hard-working, and determined in their fight for space. Beneatha pursues her interests without inhibitions; whether it is guitar-playing or sports, she understands that she has to experiment to fulfill herself. With similar zest, Bigwapi fights to remain above board in the bleak situation of colonial poverty and childlessness. She uses her ingenuity to make her farm yield rich harvests. She tends her farm meticulously and when "the stalks are brittle as fire sticks" in other gardens, in hers "the plants stand as high..." (10). This is because of her interest in working hard. She tells her sister Lomusa, "'I like work. I like the earth and the things that grow in it. When I plant, I feel the seed creating for me... I do not read a book, but from the earth I learn of many things. Had I a child I could teach him much'" (12). Similarly to Bigwapi's determination and creaticity, Beneatha possesses traits that are admired by those around her: her mother thinks she is spirited, Asagai admires her talent and purposefulness. Even the seemingly antagonistic Walter loves his sister and copes with her "uniqueness" or stubbornness. But while Beneatha's talents are appreciated by her relations in the parental home, Bigwapi's are scorned by her in-laws because she is childless. On the beautiful beaded stick she makes for her husband, her mother-in-law sarcastically comments that "a man wants more than sticks" from a woman, alluding to her inability to have a child. Of her well-tended and rich garden, the wives say that she casts a spell on their farms, because they do not compare to hers. The excitement she felt in her parental home at marrying and being happy as a wife changes to pain in the marital abode. This is because of the added levels of separation created by her outsider position and her childlessness.

Both heroines value relationships with the opposite sex, but while Beneatha's relationship with a man is one aspect of her desires, becoming a doctor being her main goal, Bigwapi's main desire is to be with her husband and have his children. Her background, a traditional homestead plagued by hunger and fear of extinction, perhaps makes her focus on motherhood urgent. In addition, portrayal of motherhood as an important and necessary experience recurs in Swazi and many other African literatures of the colonial and postcolonial era. The setting of *Raisin* in the U.S. of the 1950s with its stirrings of emancipation makes the depiction of both women supportive of patriarchy and women with emancipatory agendas possible. Ruth's patrilocal marriage and patriarchal agendas find some parallels in Bigwapi, while Beneatha's struggles point to female self-assertion and self-definition outside marriage or in addition to marriage and motherhood.

Separateness cuts across spatial settings as well as social structures as illustrated in the plays. Although Bigwapi of *Witch* lives in a hut where no cars or bicycles disturb the traditional atmosphere of the open veld and Benatha of *Raisin* lives in a modest apartment building with modern amenities, both characters are confined by the social structures they inhabit. Social expectations are explicit in the patriarchal societies of the plays and many women, such as Ruth of *Raisin* and Nabosikova of *Witch*, conform to the expected pattern of behavior—yet exceptions do occur. The heroines represent the exceptions who deviate from such patterns. They not only deviate from norms but grapple with the fetters of restriction that prevent them from engaging the world as main actors capable of shaping their own destinies instead of allowing others to shape it for them. They do so by engaging ordinary life experiences such as love, marriage, and work in their own chosen manner as active participants, directing their destinies in spite of the traditional pattern mapped out for them. Through this, one appreciates how their ordinary lives are problematized by their gender as well as by their courage and ability to resist the antagonism of their societies because of what they regard as the heroines unwillingness or inability to succumb to traditional expectations. The feminist concerns of the playwrights are shown through their depiction of gender inequities and options for resistance. Refusing to bow down to intimidation, reaching out to fellow women, rejecting antagonists, and challenging oppressive structures are some of the alternatives to restrictive expectations offered in the plays.

Beneatha largely operates from the basis of her natal home where she is a daughter and insider, while Bigwapi is mostly based in her marital home, where she is a wife and outsider, yet both understand the nature of women's life as daughter and wife. Bigwapi as wife longs for her life of freedom in her parental home where her actions are understood and her mistakes condoned. Beneatha does not marry and dislocate, yet she has glimpses of marital subordination through the relationship between Ruth and the chauvinistic Walter. This partly makes her question marriage as a workable option, especially marriage as a sublimation of a woman's personality, as could be the case in a marriage with the rich and shallow George Murchison. In spite of her knowledge and empathy, she still finally sees marriage and its accompanying dislocation to Africa as a viable option, for Africa offers another opportunity for her to realize her dreams.

The above discussion shows that the location of women provides the basic difference in the structure of their subordination because of the extra levels of separation created by the change from insider to outsider positions, from natal to marital abodes. Women operate within the structures and norms of two basic locations and backgrounds, the natal and the marital, within the larger colonial or postcolonial society with its own racial structures. The natal home is the first family, the birth environment where a woman is a daughter. As the plays show, this environment is antagonistic to the woman because it subordinates her, yet it is also familiar and often supportive of her exploits. It is the environment from which the heroines expand their gendered spaces with relative success. The heroines embrace certain gendered values and attitudes, yet they exhibit independence of will and personal ethics at the same time. These contradictory positions help to illustrate the way women give and take, adjust and negotiate their spaces with successes and failures. It is part of the contradiction women contend with in a world whose structure alienates them and in which change is slow.

The plays also show that gender is not the only obstacle that separates—the barriers of separation are multi-dimensional. Bigwapi engages gender barriers while Beneatha's obstacles include gender, racial, cultural and class segregation. This, however, does not imply the absence of other dimensions of separateness in Bigwapi's world. For example, the racial and political presence of colonialism forms part of the setting of the larger world around the homestead. It influences her life and contributes to the economic depression that forces her husband to the "place of death." His experience in Johannesburg, for instance, illustrates the racial and class inequalities in the Apartheid region of Africa, which is the background of the dramatic action; however, the heroine does not show awareness of the influence of racism or query racial and colonial structures as she does her gender-based exclusions. One may easily suspect that the fact of the playwright being white might have hindered her view of the impact of colonial structures on the lives of the characters she depicts—yet her other writings indicate her awareness of the impact of colonialism on traditional African social structures. Her novel *Bite of Hunger*, for example, portrays colonialism as a strong adversary that dominates, exploits, and violates traditional social structures and the characters living in them.

Beneatha of *Raisin*, however, does show an awareness of the links between gender oppression and other oppressive ideologies, such as racial and cultural politics. In the play, she plays an important role in theorizing racism, an activity that proves useful in her family's fight for space in the neighborhood of their choice, which is maintained as a prerogative of whites. As Americans, they fight their marginalization by the mainstream white community and team up to place themselves in the previously barred center. It is a familiar struggle for the heroine whose life is a constant war for space in prohibited territories. In this fight, unlike in her fight against gender subordination, her brother is an enthusiastic ally, for he understands racial marginalization even while he upholds gender subordination. The interrogation of sociopolitical space is a recurrent theme in Hansberry's writings. Problems which she tackles in *Toussaint* are the suppression of slaves, servants, wives, amd the objectification of slaves as non-persons, inanimate objects without feeling and intelligence.

The playwrights examined here extol women's struggle no matter the location, whether in the natal home or the marital abode, or in a racist and classist society with multiple separations of gender, racial, class and cultural levels. The struggles are explored through women's voices and women-centered perspectives. They therefore join other women playwrights in providing new voices, new stories, and new structures of women's experiences in different worlds. Whether childless or with child, young or old, African or American, the women in these plays experience restrictions and degradations because the world is gendered and male-oriented.

The heroines represent women who redefine their spaces, and since they share the spaces with men and are revealed in their relationships with them, they also progressively redefine men's spaces as well as how spaces are structured societally. The plays portray rebellion against subordination as a viable alternative for breaking down the walls of separation and subordination. The heroines achieve relative successes in their natal homes because of the bonding of women and the support of the family. While such bonding and support are strong and help to liberate women in the natal home, they are weak and do not liberate women in the marital abode because of their outsider status.

Finally, the plays show that there is a gender convergence that cuts across geographical and racial boundaries because, although the playwrights are of different races, white and black, they are able to empathize with and convincingly represent women's lives in their respective societies because of their common bond and understanding as women. On the surface, the works are about gender and how women negotiate gender oppression, but a deeper look reveals their socio-political intention. The playwrights are engaged in the politics of positionality and transformation through dramatic representation. Bigwapi's failure and Beneatha's success make political statements about gender in both natal and marital homes as well as in society at large, if we understand politics in its proper perspective as negotiation and renegotiation of the existing order. The playwrights expose social, economic, and political boundaries of the existing order, its inequalities, injustices, and antagonism towards women, and women's values, contributions, and their resistance to that order.

Notes

1.   Referred to as *Witch* in the text.

2.   Referred to as *Raisin* in the text.

3.   A focus on language itself and its movement rather than of the pattern of migration of people would reveal that, in settler colonies, language is transported by people to a new environment where it changes in the process of adaptation. In the case of non-settler colonies or invaded territories, the language overwhelms and supplants the indigenous one and occupies the prime linguistic space.

4.   This cultural practice persists in colonial and to some extent post-colonial Swaziland.

5.   The influence of feminism has diminished this practice. Modern women have reacted in a number of ways which include retaining their surnames and adopting a double barrel name made up of both surname and marital name.

6.   This is why, in some cultures, the corpse of a married woman is carried back to her father's home. Sometimes, the birth of a son might qualify the corpse to get a space in the marital abode.

7.   This is different in matrilocal marriages where women do not dislocate. Men do experience a separation when they dislocate to a matrilocal abode. However, their superior status as men in the society as a whole gives them greater confidence than a woman who is dislocated.

8.   This does not imply that the natal family ceases to love and support their daughter when she relocates but that the structure of her marital location does not endorse what might be regarded as interference from her parental family and such support or interference usually decreases. Part of the problem which Diana, the princess of Wales, faced was that she found it difficult to fit into the new structure of the British royal family and that

she had lost the daily backing of her natal family because of dislocation. Her husband operated within the same structure he was used to from birth and did not have the problem of adaptation which the outsider faced. As an insider, his actions and motives were easily appreciated by members of the family because they understood him and were part of his background.

9.   The South African mines earned such a notorious name because of the high death rate of their workers. Sikova's brother died in one of the holes in the mines. Minework is also a source of wealth because those who survive return with some money.

10. In a patriarchal system, a colonized daughter is subjugated by both patriarchal and colonial systems. Another level of separation is added when she relocates to a marital abode.

Works Cited

Aidoo, Ama Ata. *Anowa*. London: Longman, 1965.
———. *The Dilemma of a Ghost*. Harlow: Longman, 1965.
Arua, A. E. "Marital Naming in the Ohafia Igbo Society." *Women and Language* XV. 2 (1992): 8-10.
Ashcroft, Bill, Gareth Griffiths and Helen Tiffin. *The Post-Colonial Studies Reader*. London and New York: Routledge, 1995.
———. *The Empire Writes Back: Theory and Practice in Post-Colonial Literatures*. London and New York: Routledge, 1989.
Baraka, Amiri. *"A Raisin in the Sun*'s Enduring Passion." *A Raisin in the Sun and The Sign in Sidney Brustein's Window by Lorraine Hansberry*. Ed. Robert Nemiroff. New York: Plume, 1987. 9-20.
Booth, A.R. "European Courts Protect Women and Witches: Colonial Law Courts as Redistributor of Power in Swaziland, 1920-1950." *Journal Of Southern African Studies* (1992): 7-16.
Bren, N. "It's Legal—A Woman Can Marry Another Woman." *Pace*, April 1992, 109.
Coryell, J. "What's in a Name?" *Women: A Journal of Liberation* 2 (1971): 59.
Davies, Carole Boyce. *Black Women, Writing and Identity*. London: Routledge, 1994.
Derman, J.P. "Stock and Aristocracy: The Political Implications of Swazi Marriage." *African Studies* 36.2 (1977): 119-129.
De Veaux, Alexis. *The Tapestry. 9 Plays by Black Women*. Ed. Margaret Wilkerson. New York: Mentor, 1986.
Engelbrecht, J.A. "Swazi Customs Relating to Marriage." *Annals of the University of Stellenbosch* 8.612 (1930): 1-27.
Epprecht, M. "Women's 'Conservatism' and the Politics of Gender in Late Colonial Lesotho." *Journal of African History* 36 (1995).
Graddol, D. and Joan Swann. *Gender Voice*. Oxford: Basil Blackwell, 1989.
Hansberry, Lorraine. *A Raisin in the Sun*. New York: Random House, 1959.
———. *Toussaint: Excerpt from Act I of a Work in Progress. 9 Plays by Black Women*. Ed. Margaret Wilkerson. New York: Mentor, 1986.
Kuper, Hilda. *A Bite of Hunger*. New York: Harcourt, Brace, and World, 1965.
———. *A Witch in My Heart*. London: Oxford UP, 1970.

Mhlophe, Gncina, T. Mtshali and M. Vanrenen. *Have You Seen Zandile*. Johannesburg: Skotaville, 1988.

Minh-Ha, Trinh T. "Writing Postcoloniality and Feminism." Ashcroft, Griffiths and Tiffin, 264-268.

Onyekachukwu, O. F. *Sons for My Son*. Obosi, Nigeria: Pacific, 1990.

Petersen, Kirsten Holst. "First Things First: Problems of a Feminist Approach to African Literature." Ashcroft, Griffiths and Tiffin, 251-254.

Rich, F. "*A Raisin in the Sun*: The 25th Anniversary." *A Raisin in the Sun and The Sign in Sidney Brustein's Window by Lorraine Hansberry*. Ed. Robert Nemiroff. New York: Plume, 1987. 21-42.

Smith, P.M. *Language, the Sexes and Society*. New York: Basil Blackwell, 1985.

Wilson-Tahoe, Nana. "Reading towards a Theorization of African Women's Writing: African Women Writers within Feminist Gynocriticism." *Writing African Women*. Ed. Stephanie Newell. London: Zed, 11-28.

Sherry, Ruth. *Studying Women's Writing*. London: Edward Arnold, 1988.

Zirimu, Elvania N. *Family Spear*. *African Theatre*. Ed. Gwyneth Henderson. London: Heinemann, n.d.

.

INDEX